LEARNING LATIN AND GREEK FROM ANTIQUITY TO THE PRESENT

This volume provides a unique overview of the broad historical, geographical, and social range of Latin and Greek as second languages. It elucidates the techniques of Latin and Greek instruction across time and place, and the contrasting socio-political circumstances that contributed to and resulted from this remarkably enduring field of study. Providing a counterweight to previous studies that have focused only on the experience of elite learners, the chapters explore dialogues between center and periphery, between pedagogical conservatism and societal change, between government and the governed. In addition, a number of chapters address the experience of female learners, who have often been excluded from or marginalized by earlier scholarship.

ELIZABETH P. ARCHIBALD is Visiting Teaching Professor at the Peabody Institute of the Johns Hopkins University. Her research focuses on early medieval education, medieval Latin, and the reception of classical texts in the Middle Ages.

WILLIAM BROCKLISS is Assistant Professor of Classics at the University of Wisconsin-Madison. His research encompasses the interactions between literature and the natural environment, the history of classical pedagogy, and the classical tradition. The latter interest is reflected in his previous Yale Classical Studies volume, *Reception and the Classics*, Cambridge (2011) edited with Pramit Chaudhuri, Ayelet Haimson-Lushkov, and Katherine Wasdin.

JONATHAN GNOZA is an adjunct instructor in the Medieval and Renaissance Center at New York University. He has previously contributed as a translator to *The Virgilian Tradition: the First Fifteen Hundred Years*, (2008).

YALE CLASSICAL STUDIES

VOLUME XXXVII

LEARNING LATIN AND GREEK FROM ANTIQUITY TO THE PRESENT

EDITED FOR THE DEPARTMENT OF CLASSICS BY

ELIZABETH P. ARCHIBALD

*Visiting Teaching Professor at the Peabody Institute
of the Johns Hopkins University*

WILLIAM BROCKLISS

Assistant Professor of Classics, University of Wisconsin-Madison

JONATHAN GNOZA

*Adjunct Professor in the Medieval and Renaissance Center,
New York University*

CAMBRIDGE
UNIVERSITY PRESS

University Printing House, Cambridge CB2 8BS, United Kingdom

Cambridge University Press is part of the University of Cambridge.

It furthers the University's mission by disseminating knowledge in the pursuit of education, learning and research at the highest international levels of excellence.

www.cambridge.org
Information on this title: www.cambridge.org/9781107051645

© Cambridge University Press 2015

This publication is in copyright. Subject to statutory exception and to the provisions of relevant collective licensing agreements, no reproduction of any part may take place without the written permission of Cambridge University Press.

First published 2015

Printed in the United Kingdom by Clays, St Ives plc

A catalogue record for this publication is available from the British Library

Library of Congress Cataloging in Publication data
Learning Latin and Greek from antiquity to the present / edited for the Department of Classics by Elizabeth P. Archibald, William Brockliss, Jonathan Gnoza.
pages cm
Includes bibliographical references and index.
ISBN 978-1-107-05164-5 (Hardback)
1. Latin language–Study and teaching–History.   2. Greek language–Study and teaching–History.
I. Archibald, Elizabeth P.   II. Brockliss, William.   III. Gnoza, Jonathan.
PA74.L43 2014
488.0071–dc23   2014002419

ISBN 978-1-107-05164-5 Hardback

Cambridge University Press has no responsibility for the persistence or accuracy of URLs for external or third-party internet websites referred to in this publication, and does not guarantee that any content on such websites is, or will remain, accurate or appropriate.

Contents

List of illustrations		*page* vii
Notes on contributors		viii
Acknowledgements		xii
1.	Introduction: "Learning me your language" Elizabeth P. Archibald, William Brockliss, Jonathan Gnoza	1
2.	Papyri and efforts by adults in Egyptian villages to write Greek Ann Ellis Hanson	10
3.	Teaching Latin to Greek speakers in antiquity Eleanor Dickey	30
4.	Servius' Greek lessons Félix Racine	52
5.	Pelasgian fountains: learning Greek in the early Middle Ages Michael W. Herren	65
6.	Out of the mouth of babes and Englishmen: the invention of the vernacular grammar in Anglo-Saxon England Jay Fisher	83
7.	First steps in Latin: the teaching of reading and writing in Renaissance Italy Robert Black	99
8.	The teaching of Latin to the native nobility in Mexico in the mid-1500s: contexts, methods, and results Andrew Laird	118
9.	*Ut consecutivum* under the Czars and under the Bolsheviks Victor Bers	136

10.	Latin for girls: the French debate Françoise Waquet	145
11.	Women's education and the classics Fiona Cox	156
12.	"Solitary perfection?" The past, present, and future of elitism in Latin education Kenneth J. Kitchell, Jr.	166
13.	Exclusively for everyone – to what extent has the *Cambridge Latin Course* widened access to Latin? Bob Lister	184
14.	Epilogue Emily Greenwood	198

Bibliography 209
Index 232

Illustrations

Fig. 2.1: *P.Petaus* 121, TM no. 12630. Inv. Nr. Cologne 328, Recto Permission for this and the two following images granted by Dr. Robert Daniel, Kustos, Papyrus-Sammlung, Cologne. *page* 16
Fig. 2.1a: *P.Petaus* 77.18, TM no. 12687. Inv. Nr. Cologne 310 b, Recto 17
Fig. 2.1b: *P.Petaus* 60.42, TM no. 8762. Inv. Nr. Cologne 312, Recto 17
Fig. 2.2: *SB* XIV 11585, TM no. 14491, P.Corn. Inv. I 11, Recto. Image digitally reproduced with the permission of the Papyrology Collection, Graduate Library, University of Michigan. 24
Fig. 5.1: Vienna, Österreichische Nationalbibliothek, MS 795, f. 19r. Permission granted by Österreichische Nationalbibliothek. 71
Fig. 5.2: Schaffhausen Stadtbibliothek, MS Gen. 1, p. 137. Permission granted by Schaffhausen Stadtbibliothek and Codices Electronici AG, www.e-codices.ch. 71
Fig. 5.3: Metz, Bibliothèque Municipale, MS 145, f. 204, from J. Becker, *Textgeschichte Liudprands von Cremona*. Munich, 1908, Taf. 1. (The original manuscripts of this and the next image were destroyed; the reproductions are from public domain works.) 72
Fig. 5.4: Dresden, Sächsische Landesbibliothek, MS A 145b, f. 1r.; from Alexander Reichardt, *Der Codex Boernerianus. Der Briefe des Apostels Paulus*. Leipzig, 1909. 74
Fig. 5.5: Leiden, Universiteitsbibliotheek, B.P.L. 67, f. 32v. Permission granted by Leiden, Universiteitsbibliotheek. 79
Fig. 13.1: Cambridge Latin Course Stage 21 model sentence: *faber primus statuam deae Sulis faciebat*. Reproduced with the permission of University of Cambridge School Classics Project. 189

Notes on contributors

ELIZABETH P. ARCHIBALD is Visiting Teaching Professor in the Department of Humanities at the Peabody Institute of the Johns Hopkins University. Her research deals with various aspects of the history of Latin education in the early Middle Ages.

VICTOR BERS is Professor of Classics at Yale University. His publications include *Greek Poetic Syntax in the Classical Age* (1984), *Speech in Speech: Studies in Incorporated* Oratio Recta *in Attic Drama and Oratory* (1997), and Genos Dikanikon: *Amateur and Professional Speech in the Courtrooms of Classical Athens* (2009).

ROBERT BLACK is Professor of Renaissance History at the University of Leeds. His books include *Benedetto Accolti and the Florentine Renaissance* (1985), *Studio e scuola in Arezzo durante il medioevo e il rinascimento* (1996), *Humanism and Education in Medieval and Renaissance Italy* (2001), *Education and Society in Florentine Tuscany* (2007), and *Studies in Renaissance Humanism and Politics* (2011). Together with Louise George Clubb, he has written *Romance and Aretine Humanism in Sienese Comedy* (1993), and with Gabriella Pomaro, *Boethius's Consolation of Philosophy in Italian Medieval and Renaissance Education* (2000). He has edited *Renaissance Thought: A Reader* (2001) and *The Renaissance: Critical Concepts in Historical Studies*, 4 vols. (2006). His new biography, *Machiavelli*, was published in August 2013. In 2014, he has been Robert Lehman Visiting Professor at Villa I Tatti, the Harvard University Center for Italian Renaissance Studies in Florence, Italy.

WILLIAM BROCKLISS is Assistant Professor of Classics at the University of Wisconsin-Madison. His previous publications include the volume *Reception and the Classics: Interdisciplinary Studies* (Cambridge University Press, 2012; Yale Classical Studies 36), which he co-edited with Pramit Chaudhuri, Ayelet Haimson-Lushkov, and Katherine Wasdin.

FIONA COX is Lecturer in French at the University of Exeter. Her research focuses on the reception of classical literature in the nineteenth, twentieth, and twenty-first centuries, with a particular emphasis on Virgil and Ovid. Her publications include *Aeneas Takes the Metro: Virgil's Presence in Twentieth Century French Literature* (1999), and *Sibylline Sisters: Virgil's Presence in Contemporary Women's Writing* (2011).

ELEANOR DICKEY is Professor of Classics at the University of Reading. She is the author of more than eighty scholarly publications, including *The Colloquia of the Hermeneumata Pseudodositheana* (2012), *Ancient Greek Scholarship* (2007), *Latin Forms of Address* (2002), and *Greek Forms of Address* (1996).

JAY FISHER is Visiting Assistant Professor of Classics at Rutgers University. His publications include the monograph *The Annals of Quintus Ennius and the Italic Tradition*, shortly to be published by Johns Hopkins University Press. His current research focuses on cultural and linguistic aspects of the reception of Latin literature.

JONATHAN GNOZA is an adjunct instructor in the Medieval and Renaissance Center at New York University, where he teaches courses on medieval and Renaissance Latin. He previously contributed to *The Virgilian Tradition: The First Fifteen Hundred Years* (2008).

EMILY GREENWOOD is Professor of Classics at Yale University. She is the author of *Thucydides and the Shaping of History* (2006), and *Afro-Greeks: Dialogues between Anglophone Caribbean Literature and Classics in the Twenty-First Century* (2010). She has also co-edited *Reading Herodotus: A Study of the* Logoi *in Book 5 of Herodotus' Histories* (with Elizabeth Irwin), and *Homer in the Twentieth Century: Between World Literature and the Western Canon* (with Barbara Graziosi).

ANN ELLIS HANSON is Senior Research Scholar at Yale University. Her extensive publications apply papyrological findings to the study of ancient medicine, physiology, and social history, with a particular focus on the lives of women. Her achievements were recognized by a MacArthur fellowship in 1992. After being sidelined for 2012 and the better part of 2013, she is now back at work, bringing to completion two major projects: – publication of the papyrus archive of Nemesion, son of Zoilos, collector of money-taxes at Philadelphia (Fayum) for Julio-Claudian emperors; editing and translating the Hippocratic treatise in two books, *Diseases of Women*.

MICHAEL W. HERREN is Distinguished Research Professor of Classics emeritus at York University and a member of the Graduate Programme in Medieval Studies at the University of Toronto. He is a fellow of the Royal Society of Canada and the Medieval Academy of America, an Honorary Member of the Royal Irish Academy, and has twice been a research prize recipient of the Alexander-von-Humboldt Foundation. The founding editor of *The Journal of Medieval Latin*, his publications include editions/translations of *Aldhelm: The Prose Works* (1979, with Michael Lapidge), *The Hisperica Famina* (1974, 1987), *Iohannis Scotti Eriugenae Carmina* (1993), *The Cosmography of Aethicus Ister* (2011), and the monograph (with Shirley Ann Brown) *Christ in Celtic Christianity* (2012). Most recently he published the Oxford Online Bibliography entry "Classics in the Middle Ages."

KENNETH J. KITCHELL, JR. has been Professor of Classics at University of Massachusetts, Amherst for sixteen years. Prior to that he taught at Louisiana State University for twenty-two years and Quigley Preparatory Seminary South in Chicago for two years. He has served as president of the Classical Association of the Middle West and South (CAMWS) and the American Classical League (ACL), and as vice president for education for the American Philological Association (APA). He has published on Catullus, Latin and Greek pedagogy, the history of Latin teaching, and on classical and medieval animal lore.

ANDREW LAIRD is Professor of Classical Literature at Warwick University. He is author of *Powers of Expression, Expressions of Power* (1999) and *The Epic of America* (2006), and co-editor of *Italy and the Classical Tradition: Language, Thought and Poetry 1300–1600* (2009) and *The Role of Latin in the Early Modern World: Linguistic Identity and Nationalism* (2012). His most recent publications include a series of articles presenting editions, translations, and studies of Latin texts by Spaniards and native authors from sixteenth-century Mexico.

BOB LISTER retired from his post as Lecturer in Classics and Education at the University of Cambridge in 2008 and was Director of the Cambridge School Classics Project from 1996 to 2003. He continues to teach Latin and Greek at undergraduate level and is also director of a project on teaching classical mythology through storytelling. He is the author of *Changing Classics in Schools* (2007) and edited *Meeting the Challenge: International Perspectives on the Teaching of Latin* (2008).

FÉLIX RACINE is a research affiliate at McGill University specializing in ancient and medieval travel literature and geography, educational history, and the medieval reception of Greek literature. His monograph, *Know Your Places: Teaching and Writing Geography in Late Antiquity*, will appear shortly from the University of Michigan Press.

FRANÇOISE WAQUET, docteur ès lettres, is Directrice de recherche at the Centre national de la recherche scientifique, Paris. Her research focuses primarily on western intellectual culture in the early modern and modern period. Her principal publications are *Le modèle français et l'Italie savante. Conscience de soi et perception de l'autre dans la République des Lettres, 1660–1750* (1989); *La République des Lettres* (1997, with Hans Bots); *Le Latin ou l'empire d'un signe, XVIe–XXe siècle* (1998); *Parler comme un livre. L'oralité et le savoir (XVIe–XXe siècle)* (2003); *Les enfants de Socrate. Filiation intellectuelle et transmission du savoir, XVIIe–XXIe siècle* (2008); *Respublica academica. Rituels universitaires et genres du savoir (XVIIe–XXIe siècle)* (2010).

Acknowledgements

The editors would like to thank Michael Sharp, Elizabeth Hanlon, Gillian Dadd, and Charlotte Thomas of Cambridge University Press for steering this volume to completion. We also thank the anonymous readers of Cambridge University Press for providing feedback that improved the volume in countless respects. Since this book grew out of a conference offered at Yale University, we extend our thanks to those Yale individuals and organizations who supported and sponsored that event: the Department of Classics, especially its former chair Christina Kraus; the Woodward Fund; the Deputy Provost for the Arts; the Edward J. & Dorothy Clarke Kempf Fund; the Beinecke Library; the Graduate School of Arts and Sciences; the Hellenic Studies Program; the Renaissance Studies Program; the Departments of English, Italian, French, and History; and Félix Racine, who in addition to contributing a paper also worked with the editors to organize the conference. Portions of Robert Black's *Education and Society in Florentine Tuscany: Teachers, Pupils and Schools, c. 1250–1500* (2007) appear in this volume courtesy of Koninklijke Brill NV, and portions of the same author's "Italian education: Languages, syllabuses, methods" in *Language and Cultural Change: Aspects of the Study and Use of Language in the Later Middle Ages and the Renaissance*, ed. Lodi Nauta (2006), appear courtesy of Peeters. Most of all we thank the contributors for their dedication to this project.

CHAPTER I

Introduction: *"Learning me your language"*

Elizabeth P. Archibald, William Brockliss, Jonathan Gnoza

> You taught me language, and my profit on't
> Is I know how to curse. The red plague rid you
> For learning me your language!
>
> (*Tempest* 1.ii.364–6)

Caliban's memorable rant against Prospero in Shakespeare's *Tempest* introduces a number of issues pertinent to a history of second language instruction: the differing motivations of pupil and master, the various uses to which the acquired language might be put (in Caliban's case, "to curse"), and the renegotiations of existing power structures that result from such education – whether through the teacher's empowerment of the pupil or the pupil's subversion of the master's authority. These and other sources of "profit" for master and pupil characterize the history of second language instruction. Instructors might seek to consolidate control over their pupils, drawing on language as an instrument of "civilization," or they might teach for more altruistic purposes. Students of second languages might expect to gain increased social standing, intellectual respect, or spiritual virtue – or, like Caliban, they might harness their "profit" for rebellion.

The present volume, which emerged from a conference held at Yale University in March 2009 entitled "Learning Me Your Language," seeks to explore such themes over a broad historical, geographical, and social range: it considers the teaching and learning of Latin and Greek as second languages from antiquity to the present day, elucidating both the techniques of Latin and Greek instruction across time and place, and the contrasting socio-political circumstances that contributed to and resulted from this remarkably enduring field of study. Throughout this broad historical range the papers explore dialogues between center and periphery, between pedagogical conservatism and societal change, between government and the governed.

These dialogues result from the fact that the acquisition of a second language, unlike mastery of a native tongue, is always the result of a decision, whether on the part of the learner or an authority figure – and while the end result may remain the same, the forces behind this decision can change radically. The papers in this volume interrogate these forces in diverse contexts, where the learning of these languages served very different purposes. Latin and Greek offer particularly promising material for such studies: they have had unusually enduring influence as "second languages" – that is, languages that are learned by a person already proficient in another language.

Consideration of the history of Latin and Greek as second languages has the potential to enrich several areas of scholarly discourse. Firstly, such a history promises both to complement and profitably to recalibrate the perspectives offered by current research into second language acquisition. Recent SLA studies have explored a number of the themes to be addressed by this volume – the mechanics of learning (conscious and subconscious learning;[1] teaching in the target language or the native language[2]) and the broader social aspects of language study (the interplay of language, power, and status;[3] the role of gender in language study[4]); however, the historical context that could have been provided by the history of education in the classical languages has not entered into these conversations. The long context offered by this volume promises to enrich investigations of second language acquisition and the cultural issues associated with it, through explorations of questions such as: Who has access to second language study? Is such access earned despite restrictions or imposed despite reluctance? What circumstances create "secondary" learners of languages, who are assigned a subordinate position within linguistic hierarchies?[5] What is the ultimate goal of second-language study, and how much mastery is enough?

Secondly, within the humanities we lack studies that offer an overview of the complete histories of education in Latin and Greek. Scholars have previously examined the nature of instruction in the two languages, together with themes such as the multiple identities of the second language learner,[6] the interaction between Christianity and pagan learning,[7] the

---

[1] Cf. Krashen 1981.   [2] Cf. Johnson and Swain 1997.
[3] Cf. Tollefson 1995, Slade and Möllering 2010.   [4] Chavez 2001.
[5] On "secondary" learners, see p. 8 below, and Greenwood in this volume.
[6] Adams (2003a), for instance, has explored how the subjects of the Roman Empire used their native language alongside Latin to negotiate their complex identities.
[7] Cf. Contreni 1980 and Sullivan 1995.

evolution of pedagogical styles as the two languages encountered new educational contexts,[8] the decline in classical learning,[9] and recent attempts to revive it[10] – all areas that are further explored in this volume. Such scholarship, however, has been restricted to specific time-periods, entailing a disconnect between their various perspectives on education in the languages. No study has yet examined the history of instruction in Latin and Greek over time, as it responded to changing social, political, linguistic, and religious factors.[11] The essays in this volume promise to achieve just that: they span two millennia of instruction, bringing into focus both shifts and continuities in Latin and Greek pedagogy.

Lastly, as a study of second- rather than first-language speakers, this volume covers an unusually large range of places, peoples, and social groups, and thus encompasses the complete breadth of the histories of Latin and Greek. As Joseph Farrell has shown, Latin has consistently been identified with the culturally normative – with those in political power, with the masculine gender.[12] Similar observations might be made regarding Greek, the language of the eastern Roman Empire and subsequently of the Byzantine Empire. If we gain, however, a proper appreciation of engagement with the classical languages not only by privileged learners but also by marginalized groups, we have the chance to rewrite the traditional narrative of the languages' histories.

The education of women forms a central thematic strand to this volume, challenging the patriarchal bias that has until recently characterized studies

---

[8] Recent research on Latin and Greek education in the Middle Ages has focused on issues such as the methods of Latin pedagogy, particularly in Germanic speaking regions: cf. Grotans 2006 on the development of bilingual pedagogy around the year 1000. The essays in Corso and Pecere 2010 elucidate pedagogy in many learning contexts before the Renaissance. Grafton and Jardine (1986) analyze the emergence of humanist education in its social and political context. Black (2001) and Rizzo (2002) have emphasized continuities between the educational methodologies of the Middle Ages and the Renaissance. Other important studies of changing educational contexts and pedagogical techniques for the study of Latin and, to a lesser extent, Greek include Hunt 1991, Law 1997, Lanham 2002, Law 2003, Orme 2006, and Cannon, Copeland, and Zeeman 2009.
[9] Françoise Waquet (1998), for example, has explored the failures of Latin pedagogy from the Enlightenment to the mid-twentieth century.
[10] Two volumes that appeared either side of the millennium, LaFleur 1998 and Morwood 2003, assessed the current state and possible future developments of Latin education in the English-speaking world. See further Lister 2008, which also embraces non-Anglophone countries.
[11] Too and Livingstone 1998 might appear an exception to this rule, but is avowedly ahistorical. Although it covers a broad historical range, its arrangement in reverse temporal order was explicitly chosen to disrupt any sense of historical progression from antiquity to the present (see "Introduction").
[12] Farrell 2001. See pp. 1ff. and 123ff. on the association of Latin and power, and pp. 52–83 for a discussion of the perceived masculinity of Latin.

of education in the classical languages.[13] Ann Hanson, for instance, examines the use made of acquired Latin and Greek by women in ancient Egypt; Françoise Waquet considers French debates over the place of Latin in the education of girls; Fiona Cox sees a future for Latin freed from traditional, patriarchal power structures and dominated instead by female learners and scholars.

The study of second-language learners in this volume also serves to challenge traditional focuses on the political center as opposed to the margins of empire, of rulers as opposed to subjects.[14] The papers cover an extraordinarily wide geographical range, and address learning contexts not often juxtaposed such as Roman Egypt and sixteenth-century Mexico. Such studies offer the opportunity to view similarities – including the continued use of the classical languages by those attempting to gain access to political elites – but also to explore the full diversity of the experiences of peoples on the periphery of Latin and Greek culture – the imperial subjects not only of ancient Rome but also of colonial Spain. At the same time, the essays recast the discourse of rulers and ruled within those areas by giving voice to groups that would normally be silenced. Kenneth Kitchell's paper, for instance, considers the complex relationship of American slaves and their descendants with the classical languages – and Shakespeare's Caliban, as Kitchell notes, is himself a slave, forced to learn what purports to be a language of civilization.

The history of Latin and Greek presented by this volume can be imagined in terms of the competing claims of elites who would see the two languages as their own possession – originally as first languages or, later, as if they were such – and of those who saw them as second languages – as a possession of none but a potential resource for all, or as a desirable but hardly attainable goal. This relationship, as will be made clear, altered over time: a survey of the history of education in Latin and Greek reveals the increasing distance of the learner from the two languages, the eventual readiness with which they were acknowledged as second languages, and the changing educational techniques and philosophies that responded to these shifting perceptions.

---

[13] It is only in recent decades that serious attempts have been made to address this deficiency, but these attempts have been restricted to particular time periods. On the ancient world, cf. Cribiore 2001, pp. 74–101. Important studies of women's education in the Middle Ages include McKitterick 1994, Clanchy 1984, and Desmond 1994. For the Renaissance, cf. Stevenson 1998.

[14] In addressing such themes, this volume follows on from Adams 2007, in which he finds some evidence for influence of local languages on the varieties of sub-elite provincial Latin. Adams' volume, however, considers only the ancient world.

In the Roman Empire Latin and Greek were languages of power and prestige. In both the west and the east the acquisition and demonstration of knowledge of the languages was essential for local populations in their attempts to negotiate their place in imperial power structures. Ann Hanson's examination of the role of Greek in the discourse of power in Ptolemaic and Roman Egypt draws on two archives of papyri from the Arsinoite nome to illustrate the strategies employed by villagers to acquire the language and particular idioms of their conquerors, a process that was often laborious. These papyri demonstrate the pressure felt by speakers of non-prestige, parochial languages of the empire to learn Greek. On the other hand, Eleanor Dickey shows that, contrary to the beliefs of many scholars, Greeks in the Roman Empire also sought to learn Latin, both informally and through organized classes. The texts with which they acquired their knowledge of the language (bilingual phrase books, elementary dialogues, a copy of Virgil for learners of Latin) exemplify the beginnings of Latin pedagogy.

After the fall of the Roman Empire, a situation of diglossia gradually developed in western Europe: Latin and, to a lesser degree, Greek became second languages devoted specifically to learning and culture. Late antique classrooms in the west engaged with Greek as well as Latin; however, Félix Racine argues that school texts like Servius sought to equip students with the ability to allude authoritatively to Greek language and lore, rather than seeking to impart real mastery of the language. By the early Middle Ages, knowledge of Greek was such a rarity that scholars with even the shakiest grasp of the language could flaunt it as an exotic achievement, though it also served as a point of access to the prestige of the classical past and as a means of following in the footsteps of the church fathers. Michael Herren demonstrates that, despite the scarcity of Greek learning in the early medieval west, the enthusiasm of scholars who coined neologisms and composed the occasional Greek verse demonstrates that their study was not motivated solely by a desire to better understand scripture. Rather, they studied Greek for the fun of it, and used it to show off their erudition.

Meanwhile, the changing relationship of Latin and the vernaculars led to new styles of Latin pedagogy. Places where Germanic languages were spoken saw the earliest development of bilingual education in the Middle Ages.[15] Jay Fisher clarifies the ways in which the *Excerptiones de arte grammatica Anglice* of the Anglo-Saxon scholar Aelfric sought to bridge

---

[15] Cf. Law 1984; for a later example of bilingual Latin pedagogy in Romance-speaking regions, see Merrilees 1987.

the pedagogical gap between the world of the sixth-century grammarian Priscian (a pagan whose pedagogy was designed for native Greek speakers) and his own world of Christian Anglo-Saxons. In response to this pedagogical challenge, Aelfric pioneered techniques of bilingual grammatical pedagogy, deftly navigating the differences between the two languages and thus setting the stage for a new pedagogical relationship with Latin even among Romance speakers.

As Latin and Romance drifted farther apart, new theoretical models emerged for Latin pedagogy, and for the cultural and intellectual role of the language. Though it was clearly no longer a native tongue, Latin was regarded as synonymous with grammar, an analytical and instructional system for teaching generalized concepts of language and literacy.[16] Indeed Latin became so entrenched in the educational systems of medieval and Renaissance Italy that, until the eighteenth century, students were taught reading through the medium of the language; an example of this practice is offered by Robert Black, who elucidates the mechanics of the process by which young students became literate in Renaissance Italy. The well-established tradition of acquiring literacy and Latinity together was also exported from Europe to the New World. Andrew Laird examines this phenomenon in the context of Latin study among native Nahuas in Mexico in the decades after the Spanish conquest. Franciscan missionaries brought with them well-established pedagogical traditions and the idea of Latin as *grammatica* – the proper tool for understanding generalized concepts of language and literacy. Ultimately, this complex educational initiative resulted not only in native Nahuatl-speaking nobility acquiring enough Latin to read, converse, and compose elegant letters and verse, but also in the preservation and creation of literature in Nahuatl.

The persistent identification of Latin with *grammatica* itself gave it a status even beyond a privileged second language – not exactly a mother tongue, but the mother of tongues, and a kind of first language in the context of an elite intellectual class. However, the language could only be regarded as a quasi-first language by expert teachers and scholars:[17] the experience of the learner, by contrast, was increasingly one of alienation and mental struggle. As Kenneth Kitchell notes, Enlightenment thinkers came to question the value of education in a dead language and the elitist attitudes of its champions. On the other hand, this recognition of the

---

[16] On the centrality of *grammatica* to literary culture in this period, cf. Irvine 2006. On the grammatical underpinnings of medieval philosophy, see for example Kelly 2002. Voigts (1996) examines the respective roles of Latin and English in late-medieval bilingualism. For assessments of the social role of grammar, see also Gehl 1993 and 1994 on trecento Tuscany.

[17] For the attitudes of such experts prior to the twentieth century, cf. Stray 1998, pp. 1–82.

otherness of Latin meant that the mental anguish of the learner could be recast as a virtue, and pedagogy accordingly as an act of discipline.[18] In her essay on nineteenth- and early twentieth-century French debates about the place of Latin in the education of girls, Françoise Waquet chronicles the remarkable arguments of educationalists who proposed that the female Latin student's feelings of "perpetual, painful inadequacy" would inculcate the modesty appropriate to her future place in society. In France, then, some teachers saw Latin as a means to promote docility in their female charges, providing a stark contrast to the missionaries studied by Laird: they had taught young Nahua men the classical languages in the hopes of forming a new patriarchal, "gubernatorial class."

Whether in spite of or because of such attempts to defend Latin education, the language proceeded to lose its place at the center of the western curriculum and its elite status in western culture. In the late twentieth century, even experts could no longer claim to have Latin as a first language.[19] Both Latin and Greek had acquired an aura of otherness; nowadays, all who approach the languages do so from the alienated position of the second-language learner.

The alienation of learners, however, has had the welcome consequence of relaxing the control of elites who traditionally controlled classical education and of opening up the languages to previously marginalized groups. Bob Lister notes that champions of classical education in Britain saw opportunity in the reassessment of the status of the languages. They had been the preserve of elite social classes, but now that they were no longer the possession of any one group they could be made available "exclusively for everyone." Moreover, as educational contexts became more inclusive, female students have increasingly adopted Latin and Greek. Fiona Cox argues that, whereas educated nineteenth-century women tended to regard the male world of Latin and Greek with wistfulness or frustration, the gradual opening of educational opportunities to women paved the way for a new era of classical reception in the twentieth century, this one defined largely by female authors mapping the classics onto female experience for the first time. As the study of Latin and Greek undergoes new transformations in the twenty-first century, women are playing an instrumental role in determining the future shape of the classics.[20]

---

[18] Cf. Stray 1998, chs. 9 and 10 on the "Indian Summer" of classical education in Britain, during which the learning of Latin was recast as a mental discipline.
[19] Cf. Clarke 2010, pp. 120ff.
[20] Cf. Farrell 2001, pp. 97ff. on the "feminization of Latin studies" in the twentieth century.

This constitutes a significant change in attitudes to the classics but not, as Emily Greenwood notes in her epilogue, in the true nature of the relationship of learners to the languages. Despite the belief of elites that their privileged knowledge amounted to a first-language acquaintance with Latin or Greek, this has never truly been the case in the post-antique world. Rather, a distinction has existed between insiders who have jealously guarded their (imperfect) knowledge of the languages, and those whom they have regarded as "secondary" users of what is for all a second language – Greenwood offers the figure of Caliban as an example of the latter group. A recent reassessment of the status of the languages offers a more accurate perspective on classical education, promising a "shift away from classics as an inherited tradition towards an understanding of the different political, social and cultural factors that have shaped the teaching and study of Greek and Latin." The present volume continues that movement: it challenges the claims of elite, supposed first-language speakers by recasting the histories of the two languages in terms of second language acquisition.

Alongside the changing attitudes of learners to Latin and Greek, the essays of this volume present continuities in classical education from antiquity to the present, particularly in pedagogical techniques and in social attitudes to the two languages at the margins of classical culture. In countries outside what was the Roman Empire Latin and Greek could never be regarded as first languages, and served instead as symbols of western European civilization. Complementing Judith Kalb's recent study of the notion of the Third Rome in late imperial and early Soviet literature,[21] Victor Bers surveys the history of classical education in Russia, where the languages and their attendant cultures were a reference point in debates between westernizers and Slavophiles, and in the political discourse of Czarists, Bolsheviks, and their respective critics. In the United States, as Kenneth Kitchell shows, some revolutionary leaders were suspicious of Latin and Greek for their aura of European elitism; bearing out the fears of those men, the languages came to represent educational and social privileges from which certain groups, such as African-Americans, were excluded.

In every age, however, alongside those experts who seemed more eager to assert their own superiority, there have been innovative teachers and writers who have attempted to ease the painful journey of the second-language learner. Bilingual texts helped the Greek speakers of the Roman Empire to learn their Latin (Dickey), and scholars of the medieval west to

---

[21] Kalb 2008.

learn Greek (Herren). Learning manuals have shown an awareness of the needs of younger learners. Aelfric, for instance, conscious of his young readership, appears to have incorporated elements of child-directed speech into his grammar (Fisher).[22] Recently, the writers of the *Cambridge Latin Course* have attempted to accommodate the needs of children more effectively by focusing on child-centered, inductive methods of learning, where grammatical rules are at first intuited rather than learnt by rote (Lister).

Together, these case studies outline a new narrative that focuses on classics not as a pure and unchanging tradition but as a complex matrix of political, social, and cultural influences, shaped and reshaped by these forces. The history of Latin and Greek as second languages emerges as a dynamic network of tensions: between native speakers, those casting themselves as native speakers, and secondary learners; between center and periphery; between pagan traditions and Christian receptions; between Caliban and Prospero; between *auctoritas* and innovation.

And perhaps by recognizing the dynamic tensions surrounding Latin and Greek, we come closer to a new kind of dialogue in which the languages emerge as a center of gravity for connections between times, places, and disciplines. Expertise in Latin and Greek might then, rather than operating as a means to exclude, serve to open up opportunities for interdisciplinary scholarly collaborations that would not be possible through the study of other tongues. We hope that the current volume will be seen as a move in that direction.

---

[22] Cf. Kitchell 1998, pp. 6ff. Kitchell argues that Aelfric's book anticipated the emphasis of recent Latin courses on fluency rather than grammatical correctness, and also modern pedagogical techniques such as substitution.

CHAPTER 2

Papyri and efforts by adults in Egyptian villages to write Greek

Ann Ellis Hanson

Homer's Menelaus spent time in Egypt on his way home to Mycenae after the Greeks sacked Troy, and the king of Egyptian Thebes gave him glorious gifts as he departed, including a silver weaving basket for his wife and a golden distaff. Helen kept Egyptian medicaments and anodynes among her possessions, for Homer pictured Egypt a country of fabulous wealth, a treasure trove of the wisdom of the ancients, and, as he had done with the Trojans, he imagined no language barrier to prevent his Greeks from communicating with Egyptians. In the seventh century BCE trade flourished in and around Naucratis, a Greek enclave on the Canopic branch of the Nile, and by the time of the historian Herodotus' visit in the mid-fifth century Egypt had been absorbed into the aggressively expanding Persian Empire. Two centuries later Alexander the Great and his Macedonians arrived in Egypt as welcome conquerors of the unpopular Persian king and they became the country's masters, gradually opening up fertile areas to exploitation by fellow Greeks and building the cosmopolitan city on the Mediterranean coast whose outlines Alexander had merely sketched out before his departure for conquests further east. He never revisited this Alexandria again while still alive. Hellenophones from the islands and the littoral of the eastern Mediterranean eagerly immigrated into Egypt: many stayed near the coast in the first years, as Alexandria developed into a commercial hub that linked the Nile valley and eastern emporia on the Red Sea and beyond to the Mediterranean. A dazzling intellectual and cultural capital came into existence and it speedily eclipsed the glories of Athens. By the middle of the third century BCE improved irrigation encouraged settlements into the country districts and small villages of the Delta and further south into the large oasis called the Arsinoite nome.

Ptolemaic monarchs encouraged Egyptians of the wealthier strata to learn the language of their conquerors, and in the cities and larger towns Greek was the language most often heard on the boulevards and colonnaded streets, although the Egyptian language remained dominant in the countryside and its hamlets. Roman influence spread into the eastern Mediterranean during the second century BCE along with Roman armies, and interventions became frequent in the first century, culminating in the struggle for supremacy among the Triumvirs who assumed power at Rome after the assassination of Julius Caesar (44 BCE). Cleopatra VII, the last of the Ptolemaic dynasty, and Marcus Antonius (Marc Antony), were defeated on 2 September 31 BCE at the naval battle of Actium by Caesar's great nephew Octavian, who would become Augustus. Egypt was thereafter a province of the Roman Empire, but Romans neither pressured nor encouraged Egyptians to learn Latin. Rather, in common with the rest of the eastern Mediterranean, Greek continued as the language of documents and other written communications, both public and private, and those Egyptians with property to protect needed either to know enough Greek to read texts prepared for them by professional scribes and to append their signature, or, if illiterate in Greek, to engage trustworthy others to read and write for them. Illiterates in Egypt inhabiting peasant villages of the countryside repeatedly relied on the same person, or persons, year after year, chosen from a work environment, from the neighborhood, or from the family, and in the Roman period capable individuals were present in sufficient numbers to do some writing and reading of Greek for those unable to do so for themselves.[1] To be sure, a new hierarchy of status was instituted under the Emperor Augustus, with Roman citizens at the top; also privileged were citizens of Alexandria and the other cities with Greek constitutions and governmental structures (four such, after Hadrian founded Antinoopolis about 130 CE). The rest of the population was lumped together as "Egyptian," and the special status the Ptolemies had awarded those of Greek and Macedonian descent evanesced and eventually disappeared. The more Hellenized inhabitants of the capital cities, or metropoleis, of the nomes, nonetheless enjoyed tax benefits denied other Egyptians, and they enjoyed a more sophisticated life-style. The Greekness of these metropolitans became more pronounced over time, as local and imperial euergetism fostered the development of the accoutrements of Greco-Roman daily living – aqueducts and baths, gymnasia, theaters, civic buildings of many types.[2] Most male inhabitants in Roman times were bilingual to some degree, able to understand at least a bit of Greek, as well as their native Egyptian, depending, of course, on how vital what was being said was to an oral conversation. Peasant men of the farming villages

---

[1] Hanson 1991: 166–70.   [2] Lewis 1983.

had greater opportunity to acquire Greek, no matter how poor or disadvantaged, than did their womenfolk, who sometimes required that letters in Greek even from kin be translated for them.³

The Egyptian language was represented in different scripts over the course of millennia, beginning about 3000 BCE with the pictographic hieroglyphs, painted on walls of temples and tombs or incised on blocks of stone for display; the later scripts, such as hieratic and from the seventh BCE onward demotic, were better suited to rapid writing executed with a brush on papyrus. Demotic continued to represent Egyptian in everyday communications throughout the Ptolemaic period and into the reigns of Julio-Claudian emperors, but then it peters out as a script of daily use, retreating into temple enclaves for the copying of religious and literary texts.⁴ That the Egyptian language continued to maintain a vigorous presence, even when not being written, is demonstrated by the speedy acceptance of the new Coptic script in the third century CE, based on the Greek alphabet plus letters from demotic to represent Egyptian phonemes not present in Greek. So dominant had Greek become that the statement "he or she does not know letters" characterized those illiterate in Greek and ignored competence in Egyptian. Employing documentary papyri as a means to investigate levels of literacy in Roman Egypt had its beginnings with Ernst Majer-Leonhard and his catalog of illiterates and semi-literates early in the twentieth century.⁵ In the decades that followed, the topic of literacy has been probed with ever-greater intensity and sophistication, drawing literary and subliterary papyri into the equation and problematizing anecdotal evidence from the many documents that continue to accumulate to this day.⁶ The last quarter of the twentieth century, in particular, was crowded with important and nuanced observations, such as R. Thomas's insistence in 1992 that while the Greek and Roman worlds give the impression of being literate societies, evidence for orality persists at many levels, underscoring its primacy. Equally important for dealing with papyri from the ancient schools have been Raffaella Cribiore's

---

³ Rowlandson 1998: 311, papyrus no. 246, translation of *SB* XVIII 13867, TM no. 27679. For bibliographical references to editions of papyri referred to in this paper only by their conventional abbreviations of titles, see Oates *et al.*
⁴ Bagnall 2011: 32–9, for the writing of Greek and Egyptian in the Hellenistic period, and pp. 74–94, for the emergence of Coptic.
⁵ Majer-Leonhard 1913: 69–73, who isolated the documentary formulae expressing inability to write. See now Werner 2009: 333–52.
⁶ See Papaconstantinou 2010, for a recent overview of multilingualism in Egypt from the Ptolemies to the penetration of Arabic under the Abbasids, punctuated with evidence from individual case studies.

identifications and descriptions in 1996 of the various levels of handwriting, especially the hand teachers used when producing attractive, yet legible models for their pupils to copy. The provocative question with which W. V. Harris began his wide-reaching study of literacy in the Mediterranean basin, "How many people could read, how many people could write in the Graeco-Roman world?," has remained of necessity unanswered, for Harris's intention was not to urge a scholarly consensus that would coalesce on a specific percentage. Rather, he demonstrated beyond shadow of a doubt that modern guesses about literacy levels in the ancient world often lack grounding in the ancient evidence and also tend to be overly optimistic, even for the Roman period, when evidence is most abundant. The vast majority of ancient peoples were unschooled and lacking opportunities for extensive writing and reading. Low socio-political status and poor economic prospects marked those thus disadvantaged: they were the inhabitants of small villages, hamlets, isolated farmsteads, not those living in large towns and cities; they were borrowers, renters, hired laborers, and women, and not the propertied. There were, of course, exceptions, and their stories embellish and enliven Harris's text and footnotes.

Early on Harris alerted his readers to the possibility that not only was some basic learning likely to take place in the home, as literate and semi-literate fathers and mothers, perhaps aware of the role writing and reading played in their own lives, passed on whatever knowledge they had to their own children (pp. 15–16, 274). A cross-generational example has been identified through resemblance between the signatures penned on papyrus by Aurelia Charite, a wealthy landowner at Hermopolis in the middle of the fourth century CE, and the penmanship of her mother Demetria.[7] Demetria has seemed the more skillful writer of the pair, although both women write slowly, giving individual articulation to many of their letters. Neither woman was in the habit of writing on a daily basis, and both mother and daughter took up papyrus and reed pen only when the need arose. Nonetheless, the women were able to read and sign documents for themselves without additional assistance. Copies of ancient school books suggest that beginners, whether children or adults, learned writing separately from reading: of necessity they copied the Greek alphabet over and over again, before going on to master

---

[7] For Demetria's penmanship as she writes the first eleven lines on the papyrus sheet, instructing a bank clerk to transfer four talents to her daughter Charite, see Bagnall and Cribiore 2008: 2B.5, letter no. 168 = *P.Charite* 38, TM no. 15617 (legible scan at Österreiche Nationalbibliothek Katalog der Papyrussammlung with inventory no. G 13111 + G 36743). For Charite's own signature at the bottom of a papyrus sheet, acknowledging receipt of produce owed her as rent, see plate 27, and translation of text 179(b) in Rowlandson 1998: 242–3 = *P.Charite* 8, TM no. 15564; Aurelia Charite employed a professional scribe to write the first twenty-three lines of text that preceded her signature.

more difficult material. Repetition and rote learning were prominent features in ancient education, yet not all language learners were children. The later Roman period witnessed the widespread use of educational materials that would have catered more to the needs and interests of adults, particularly important of which are the bi- and trilingual glossaries well-attested in papyrus examples.[8] Curricular materials available to those beginning the study of medicine were likewise in plentiful supply, in addition to apprenticeship with a practitioner.[9] Galen tells us something about the curricular paths available, while papyri likewise provide examples of texts designed for those beginning the study of medicine – medical definitions and catechisms, or question-and-answer exercises, that not only played a role in the medical education of antiquity, but continued to serve for more than a millennium thereafter in Latin translations. Adults with sufficient motivation for acquiring the rudiments of a second language may have turned to friends and family members of greater linguistic accomplishment and they also listened carefully when in the presence of others speaking the target language. Of the more than seventy-five examples of Greek alphabets written on papyri and ostraca catalogued by Cribiore in 1996, some were written more skillfully and others less so. There is no way to tell from the writing alone whether the writer was a child at school, or a struggling adult, although when text is copied, what is written may distinguish the boy from the man, the girl from the woman.

When Harris was probing the evidence for the diffusion of literacy among adults in the Roman world, he appealed to Artemidorus' *Dreambook* and Artemidorus' claim that the dream in which the sleeper was learning his letters had one meaning for the literate person and a different meaning for an

---

[8] For bi- and trilingual glossaries on papyrus, see initial collections by Kramer 1983: 7–27 (introduction) and Kramer 2001: 1–30 (introduction); for the important republication of *C. Gloss. Biling.* I 2 Kramer (= P.Sorb.inv. 2069 verso, *MP³* 3006, *LDAB* 5438), see Dickey and Ferri 2010: 177–8. For antecedents and developmental history of P.Sorb.inv. 2069 verso, see Dickey 2010a: 195–201. For the re-publication of *C. Gloss. Biling.* II 8 Kramer (= *P.Prag.* II 118, *MP³* 3004.22, *LDAB* 6007), see Dickey and Ferri 2012, 129–32. This latter papyrus contains a bilingual Latin-Greek *sermo cottidianus*, part of the so-called *Hermeneumata Pseudodositheana* with textual connections to the *Colloquium Harleianum*, see Dickey 2012: 7–10 (#32 on figure 1.1), 18. Dickey 2012 re-edits the *Colloquia Monacensia-Einsidlensia*, 100–84, *Colloquium Leidense-Stephani*, 185–215, and *Colloquium Stephani*, 219–45, equipping each edition with introduction and description, translation, and critical commentary. Thus she makes these texts more accessible to a modern audience than do the presentations by G. Goetz in his *Corpus Glossariorum Latinorum* vols. 2 (1888) and 3 (1892). See also Dionisotti 1982a and Schironi 2009: 14–24.

[9] For study materials directed toward beginners, see Hanson 2010: 192–7; of particular interest are *PSI* XII 1275 (*MP³* 2345.1, *LDAB* 4608) and *P.Oxy.* LXXIV 4970 (*MP³* 2354.11, *LDAB* 119315), both seemingly proëmia to medical manuals advising beginners about the appropriate subject matter with which to initiate their medical studies – learning either the names of the parts of the body in the *PSI* text (also advocated by Rufus of Ephesus), or the Hippocratic Oath in the papyrus from Oxyrhynchus (also urged by Scribonius Largus, *Compositiones* praef. 5). For Latin versions of Greek medical catechisms on papyrus, see e.g. the Pseudo-Soranus, *Quaestiones medicinales*.

illiterate one (pp. 274–5).[10] Artemidorus neglected to clarify in which way the meanings differed, and Harris himself – although he appealed to Lucian's sarcastic remark about widespread ignorance among orators and teachers, and though he emphasized Soranus' assertion in his *Gynaikeia* that the best midwife should know letters and be able to read, so as to combine medical theory with her knowledge of gynecological practices – probed papyrus documents for evidence on ancient literacy only on occasion. Thus, in what follows I examine two adults, each living in an Arsinoite village during the early and middle years of the Roman Principate, and sketch out what I think can be said about their attempts to enhance their writing skills on the basis of the papyri on which they wrote. I also think it very likely that both benefitted from the influence of a close family member.

Petaus, son of Petaus, has often figured as a poster child for illiterates in the Roman world, becoming something of a celebrity in the years after 1966, when H. C. Youtie introduced him to the scholarly world as the scribe who did not know how to write.[11] That is, Petaus was appointed the village scribe, *komogrammateus*, of Ptolemais Hormou and nearby villages in the southern Arsinoite nome for a three-year period beginning in 183/184 CE, and his archive of some 130 business documents and other records reveal him repeatedly practicing the essential phrase a village scribe was required to append to a document he then forwarded to government officials in the capital of the nome; his signature guaranteed that the proper authority in the village had scrutinized the text prior to its being dispatched. He had to be able to write "I Petaus, village scribe, submitted [this]," and was aiming for Πεταῦς κωμογρ(αμματεὺς) ἐπιδέδωκα, or the shorter version, "I Petaus submitted [this]," Πεταῦς ἐπιδέδωκα.[12]

---

[10] Artemidorus, *Oneirokritika* 1.53.
[11] Youtie 1966, as he and his colleagues were preparing Petaus' archive for publication in 1968. Two additional articles by Youtie elucidated the language papyri employed for varying degrees of literacy, from the person illiterate in Greek, ἀγράμματος and μὴ εἰδὼς/εἰδυῖα γράμματα, to the slow writer, βραδέως γράφων/γράφουσα, and underscored the general tolerance toward illiteracy: Youtie 1971a and 1971b. For the edition, see U. Hagedorn *et al.* 1968, *Das Archiv des Petaus*.
[12] The parentheses indicate that the word *komogrammateus* was not written out in full, but was abbreviated in a conventional manner. Petaus continued to practice Πεταῦς κωμογρ(αμματεὺς) ἐπιδέδωκα and Πεταῦς ἐπιδέδωκα, and his practice sheets were kept along with his business papers: *P.Petaus* 122d (TM no. 12634, scan not available) and *P.Petaus* 114 (TM no. 12624), image of the latter online www.uni-koeln.de/phil-fak/ifa/NRWakademie/papyrologie/PPetaus/bilder/PK366r.jpg, in which Petaus (line 2, hand 2) wrote out no more than his name and the first two letters of κω(μογραμματεύς), but he did not even attempt the verb ἐπιδέδωκα. The version of his name on *P.Petaus* 115 (lines 4–5, TM no. 12625) was written more expansively, so perhaps Petaus was employing a different model from which to copy, image online at www.uni-koeln.de/phil-fak/ifa/NRWakademie/papyrologie/PPetaus/bilder/PK378r.jpg. Here, however, Petaus allotted the available space poorly and was forced to set the final two letters of the verb on a second line.

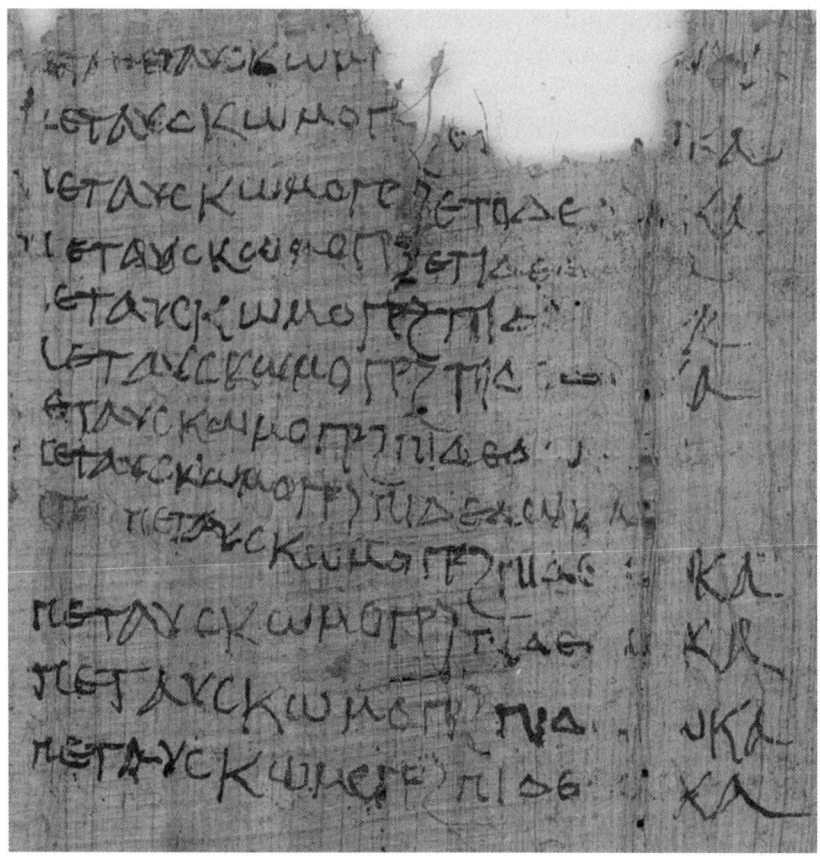

Figure 2.1: *P.Petaus* 121, TM no. 12630

The largest sheet of papyrus on which he practiced, *P.Petaus* 121, TM no. 12630, reproduced in Figure 2.1 but with the blank space in the lower half truncated, shows him copying, and his efforts amply display the difficulties he has when manipulating papyrus and reed pen.[13] He wrote

---

[13] This sheet on which Petaus practiced his signature has often been reproduced: Youtie 1966: 127–43, with plate of *P.Petaus* 121, TM no. 12630, image online at www.uni-koeln.de/phil-fak/ifa/ NRWakademie/papyrologie/PPetaus/bilder/PK328r.jpg. For Petaus' subsequent fame as the scribe who could not write, see Turner 1968: 83; Lewis 1983: 81; Montevecchi 1988: 255, 400; Harris 1989: 278–9; Hanson 1991: 171–4; Cribiore 1996: 150–1; Horsley 1989: 12–13; Kraus 2000: 329, 334–8; Cribiore 2009: 327; Vandorpe 2009: 217 and fig. 10.1.

the beginning of his name twice in both lines 1 and 9, and then excising the first letters and starting anew; in the ninth line as in the first he seems to have noticed he omitted the second letter of his name (having written Πτ, instead of Πετ). In line 3 he also became aware of his omission of the third letter from the verb (writing ἐπδέδωκα, instead of the correct ἐπιδέδωκα) and squeezed in the missing iota in between the two letters he had already written. In line 4, however, he failed to observe his omission of the right leg of the π in ἐπι- and wrote ἐτι- instead. More serious, he was never aware that he dropped the initial vowel from the verb ἐπιδέδωκα beginning in line 5, continuing to the end with only πιδέδωκα. A thumbprint appears to the right at the point where Petaus abandons his task in frustration after his twelfth try, leaving the bottom half on the front of the papyrus still blank. One supposes that Petaus got ink on his right thumb, making the thumbprint when turning over the sheet to the reverse side, where he twice tried to write out the practice sentence, again botching it.

Petaus' penmanship in his practices is ugly, marred by unevenness and unnoted omissions; his letters are large and awkward, his writing sometimes moving erratically up and down. While practice never made perfect, the seven papyrus documents from the archive to which Petaus appended the shorter version of his formal signature, "I, Petaus, submitted [this]," seem to display improvement of a sort: his letters become smaller and his written line becomes more straight over the year from 4 May 184 to 28 May 185.[14] By setting the bar for accomplishment low, Petaus was able to show improvement.

Repeated copying was a pedagogical technique frequently encountered in school texts from Egypt: the student begins by copying a model written out by his teacher in clear, attractive, and relatively large letters, but he then uses each line of his own copying as model for the following line.[15] Had Petaus' practices not been unearthed with the rest of the archive that

---

[14] Cf. the earliest and latest dated documents bearing Petaus' signature: P.Petaus 77.18, 4 May 184, TM no. 12687, online at www.uni-koeln.de/phil-fak/ifa/NRWakademie/papyrologie/PPetaus/bilder/PK310br.jpg (accessed 8 May 2013) and P.Petaus 60.42, 28 May 185, TM no. 9762, online at www.uni-koeln.de/phil-fak/ifa/NRWakademie/papyrologie/PPetaus/bilder/PK312r.jpg (accessed 8 May 2013). Cf. also P.Petaus 46.34, 10 Jan. 185, TM no. 8817, online at www.uni-koeln.de/phil-fak/ifa/NRWakademie/papyrologie/PPetaus/bilder/PK311r.jpg (accessed 8 May 2013); P.Petaus 47.54, 25 Jan. 185, TM no. 8818, image not available; P.Petaus 49.22, 28 March 185, TM no. l 8758, online at www.uni-koeln.de/phil-fak/ifa/NRWakademie/papyrologie/PPetaus/bilder/PK340r.jpg.

[15] E.g. Cribiore 1996: 204–14, writing and copying exercises, especially nos. 129, 130, 132, 135, 138, 139, 146, 159; see also 250, no. 313, side 2, with *Iliad* 2.244 written nineteen times (republication of *T.Varie* text 80, with photo on tavola xciii, *Pap.Flor.* XVIII, p. 172).

bears his name, his copying might have been interpreted as the halting penmanship of a schoolchild just learning how to form letters. The content of what he was practicing, however, "I Petaus submitted [this]," was not a customary assignment for a boy or girl, whose exercises more often involved copying a line or two from high literature – Homer, Euripides, Demosthenes, or a maxim from Menander to urge them on. Petaus' appointment as village scribe in Ptolemais Hormou and other villages for a term of three years was assigned him by government officials in the Roman bureaucracy of the nome only because Petaus possessed sufficient property to guarantee that he could make good any shortfalls owed to the fisc once his three-year term in office was completed.[16] Among the peasants in his natal village Karanis, Petaus was a relatively wealthy man, and literacy in Greek was not a requirement for the office of village scribe. It was the value of his property that had been scrutinized by authorities, not his ability to read and write, and the tacit assumption was that either Petaus could function efficiently enough as village scribe to satisfy villagers and government officials alike, or that he could afford to hire a secretary to perform the job of *komogrammateus* in his stead. The duties included directing the local office responsible for keeping property records and population data on births and deaths up to date; implementation at the local level of fiscal and agricultural decisions taken in Alexandria or the metropolis of the nome; and making recommendations to the *strategos* as to which fellow villagers possessed property sufficient to undertake liturgic appointments, or even replace Petaus himself when his three-year stint as *komogrammateus* was over.[17] Petaus' bureau employed about ten or so professional scribes to handle the writing of official documents, with two being responsible for some 20 percent of the writing. Petaus was twice called upon to investigate charges laid against two village scribes serving in other villages, each of whom had been denounced to a nome official by some villager from the place where he was serving: the *komogrammateus* of Karanis was accused of being in debt and without requisite property (*P.Petaus* 10.4–10, TM no. 8803), while the *komogrammateus* of Tamauis was accused not only of being in debt and without requisite property, but also of being illiterate (*P.Petaus* 11.3–9). Petaus dated his replies to the two requests for verification on the same day, 2 May 184, pronouncing both

---

[16] In Petaus' day the assets a village scribe was required to declare were presumably 3,000 drachmas, or half a talent (*P.Petaus* 10.18, TM no. 8803); the collector of money taxes at Philadelphia, Nemesion, son of Zoilus, apparently possessed assets approaching 4,500 drachmas in the middle of the first century CE (*P.Gen.* II 91, TM 11262).

[17] Lewis 1997: 35.

men as possessors of sufficient property to prevent losses to the fisc. As to the charge that the *komogrammateus* of Tamauis was illiterate, however, Petaus added, "No, he is not illiterate, because he appends his signature to the documents he dispatches to the *strategos* and others."[18] The definition Petaus gives, of course, applies equally to himself, and this episode perhaps motivated Petaus to pursue his practicing all the more vigorously.

Youtie likewise drew attention to a private document in the archive in which Petaus' brother Theon asserts that he has written out the text and subscription on the papyrus acknowledging to Heron, son of Heraclides, that the two brothers, sons of their father likewise named Petaus, had back home in Karanis received a loan of one hundred drachmas in the course of the twenty-fourth regnal year of the Emperor Commodus (183/184 CE).[19] As the literate family member, Theon was the person most likely to have produced the models for his older brother Petaus to copy and he would have written out the signature that Petaus practiced over and over again. The repeated copying ultimately made Petaus a writer skillful enough to avoid accusations of being illiterate, for he had learned how to imitate literacy through the writing of a proper signature. Petaus could authenticate the documents that passed through his hands in a convincing manner, and no one really cared whether or not Petaus was able to read what he wrote. Others took care of the complicated writing and reading.

Most of the scribal hands in the archive represent the work of professionals. But Hand B eventually proved to be that of Theon; he was responsible for writing at least eleven papyri in the archive, mostly lists.[20] The editors noted moreover that Theon was a more confident writer than his brother, and his penmanship the more fluid; nevertheless his writing resembled that of Petaus in its awkwardness and uncertain orthography. There can be no question, however, but that Theon could read and write as he asserted in the contract of loan (*P.Petaus* 31.13–14). It is hard to resist a scenario such as the following: the two brothers, when young, had several years of schooling, most likely in Karanis. The older son found lessons tiresome, but by contrast the younger son enjoyed his school assignments and continued to use what he had learnt in subsequent years. In adulthood

---

[18] *P.Petaus* 11.36–8, TM no. 8804: Turner 1968/1980: 83 suggested reading μή (instead of .η in the *editio princeps*). Thus, μὴ εἶναι δὲ καὶ ἀγράμματον αὐτόν, ἀλλὰ | ὑπογράφειν οἷς ἐπιδίδωσι στρα(τηγῷ) καὶ ἄλλοις | βιβλίοις τῆς κωμογρα(μματείας).

[19] *P.Petaus* 31.13–14, TM no. 8850: "I Theon wrote out the greater part (of this document) also on behalf of Petaus," Θέων ἔγραψα | καὶ ὑπὲρ τοῦ Πεταῦτος τὰ πλ⟨ε⟩ῖστα, image online at Michigan APIS 2983 = P.Mich.inv. 6878 recto. For discussion of Theon's command of Greek, see Youtie 1971b: 241–62.

[20] *P.Petaus*, pp. 34–9, with Hand B described on p. 37.

Petaus relied on the skills of his literate brother, and Theon did the writing for him. Theon's writing of business papers for Petaus' *komogrammateia* appears to have been restricted for the most part to gathering preparatory material for the lists that professionals in the bureau subsequently copied to become the formal submissions which Petaus authenticated by appending his signature and then dispatched. Deciding which villagers were to be on which lists displays Theon as carrying out sensitive tasks for his brother, Petaus the scribe who did not know how to write.[21]

The second example likewise involves an archive, and the character on whom we now focus resembles Theon, for the woman Thermouthis is but a minor figure in the archive of business papers assembled by her husband Nemesion, son of Zoilus, collector of the money taxes owed to Rome by the peasant villagers of Philadelphia during the reigns of the Julio-Claudian emperors. Thermouthis' only known contribution to survive among her husband's business papers is a letter she wrote to Nemesion on 7 July 59 CE, while he was away from the village presumably in consequence of his responsibilities as tax-collector. He may have journeyed as far north as Alexandria, since she spoke of his "coming back down" to Philadelphia, but the same phrase would do for his return were he to have traveled only to the metropolis of the Arsinoite nome.[22] In his official capacity Nemesion oversaw the preparation of the yearly *synopsis* for Philadelphia, the calculation which determined how much the some 900 male villagers between the ages of fourteen and sixty-two owed to the imperial bureaucracy during that year.[23] He monitored the work of collectors as they canvassed the village and nearby hamlets for installments of capitation taxes, as well as collecting payments from villagers currently resident elsewhere than Philadelphia; and he kept records of arrears still owing after the books for the current tax year were closed. The *komogrammateus* of Philadelphia supplied Nemesion with changes in population data, and from notices for the births and deaths Nemesion composed lists of male villagers in the ages of tax liability; he noted changes in domicile and status for the men and youths listed in his records, as when young men of the

---

[21] Cf. two lists with names of villagers from Herakleonos Epoikion: the longer (85 lines), but less detailed list written by Hand B (Theon's), *P.Petaus* 117, TM no. 12627, and the shorter (17 lines) list with fuller information apparently written by Hand G, *P.Petaus* 116, TM no. 12626.

[22] *SB* XIV 11585, TM no. 14491. It seems to me unlikely that Nemesion journeyed as far as Alexandria on this occasion, although tax-collectors under his direction did go to the capital city on the Mediterranean coast to collect taxes from villagers of Philadelphia currently resident there. For additional discussion, see Osgood 2011: 135–7.

[23] *P.Sijp*. 26, TM no. 109074; the nearly complete *synopsis* that survives is for the eleventh regnal year of the Emperor Claudius, 50/51 CE.

village enlisted in the military, most likely joining the Roman fleet. He communicated with superiors in the tax bureaux of the metropolis and Alexandria. Composing and compiling tax records made Nemesion a fast and fluid writer of Greek; his control of the grammar and orthography was serviceable, although neither educated nor elegant, yet certainly within koine norms. His was not the Attic Greek of earlier times, but the Greek he wrote was that employed all over the eastern Mediterranean for everyday communications. Thermouthis too was literate in Greek, able to write and read, somewhat unusual accomplishments for a village woman. That both Thermouthis and Nemesion were able to speak Egyptian seems likely due to the fact they lived in an agricultural community, yet neither gives any indication they were able to read or write their native language, for by their day the use of demotic was fast dwindling.[24] At least two of the couple's sons survived beyond age fourteen years, for their names appear on a receipt for the dike tax they paid in 69/70 CE.[25] A letter to Nemesion from a man with the Roman gentilicial Servilius closed with greetings for Thermouthis, as well as for two other females, Ammonous and Nemesous, the latter a likely name for a daughter of the couple, since it is a feminine form of her father's name.[26] Servilius' salutations for Thermouthis at the close of his letter to Nemesion also hint that she was Nemesion's wife. For her part Thermouthis eschewed overt expressions of the couple's affinity in her own letter to Nemesion, for such emotionalism seldom characterizes family letters in the earlier centuries of Roman rule.

Nemesion is attested as collector of money taxes in at least seven different regnal years between 44/45 and 57/58 CE, and this stands in sharp contrast to the three-year terms for liturgic appointments in the second century CE, such as Petaus' term as *komogrammateus*. Nemesion's office of *praktor argyrikon* became a liturgic appointment only from the reign of the Emperor Trajan onward.[27] Nemesion apparently found collecting taxes a congenial and profitable activity and he repeatedly assumed the post and may even have held it continuously in years for which we have no evidence to the contrary. His superiors show no dissatisfaction with his

---

[24] Hanson 1992: 136. The couple had no obvious connections to the local temples, for the significance of which, see Bagnall and Cribiore 2008, chapter 7, pp. 269–71.

[25] Hélène Cuvigny was the first to draw attention to this receipt (*BGU* VII 1614, frag. A, lines 7–8, TM no. 9519) as part of the proof that Thermouthis was in fact Nemesion's wife, for she was said in the receipt to be the mother of Nemesion's two sons: Ptollis and perhaps [Nemesi]on after his father, although only the -ων from the end of his name is visible.

[26] *P.Graux* II 11.10–11, TM no. 25919. Assumptions about the composition of this nuclear family are only likely guesses.

[27] Lewis 1997: 42–3 (s.v. πρακτορεία, πράκτωρ); 35 (s.v. κωμογραμματεία, κωμογραμματεύς).

performance, so far as we know, not even in years when harvests were poor and the rate of tax delinquencies high in both Philadelphia and neighboring villages.[28] Nemesion was a wealthy man by village standards (see footnote 16). He did favors for men with Roman names and received presents from them in return. In the letter from Servilius the latter assured Nemesion that his son-in-law Julius would shortly be delivering the five rolls of papyrus and the other items Nemesion asked him to purchase. Nemesion seems to have gotten on well with his superiors in the Roman bureaucracy, and when a copy of the Emperor Claudius' letter to the Alexandrians came Nemesion's way, he copied the long missive on the back of an old tax roll from the second year of the Emperor Gaius' reign (37/38 CE).[29] In addition to collecting taxes Nemesion also lent money at interest, once threatening to take into custody an old couple from Philadelphia, if their eldest son did not promptly repay the debts his parents owed him.[30] The ages of the couple are not specified, but their son was already thirty-eight years old at the time of the incident, underscoring the fact that the husband and wife Nemesion was threatening to impound with the help of Roman soldiers were well advanced in years. Nemesion's papers testified to disputes and quarrels he had with colleagues and underlings; he and the shepherds in his employ frequently argued over wages, and Nemesion was not above confiscating the shepherds' belongings. Perhaps most interesting, however, are the long-lived business arrangements he had with the Roman centurion Lucius Cattius Catullus, extending over at least thirteen years.[31] Nemesion owned grain land, as well as flocks of sheep and goats, and some of the records he kept about his properties show him dividing income from sales of animals and their skins with Cattius – he calls him Lucius – along with expenses incurred in managing the properties. Nemesion was serving as the owner of record, since Roman law discouraged Cattius from acquiring property in any province where he was serving on active duty. For his part, Cattius provided Nemesion with soldiers from the troop under his command, enabling Nemesion to settle his disputes with threats from Roman swords.

---

[28] Hanson 1986: 261–77.
[29] P.Brit.Lib.inv. 2248, of which only Claudius' letter on the verso has been published as *P.Lond.* VI 1912, TM no. 16850; for Nemesion's hand and the tax document on the recto, see Hanson 1984.
[30] Hanson 2001: 91–7, *P.Thomas* 5, TM no. 44491, and for other testimony to Nemesion's money-lending, *SB* IV 7465, TM no. 14021.
[31] Hanson 2001: 91–7.

Nemesion's busy life and diverse interests were likewise reflected in the letter Thermouthis wrote to him while he was absent from the village: her concise retelling of recent developments reveal her well able to manage whatever arises on the home front during her husband's absence, even though she was likely to be younger than he and perhaps considerably younger.[32]

> Thermouthis to Nemesion, greeting.
>
> I want you to know that Lucius has come.
>
> About his smock of coarse sackcloth which you have in the city, if you come down, bring (line 4) it. He has the hood here. I gave it to him some time ago on his word alone, so that he might have it until you come down.
>
> And about the shepherds' wages (line 8), he said, "I am sending a soldier ... immediately" – he says – "to seize the shepherds' belongings that remain." He has not given us their mattress (line 12), because he says, "Bring me my old one!"
>
> And about the shovel he says that you asked them for three staters per shovel.
> Farewell.
> Year 5 of Nero, Epeiph 13.
>
> *Address on the back:* Give to Nemesion
> (*SB* xiv 11585, TM no. 14491, P.Corn.Inv. I ii)

Thermouthis employed only brief greetings at the beginning and ending of her letter, condensing lines 1 and 16 to the minimum: at the outset Θερμοῦθις Νεμεσίωνι χαίρειν and at the end ἔρρωσο, followed by the date. At the same time, although her orthography is phonetic throughout the body of the letter (lines 2–15), she executes the first and last lines flawlessly, no matter what standard of Greek spelling be applied. Her competence with these four words suggests that she has composed other letters on previous occasions, opening and closing with the same or similar words, even though no other letter written by her hand seems to have survived within the rest of Nemesion's archive. The phonetic spellings that intrude into the body of her letter do not appear in the formulaic lines at beginning and end – neither the frequent and false interchange of short and long vowels,[33] and diphthongs,[34] and no iotacistic interchange of ει and ι.[35]

---

[32] For age differences among spouses, see Bagnall and Frier 1994: 118–21.

[33] Examples of omicron (o) when omega (ω) is correct: line 2 θελο; line 2 -γνοσκ-; line 5 οδε; lines 6 and 12 δεδοκ-; line 9 πεμπο.

[34] Examples of epsilon (ε) when either αι or η would be correct: line 4 -βεν- (in the correct καταβαίνεις); line 13 -λε- (in the correct παλαιάν); line 14 ετ- (in the correct ἠτήσω).

[35] Indiscriminate use of ει and ι, for which line 2 provides examples of both: οτει for ὅτι and ηκι for ἥκει. Thermouthis is consistent in invariably writing ὅτει the three times it occurs (lines 9, 12, 14)

Θερμοῦθις Νεμεσίωνι χαίρειν.
θέλο σε γηνόσκειν ὅτει ἥκι Λού-
κι⟨ο⟩ς περὶ τοῦ σάκκου αὐτοῦ τοῦ παχέως
οὗ ἔχις ἐν τῇ πόλι, ἂν καταβένις κα-　4
τένικον. τὸν σουβρικὸν ἔχι ὅδε. ἀπά-
νο αὐτοῦ δέδοκα μόνῃ μαρτυρίᾳ
αὐτοῦ [ὅ]πος ἔχι αὐτὸ ἕως καταβῇς.
καὶ περὶ τῶν μισθῶν τῶν πυμέν^ον　8
ἔλεγε ὅτει πέμπο στρατιώτη[ν...]
... παραυτόν, λέγει, εἴνα συλήσῃ
τὰ παραμεμένεκε τῶν πυμένων.
τὴν τύλην ὑμῶν οὐ δέδοκε. ὅτει　12
φέρε τὴν ἐμὴν τὴν παλεάν, λέγει.
καὶ περὶ τῆς ἄμης λέγει ὅτει ἐτήσο
αὐτοὺς τρῖς στ[α]τρες τῆς ἄμης.
ἔρροσο　16
(ἔτους) ε Νέρονος Ἐπεὶφ ιγ̄
verso/back: ἀπόδ(ος) Νεμεσίονι.

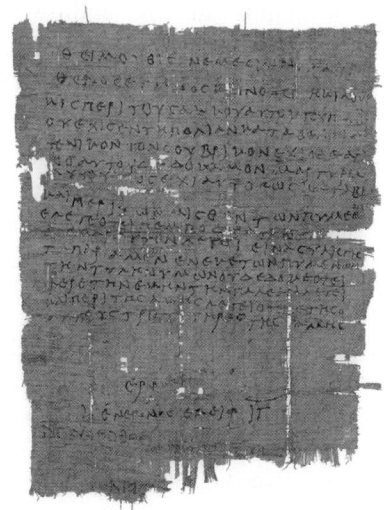

Figure 2.2: *SB* XIV 11585, TM no. 14491, P.Corn.Inv. I 11

Phonetic spellings were left uncorrected in the above transcript, except for correcting to Λούκι<ο>ς; both Thermouthis and Nemesion write his Roman name as Λοῦκις, as do an increasing number of Greco-Egyptians as time goes by.³⁶

If Thermouthis wrote out the letter for herself, as seems probable to those who include it in collections of papyri elucidating women's lives, not only does her penmanship and mastery of Greek syntax exceed her competence in spelling, yet the confidence and verve with which she expresses herself remain impressive.³⁷ In their description of Thermouthis' letter as B4.34, letter no. 233, Bagnall and Cribiore award positive marks to

---

and also in writing omicron, not omega, for the first person singular active ending of verbs (lines 2 and 9).

³⁶ Youtie 1976: 53–6 offered a "corrected version" of Thermouthis' entire letter that replaced her many variations from standard orthography, while still retaining her characteristic syntax. I employ corrected orthography for the lemmata of the commentary appearing below, to encourage comparison between what Thermouthis writes and more standard koine. The version of the letter in the DDbDP <papyri.info> speaks of three lines written by a second hand in the direction opposite the main text; these lines are said to be too fragmentary for translation and that someone made an attempt to expunge them. The three lines are, however, placed at the bottom of the recto or front side and not on the verso or back, as stated in the online apparatus criticus. The third line apparently reads: σὺν το θεο (leg. τῷ θεῷ) θέλων (leg. θέλοντι), "if the god is willing."

³⁷ Youtie 1976: 53. As the first editor of the text Youtie argued that the matter of Thermouthis having penned the letter herself could not be decided for certain and caution was appropriate. At the same time, he also drew attention to the fact that the concluding formula in lines 16 and 17 was written by

Thermouthis for her penmanship, because despite the fact that she employs ligatures only sparingly, her individual letters are not unattractive, occasionally moving in the direction of more cursive forms, and hence toward more fluid writing.[38] Alignment of lines is not as difficult for Thermouthis as it was for Petaus (see footnote 14). Spelling is the main impediment to immediate legibility of Thermouthis' letter; by reading her letter aloud, voicing the words she wrote on the sheet of papyrus, her husband may well have failed to notice her faulty orthography, however bothersome it is to those accustomed to Attic Greek. What makes her letter impressive is not so much its overall physical appearance, but rather her command of serviceable Greek and the rhythm she establishes to shape a coherent and efficient missive, beginning with her opening declaration of the most important event in the household since Nemesion's departure: θέλω σε γινώσκειν ὅτι ἥκει Λούκιος, "I want you to know that Lucius has come."[39] In the formal language of official documents Nemesion refers to him as "Cattius, our local centurion," or as "Cattius Catullus."[40] But in the agricultural records that detail their financial cooperation, intended for their eyes alone, Nemesion uses his praenomen Lucius, writing Λοῦκις. Thermouthis likewise writes Λοῦκις in her letter, perhaps highlighting the fact that the centurion was a figure familiar to Nemesion's household.

Thermouthis structures her letter around three περί-clauses that explain developments resulting from Lucius' arrival at Philadelphia. The first two

---

the same hand as lines 1–15, because a change of hand at this point is a common marker that the sender of the letter is employing a scribe to write the body of the letter, for senders who were themselves literate yet are also making use of a scribe prefer to write the closing greeting in their own hand, penmanship that might well be familiar to the recipient. A photo of Thermouthis' letter in Rowlandson 1998: 326–7, text 259 and plate 41.

[38] As of 18 June 2013 the scan of Thermouthis' letter (*SB* XIV 11585, TM no. 14491), letter no. 233, B4.34 in Bagnall and Cribiore 2008, does not illustrate that papyrus, but rather another one, published as *P.Corn.* I, TM no. 2301, a two-columned text from the mid-third-century BCE archive of Zenon, currently housed with the University of Michigan collection as Michigan APIS 1239, an extensive account of kiki oil for the lamps of Apollonius' scribes. The reason for the confusion of an early Ptolemaic papyrus with a letter written in the mid-first century CE involves the inventory numbers assigned to the two papyri at Cornell University when the papyri were originally inventoried: the Ptolemaic account was designated P.Corn.Inv. II i, while Thermouthis' letter was inventoried as P.Corn.Inv. I ii, numbers easily confused. A scan of Thermouthis' letter is available at Michigan APIS 1203; and despite the fact that her letter is now housed in Ann Arbor MI (not Ithaca NY), its inventory number remains P.Corn.Inv. I ii.

[39] Thermouthis' orthography has been corrected here and in the lemmata that follow in order to facilitate comparisons with the uncorrected version.

[40] *P.Mich.* X 582 (= P.Mich.inv. 886, TM no. 12269), with improvements to the Greek text recorded at Michigan APIS 3150. See also Hanson 2001: *P.Thomas*, papyrus 5, pages 91–7. The centurion is addressed as Lucius Cattius Catul<l>us in the petition directed to his attention by a Philadelphia villager in 50/51 CE, *P.Sijp.* 15.1, TM no. 110149.

topics afford her an opportunity to add details that were apparently unknown to Nemesion because he departed before Lucius' arrival:

Lines 3–7: περὶ τοῦ σάκκου αὐτοῦ τοῦ παχέως | οὗ ἔχεις ἐν τῇ πόλει, ἐὰν καταβαίνῃς κα-|τένεικον· τὸν σουβρικὸν ἔχει ὧδε. ἐπά-|νω αὐτῷ δέδωκα μόνῃ μαρτυρίᾳ | αὐτοῦ ὅπως ἔχῃ αὐτὸν ἕως καταβῇς, "About his smock of coarse sackcloth which you have in the city, if you come down, bring it. He has the hood here. I gave it to him some time ago on his word alone, so that he might have it until you come down."

Lucius has apparently left one of his garments in the city where Nemesion currently is, most likely in the metropolis of the Arsinoite nome. Thermouthis conveys to Nemesion Lucius' desire that he bring the smock back with him when he returns home to Philadelphia. Subordinate and contingent topics occur to her, and she continues with the fact that Lucius is able to use the hood (σουβρικός) while he is in Philadelphia, for when he asked her for it, she gave it to him without taking a receipt, but on his word alone. In the process Thermouthis practices the term Lucius used for this item of clothing which shades his head.[41] She apparently takes some pleasure in displaying to Nemesion the word she has acquired for her vocabulary, and because the word *subricus* was mentioned to her by the Roman, she no doubt thinks it proper Latin.

Lines 8–11: καὶ περὶ τῶν μισθῶν τῶν ποιμένων, | ἔλεγε ὅτι "πέμπω στρατιώτη[ν ±3] | ... παραυτά," λέγει, "ἵνα συλήσῃ | τὰ παραμεμένηκε τῶν ποιμένων," "And about the shepherds' wages, he said, 'I am sending a soldier immediately' – he says – 'to seize the shepherds' belongings that remain.'" The insertion of ἔλεγε and λέγει followed by quotations of Lucius' own words in direct discourse heighten the vividness of her narrative.

It may be that Nemesion encouraged his wife's efforts to enhance her skills in penmanship and composition, and he may have influenced her writing. That is, while Nemesion was by no means the sole writer of Greek in Philadelphia in the middle of the first century CE, a passably literate neighbor, however many there may have been, could just as well have pushed upon Thermouthis the phonetic spellings she produced in her letter, infelicities and all. Husband and wife, nonetheless, do share a number of orthographic errors and it seems worthwhile to point these out, since it seems not impossible that Nemesion's notions of proper

---

[41] Youtie 1976: 53–4, where he noted that this was the first occurrence of σουβρικός in the papyri. He canvassed previous occurrences of other forms, a diminutive and several compounds, all designating garments for the upper body. While Youtie suggested an ultimate derivation from *sub* and *rica*, see Daris 1991: 105, for an alternative derivation.

spelling influenced what Thermouthis was writing: in the two times Thermouthis mentions "of the shepherds" (πυμέν^{ον}, with short vowel instead of long in the case ending of line 8 and correctly with omega in line 11), she spells the first syllable of the Greek word ποιμένων as πυ-, because she pronounces ποι- and πυ- identically. Although the interchange of υ- and οι- is becoming a common infelicity that begins in the later first century CE, the mistake is likewise a prominent one in Nemesion's copying of Claudius' letter to the Alexandrians, and appears elsewhere in his papers. Someone else might have introduced this and other orthographic errors into the text of Claudius' letter in the course of its transmission, but even if spelling mistakes in the Emperor's letter are not to be blamed upon Nemesion with certainty, it is nonetheless the case that as he copied he made no obvious attempts to improve orthography in his model. Nemesion may also have influenced Thermouthis' spelling through his own habit of interchanging the short and long vowels ο and ω; so far as I am aware, however, he never employed omicron for the correct omega in the final syllable of first-person active verb forms as Thermouthis does twice in her letter (lines 2 and 9).[42] Another infelicity shared by the couple along with Greco-Egyptian neighbors involves their failure to distinguish ἡμ- from ὑμ- in the initial syllable of first- and second-person plural pronouns and pronominals, treating the syllables as homophonous. Thus, for example, in Claudius' letter Nemesion writes ἡμᾶς (line 21) which the modern editor corrects to ὑμᾶς; ἡμῶν (lines 28 and 106) which the modern editor corrects to ὑμῶν; ἡμεῖν (line 65) which the modern editor corrects to ὑμῖν; and ἡμετέρων (line 75) to ὑμετέρων. Thermouthis may have committed a somewhat similar mistake in line 12 of her own letter, writing ὑμῶν, when she intends the first-person plural and, I suggest, confusing in addition genitive for dative, as Thermouthis also does when she writes αὐτοῦ δέδοκα in line 6, instead of the correct αὐτῷ δέδωκα. (See next paragraph and footnote 43).

Lines 12–13 are apparently tangential to the larger topic of the soldier's confiscation of property left behind by the shepherds: τὴν τύλην ἡμῖν[43] οὐ δέδωκε, ὅτι | "φέρε τὴν ἐμὴν παλαιάν," λέγει, "He has not given us their mattress, because he

---

[42] Gignac 1976: vol. I, 197–9 (interchange of υ and οι) which occurs in *P.Lond.* VI 1912.20, 64, 87. Gignac 1976: vol. I, 275–7 (substitution of ο for ω) which occurs in *P.Lond.* VI 1912.29 (πρότα), 49 (ἀνθρόποις), 102 (φιλανθροπείας).

[43] ὑμῶν pap., Youtie corrected to ἡμῶν, but perhaps dative ἡμῖν was actually Thermouthis' intention. That is, with Lucius saying, "I have not given their mattress to you (Thermouthis and Nemesion), because (you must first) bring me my old one!," Thermouthis transfers his words to a report in the third person, "He has not given their mattress to us, because he says, 'Bring me my old one'!" Youtie's note to lines 12 and 13 suggests keeping the final two phrases together and relating them to lines 8–11.

says, 'Bring me my old one'!" Apparently a swapping of mattresses was to take place, with Lucius unwilling to surrender the mattress in his possession to Nemesion's wife prior to receiving the replacement.

Lines 14–15: καὶ περὶ τῆς ἄμης λέγει ὅτι ᾐτήσω | αὐτοὺς τρεῖς στατῆρας τῆς ἄμης, "And about the shovel, he says that you asked them for three staters per shovel."

The terseness of Thermouthis' words on this last topic is perhaps at first surprising, but by her own account she was not involved in the matter of shovels, nor in their pricing. This was of concern to Nemesion and Lucius, and whenever they discussed shovels and their cost she did not take part. Therefore she has nothing of her own to add. But to whom does her αὐτούς (line 15) refer, since the shepherds presumably decamped upon the arrival of the soldier Lucius dispatched, if the shepherds had not fled already?[44]

As a young woman born and raised in a village dominated by farming interests, Thermouthis was unlikely to have been subjected to lengthy formal schooling, but in common with Petaus' younger brother Theon, she too seems to have profited from whatever educational opportunities came her way. She listened carefully to those speakers of Greek whose command of the language she admired and she refined her own capabilities through absorption and practice. Much of her language learning was demonstrably oral, as the style in which she composed her own letter makes clear, and repeating another's words verbatim not only heightens the vivacity of her narrative, but also can supply her with proper vocabulary and syntax for the sentences she is attempting to replicate. Nemesion – collector of money taxes owed by villagers of Philadelphia to Rome, money-lender, business partner of the centurion Lucius and other Romans – though stern to those who owe him money and sometimes threatening violence to those in his employ, was apparently indulgent to members of his own family, using his contacts in the metropolis and Alexandria to acquire luxury goods for their use, as well as his own.[45] He may well have encouraged Thermouthis' efforts to attain greater fluency and sophistication in writing, speaking, and perhaps even reading Greek.

---

[44] One can imagine various scenarios for the shovel, or shovels, and the αὐτούς. For example, if Lucius dispatched more than a single soldier, perhaps they intended to perform demolition work on an enclosure in which the shepherds lodged their gear and needed additional shovels for the task.

[45] *P.Graux* II 10.3–13, TM no. 25918, Servilius mentions to Nemesion various items the latter asked him to buy, such as things of interest to grownups (five rolls of papyrus, best quality Italian rose oil, perhaps the ring, etc.); and pleasurables (στρόβιλοι) for children. Servilius encourages Nemesion to make other requests of him: "If you need something, just write and I shall do it," ὃ ἐὰν χρῄζῃς γράφε καὶ ποιήσω.

Because Nemesion was relatively wealthy, he could encourage his wife either by turning a benign gaze toward her and other womenfolk in his household, should they desire to spend time in what would have been for them a leisure pursuit. Or he may even have been involved more directly, monitoring and correcting some of Thermouthis' attempts to the extent his own attainments enabled him. Nemesion was, after all, the more experienced at composing documents and letters, while his work in the tax bureau on a daily basis forced him to become a fluent writer.

CHAPTER 3

Teaching Latin to Greek speakers in antiquity
Eleanor Dickey

When we think of ancient Latin teaching, we tend to think of little Roman children reading Latin poetry and learning about rhetoric in schools where everyone was a native speaker of Latin.[1] Such ancient schools seem utterly different from modern Latin teaching, which since it is always directed at non-native speakers has to concentrate most of its efforts on building basic language skills that Roman children had already acquired before they were old enough to go to school.

Yet not all Latin learners in the ancient world were native speakers: as the Romans conquered other peoples their language spread rapidly around the Mediterranean. The learning of Latin by these other peoples took place in different ways in the various parts of the empire. In the west, entire populations shifted to become Latin speakers: men and women who had grown up speaking Oscan or Gaulish raised their children speaking Latin, and their own native languages died out. In such areas any large-scale non-native-speaker Latin teaching could have occurred only before the shift was complete, for once the non-Roman populations became native Latin speakers the need for teaching geared to non-native speakers would have disappeared.

In the east, by contrast, populations conquered by the Romans did not switch to Latin and instead relied primarily on Greek. Greek was of course not the original language of this whole area, having been imported into most of it by Alexander and his successors, and indeed many people in the eastern empire were not native speakers of Greek. Nevertheless, when populations in the east gave up their native languages and switched to another language for raising their children, the language to which they switched was usually Greek rather than Latin, and therefore native speakers of Latin continued to be relatively rare in that portion of the world.

[1] I am grateful to Daniela Colomo, Rolando Ferri, Anna Morpurgo Davies, Siam Bhayro, Philomen Probert, and Jim Adams for assistance with this project.

Nevertheless, knowledge of Latin as a second language was not uncommon among Greek speakers during the empire (cf. Rochette 1997; Rizakis 2008). The Roman army, a common path to citizenship and social advancement, was a major source of Latin learning for recruits from the eastern empire and may even have conducted organized Latin classes for these recruits (Adams 2003a: 617–21). The Roman legal system was another source of such learning; prospective lawyers needed to know Latin and for this reason major universities in the east, such as Beirut, offered lectures from professors of Latin. The higher levels of the Roman provincial administration were also Latin-speaking, and of course anyone who travelled to the western empire, or interacted regularly with merchants or other travellers from the west, would find Latin useful. The result was that systematic, organized teaching of Latin as a foreign language was far more common in the east than in the west.

How was this teaching conducted? What was the experience of the ancient Latin learner? Our evidence on this point comes principally from Egypt, where numerous papyrus fragments preserve the texts that ancient students used to learn Latin. These texts fall into several distinct groups: transliterated texts geared strictly to oral proficiency; elementary materials for those attaining literacy in the Roman alphabet; and more advanced texts. Most of them have been studied individually,[2] but we have little sense of how the different kinds of text fitted together in the ancient curriculum. In what follows I attempt to pull together the information we have about different types of Latin-learning materials and suggest how they complemented each other and what kind of learning experience they gave the ancient Latin student.

Berlitz Latin for Travellers: **transliterated texts**

A significant number of preserved Latin learning materials have the Latin transliterated into Greek script.[3] These texts resemble the phrase books that English speakers sometimes use to get around on short trips to Russia,

---

[2] There has been extensive work on the glossaries (e.g. Kramer 1983, 2001, 2004; Dickey 2010a), on the bilingual Virgil and Cicero materials (e.g. Gaebel 1970; Maehler 1979; Rochette 1990; Scappaticcio 2013), and on the *Hermeneumata* (e.g. Dionisotti 1982a; Korhonen 1996; Ferri 2008; Dickey 2012), but much less on the grammatical material (though Bonnet 2005 provides discussion as well as a text and translation of Dositheus) and the annotated literary texts (though McNamee 2007 is very helpful). Rochette (1997: 165–210) offers a useful overview of much of the material. For a complete list of the surviving ancient Latin-learning materials, see Dickey 2012: 7–10.

[3] More than a dozen papyri, including numbers 1, 5–9, 11–13, and 15 in Kramer 1983 and numbers 3, 6, and 7 in Kramer 2001.

China, or another country where a non-Roman alphabet is used; they were clearly designed for use by people literate in Greek who needed some oral proficiency in Latin but did not want to invest time and energy in learning a different alphabet. The transliterated texts are most often classified vocabulary lists; just as a modern Berlitz phrase book might have sections on airport vocabulary, hotel vocabulary, and restaurant vocabulary, so its ancient equivalents might have sections on army vocabulary, religious vocabulary, and terms for different vegetables. Example 1 is an extract from such a classified vocabulary list, from the beginning of a section on military vocabulary; the Greek terms are on the left and the Latin on the right.[4]

1. [περ]ι στρ[ατιωτων]   δη μι[λιτι]βους   About soldiers:
   [στ]ρατι[α]   μιλ[ιτι]α   warfare
   παρε[μβολη]   καστρα   camp
   ταφρ[ος]   φοσσα   ditch
   ηγεμ[ων]   δουξ   leader
   αυτοκ[ρ]ατωρ   ιμπερατωρ   emperor
   χιλιαρχος   τριβουνους μελιτουμ   military tribune
   στρατοπεδαρχης   φρενεκτους κα[στ]ρωρου[μ]   camp prefect[5]
   πρωροστατης   πρινκιψ   commander
   σκηναι   ταβερνακουλα   commander's tent
   στρατοπαιδον   εξερκιτους   army

(P.Strasb.inv. g 1173 (*M-P³* 2134.61, *LDAB* 9218),[6] III–IV CE, ed. Kramer 2001: no. 6, lines 24–34)

Another standard feature of a modern phrase book is a conversational section giving the basic greetings and other phrases necessary for having civil interaction with speakers of the other language. Such works also existed in antiquity; example 2 is an extract from the Latin and Greek sections of a trilingual conversation manual. This work now survives in three columns: Latin on the left (in Greek script), Greek in the middle,

---

[4] In transcriptions of papyri, dots under letters indicate that only part of the letter is preserved, square brackets indicate letters no longer visible on the papyrus but presumed to have originally been present, and round brackets indicate expansion of abbreviations.

[5] Surprisingly, φρενεκτους is for Latin *praefectus*. This is not the place to discuss the spellings of the transliterated Latin and how much they can tell us about the evolution of spoken Latin in the later empire, but much has been written on this important aspect of these texts; see Adams (2003a: 40–63) and the commentaries by Kramer (1983, 2001).

[6] Because papyri are often difficult to identify precisely, for all papyri quoted I shall give both the number in the Mertens-Pack database of literary papyri (*M-P³*) and the number in the Leuven database of ancient books (*LDAB*); the former database can be found at www2.ulg.ac.be/facphl/services/cedopal/pages/mp3anglais.htm and the latter at www.trismegistos.org/ldab/index.php.

and Coptic on the right. The Coptic seems to be a translation of the Greek, and it is thought that the work was probably adapted from a bilingual manual by the addition of the Coptic column for the benefit of Copts whose Greek was not up to learning Latin through the medium of Greek. The columns are very narrow, containing only one to three words per line and thereby causing individual phrases to be divided between two or more lines; on each line the Greek exactly matches the Latin. This type of layout was the norm in ancient phrase books. It has the advantage of allowing the reader to understand each component of the phrase and thereby to modify it if necessary.

2. σερμω   ομιλια   Daily conversation:
    κω[τιδια]νους·   καθημερινη·
    κοιδ φακιμους,   τι ποιουμεν,   What (shall) we do,
    φρα[τε]ρ;   αδελφε;   brother?
    [λι]βεντε]ρ τη   ηδεως σε   I am glad
    βιδεω.   ορω.   to see you.
    ετ εγω δη,   καγω σε,   And I (am glad to see) you,
    δομινε.   δεσποτα.   sir.
    ετ νως   και ημεις   And we (are glad to see)
    βως.   ημας.   you (plural).
    νεσκ[ιω]   ουκ οιδα   Someone
    κοις   τις
    οστιουμ   την θυραν   is knocking on the door;
    πουλσατ·   κρουρει·
    εξιειτο   εξελθη   go
    κιτω φορας   ταχεως εξω   quickly outside
    ετ δισκε   και μαθε   and find out
    [κο]ις εστ.   τις [εσ]τιν.   who it is.

(P.Berol.inv. 10582 (M-P³ 3009, LDAB 6075), VI CE, ed. Kramer 2010: lines 42–64. Diacritics are original but punctuation editorial.)

Another feature of the transliterated texts is grammatical information. Greek speakers, being used to an inflected language with even more verb forms than Latin, were not frightened by the concept of foreign inflections. Even learners who did not want to read and write felt a need to know some grammar, as illustrated by the alphabetically ordered verb conjugation table in transliterated Latin given as example 3.[7]

---

[7] Morgan (1998: 162–9) has argued that the ancients did not use grammatical tables as a part of basic language instruction, but this view is difficult to reconcile with the existence of documents such as this one and that in example 7. Such evidence clearly indicates that Greek speakers learning Latin did

3.

ασπαζεται	σαλουτατ	he greets
ασπαζεις	σαλουτας	you greet
ασπαζομαι	σαλουτω	I greet
βασιλ[ε]υ[ει]	ρηγνατ	he rules
βασιλ[ε]υ[εις]	[ρ]ηγνας	you rule
βασιλευ[ω]	ρηγνω	I rule
βα[σ]ανι[ζει]	τορκ[ε]τ	he tortures
βασανι[ζει]ς	τορκες	you torture
βασαν[ιζ]ω	τορκεω . . .	I torture
γινωσκει	νοουιτ	he knows
γινωσκεις	νοουις	you know
γινωσκω	νωουι . . .	I know
γηρασκει	σ[ε]νησκιτ	he grows old
γηρασκεις	σενησκις	you grow old
γηρασκω	σ[ε]νησκω	I grow old
γενναται	ν[α]σκιτουρ	he is born
γεννασαι	νασκαιρης	you are born
γεννωμαι	ν[ασκορ]	I am born

(P.Strasb.inv. g 1175 (*M-P³* 2134.71, *LDAB* 9217), III–IV CE, ed. Kramer 2001: no. 3, lines 3–11, 60–2, 72–7)

This table shows a good knowledge of both Latin and Greek idiom. Verbs in both languages are given in the tense and voice that would actually be used, even if those do not match each other: thus Latin *novit* is correctly given in the perfect as the equivalent of the Greek present γι(γ)νώσκει, and *salutat* is correctly active as the equivalent of the Greek middle ἀσπάζεται, while *nascitur* is correctly deponent. At the same time, the table is unusual in a number of ways: it has only singular verbs, and it presents the forms in the order third person, second person, first person. In both Greek and Latin grammar the normal order is first person, second person, third person, but in Semitic languages it is traditional to start with the third person singular.[8] It is possible that this text was designed by, or designed to be used by, someone whose main education had been in a Semitic language (Aramaic?) rather than in Greek – though the writer must have been literate in Greek as well.

---

use grammatical tables, even at a stage when they were not yet learning the alphabet. See also Rochette 1997: 179–81.
[8] Personal communication from Siam Bhayro.

Elementary Latin literacy

The number of transliterated texts could give the impression that Egyptian Greek speakers were only interested in oral proficiency in Latin and never learned to read it, but such was not the case. The majority of Latin-learning papyrus texts have the Latin in its own alphabet, and a number of fragments show how Greek speakers learned that alphabet. The teacher would write out the new alphabet, either in capitals or both in capital and in lower-case forms, and the student would then copy it out repeatedly; students also copied out one or two lines of verse to help them learn to use the letters in context.[9]

Example 4 shows such a learner's alphabet and line of verse (Virgil, *Aeneid* 4.129); someone (one hopes it was the student rather than the teacher) has written Greek equivalents over the Latin letters but made the mistake of equating Greek η (a vowel) with Latin *h* (a consonant).

4. [α   β   κ   δ]   ε   φ   γ   η   ι   κ   λ[
    [A] B   C   D   E   F   G   H   I   [K] L]

    ]V   X   Y   Z

    [α   β] κ   δ   ε   φ   κ   η   ι   κ[
    a   b   c   d   e   f   g   h   [i] k   l   m   n   o   p   q   r[

[Oceanum inter]ea surgen⟨s⟩ Aurora [reliquit]

(*P.Oxy.* 10.1315 (*M-P³* 3013, *LDAB* 4163), V–VI CE, ed. Kramer 2001: no. 2)

The student also learned the Latin letter names; an alternative way of learning the alphabet was to write these over the Latin letters in Greek script, as in example 5.[10]

5.]γη ʽι κα ιλ μ εν ω ππ κου ρ ες ττ ου ξη
    ]G   H   I   K   L M   N O   P   Q R   S   T   U   X   Y   Z

(*O.Max.* 356 (*M-P³* 3012.01, *LDAB* 10791), I–II CE, ed. Cuvigny 2003: 445)

Once the ancient Latin student had learned the alphabet, he (or perhaps she?) needed the same basic materials as a modern student: some grammar, some vocabulary, and a text to read. All these types of material have been found both

---

[9] Clarysse and Rochette (2005: 75) propose a different system of alphabet learning, but their arguments have been refuted by Feissel (2008).
[10] The most famous example of the writing of Latin letter names in this fashion is *P.Ant.* 1 fr. 1 verso (= Kramer 1999, 2001: no. 1). But because this example occurs in a shorthand manual, it is not clear that it was a teaching tool.

on papyrus and in medieval manuscripts whose contents are likely to be ancient. Example 6 comes from a manuscript copied around 900 CE, but the material in it is certainly ancient, because part of this text has also been recovered on papyrus (see Dickey and Ferri 2012). It is an extract from the *Colloquium Harleianum*, one of a group of six colloquia that contain dialogues and narration of scenes from everyday life. In medieval manuscripts the colloquia are part of a body of bilingual language teaching materials known as the *Hermeneumata Pseudodositheana* (because in some manuscripts they are attached to the grammar of Dositheus, for which see below, though they were not composed by Dositheus). In the medieval west the *Hermeneumata* collection was used as a unit to teach Greek to Latin speakers, but the different elements of which it is made up were probably separately composed, and many of them were originally created in antiquity for teaching Latin to Greek speakers.[11] The colloquia include descriptions of getting up in the morning, going to school, having lunch, visiting friends, banking, shopping, going to court, trips to the public baths, dinner parties, and finally going to bed in the evening; they also contain collections of phrases to use in various situations, such as when engaged in a brawl, dealing with a recalcitrant servant, excusing oneself for not having done something, etc.

6. Χαῖρε,   *Ave,*
   κύριε   *domine*
   διδάσκαλε,   *praeceptor,*
   καλῶς σοι   *bene tibi*
   γένοιτο.   *sit.*
   ἀπὸ σήμερον   *ab hodie*
   φιλοπονεῖν   *studere*
   θέλω.   *volo.*
   ἐρωτῶ σε οὖν,   *rogo te ergo,*
   ⟨δίδαξόν με⟩ Ῥωμαϊστὶ   *⟨doce me⟩ Latine*
   λαλ⟨ε⟩ῖν.   *loqui.*
   Διδάσκω σε,   *Doceo te,*
   ἐάν με πρό⟨σ⟩σχῃς.   *si me attendas.*
   Ἰδού, προσέχω.   *Ecce, attendo.*
   καλῶς εἶπας,   *Bene dixisti,*
   ὡς πρέπει   *ut decet*
   τῇ εὐγενείᾳ σου.   *ingenuitatem tuam.*
   ἐπίδος μοι, παῖ,   *porrige mihi, puer,*
   τὸ ἀναλογεῖον.   *manuale.*

---

[11] On the nature and history of the *Hermeneumata* see Dickey 2012: 16–44, Korhonen 1996, Dionisotti 1982a, and Goetz *et al.* 1888–1923: vols. 1 and 3.

ταχέως οὖν	*cito ergo*
ἐπίδος	*porrige*
τὸ βιβλίον,	*librum,*
ἀνείλησον,	*revolve,*
ἀνάγνωθι	*lege*
μετὰ φωνῆς,	*cum voce,*
ἄνοιξον	*aperi*
τὸ στόμα,	*os,*
ψήφισον.	*computa.*
ἄρτι καλῶς	*modo bene*
ποίησον	*fac*
τόπον,	*locum,*
ἵνα γράψῃς	*ut scribas*
ἅμιλλαν.	*dictatum.*

(*Colloquium Harleianum* 4a–5d, ed. Dickey forthcoming. Diacritcs and punctuation are editorial.)

"Hello, sir teacher! May (all) be well for you. From today I want to work hard. So please teach me to speak Latin." "I (shall) teach you, if you pay attention to me." "Look, I'm paying attention." "You have spoken well, as befits your good birth. Boy, hand me the book-stand. So, quickly hand (me) the book, turn (to the right page), read aloud, open your mouth, count. Now mark the place well, so that you may write an exercise."

These colloquia have short sentences, simple syntax, and common everyday vocabulary. (The words in them often appear strange to modern readers, because most of the Latin we are used to is both earlier in time and concerned with other topics, but in most cases the words that appear unfamiliar to us can be shown to have been in use during the empire.) They are thus ideal reading material for the early stages of learning the language.[12] It is likely that students memorized sections of the colloquia in Latin, using the Greek translation to make sure they understood the Latin, and then recited these extracts to the teacher, either individually or with several students performing a dialogue.[13]

This system was an excellent way to learn basic vocabulary in context, but nevertheless the colloquia were no substitute for a real dictionary, as they could not easily be used to look up a specific word. Lexica, therefore,

---

[12] Although the colloquia have generally not been used for language teaching since the sixteenth century, they remain potentially useful even today: see Debut 1987 on the advantages for today's Greek teachers of the Greek half of the colloquium. I have used slightly adapted extracts from the Latin half of the colloquia with a first-year Latin class at the University of Exeter and found the material to be excellent for modern students, provided the vocabulary is adequately glossed.

[13] See Dickey 2012: 52–4.

existed in abundance.[14] Many were classified word-lists, like the transliterated text in example 1; others arranged words in alphabetical order. (Ancient alphabetical order did not necessarily mean full alpabetical order of the kind used today; often words were grouped together by their first two or three letters without regard for the other letters in the words, as in example 3 above. See Daly 1967.) Ancient lexica, like modern ones, came in a variety of sizes, ranging from small to large. Example 7 is a short extract from the largest known ancient bilingual lexicon; this work is not fully preserved, but it can be estimated that when complete it had c. 32,000 entries, divided roughly equally between Latin-Greek and Greek-Latin sections.[15]

7.	παρες	*omitte*	let go!
	παρεσκευασατο	*adparuit* π̄ *adiunxit*	he prepared, he added
	παρεστη	*ads*[*i*]*stit*	he stood by
	παρεστησεν	*obtuli̭t adprova*[*v*]*i̭*[*t*]	he offered, he agreed
	παρεστω	*adsit praesto sit*	let him be present
	παρεστραμμενον	*reviminatum*	hemmed
	παρετυχεν	[*inter*]*fuit*	he was present
	παρευρησις κ[αιρος]	[*o*]*c̭c̭asio*	pretext, opportunity
	παρεχει	*praestat praebet*	he provides

(*Folium Wallraffianum* (M-P³ 2134.4, *LDAB* 6279), VI CE, ed. Kramer 1983: no 4, lines W48–56)

In addition to vocabulary, an ancient Latin learner needed grammar. Example 8 comes from a table of noun inflections designed for Greek speakers learning Latin. The text, as usual in antiquity, is written in the target language rather than the learner's native language; not only the noun declensions themselves, but also the headings and accompanying

---

[14] For further information on them and on example 7, see Bataille 1967; Kramer 1983, 1996, 2001, 2004; Dickey 2010a, 2010b, 2012: 11–12, 20–4.

[15] From the distribution of words on the three preserved fragments, it has been calculated that the Greek-Latin half would have comprised approximately 200 folios or 400 pages (Preisendanz 1933: 25), and it is believed that the Latin-Greek half could not have been much shorter (Kramer 1983: 45). The only intact leaf has 80 entries (40 on each side), yielding a calculation of 800 x 40 = 32,000. Preisendanz does not state how he arrived at the figure of 200 folios, but he may have used Heraeus' Greek-Latin index to the *Corpus Glossariorum Latinorum* (Goetz *et al.* 1888–1923, vol. 7, pp. 441–687). The surviving leaf of the Greek-Latin half of the ancient lexicon, containing 80 lines with entries from παραχιμαζει to παροιμεια, covers material that takes up one and a quarter of the 246 pages of Heraeus' index; if the complete lexicon had approximately the same percentage of words beginning with παρ- as the index, it would have had 246/1.25 = 197 leaves. But such figures can only be very approximate, as different results are obtained from different Greek lexica: the ninth edition of LSJ, for example, yields a result of 2042/11.3 = 181 leaves, while the smaller abridged edition (Oxford 1871) gives 804/4.7 = 171 leaves.

Teaching Latin to Greek speakers in antiquity

grammatical information are in Latin. The text's orientation towards Greek speakers is revealed only by the Greek glosses that accompany each word.

8. *Neutralia in o̅r̅*   Neuter nouns in -*or*:

hoc aequor.	τοπελαγος	nom.	*aequor* "sea"
huius	*aequoris*	gen.	*aequoris*
hui̧c	*aequori*	dat.	*aequori*
hoc	*aequor*	acc.	*aequor*
o	*aequor*	voc.	*aequor*
abhoc	*aequore*	abl.	*aequore*
Pł haec	*aequora*	Plural, nom.	*aequora*
horum	*aequorum*	gen.	*aequorum*
his	*aequorib(us)*	dat.	*aequoribus*
haec	*aequora*	acc.	*aequora*
o	*aequora*	voc.	*aequora*
abhis	*aequorib(us)*	abl.	*aequoribus*
In m̅a̅ *hoc poema*		(Neuter nouns) in -*ma*: nom. *poema*
	τοποιημα		"poem"
huius	*poematis*	gen.	*poematis*
huic	*poemati*	dat.	*poemati*

(papyrus of v–vi ce (*M-P*³ 2997, *LDAB* 6148), ed. Dickey, Ferri, and Scappaticcio 2013: lines 42–58. Diacritics and punctuation are original.)

The nouns are divided into categories by their genders and terminations, as usual in both Greek and Latin grammar, since words with the same gender and the same termination normally decline in the same way. The cases are indicated by forms of the demonstrative *hic, haec, hoc*; again this is a standard feature of Latin grammars. In ancient Greek grammars inflected forms of the article are used as an efficient way of indicating gender, number, and case; whereas a modern teacher has to spell out "feminine dative plural," our ancient counterparts could simply use ταῖς. The Romans, whose grammatical tradition was heavily influenced by the Greeks, borrowed this practice but, since Latin has no article, used *hic* "this" instead.[16] Because the ablative *hoc* was graphically indistinguishable from the neuter nominative and accusative *hoc*, the ablative was indicated by putting *ab* "from," a preposition that can only take the ablative, in front of the ablative *hoc*. The vocative was indicated by the vocative particle *o*, as in Greek where ὦ was used the same way.

---

[16] Latin had no word as useful for this purpose as the Greek article, which has seventeen distinct forms (not counting duals); *hic* is the best, as it has a total of fifteen graphically different forms, whereas *is* and *ille* have only fourteen each.

In this papyrus the Latin cases appear in their original order. The Greek order was nominative, genitive, dative, and accusative, to which the vocative could be added at the end as necessary; Latin grammarians adapted this by adding the ablative case, which Latin has but Greek does not, at the end of the cases shared with Greek. The order of cases illustrated here is still used in many countries, though in others it has been replaced by one partially derived from Sanskrit (see Allen and Brink 1980).

Learning forms, however essential, is only part of Latin grammar: the student also has to understand how to use those forms. Many Latin constructions posed no difficulty for Greek speakers, as identical or very similar uses occurred in their own language. For example, the employment of the nominative, genitive, dative, accusative, and vocative cases was largely self-evident to the Greeks, and there are no ancient counterparts of the efforts expended by modern Latin teachers exhorting students to pay attention to the endings and take the nominative rather than the word that happens to come first as the subject of the sentence. The ablative case, however, was a different matter. Although Greek does not have an ablative, many of the Latin constructions using the ablative are recognizably present in Greek as well, where they take either the genitive (when the use in question is descended from the original Proto-Indo-European ablative, which merged with the genitive in Greek) or the dative (when the use in question is descended from an original Proto-Indo-European instrumental, which merged with the ablative in Latin and with the dative in Greek). Therefore from a Greek perspective the Latin ablative was sometimes the equivalent of a genitive and sometimes the equivalent of a dative; the trick was to distinguish which was which.

Example 9 comes from a Latin grammar written by a Greek speaker named Dositheus in the fourth century CE and preserved via the western manuscript tradition. We are accustomed to think of the Latin grammarians as Latin speakers writing for other Latin speakers, because in conformity with ancient custom they wrote entirely in Latin. Yet many of the most important Latin grammarians, including Charisius and Priscian, worked in the eastern empire and wrote for Greek speakers. Most of these grammars, of course, are not usable by beginners in Latin, because one needs to know a considerable amount of Latin before one can understand them. It is possible that elementary Latin teachers used these grammars and provided an oral translation into Greek for the benefit of pupils whose Latin was not yet up to reading the original, but it is also possible, particularly in the case of the more complex material, that these grammars were not used until pupils reached a higher level. In that case teachers must have found some other way of conveying to their students basic syntactic information like the use of the ablative.

One such means of conveying that information was provided by the grammar of Dositheus (fourth century CE), which unlike the other Latin grammars is accompanied by a running Greek translation. The Greek is clearly intended to assist in reading the Latin rather than to replace it: the Greek version omits the examples, so that it does not make sense on its own. The translation is complete only at the beginning of the work and is gradually reduced as the grammar progresses. Dositheus evidently expected that students would use the information he provided in the early sections of the work, such as the explanation of the ablative case, at early stages of Latin study. Example 9 is an extract from the beginning of his discussion of the Latin cases:

9. Πτώσεις εἰσὶν ϛ΄·
ὀνομαστική, γενική, δοτική,
αἰτιατική, κλητική,
ἀφαιρετική, ἢ καὶ ἀπενεκτική.
προσβάλλεται
παρὰ τῶν ἐπιμελεστέρων
καὶ ἑβδόμη πτῶσις.
ἀεὶ ἡ ἀπενεκτικὴ
ἑνὶ τρόπῳ ἐκφέρεται,
ὅταν ἀπὸ προσώπου
ἢ ἀπὸ τόπου
ἢ ἀπὸ πράγματος
ἀφαιρεθέν τι ⟨σημαίνεται⟩,
οἷον ἀπὸ Αἰνείου
τὴν ῥίζαν ⟨τὸ γένος⟩
κατάγει Ῥωμύλος,
ἀπὸ Ῥώμης εἰς Ἀφρικὴν
ἐπάνεισιν,
ἀπὸ τῶν βιβλίων τῶν Κικέρωνος
νενόηται.
ἡ δὲ ἑβδόμη πτῶσις
τρόποις τέτρασιν ἐκφέρεται·
πρώτῳ, ὅταν ἐν προσώπῳ
⟨ἢ ἐν τόπῳ⟩
ἢ ἐν πράγματι νοῆται,
οἷον ἐν τῷ Σκηπίωνι
ἡ στρατιωτικὴ ἀρετὴ

Casus sunt VI:
nominativus, genetivus, dativus,
accusativus, vocativus,
ablativus.
adicitur
a diligentioribus
etiam septimus casus.
semper ablativus
uno modo profertur,
cum a persona
aut a loco
aut a re
ablatum quid ⟨significetur⟩,
veluti ab Aenea
stirpem
deducit Romulus,
ab urbe in Africam
redit,
a libris Ciceronis
intellectum est.
septimus vero casus
modis IIII profertur:
primo, cum in persona
⟨aut in loco⟩
aut in re intelligitur,
veluti in Scipione
militaris virtus

ἐξέλαμψεν,   enituit,
ἐν τῷ ὄρει τῷ Καυκάσῳ   in monte Caucaso
ποινὰς ἔτεισεν Προμηθεύς,   poenas luit Prometheus,
ἐν τῷ ἀνδριάντι Κικέρωνος   in statua Ciceronis
ἡ νίκη ἡ τῶν συνωμοτῶν   victoria coniuratorum
ἐγγράφεται,   ⟨in⟩scribitur,
καὶ ἑρμηνεύεται τὸ τοιοῦτο σχῆμα   et interpretatur talis figura
διὰ τῆς δοτικῆς.   per dativum:
                                                  ἐν τῷ Σκηπίωνι,
                                                  ἐν τῷ Καυκάσῳ,
                                                  ἐν τῷ ἀνδριάντι.

ὃς κανὼν καὶ ἐν τοῖς ὀνόμασιν   quae regula etiam in nominibus
τῆς δευτέρας κλίσεως,   secundae declinationis,
ὧν καὶ ἡ ἀφαιρετικὴ   quorum ablativus
καὶ ἡ δοτικὴ ἡ αὐτή ἐστιν,   et dativus idem est,
παραφυλάττεται   observatur
καὶ ἐν τοῖς ὀνόμασιν   et in nominibus
τῆς τρίτης κλίσεως,   tertiae declinationis,
ὧν ὁμοίως ἡ ἀπενεκτικὴ   quorum item ablativus
καὶ ⟨ἡ⟩ δοκτικὴ ἡ αὐτή ἐστιν,   et dativus idem est,
οἷον   veluti ab hac securi,
                                                  ⟨ab hoc⟩ suavi.

(Dositheus chapter 18, ed. Bonnet 2005: 35–6. Diacritics and punctuation are editorial.)

"There are six cases: nominative, genitive, dative, accusative, vocative, ablative; also a seventh case is added by more meticulous people. The ablative is always used in a single way, when it indicates that something is coming from a person or a place or a thing, as *ab Aenea stirpem deducit Romulus, ab urbe in Africam redit, a libris Ciceronis intellectum est*. But the seventh case is used in four ways: first, when it is understood as being in a person, place, or thing, as *in Scipione militaris virtus enituit, in monte Caucaso poenas luit Prometheus, in statua Ciceronis victoria coniuratorum ⟨in⟩scribitur*, and such a construction is translated with the dative: ἐν τῷ Σκηπίωνι, ἐν τῷ Καυκάσῳ, ἐν τῷ ἀνδριάντι. This rule is observed even in nouns of the second declension, whose ablative and dative is the same, and in nouns of the third declension, whose ablative and dative are also the same, as *ab hac securi, ⟨ab hoc⟩ suavi*."

The discussion continues at considerable length, going over the different uses of the "seventh case" (which is clearly a subdivision of what we would call the ablative); the second use is the ablative absolute, the third is the ablative of means, and the fourth a group of ablatives that we would consider heterogeneous.

Reading "real" Latin literature

The goal of modern Latin instruction is almost always the reading of Roman literature in the original language. Although other material is normally used at the very early stages of Latin study, it is a great day for both student and teacher when the student meets his or her first piece of authentic ancient literature. For Greek speakers the situation was somewhat different because many of these Latin learners had practical goals, such as the practice of law, and were not interested in Latin literature primarily for its own sake (cf. Rochette 1997: 196). Nevertheless, a substantial number of Greek speakers evidently made some effort to read Latin literature, and at least a few of these progressed to an advanced level.

A considerable number of Latin literary papyri survive from Egypt (see Cavenaile 1958), but most of these offer no clues as to who used them. We know that some native Latin speakers lived in Roman Egypt, and others travelled there temporarily; members of both these groups could have owned works of literature in their native language and occasionally discarded them where a modern excavation could retrieve the remains (cf. Thomas 2007). Therefore the fact that a papyrus found in Egypt contains a work of Latin literature does not constitute clear evidence that that work of literature was read by a Greek speaker. It is likely to be the case that a significant number of such papyri were in fact read by Greek speakers, just as a significant number of the French books in an English-speaking country are owned and read by native speakers of English, but proof is lacking as to which papyri these were.

The situation is different, however, with Latin texts that also contain material in Greek. Latin literary texts with Greek translations, glosses, or annotations were clearly read by Greek speakers, and by inspecting those texts one can get a fair impression of what sort of Latin literature these Greek speakers read. Among prose authors their first choice was Cicero, and among his works the Catilinarian orations figure prominently. Among verse authors there was a strong preference for Virgil, and within the works of Virgil a preference for the *Aeneid*, particularly the earlier books.[17]

---

[17] We have fourteen papyri of Latin literary texts (not counting works on Roman law, of which we also have numerous bilingual examples) with Greek translations, of which eleven are of Virgil and three of Cicero's *Catilinarians*; six papyri of Latin literary texts with Greek annotations (Terence, Cicero, Sallust, Seneca, Juvenal); and two papyri of Latin literary texts without Greek words but with diacritics added by Greek speakers (both Virgil). There is no evidence for any use of Caesar by Greek-speaking Latin learners. Of the thirteen Virgil papyri, one is of the *Georgics* and twelve are of the *Aeneid*; of the latter, five include material from the first book and none includes any material

Evidently many an ancient Latin student, like many a modern one, began at the beginning of the *Aeneid* and did not get very far.

At the early stages of reading literature ancient students made use of bilingual materials that are now sometimes called texts and sometimes glossaries. These are works arranged in two very narrow columns (like a glossary, and like the colloquia: see examples 2 and 6 above) with the Latin on the left and the Greek on the right. Each line is one to three words long, and the Greek is arranged so that each line in the right-hand column translates exactly the words that appear on that line in the left-hand column. The restrictions on translation imposed by this system, which would produce nonsense in English, generally work in Greek in the sense that a comprehensible translation can be achieved. But the translation is not elegant; it is clearly intended as an explanation of how the Latin works, not as a substitute for the Latin that might be read in its own right. Occasionally the translation is simply wrong.

Example 10 is an extract from one such Virgil text. This text contains every word of the Latin in the passages it covers, so that one can read the *Aeneid* by going down the left-hand column and a translation of it by going down the right-hand column.

10. *restitit ænēas*   ἀπέστη ὁ αινείας
    claraque in luce   και εν καθαρῶι τωι φωτι
    rĕfulsit   αντελαμψεν·
    ŏś: umerōśque   το προσωπον: και τους ωμους
    dĕo símilis   θεῶι ομοιος
    namque ípsa: dēcoram   και γαρ αὐτη: ευπρεπη
    cæsariem natō   την κομην τωι παιδι
    génetrix: lumenque   ἡ γεννητιρα: και φως
    iuventae   τῆς νεότητο[ς]
    purpúreum et laetōś   προφύρεον και ἱλαρας
    óculis   τοῖς οφθαλμοῖς
    adflarat: honōres   προσπεπνευκει: τιμᾶς

(Ambrosian Palimpsest (M-P^3 2943, *LDAB* 4156), IV–V CE, ed. Scappaticcio 2009: lines 1–12 = *Aen.* 1.588-91. Diacritics and punctuation are original.)

"Princely Aeneas stood and shone in the bright light, head and shoulders noble as a god's. For she who bore him breathed upon him beauty of hair and bloom of youth and kindled brilliance in his eyes..." (trans. Fitzgerald 1981: 24)

from the second half of the poem. For details see Dickey 2012: 7–10; further useful information can be found in Rochette 1996, Parker 1992, esp. p. 52, and for the annotated papyri McNamee 2007: 473–92.

Some of the Virgil texts, however, do not contain all the words of the original, but rather a selection, with the Greek translations of those words. It is the existence of those partial texts that gives rise to the term "Virgil glossaries" as designations for this group of materials. Example 11 comes from one of these selective glossaries; my translation reflects the Greek rather than the Latin when the two differ.

11. | | | |
|---|---|---|
| revolúta est | ενεκυλίσθη (corrected to ενεκυλείσθη) | was revolved |
| quaesivit | εζήτησεν | sought |
| reperta | ευρεθέντα (corrected to ευρηθέντα) | found |
| difficilis | δυσχερής | difficult |
| obitus | απεδρυσις (corrected to αποδυσεις) | death |
| luctantem | αντιπαλέουσαν | struggling |
| nexaeq(ue) | και δεδεμέναι | and bound |
| ártus mérita | μέλη άξια | limbs worthy |
| períbit | απόλλυτο (corrected to απόλλυται) | perished[18] |
| nóndum | ουδωπω | not yet |
| flávum | ξανθόν | yellow |
| prosérpina | περσεφ[ονη] | Persephone |
| abstulerat | αφιλα[το] (corrected to αφειλατο) | had taken away |
| damnáverat | κατέκ[ρινεν] | had condemned |
| órco | χαρ[ωνι] | Charon |

(*P.Oxy.* 8.1099 (*M-P³* 2950, *LDAB* 4162), v ce, ed. Fressura 2009: lines 38–52 = *Aen.* 4.691–9. Diacritics and punctuation are original.)

Cf. actual text of *Aeneid* 4.691–9 (glossed words underlined):

ter <u>revoluta</u> <u>toro</u>[19] <u>est</u> oculisque errantibus alto
<u>quaesivit</u> caelo lucem ingemuitque <u>reperta</u>.
tum Iuno omnipotens longum miserata dolorem
<u>difficilisque obitus</u> Irim demisit Olympo
quae <u>luctantem</u> animam <u>nexosque</u> resolveret <u>artus</u>.
nam quia nec fato <u>merita</u> nec morte <u>peribat</u>,
sed misera ante diem subitoque accensa furore,
<u>nondum</u> illi <u>flavum</u> <u>Proserpina</u> vertice crinem
<u>abstulerat</u> Stygioque caput <u>damnaverat</u> <u>Orco</u>.

"Three times she . . . fell back on the bed. Her gaze went wavering as she looked for heaven's light and groaned at finding it. Almighty Juno, filled with pity for this long ordeal and difficult passage, now sent Iris down out of Olympus to set free the wrestling spirit from the body's hold. For since she died, not at her

---

[18] Assuming that *peribit* is intended to be *perivit* (the correct reading is *peribat*) and taking the original Greek rather than the correction.
[19] Glossed on line 37 of the papyrus.

fated span nor as she merited, but before her time enflamed and driven mad, Proserpina had not yet plucked from her the golden hair, delivering her to Orcus of the Styx." (trans. Fitzgerald 1981: 121)

In addition to translations, some of the Virgil papyri provide other reading aids. Diacritics such as accents, macrons, and diaereses are sometimes supplied to indicate correct pronunciation (cf. examples 10 and 11), and words may be re-arranged to make the sense clearer (like the grouping together of *revoluta est* at the beginning of example 11, but more systematically).[20]

It is generally agreed that these Virgil reading aids were produced (largely independently of one another) by looking up words in lexica and writing down their meanings; there is, however, considerable debate about who created them and how they were used.[21] Some, like example 10, could be used as a text of Virgil for students without enough Latin to read the original itself, rather like a modern Loeb Classical Library text. Indeed if example 10 was not intended to be used on its own, the repeated inclusion of obvious words like *et*, for which a reader with even the most rudimentary knowledge of Latin was unlikely to need a gloss, is difficult to explain. On the other hand texts like example 11 could not be used independently as copies of Virgil. How were they used?

One theory is that they are word-lists composed by students reading Virgil from a separate text. Latin students today sometimes make two-column vocabulary lists when preparing a text they will need to translate in class; they do not write down every Latin word in the left column, only the ones with which they have difficulty, and then they use a dictionary to look up the definitions and write those in the right-hand column. The Virgil glossaries could be the ancient equivalents of such student word-lists. In that case the mistranslations would be the natural result of the students' not knowing very much Latin yet: the mistakes are no worse than many modern students make in reading the same texts.

The other possibility is that teachers produced the glossaries as aids for their students. This practice too has modern parallels: teachers sometimes make running vocabulary lists to allow students to read difficult texts quickly, without spending hours poring over a dictionary. In antiquity,

---

[20] See *P.Fouad* I.5 and Rochette 1997: 193–6. Such rearrangement of course ruins the metre, but there is no evidence that Greek-speaking Latin learners thought about the metrical aspects of Virgil's poetry. Diacritic marks, while numerous, never seem to indicate ictus, foot division, or other metrical features.

[21] See especially Rochette 1997: 188–98, 1990; Axer 1983; Maehler 1979; Gaebel 1970; and Reichmann 1943.

when dictionaries would have been more difficult to acquire in large quantities, the practical need for such running vocabulary lists might have been even stronger than it is today.[22] If the Virgil glossaries were produced by teachers rather than by students, the mistakes in them assume a different significance; they then become rather damning evidence of poor knowledge of Latin on the part of (at least some) ancient Latin teachers.

If we assume that all the bilingual Virgil papyri – which seem very similar to one another despite the fact that some include all the words of the poems and others do not – were produced under the same circumstances, the case for student efforts seems stronger. Modern students are heterogeneous in their preparation techniques: even within a single class of students learning Latin for the first time, different individuals tend to have strong inclinations to prepare in different ways. Some prefer to copy out the Latin before translating it, and others do not do so; some make wordlists while others prefer to write out a complete translation. So if the Virgil glossaries are all student efforts, the differences between them might have to do with such individual preferences on the part of their authors.

On the other hand there is no real reason to assume (though nearly everyone does) that the full Virgil texts and the partial ones must belong to the same genre. Moreover, the dividing line between word-lists produced individually by students and those produced by others for students need not be absolute. A teacher may distribute a word-list originally prepared by a student for individual preparation, with or without corrections;[23] it may also, of course, circulate unofficially among students, perhaps accumulating corrections or additional errors in the process. Different teachers, or even the same teacher under different circumstances, may sometimes provide students with a word-list and sometimes ask the students to produce their own. Given the poor quality of some of the Virgil materials,

---

[22] It has been argued (Rochette 1997: 196) that the fact that the Virgil glossaries are all written in practiced hands (rather than the clumsier "school hands" of less accomplished writers) shows that teachers must have produced them. But *all* Latin learning materials are written in practiced hands (Cribiore 1996: 30), so this argument cannot be admitted unless one assumes that it applies equally to the other surviving Latin learning materials, i.e. that all the Latin-learning papyri we possess were written by teachers rather than by students. This is not, however, the usual explanation for the practiced hands of the Latin materials; rather it is thought that Greek speakers typically learned Latin when they were old enough, and well enough trained in Greek literacy, to produce practiced-looking handwriting from an early stage of study (Cribiore 1996: 30).

[23] As a teacher I have used student-prepared word-lists on a number of occasions. Sometimes I have asked each student to prepare a different section of a text and then distributed all the results to the whole group, and sometimes I have distributed word-lists that I made as a student. In both cases some errors slipped through despite checking before distribution, though the results were not as bad as the worst of the Virgil glossaries.

it seems to me very likely that students produced at least some of them, but it is not impossible that teachers produced others.

The reading of Virgil may not have progressed very efficiently under these circumstances, but nevertheless some students learned Latin well enough to go on to reading monolingual texts. Example 12 comes from a papyrus copy of Sallust's *Catiline*, another text that is often read with undergraduate classes today. The student who used this copy had evidently reached the level where he (or she) did not need to write out a complete Greek translation, but nevertheless Greek equivalents of the hard words have been written in above the lines.

12.
      πρα]σιμα
    ve]ṇalia, habēre edocuit· am[bitio
     κατηναγκασεν
  multos mortales falsos fie]ṛi subēgit· aliud clausu[m in
      εν τω προχιρωι
  pectore, aliud in lingua i]n promptum habēre· [ami-
  citias inimicitiasque] non ex rē, sed ex com[modo
  aestumare, magisqu]e volṭum quam in[genium

(*PSI* 1.110 (*M-P*³ 2932, *LDAB* 3877), iv–v ce, recto, ed. Funari 2008 = Sal. *Cat.* 10.4–5. Diacritics and punctuation are original.)

In addition to the glosses, macrons have also been added above some of the long vowels in this text. The marking of long vowels, while not completely unknown in texts from Latin-speaking areas, is very rare in surviving Latin documents from the western empire: native speakers knew which vowels were long and which were short and did not need that information in writing. Greek speakers, on the other hand, had difficulty with Latin quantities just as modern students do. But unlike modern students, who generally prefer to ignore the whole issue, Greeks were used to distinguishing between long and short vowels both in pronunciation and (in the case of *e* and *o*) in writing. They therefore found the limitations of the Latin alphabet disconcerting, especially when they needed to pronounce something accurately. Latin papyri used by Greek speakers often have macrons over long vowels, particularly long *e* and *o*, and indeed in this text all the vowels marked as long are *e* vowels.[24] The text was evidently prepared by a student who intended to read it aloud in Latin as well as translating it.

---

[24] Most of the vowels with macrons (all but *militēs* in line 9 of the back of the fragment) are also in penultimate syllables and therefore relevant for accentuation. It is likely that correct pronunciation of the accent as well as the usual Greek desire to know the quantity of *e* and *o* played a part in determining the distribution of macrons in this text.

There remains one major area of modern Latin instruction for which we have found no parallels: prose composition, or indeed any translation into Latin by learners of the language. In general such translation would be difficult to identify, for there are numerous documents written in non-native-speaker Latin, and while some of those may have been written as educational exercises, it is usually impossible to know the conditions under which a given piece of Latin was produced. Nevertheless, there is some evidence pointing in the direction of Latin composition exercises. Example 13 is an extract from a papyrus containing a set of fables of Babrius in Greek and translations of them into Latin by someone who, though relatively advanced in the study of the language, was clearly not a native speaker.[25] Fables were standard easy-reader material in antiquity (not only because they are short and usually simple, but also because of their moral content), and their use for second-language learning is well documented (see Dickey 2012: 24–5). Therefore when a non-native speaker has translated an entire set of fables into Latin, an educational exercise is the most likely explanation.

13. ἄγροικος ἠπείλησε νηπίῳ τίτθῃ κλαί[οντι·]
"σίγα, μή σε τῷ λύκῳ ῥίψω."
λύκος δ' ἀκούσας τήν τε γραῦν ἀληθύειν
νομίσας ἔμεινεν, ὡς ἕτοιμα δειπνήσων.
ἕως ὁ παῖς μὲν ἑσπέρας ἐκοιμήθη,
αὐτὸς δὲ πινῶν καὶ χανὼν λύκος ὄντως
ἀπῆλθε ψυχραῖς ἐλπίσιν ἐνεδρεύσας.
λύκαινα δ' αὐτὸν ἡ σύνευνος ἠρώτα
"πῶς οὐδὲν ἦλθες ἄρας, ὡς πρὶν εἰώθεις;"
κἀκεῖνος εἶπε "πῶς γάρ, ὃς γυναικὶ πιστε[ύ]ω;"

[2 lines of Latin missing]
luppus autem auditus, anucellam vere dictu[m]
putatus, m[a]nsit quasi parata cenaret.
dum puer quidem sero dormisset,
ipse porro esuriens et luppus enectus ver[e]
redivit frigiti⟨s⟩ spebus frestigiatur.
luppa enim eum coniugalis interrogabat,
"quomod[o n]ihil tulitus venisti, s[i]cut sole[bas?]"
et ille [dix]it, "quomodo enim, quis mulieri cr[edo?]"

(P.Amh. 11.26 (M-P³ 172, LDAB 434), III–IV CE, ed. Cavenaile 1958 no. 40: lines 1–8, 15–24 = Babrius fable 16. Diacritics and punctuation are editorial.)

---

[25] The translator had a good grasp of vocabulary, morphology, and orthography, but had trouble with syntax and made mistakes with participles that no native speaker would have made. For a detailed analysis of this text, see Adams 2003a: 725–41.

"A country nurse threatened a crying baby, 'Be quiet, lest I throw you to the wolf.' And a wolf, hearing (this) and thinking that the old woman was telling the truth, waited, in order to dine on the ready meal. When the child was put to bed in the evening, the wolf himself, hungry and really exhausted, returned having lain in ambush for cold hopes. His wolf wife asked him, 'How come you don't come bringing anything, as you used to?' And he said, 'How could I, who trust(ed) a woman?'"

There is however a complication with seeing this text as a Latin composition exercise: the papyrus we have is evidently a copy rather than the page on which the original translation was first done. Both the Latin and the Greek contain transmission errors, and some of the transmission errors in the Greek must have been introduced after the text was translated into Latin.[26]

Although most ancient educational exercises do not show signs of such textual transmission, copying is not really surprising in an educational context. The text we have could be a fair copy made for displaying the student's work to best advantage; it is also possible, since language teachers are not always native speakers themselves and the Latin teachers of Roman Egypt may not have been above making the kind of mistakes found in this text, that this papyrus is a set of fair copies kept by a teacher. Alternatively, of course, the "translator" could have cheated by copying his Latin version from another student; there is no reason to believe that plagiarism was less common in the ancient classroom than it is today. The chances are thus excellent that this text was translated into Latin as part of a Latin learner's educational exercise.

Ancient Latin students thus seem to have engaged in most of the elements of language learning practiced in today's Latin classrooms: they used dictionaries, learned paradigms, studied syntax, started reading on easy texts specially created for them, read Virgil and other canonical authors, and translated paragraphs into Latin. They also did a few things that modern Latin learners are less likely to do, such as working on the alphabet and on oral proficiency. At the same time, there are a number of elements of modern Latin teaching that appear not to have been used in antiquity. There is no evidence for the translation of individual sentences (either into Latin or out of Latin) as a learning technique, no evidence for scansion or reading in metre, and no evidence for provision of the kind of

---

[26] For example, the word order in the sixth line of the Greek is wrong (χανών and λύκος have been inverted): it does not scan, and it is not the order in which that line appears in other texts of this fable. The Latin, which elsewhere keeps exactly to the word order of the Greek, here has the words in the order that they should occur in Greek rather than in the order that they do occur: the Greek word order must therefore have been changed after the translation was made.

student commentary that provides clues to the grammar or syntax of a difficult sentence without translating it. Clearly there have been some important advances in language teaching since the Roman Empire – but nevertheless there is much that today's Latin students could use in the fragments of their ancient predecessors' materials.

CHAPTER 4

Servius' Greek lessons

Félix Racine

Bilingual education among the elites of the western Roman Empire was alive and well until the fourth century CE. At Rome itself, where our information is at its fullest, children of the highest social strata had been simultaneously educated in both Latin and Greek since the late Republic, a practice that Quintilian also took for granted.[1] Until at least the days of Aulus Gellius a stream of well-born Romans travelled to Athens to attend the lectures of renowned Greek teachers, and Greek philosophers found a receptive audience at Rome, most notably Plotinus and Porphyry in the third century. For a Roman with ambitions, there was no better claim to cultural achievements than to be deemed expert "in both languages" (*utraque lingua*), as the Younger Pliny said of his equestrian protégé Terentius Junior, recommending him to a friend, and as Apuleius claimed for himself, speaking to an audience in Carthage.[2] It is true that Greek instruction in Latin-speaking areas was unevenly pursued, for example in Africa, where Apuleius disparaged his accusers from Oea for their crass ignorance of Greek: they could not read a letter written in Greek by his wife and made several errors of diction and barbarisms in their feeble attempt to forge a Greek letter themselves.[3] Yet if Apuleius could make fun of his accusers it was because proficiency in Greek remained an attainable goal of well-to-do Romans. There were enough students of Greek at Carthage to hear him deliver speeches in that language, and other cities of the empire also attracted eager students of Greek, for example Marseilles and Autun in Gaul.[4]

---

[1] Quint. *Inst.* 1.12–13.
[2] Plin. *Ep.* 7.25.4, cf. 3.1.7 on the venerable Vestricius Spurinna; Apul. *Fl.* 18.
[3] Apul. *Apol.* 30.11, 87.4, 98.8. Cf. Sandy 1997: 9–12.
[4] Marseilles: Strabo 4.1.5; Tac. *Agr.* 4.2–3. In late third-century Autun, the rhetorician Eumenius reminisced about his Athenian grandfather's coming to the city to teach rhetoric: *Pan. lat.* 9 (4) 17.3. A second-century mosaic featuring two poems of Anacreon bears witness to the prestige of Greek culture in this city: Blanchard and Blanchard 1973: 268–79.

By the end of the fourth century, however, Greek instruction in the west had suffered a steep decline. A rescript of Gratian dated 376 CE admits to the difficulty of finding suitable candidates for subsidized posts in Trier, suggesting a lack of properly trained grammarians in the whole of Gaul.[5] The famous case of Augustine has often been taken as emblematic of this decline: although he was an accomplished teacher of rhetoric and had studied some Greek in his youth ("very little, in fact scarcely at all," *perparum assecutus sum et prope nihil*), he had much difficulty reading a Greek text until further studies later in his life.[6] But just as the penetration of Greek in the early empire had been uneven, so was its retreat. Ever since Pierre Courcelle's magisterial *Les lettres grecques en Occident*, the aristocracy of Rome has been seen as willfully pushing back against this trend and even fostering a revival of Greek culture with pagan overtones. Much of the evidence for this rests on Macrobius' *Saturnalia*, a fictional conversation where the great Roman senator Praetextatus (c. 315–84 CE) and his guests display their extensive Greek and Latin erudition.[7] Despite the merits of Courcelle's study, this has turned out to be a very weak basis upon which to build a portrait of Greek learning in late-fourth-century Rome: Macrobius has now been re-dated to the 430s, and in the last analysis the *Saturnalia*'s protagonists can only be used as evidence for his own Greek culture and education.[8]

One of Praetextatus' guests, the grammarian Servius, allows us a better point of entry into Greek instruction at Rome c. 400 CE. His influential commentary on Virgil, the focus of the present chapter, features many entries on Greek language and mythology, and allows us to see a Latin grammarian facing up to Greek culture and selecting elements deemed worthy of teaching. My goal in this chapter is to look not only at the role of Greek in Servius' commentary, but also at the place held by Greek in Roman education and culture as defined by the grammarian.

Servius has always had a reputation as a Greek scholar, in no small part thanks to the repeated assertion in the *Saturnalia* that he surpassed even teachers of old.[9] The many Greek citations founds in the real Servius'

---

[5] *CTh.* 13.3.11.   [6] Aug. *Contra litteras Petilliani* 2.38.91.
[7] Courcelle 1943: 3–36. Besides the cast of the *Saturnalia*, who are in any case literary constructs of Macrobius, evidence for the cultivation of Greek letters at Rome at the turn of the fifth century includes among others Symmachus' friend Naucellius, who translated into Latin a Greek *On Ancient Constitutions* (Symm. *Ep.* 3.11.3); the translation of a Greek epigram by Probinus, consul in 395 (*Ep. Bob.* [ed. Speyer 1963] 65, cf. Symm. *Ep.* 9.12.13 on Probinus' bilingualism); and Greek scholia in a fifth-century manuscript of Livy (Mommsen 1909: 106–7).
[8] Cameron 1966 and more recently Cameron 2011: 531–2.
[9] Macr. *Sat.* 1.24.8, 20, 7.11.2.

commentary on Virgil seem to support this vision of a Latin grammarian steeped in Greek culture, and since Courcelle's day he has furthermore been seen as a Neoplatonist well-versed in the works of Porphyry.[10] In fact, scholars have given so much credence to Servius' Greek learning that he has been mined for fragments of Bacchylides, Euphorion, Sophocles, and a few others.[11]

Yet two factors cast doubts on the extent of Servius' readings. First, it has long been realized that his commentary on Virgil draws extensively upon an earlier one composed by the fourth-century grammarian Aelius Donatus. Donatus' commentary is lost but survives in a modified guise, integrated into a seventh-century manuscript of Servius by an Irish compiler (together with other elements). This extended commentary is variously known as Servius Auctus, Servius Danielis, or DS.[12] Reading Servius, then, does not so much open a window on his readings and erudition but rather reveals his choices as a teacher abbreviating, selecting, and criticizing Donatus. If DS is any indication, Donatus' variorum commentary was a bulky affair, ill-suited to the classroom. We may take as typical the following entry concerning Virgil's use of the adjective "Trinacrian" to designate Sicily, where Servius left out Greek material originally found in Donatus (Serv. A. 1.196.):

TRINACRIO – *Graecum est propter tria* ἄκρα, *id est promunturia, Lilybaeum, Pachynum, Pelorum. Latine autem Triquetra dicitur.* (DS: *sane Philostephanus* περὶ τῶν νήσων *sine r littera Trinaciam appellat* ὅτι Τρίνακος αὐτῆς πρῶτος ἐβασίλευσεν).

TRINACRIAN – This is Greek from three *akra*, i.e. promontories: Lilybaeum, Pachynum, Pelorum. In Latin however it is called Triquetra. (DS: Of course Philostephanus in his *On islands* calls it Trinacia without the letter R, "because Trinacos was the first to reign over it.").

By omitting details such as Philostephanus' etymology of Trinacia, Servius shows himself aware of the needs and capacities of fifth-century schoolchildren. It was useless for them to learn this alternate Greek spelling. On the other hand, they needed to know both the correct Latin term Triquetra (also deemed correct by Quintilian)[13] and the Greek-inspired

---

[10] Courcelle 1943: 18–34; Flamant 1977: 657–67.
[11] E.g. Bacchyl. fr. 51 J = 32 B (Serv. *A.* 2.201); Euph. fr. 69, 150, 152, 154 (Serv. 2.79, 2.32, 2.541, 6.618); Soph. *Laocoon* fr. 372 (Serv. *A.* 2.204).
[12] Goold 1970: 102–5 offers the best account of the formation of DS and its relationship to Servius and Donatus.
[13] Quint. *Inst.* 1.6.30.

Trinacria made familiar by Virgil, which they could encounter in newly fashionable silver-Latin poets or use in their own poetry as Avienius or Claudian did.¹⁴ Servius provides a Greek etymology to help his students remember this place-name but does not assume them to understand the meaning of ἄκρα, promontories, which he translates into Latin.

Second, Alan Cameron has recently shown that Servius had no familiarity with classical Greek authors outside of what had been handed down to him by the grammatical tradition and by mythographers.¹⁵ Indeed, how to explain that a grammarian familiar with Greek literature could have stated flatly that Virgil had translated the whole of *Aeneid* IV from Apollonius' *Argonautica* III, or that the whole seventh *Eclogue* came from Theocritus?¹⁶ Servius also reveals his unfamiliarity with Callimachus and Aratus – although they are mentioned on occasion in his commentary – by failing to attribute to the respective author information he found in works of mythography and copied from the *Hymn to Apollo* or the *Phaenomena*.¹⁷ Ultimately, most of the Greek lore found in Servius seems to have been drawn by Donatus or his predecessors from early imperial monographs discussing Virgil's debt to Greek literature (such as Carvilius Pictor's *Aeneomastix* and Asconius Pedianus' *Contra obtrectatores Vergilii*).¹⁸ Servius himself is far removed from these early engagements with Virgil and his Greek models, and he has neither the inclination not the opportunity to double-check the information he inherited, for example at *A.* 11.31, where he hesitates to censor Donatus for deriving the name of the Arcadian town Parrhasia from the bird *parra*, suspecting without knowing that it is an indigenous Latin bird name.

We should then minimize the extent of Servius' Greek culture acquired at first hand. But this is not to say that he does not care about Greek literature and the Greek language. The sheer number of Greek technical terms of grammar or rhetoric found in his commentary, as well as his general understanding of the Greek citations he reproduces confirms that he read Greek himself. More importantly, Servius and his contemporaries could not ignore Virgil's debt to Greek literature, a debt that was extended by some late Roman scholars to the whole Latin language.¹⁹

Greek learning in Servius takes first and foremost the form of etymology and mythography, but we can also see the grammarian's concern with the

---

¹⁴ Ov. *Fast.* 4.287; *Pont.* 15.15; Sil. *Pun.* 4.494, 13.93; Stat. *Theb.* 10.622; V. Fl. *Arg.* 1. 579; Avien. *Per.* 117; Claud. *Rapt.* 1.141, 2.186, 3.119.
¹⁵ Cameron 2011: 532–4.   ¹⁶ Serv. *A.* 4.1, *Ecl.* pr.   ¹⁷ Cameron 2004: 195–6.
¹⁸ Görler 1987.   ¹⁹ Macr. *Sat.* 1.17.39.

correct orthography and scansion of Latin words, deduced from Greek models, as well with technical terms of grammar in Greek.[20] The following pages will consider Servius' use of Greek etymologies and his use of the Greek language to strengthen Latin instruction.[21] But since much of Servius' Greek lessons also mention Greek authors, we must first consider his familiarity with these Greek authorities, both as source of knowledge and as objects of teaching.

Servius invokes two types of authors to support his interpretations. First are the "qualified authorities" (*idonei auctores*), mostly Latin poets of the republican and early imperial age, whom Servius adduces as examples of proper Latin.[22] The second group includes authorities who provide justifications for his interpretations: Latin scholars and Greek prose writers and poets. Unsurprisingly, Homer looms very large among these authorities, with more than two hundred separate entries. It was of course common knowledge that Virgil studied Homer closely in order to imitate him in the *Aeneid*, a fact Servius acknowledges at the beginning of his commentary.[23] It was the view of Gino Funaioli and Eduard Fraenkel that Servius (or in my view the grammatical tradition which he abridged) made extensive use of the Homeric scholia, and a number of parallels fully support this hypothesis.[24] Some Greek authors mentioned by Servius can even be traced to the Homeric scholia, as in the following Servian entry featuring Aeschylus, which parallels Eustathius' commentary on Homer, based on ancient scholia:

Serv. A. 1.95: *MOENIBUS ALTIS – propter Pergama, quae altissima fuerunt, ex quibus omnia alta aedifica "pergama" uocantur, sicut Aeschylus dicit.*

LOFTY WALLS – on account of Pergama, which was very high and from which the whole structure was called Pergama, as Aeschylus says.

Eustathius 503 in *Il.* 1.507–8: Ὅτι Ὅμηρος μὲν μόνον τὴν τῆς Ἰλίου ἀκρόπολιν Πέργαμον ὀνομάζει θηλυκῶς, οἱ δέ νεώτεροι πάσας τὰς ἀκροπόλεις οὕτω καλοῦσιν, οἳ καὶ οὐδετέρως "τὰ πέργαμά" φασιν, ὡς καὶ Αἰσχύλος Προμηθεῖ.

---

[20] See Thomas 1879: 184 for a different division.
[21] On mythography, Cameron 2004: 184–216.
[22] Quint. *Inst.*1.8.18 calls them *clari auctores*, "good authorities." Kaster (1978) establishes that *idonei auctores* are for Servius examples and illustrations of his own prescriptions to the students rather than guidelines he follows in making his own judgements. See Wessner 1929: 335 for an earlier articulation of this idea.
[23] Serv. A. pr.: *intentio Vergilii haec est, Homerum imitari et Augustum laudare a parentibus.* Cf. Knauer 1964 and Kaster 2011.
[24] Funaioli 1930: 234; Fraenkel 1949: 153. See most recently Farrell 2008.

While Homer called only the citadel of Ilium Pergamon in the feminine, later poets use it for all citadels, while neither say "Pergama," as in Aeschylus' *Prometheus*.

Theocritus is another Greek poet frequently mentioned by Servius, this time as Virgil's model for his *Bucolics*.[25] It is improbable that Servius had recourse to the Theocritus scholia, or even less Theocritus himself. Other Greek poets are cited as authorities on mythological subjects, chiefly Apollonius, Aratus, Euphorion, Euripides, and Hesiod. More rarely, Servius invokes the name of a Greek scholar to support mythological, linguistic or scientific claims. Aristotle, for example, testifies that nymphs and divine children are mortal (Serv. *A*. 1.372, 10.551), while the geographer Ptolemy supports the opinion that climate influences human nature (Serv. *A*. 6.724), and the astronomer Hipparchus is named as an authority on constellations (Serv. *G*. 1.137). It is not uncommon for Servius to name Greek scholars in succession together with Latin ones, a clear sign that his information may derive in the last analysis only from these Latin authors. Thus, we find Thucydides paired with Sallust as a source for Minos' war against Carian pirates (Serv. *A*. 8.725), and from Servius' fumbling of Thucydides' claim that Italy was named after the Sicel king Italus we can be fairly certain that he never read the Greek historian (Serv. *A*. 8.328; cf. Thuc. 6.2.4). The mention of the Greek scholars Meton, Eudoxus, Ptolemy together with Cicero inspires even less confidence (Serv. *A*. 3.284). We can glimpse in these passages the composition technique of the commentary or commentaries used by Servius: grammarians and scholars amassed over time lists of authorities on subjects related to Virgil's text, and arranged them in rough chronological order, which gave Greek authors chronological and textual precedence. Thus, although Servius lists Xenophon, the Punic Mago, Cato, Varro, and Cicero as authors of agricultural treatises read by Virgil (Serv. *G*. 1.43), we can doubt whether he even laid eyes on any of these works: otherwise, he would have known that Cicero's *Oeconomicus* was a translation of Xenophon's.[26]

How are students to remember Greek authors? Servius does not evoke Greek authors for themselves but as justifications for his own interpretations, and as models for his students to justify their own literary interpretations. Let us take the example of Herodotus. Commenting on Virgil's treatment of the herd of Juno at *G*. 3.532, Servius evokes the story of Cleobis and Biton, sons of an Argive priestess of Hera, who pulled their

---

[25] E.g. Serv. *Ecl*. pr., 1.27, 2.21, 23–5, 51, 3.8, 10 pr., 7. [26] Cf. Jerome, *Chron*. pr.

mother's cart, adding that "among the Greeks, Herodotus treats this fully in his first book of history" (*Herodotus apud Graecos plenissime commemorat in prima historia*).[27] Herodotus is also invoked as an authority to justify his misreading of Mt. Athos as Mt. Athon at *A.* 12.701. Students were certainly not expected to know the passages where Herodotus mentioned Cleobis, Biton, and Mt. Athos, but they were taught to associate this author with the declension of Greek place-names and with mythological lore. The same expectation goes for the dry and challenging geographer Ptolemy, whom Servius urges students to invoke to as an authority on world locales (*A.* 7.678). The roughly contemporary historian Ammianus learned this lesson well and named Ptolemy as an authority on geography, together with Eratosthenes, Hecataeus, "and other very accurate investigators of such problems."[28] It has sometimes been claimed that Ammianus read Ptolemy, but he is in fact simply justifying his geographic claims by adducing a Greek authority whose name would have been recognized by his Latin readers.[29]

It is possible that Servius consulted more Greek authors than he leads us to believe, as we can see from his occasional references to competing interpretations. More probably, he found these anonymous notices in Donatus' commentary or left out authorities mentioned by Donatus. Here a comparison with DS is useful. In several instances, the compiler of DS supports Servius' interpretations with named authorities, which he must have found in Donatus, just as Servius did. Servius' process of elimination is most readily visible in the following notice, reproduced here together with DS's additions:

DORSO INIQUO – *dorsum est durior harena, quae remeantibus fluctibus et euntibus* (DS: *plerumque*) *densetur et in modum saxi durescit, quod a nautis pulvinus vocatur,* (DS: *a Graecis* θῖν: *Homerus* παρὰ θῖνα πολυφλοίσβοιο θαλάσσης [*Il.* 1.34]; *Probus "vadi dorso" pro "vado" dictum putat, ut in georgicis "dorso nemoris"* [3.436]).

UNEVEN RIDGE – the ridge is harder sand, which is made thick by the (DS: frequent) coming and going of waves, and hardens like a rock, which sailors call a sand-bank (DS: from the Greek *thin,* as in Homer: "along the shore of the loud-roaring sea"; Probus thinks we must say "ridge of shallow" rather than "shallow," as in the *Georgics,* "ridge of wood").

---

[27] Cf. Hdt. 1.31.
[28] Amm. 22.8.10: *ut Eratosthenes adfirmat et Hecataeus et Ptolomaeus aliique huius modi cognitionum minutissimi scitatores.*
[29] The case against Ammianus' use of Ptolemy has been made by Brok (1975).

More frequently, Servius discarded parts of notices from Donatus that contained contradictory interpretations, and got rid of references to authorities in the process (DS is witness to Donatus' fuller notices in these instances as well).[30] Servius is in fact noteworthy for his frequent refusal to cite authorities. As Robert Kaster observes regarding matters of language, Servius has recourse to authorities only as a last resort, preferring to invoke nature and custom in his prescriptions of correct Latin usage.[31] Servius presents himself as the arbiter of language and the correct interpreter of the Virgilian text. Authorities are only tools at the grammarian's disposal to support his own interpretations and are adduced to lend credence to various etymologies, elucidation of place-names or mythographic details.

Macrobius calls Servius "an expert in etymologies" (*Sat.* 6.9.3: *uerborum naturae conscium*) and his commentary on Virgil does not disappoint in this respect.[32] Virgil's poetry was already full of Greek etymologies, which Servius only had to make more explicit for students to grasp. The bird *acalanthis*, for example, derives its name from the spiny acanthus plant. Virgil alludes to this etymology by mentioning "thorn-bushes [ringing] with acalanthis" (*G.* 3.338: *acalanthida dumi*), and Servius simply comments that "among Greeks the acalanthis is named from the acanthi, that is from its thorns, on which it feeds" (Serv. *G.* 3.338: *apud Graecos acalanthis dicta sit ab acanthis, id est spinis, quibus pascitur*).[33] Servius also elucidates many Greek names for which Virgil did not provide etymologies, such as Libya, which the grammarian understands as named either from the African wind Libs (interestingly not the other way around) or from the Greek λιπυία, which, on the authority of Varro, means "without rain."[34]

We must keep in mind that the *Aeneid* and to a lesser degree the *Georgics* are poems of origins and etiology, in which Virgil explored the provenance of customs, divinities, and peoples of the Roman world, notably through etymologies and wordplays.[35] A novice reader can easily understand some of these etymologies, but a number of them beg more explanation from the grammarian. We can therefore read that "theater"

---

[30] Additionally, some entries of Servius Danielis mention authors assuredly known to Servius, such as Cato (3.707, 4.620, 10.179, 12.134) or Varro (1.108, 9.581, 707).
[31] Kaster 1988: 176–7.
[32] For the general question of etymologies in Servius, see Thomas 1879: 222–7 and Mustard 1892.
[33] Cf. Plin. *NH* 25.168.
[34] Serv. *A.* 1.22: *dicta autem Libya uel quod inde libs fiat, hoc est africus, uel ut Varro ait, quasi* λιπυία, *id est egens pluuiae*.
[35] O'Hara 1996.

comes from "viewing" (θεωρία) and, improbably, that a large shield, *clipeus*, takes its name from "concealing" (κλέπτειν) and that the name of the promontory of Sigeum near Troy was given after Hercules attacked the city from there, in silence (σιγή).³⁶ Many etymologies relating to place-names and mythological topics notably take the form of stories, as the case of Sigeum above, the Strophades islands named after the Argonauts Zethus and Calais, who were compelled there to turn back (στροφή) from chasing the harpies, or the Myrmidons named from the ants (μύρμηκες) or king Myrmidonus.³⁷

Servius worked within a grammatical tradition heavily influenced by the etymological thinking of Varro, who set out to discover the true origins of Latin words and in so doing recapture Rome's primitive society.³⁸ He also lived at a time of renewed interest in etymologies as a tool of analysis, both for grammatical and philosophical purposes, above all for Neoplatonists such as Proclus, who tackled etymologies as a source of knowledge on the gods in his commentary on Plato's *Cratylus*.³⁹ Etymologies were tools for deciphering the true nature of places, divinities, customs, and objects, which remain hidden to the uninitiated. For Servius' students, learning to think etymologically meant first of all memorizing Virgil's and Servius' etymologies. There is for example a strong parallel between Rutilius Namatianus' depiction of the god Pan roaming through the forests near the Etruscan town of Castrum Inui and Servius' own entry on this town, to which he appended a notice linking Inuus to the Greek Πάν.⁴⁰ It is unnecessary to suppose that Rutilius read Servius. Rather, we see in parallel a teacher transmitting to his students an etymology he judged valuable to know, and a Roman aristocrat reproducing this knowledge as well.⁴¹

Servius' own examples show readers how to discover the defining characteristic of nations and gods through etymological reasoning. Thus, he derives the Amazons' name from their life without men (ἅμα ζῶσαι) or their burning of a breast (ἄνευ μαζοῦ), Apollo "from the destruction" (ἀπὸ τοῦ ἀπολλύειν, a Homeric echo), Lyaeus/Dionysus from the loosening (ἀπὸ τοῦ λύειν) due to wine, and he asserts that the Etruscans got their name (*Tusci*) from their frequent sacrifices to the gods, ἀπὸ τοῦ θύειν).⁴² Festus is witness to a similar fanciful etymology for the Etruscans,

---

³⁶ Serv. *A.* 2.312, 5.288, 7.686. ³⁷ Serv. *A.* 2.7, 3.209.
³⁸ Besides unattributed references, Varro is named as a source at Serv. *A.* 3.443 (Var. *Ling.* 7.36), 5.145 (Var. *Ling.* 5.153), 12.7 (Var. *Ling.* 7.52). Cf. Amsler 1989: 24–31.
³⁹ Van den Berg 2007.   ⁴⁰ Rut. Namat. 1.231–6; Serv. *A.* 6.775.
⁴¹ Wolff 2007, pp. 68–9 n. 103.   ⁴² Serv. *A.* 1.490, 2.781, 3.138, 4.58, 8.479.

indicating that Servius could have expected his reasoning to be shared by the conventional wisdom.⁴³

Several place-names are also defined through Greek etymologies. This is sensible enough for place-names of the Hellenic world, as we have seen in the case of Sigeum and the Strophades, or locations imported from Greek myth such as Elysium (Serv. *A.* 5.735: ἀπὸ τῆς λύσεως, "from the release"),⁴⁴ but more problematic for Africa (Serv. *A.* 6.312: *quasi* ἄτερ φρίκης, "as if, 'without chill'"), the river Nile (Serv. *A.* 9.30: *quasi* νέαν ἰλύν, "as if, 'new mud'"), Italian cities such as Volscian Atina (Serv. *A.* 7.630: *dicta Atina a morbis, qui graece* ἄται *dicuntur*, "called Atina from diseases, which are called *atai* in Greek"), or Latin Praeneste.⁴⁵

Greek etymologies raise the problem of the correct transliteration and adaptation of Greek words into Latin, and we can occasionally see Servius indicating simple morphological principles justifying his etymological interpretations, such as the transliteration of the Greek Y into the Latin U in support of the etymology of Cumae derived from κύματα, "waves," and the addition of a C in the transition from αὐλάς to *caulas*.⁴⁶ However the problem of transliteration is not confined to the realm of etymologies. As Servius notes, "Virgil is fond of Greek declensions, with a sound respect for their rules" (*A.* 3.108: *amat Vergilius declinationes Graecas, salua regulae reuerentia*), which impels the grammarian to explain some of these rules, as long as they apply to the text.⁴⁷ In this vein he indicates that Greek words in -ος can yield Latin words in *us* (as Δῆλος, *Delus*), -*er* (as ἀγρός, *ager*), or both (Εὔανδρος, *Euandrus, Euander*), or that the ablative plural of 'Cretan' is *Cretaeis*, derived from Κρήτη, as *Atenaeis* is from Ἀθῆναι.⁴⁸ As we saw above, he also invokes Herodotus to mistakenly justify his misreading of *Athos* as *Athon* at *A.* 12.701. Assuming 'Athos' to have a short 'o', he also mistakenly concludes that it belongs to the Attic second declension. Priscian, who knew Greek better, was able to render the proper Latin *Atho, Athonis*.⁴⁹

---

⁴³ Fest. *Gloss. Lat.* 537 Th (Paul): *TUSCI – a Tusco rege, filio Herculis, sunt dicti; uel a sacrificando studiose, ex Graeco, uelut* θυσκόοι.
⁴⁴ Also Tartarus (6.577: *quia omnia illic turbata sunt*, ἀπὸ τῆς ταραχῆς; *aut, quod est melius*, ἀπὸ τοῦ ταρταρίζειν, *id est a tremore frigoris*), and the river Acheron (6.107: *quasi sine gaudio*, probably referring to the Greek ἀχεύειν).
⁴⁵ The Greek etymology of Africa is also attested in Paul's epitome of Festus, with a grain of salt: *APRICUM – locum a sole apertum. a Graeco uocabulo* φρίκη *appellatur, quasi* ἀφρικῆς, *id est sine horrore, uidelicet frigoris; unde etiam putatur et Africa appellari* (Fest. *Gloss. Lat.* 2 Th).
⁴⁶ Serv. *A.* 3.441, 9.59.
⁴⁷ Interestingly, this is followed by a note on the transformation of the Greek diphthong ει into a long Latin *e*, not properly a *declinatio*.
⁴⁸ Serv. *A.* 1.374, 3.117.   ⁴⁹ Prisc. 2.255.6 Keil. Cf. Zetzel 1981: 103–4.

As should be clear by now, Servius is not interested in the Greek language for its own sake but only insofar as it helps him teach an ideal form of Latin. We see this above all in his use of Greek to establish the proper scansion of Latin words, which seems to have been problematic to his readers. For example, his note at *A.* 8.603 gives a clear indication of the problems students ran into when trying their hand at elision:

TRACHO ET TYRRHENI – *Tarcho, sic legitur, et Latinus nominatiuus est de Graeco ueniens, ab eo quod est Tarchon, perdito "n" et ω in "o" mutata, ut Apollo* Ἀπόλλων: *aliter uersus non stat.*

THRACIAN AND TYRRHENIAN – *Thraco*, as must be read. The Latin nominative comes from the Greek, which is *Thrachon*. It lost the N and the Ω became O, just as *Apollo* from *Apollon*: otherwise the verse does not scan.

We can see the limits of Servius' interest in the Greek language and Greek culture at *A.* 10.220, where he keeps Donatus' note (found in DS) that Cybele derives her name from the Greek "the turn of the head" (τοῦ κυβίσαι τὴν κεφαλήν) but deletes the Latin translation of this expression. Obviously, he does not believe students would benefit from understanding the Greek words; they only need to acknowledge the Greek justification for the Latin orthography.

All in all, Servius is interested in Greek language only to help him define good Latin practice, and this definition often takes the form of an opposition between Greek and Latin.[50] This pedagogical approach is in large part a function of the grammarian's teaching tool, Virgil's text, which was produced at a time when Greek language and culture were much more prevalent among the Roman elite and, as poetry, plays freely with Greek models. Servius therefore routinely opposes Virgil's use of Greek to his own conception of proper Latin speech, for example at *A.* 4.302, where Virgil calls Bacchic rites *orgia*, following the Greek but Servius deems it should be *caeremoniae*, *A.* 1.319, where he condemns the "Greek" use of the infinitive to convey purpose instead of a subordinate clause, and *A.* 7.125 where he opposes the use of the prefix *ac* "among us" (*apud nos*) to the use of ἀμ "among Greeks" (*apud Graecos*). Although this concern with the definition of Latin usage by opposition to Greek (*Graeca elocutio*) is found mainly in Servius' commentary on the *Aeneid*, it is also seen in other writings, for example his commentary on the *Ars Minor* of Donatus.[51] Priscian, by comparison, writing in the predominantly Greek-speaking milieu of sixth-century Constantinople, stands at odds with Servius (and

---

[50] See further Uhl 1998: 53–85.   [51] Serv. *Don. artem minorem* 4.411.24 Keil.

presumably Donatus) by affirming the primacy of Greek over Latin. For him, teaching Latin means examining Greek grammar and its influence on Latin, while noting where the Latin language differs from the Greek, for example the ablative case (which he nevertheless ties to the Homeric adverbs in -θεν with an ablative value).[52]

This comparison with Priscian raises an important yet elusive question: how much Greek did Servius' students know? Upon first reading, the commentary on Virgil contains enough Greek material to presuppose a rather proficient readership, able not only to pronounce Greek (required to make sense of Servius' notes on loan-words) but also think with key concepts such as the Attic declension and the difference between the accentuation of the Latin accusative *Cyclopas* and the accentuation of the Greek Κύκλωπες.[53] This interpretation assumes Servius wrote for schoolchildren, but this may well not have been the case: there is a strong possibility that the commentaries were written by a grammarian for schoolteachers.[54] Also, as we have seen, much of the information transmitted by Servius accumulated over centuries of grammatical practice and included strata more in touch with Greek culture, such as the Homeric scholia and the early commentaries on Virgil. Nevertheless, the number of Greek words, authors, and citations preserved by Servius indicates he assumed at least some of it (maybe most of it) to be read and understood by students who had already gone through elementary instruction. As Michael Herren details for the Carolingian period in the following chapter, basic Greek and writing abilities were much more widespread than a real understanding of Greek texts. A late Roman student whose family had the resources to send him to the grammarian's school, especially an elite and prestigious one such as Servius', would have had more than passing acquaintance with Greek word-lists and would know basic aspects of the Greek language, but Servius did not expect him to know much more than that.

I shall end by noting similarities of design and use of Greek culture between Servius' commentary on Virgil and Augustine's *Locutiones in Heptateuchum*, an explanation of Greek and Hebrew idioms found in the Latin Heptateuch. As seen above, Augustine had a limited Greek education, but following his baptism he renewed Greek studies in order to read the Scriptures in that language. The *Locutiones* and other exegetical works of Augustine aim at making clear the more obscure aspects of

---

[52] Prisc. *Inst.* 2.187.10–14. Cf. Biville 2009: 50–3.   [53] Serv. *A.* 3.569, 12.701.
[54] Marshall 1997: 20–1.

Scripture for his compatriots, who did not know enough Greek to read Scripture and exegetical works in this language.[55] The following entry on *Genesis* 6:6–7 illustrates Augustine's concerns (Aug. *Loc. Hept* 1.14):

Quod scriptum est in quibusdam latinis codicibus: "Et paenituit, et dixit Deus: 'Deleam hominem, quem feci a facie terrae'"; in graeco inuenitur: διενοήθη, *quod magis recogitauit, quam paenituit significare perhibetur; quod uerbum etiam nonnulli latini codices habent.*

What is written in some Latin codices: "And God grieved and said: 'I will erase man, whom I have made, from the face of the earth.'" In Greek we find διενοήθη, which is held to mean "reflected" rather than "grieved." Some Latin codices also have this verb.

Much as Servius deals with the *Aeneid, Bucolics* and *Georgics* as texts influenced by Greek literature, Augustine's Latin Heptateuch depends upon a Greek archetype (and ultimately a Hebrew one). He therefore uses the Greek (διενοήθη) to justify a correct Latin reading (*recogitauit*, not *paenituit*). But the *Locutiones* are not a continuous emendation of the Heptateuch. Augustine focuses on select passages arousing his curiosity (213 in Genesis, 160 in Exodus, etc.), and compares them with Greek codices not in order to recreate a pristine, original Heptateuch, but rather a Latin Heptateuch agreeing both with Greek precedents and with correct Latin. Thus, considering *Leviticus* 6:18's *sancta sanctorum est*, he considers it a literal translation of the Greek ἅγια ἁγίων ἐστίν, inferior to the more Latinate formulation *sancta sanctorum sunt*.[56] Augustine corrects the text of the Latin Heptateuch in the same way that Servius points out to his pupils instances where Virgil should not be followed. Neither teacher assumes his students to be familiar with Greek. At times, Augustine does not even bother to provide the more complicated Greek citations he discusses, offering rather Latin translations.[57]

For Servius and Augustine, then, Greek holds a marginal place in their pupils' and readers' education, and is merely one of the tools at their disposal to comment and explain foundational Latin texts. Augustine notably uses Virgil and other Latin authorities to explain his biblical text, transferring "the concrete Latin Heptateuch into a point of entry for a much larger textual universe," as Catherine Chin noted.[58] The same process is at play in Servius' commentary, which uses Virgil as a gateway into Latin but also Greek texts, which combine to define ever more closely proper Latin usage.

---

[55] As set forth in the program of Aug. *De doct. Chr.* 2.39.59. Cf. *De Trin.* 3 pr. 1.
[56] Aug. *Loct. Hept.* 10.   [57] E.g. Aug. *Loct. Hept.* 1.10–11.   [58] Chin 2008: 107.

CHAPTER 5

Pelasgian fountains: learning Greek in the early Middle Ages
Michael W. Herren

Esse velim Grecus, cum sim vix, domna, Latinus.

I would like to be a Greek, Lady, though I am scarcely a Latin.[1]

These oft-quoted words by Ekkehart IV of St Gall express the essence of westerners' desire to master the Greek language, one of the three sacred languages written on Christ's Cross at his crucifixion. Greek was the original language of the New Testament and the key to the writings of the Greek fathers. What follows is a sketch of how scholars in the Latin-speaking west were able to learn something of this difficult alien tongue and what they were able to achieve from their study. One westerner, possibly John Scottus Eriugena the Irish polymath, felt that he had achieved his desired goal when he appended these words to a Latin translation of the four Gospels:

Cerne: labore meo lingua Pelasga patet.

Behold: through my efforts the Pelasgian tongue is made clear.[2]

Bernhard Bischoff's essay, "Das griechische Element in der abendländischen Bildung des Mittelalters,"[3] laid the foundation for the study of the fortunes of the Greek language in the western Middle Ages. Walter Berschin's *Greek Letters and the Latin Middle Ages*, first published in German in 1980,[4] built on Bischoff's foundation, expanding its parameters to include Greek written in southern Italy, and widened the chronology. A number of important studies followed. I would single out Bernice Kaczynski's 1988 book *Greek in the Carolingian Age*, based on a close examination of the virtually intact collection of ninth-century manuscripts

---
[1] Ekkehart IV, *Casus S. Galli*, ch. 4 in Meyer von Knonau 1877: 344.
[2] App. 2.1–2 in Herren 1993a: 122.
[3] Originally published as Bischoff 1951; reprinted with modifications as Bischoff 1967.
[4] English translation by Frakes 1988 (Berschin 1988a). The book is prefaced by a valuable essay, *ibid.* pp. 3–17, on the history of scholarship on this topic from the Renaissance onwards.

held by the Stiftsbibliothek of St Gall. Also of special note is Carlotta Dionisotti's article "Greek Grammars and Dictionaries in Carolingian Europe," published in the same year in the collection *The Sacred Nectar of the Greeks: The Study of Greek in the West in the Early Middle Ages.*[5]

Since these works were published, Bernhard Bischoff and Michael Lapidge produced an edition and study of the biblical glosses connected to the study of Greek at the school of Canterbury in the late seventh century.[6] The work consists of mostly short notes to the Pentateuch ascribed to Theodore, archbishop of Canterbury 669–90, and his companion Abbot Hadrian, who headed the Canterbury school until his death in 710.[7] The base text for the commentary is the Latin Vulgate, but Theodore and Hadrian, both Greek speakers, interjected words and phrases drawn from parallel versions in Greek, and from other Greek sources.[8] What we have then, according to the editors, is a kind of student notebook – with all the shortcomings of such – that reflects the teaching conducted at Canterbury in the late seventh century. The commentaries mention Greek as well as Latin patristic authors, and thus provide firm evidence of the Greek sources known to the two masters. Authors quoted by name include Basil of Caesarea, Clement of Alexandria, Cosmas Indicopleustes, Epiphanius of Salamis, and John Chrysostom.

Theodore and Hadrian are among the very few names known to us of Greek-speakers teaching Greek in a western location in the early Middle Ages.[9] Paul the Deacon was engaged to teach Greek at Charlemagne's palace school, but the only trace of this is Paul's diffident remark that he did not know the language very well.[10] We learn from Ekkehart IV (*c.* 980–1060) that Greek tutors were dispatched to prepare the Duchess Hartwig for marriage to the Greek King Constantine, and that she had received an excellent tutelage.[11] Alas, we know very little of the methods, textbooks or other resources (apart from glossaries) used prior to the Carolingian age. However, we now know a good deal about teaching resources known to the Carolingians thanks to Dionisotti's study in *The Sacred Nectar of the Greeks.* There she showed that portions of a Greek

---

[5] Dionisotti 1988a. [6] Bischoff and Lapidge 1994. [7] See the studies in Lapidge 1995.
[8] Discussed by Lapidge (1988).
[9] See the references to the presence of Greeks in the Carolingian period in Berschin 1988a: 133; for Greek-Frankish relations to the eleventh century see Riché 1988, with a list of embassy missions between east and west, pp. 166–8. Almost none of this information, however, bears upon the teaching of Greek.
[10] Dümmler 1881: 49: *Graiam nescio loquellam, ignoro Hebraicam;/Tres aut quattuor in scolis quas didici syllabas,/Ex his mihi est ferendus maniplus ad aream.*
[11] Berschin 1988a: 150.

grammar survived in a group of seven manuscripts dated to the ninth and tenth centuries.[12] The paradigms include both nouns and verbs. Other paradigms of verbs, preserved in a *defloratio* of Macrobius' work on the Greek and Latin verb, are to be found in another group of five Carolingian manuscripts. The most complete of these grammatical manuscripts is that preserved as no. 444 in the Municipal Library of Laon, written by Martin of Laon (aka Martin Hibernensis, Martin the Irishman). This "Thesaurus linguae Graecae," as it is sometimes called, is the object of important studies by E. Miller, Edouard Jeauneau, and John Contreni.[13] Dionisotti gives a complete list of its Greek contents in an appendix to her article in *The Sacred Nectar*.[14] Given time constraints I can only hint at the riches contained in this great thesaurus. Additional to the paradigms one finds alphabets, several Greek-Latin glossaries, a full list of Priscian's Greek words, phrases and quotations, Greek words collected from church fathers, the Greek poetry of John Scottus with glosses, and much more. Was that all there was? Dionisotti conjectured that there was indeed more, possibly even the complete grammar of Herodian, a fragment of which with the title *Ex minore Herodiano* survives in Paris lat. 7501 from Corbie. Other traces of a more complete grammar are to be found in Sedulius Scottus's commentary on the grammar of Eutyches, which gives fuller paradigms of verbs than those found in the *De verborum Graeci et Latini differentiis uel societatibus* of Macrobius.[15]

Glossaries and word-lists form the other important component of these early Greek studies. Evidence for the use of glossaries shows up in seventh-century Ireland, where they were employed by the authors of the *Hisperica Famina*.[16] We also find Greek words put to imaginative uses in the late seventh- or early eighth-century Irish-to-Latin glossary known as "O'Mulconry's Glossary," which was doubtless dependent on one or more of the known Graeco-Latin dictionaries.[17] Between the late seventh and eighth century Anglo-Saxon scholars drew *graeca* from glossaries and glossed copies of the church fathers and inserted them into new glossaries of English manufacture. This is the series of Latin-Old English glossaries that comprises the Épinal-Erfurt, Leyden, and Corpus glossaries. As Lapidge has shown, more evidence for the teaching of Theodore and Hadrian can be wrung out of these glossaries.[18]

---

[12] Dionisotti 1988a: 21–6.
[13] Miller 1860, Jeauneau 1972, Contreni 1978 (see Index of Manuscripts, p. 204).
[14] Dionisotti 1988a: 45–54.   [15] Dionisotti 1988a: 24–6.
[16] For a list of Greek and Greek-derived words in the A-Text, see Herren 1974: 191–3.
[17] Herren 1999: 65–6; Herren 2010, esp. pp. 519–26; Russell 2000; Moran 2012.
[18] Lapidge 1986, reprinted in Lapidge 1996: 155–63.

Continental scholars during the Carolingian age had a variety of glossarial aids available to them. The largest of these, perhaps, was the Latin-to-Greek Dictionary of Pseudo-Philoxenus, which survives in one full copy, two fragmentary copies, and excerpts from Remigius of Auxerre.[19] As Dionisotti points out, this dictionary was intended for Greeks learning Latin, but it could also be useful for scholars eager to know the correct Greek equivalent of a Latin word. A substantially more useful Greek-to-Latin dictionary was also known, namely the Pseudo-Cyril dictionary, which would have provided help for reading the Bible among other tasks.[20] In addition to these large dictionaries, numerous less complete lexicons survive, some of which are organized alphabetically, others by subject matter, such as the *Hermeneumata Pseudo-Dositheana*.

In the ninth century, the centres that possessed these resources would have used them exclusively for scholarly purposes, chief among them being biblical exegesis. However, a few slightly later examples survive of a more practical type of glossary or word-list designed to serve the needs of travellers. These contained the basic phrases needed for acquiring food, drink, and lodging, as well as the basic exchange of courtesies – good day, how are you?, thank you, excuse me, and the like – but would be practically useless for anything more than that since they contained no grammatical information. One such list, published by Bernhard Bischoff, gives common words loosely arranged by category (parts of the body, food and wine, religious terms).[21] Of interest to the philologist is the fact that many of the Greek words are in their demotic form, closely resembling their modern equivalents. This shows that the list was meant to be used by persons who needed to communicate with Greek speakers. Here is a small sample:

summi   *panem*   (τὸ ψωμί)
krasin *vinum*   (τὸ κρασίν)
papais *presbiter* (ὁ παπᾶς)

Word-definitions and paradigms are sometimes combined haphazardly in the same glossary. A good example of this occurs in the so-called "Reichenauer Schulheft" ("Reichenau Notebook"), a miscellany of eight folios consisting of a life of Vergil, a Greek glossary, and some Old Irish poems including the famous "Pangur Bán." It is now housed at St Paul's Monastery in Kärnten.[22] The Greek word entries are written in majuscule, while

---

[19] Dionisotti 1988a: 7.   [20] Dionisotti 1988a: 6–15.   [21] Bischoff 1984.
[22] Unterdrauberg, Carinthia (Austria), St Paul's Monastery, MS 25.2.31, formerly 25 d. 86 (Codex Sanblasianus 86). See the description by Stern (1908–9). A digitalized version is available online:

the glosses appearing above are written in an Irish minuscule that lacks all trace of the influence of Carolingian minuscule, and thus appears to belong to the earlier part of the ninth century, or possibly even the end of the eighth. Whether it was written at Reichenau or brought there by Irish monks is hard to say. The entries are neither alphabetized, nor is there evidence of grouping by subject-matter. The glossary may represent *glossae collectae* to a Greek work, since several words are repeated. Amid the word-entries at irregular places can be found declensions of Greek nouns accompanied by their articles: Ο ΚΥΡΙΟC (glossed *dominus*), ΤΟΥ ΚΥΡΙΟΥ, etc.; Η ΓΥΝΗ (glossed *mulier*), ΤΗC ΓΥΝΗC (instead of the correct γυναικός),[23] etc.; ΤΟ ΟΝΟΜΑ (glossed *nomen*), ΤΟΥ ΟΝΟΜΑΤΟC, etc. It is obvious that these paradigms are imported from a set of noun declensions known as the "Declinationes Graecorum" represented in seven manuscripts, since the examples used in all seven are identical and a "Greek ablative singular" (!) introduced by ΑΠΟ is included.[24]

Whereas the large dictionaries and the *Hermeneumata* belong to late antiquity, one work shows several stages of compilation by Carolingian scholars. This is the *Scholica Graecarum Glossarum*, originally attributed to Martin of Laon.[25] M. L. W. Laistner, its first editor, was unaware of all the manuscripts of this work – some representing expanded recensions – but a recent detailed study by Patrizia Lendinara argues that the work was compiled in three basic stages: (1) an initial core of entry words derived largely from the *graeca* in Isidore of Seville's *Etymologiae*; (2) an expansion in the mid-ninth century incorporating the *graeca* and the interpretations found in commentaries on Martianus; (3) a late ninth-century addition of about 400 miscellaneous Greek words.[26] The activity in phase 2, in which Lendinara sees the involvement of Martin of Laon and John Scottus Eriugena, makes use of the oldest commentary tradition on Martianus and the two versions of Eriugena's commentary on Martianus.[27] The result is marked by an expansion of philosophical terms in Greek.

It should be clear from the foregoing that scholars in the early Middle Ages, particularly during the ninth century, were driven by a desire to learn Greek. This desire was fuelled primarily by a perceived need to know the original language of the New Testament, but the newly found interest in

---

http://hildegard.tristram.de/schulheft (accessed 25 April 2013). The Greek grammar and glossary were edited by Petschenig (1883). On the Old Irish poems, see Tristram 1999.

[23] Dionisotti 1988a: 22–3 on the prevalence and origin of this anomalous declension.
[24] Dionisotti 1988a: 22–3.
[25] See Laistner 1923. A new edition is being prepared by Patrizia Lendinara.
[26] Lendinara 2011.   [27] Lendinara 2011: 325–30.

secular learning, especially the interpretation of Martianus Capella's demanding work, came into play as well. This may be a good time to ask: what precisely is meant by the knowledge of Greek? There has been much uncritical use of the phrase "knowledge of Greek" particularly by an earlier generation of historians, often speaking in reference to Ireland. The question is easily answered by another question: what does it mean to know *any* language? Not a few Latin writers of the Middle Ages larded their compositions with Greek words. For the most part, these words were acquired from Greek-Latin glossaries, or from glossed copies of the Scriptures or Church fathers. But the pertinent question is: if you set a Greek text in front of someone, would he or she be able to translate it, even with a dictionary? Further, if you asked a person to translate a simple sentence from Latin (or their native language) into Greek, would the person be able to do it? I leave aside the question of whether one could speak Greek or understand it when spoken; given the absence of native speakers, it would be virtually impossible to acquire this skill without travelling to the east,[28] or otherwise having contact with Greek-speakers through trade or diplomacy. So in this instance we must be content to accept two of the four criteria as sufficient for knowing a language, namely, competence in reading and writing.

There is little question that a number of westerners were concerned to acquire the basic skill of writing words in Greek letters, as is demonstrated by the numerous examples of the Greek alphabet we find in western manuscripts, especially those written between the late eighth and the tenth century. These alphabets are frequently accompanied by their Greek letter-names, and sometimes by their Greek numerical equivalents, because the Greeks employed letters as numerals. A particularly interesting example occurs in Vienna, ÖNB 795, dated to 799 (Figure 5.1).

The example shows the letter-form with its Greek letter-name written above it in the first column, its Greek numerical value written out in letters in the middle column, and its equivalent in Roman numerals in the third column. In the left margin you will see the Latin letter equivalent: *pro a*, *pro b*, etc. The letters used are almost invariably majuscules based on the Greek hand known as "biblical majuscule." One character, namely "siglum M," approximately ")-(", is a western peculiarity, as Walter Berschin showed.[29] It is prominently displayed in lines 5–6 of the Lord's Prayer contained in the famous Schaffhausen Adomnán (Figure 5.2).

---

[28] The most famous example is Liutprand of Cremona (tenth century); see Berschin 1988a: 174–82.
[29] Berschin 1988b: 87–8.

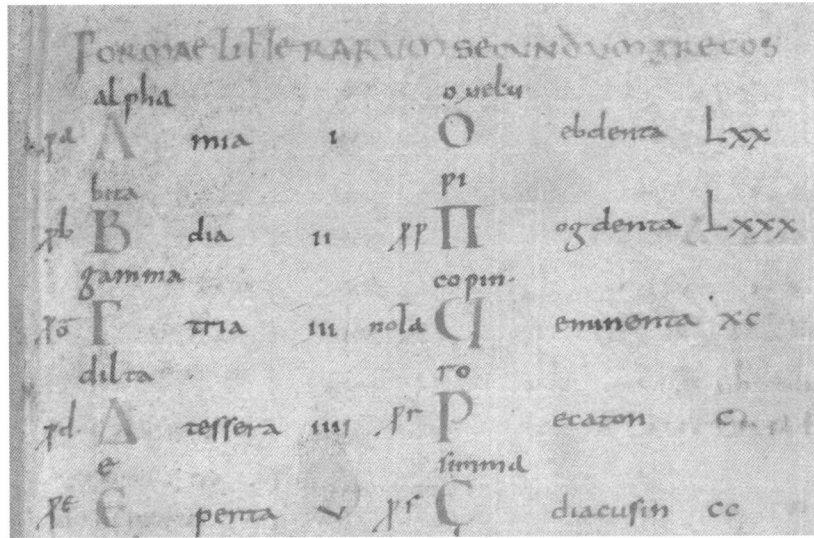

Figure 5.1: Vienna, Österreichische Nationalbibliothek, MS 795, f. 19r.

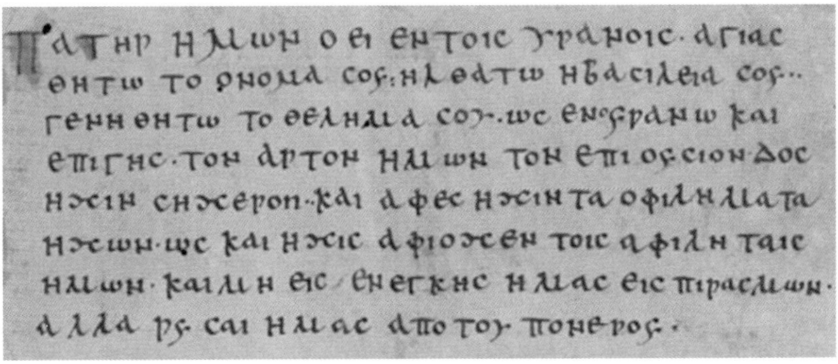

Figure 5.2: Schaffhausen, Stadtbibliothek, MS Gen. 1, p. 137.

It is also the "default form" in the "Reichenauer Schulheft."[30] In the east it was confined to epigraphic use. Bernhard Bischoff notes several instances of the use of Greek minuscule;[31] an example is found in the "Antapodosis" of Liutprand of Cremona from the late tenth century (Figure 5.3).

There are also scattered instances of letters written with accents and breathing marks.

---

[30] Consult folios 2v–4r in the online version; see n. 22.   [31] Bischoff 1967: 254–5.

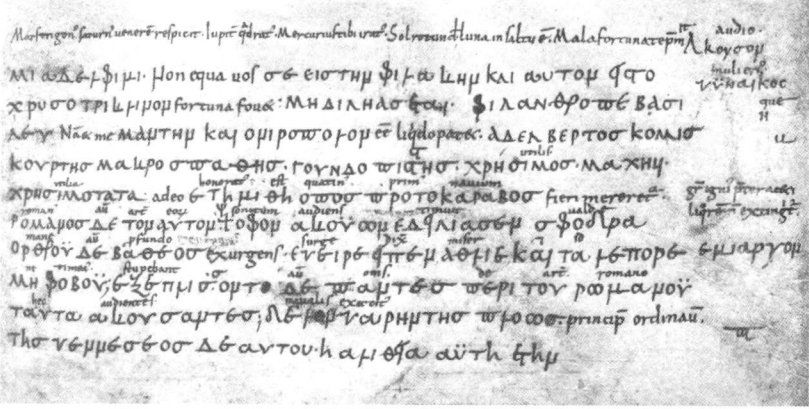

Figure 5.3: Metz, Bibliothèque Municipale, MS 145, f. 204 (Becker 1908, Taf. 1).

When Greek words were copied, they were sometimes copied completely in Greek letters, sometimes in a relatively consistent transliteration into the Roman alphabet, but frequently in a mixture of Greek and Latin letters. I recently spent some time studying the Greek *tituli* in the three Carolingian copies of Lucretius's *De rerum natura*. I discovered that these "chapter headings" are derived from small snippets of Epicurus's authentic works inserted to introduce the subject matter of the ensuing passage in the Lucretian text. I conjectured that the *tituli* were originally marginal references to passages in Epicurus (written in Greek) that were relevant to the Lucretius passages to which they were affixed (thus, a kind of *apparatus fontium*).[32] Here I shall be concerned exclusively with their written form. We find one heading at *DRN* 2.646 written mostly in Greek letters, with one manuscript replacing an alpha with a delta:

TOMAKΔPION KAIA Φ[eras.]ΘARTON

i.e. Τὸ μακάριον καὶ ἄφθαρτον ("the blessed and imperishable").

Most of the letters can be taken as Greek letters, given the overlap between Greek and Roman majuscule characters. However, the R of <A>ΦΘARTON should have been replaced by a P-shaped letter rho.

To be sure, westerners were able to do much more than write alphabets, individual words, short phrases, and *tituli*. We find examples of entire Greek texts written competently by western hands using the Greek

[32] Herren 2012.

alphabet. It is also interesting to observe that by this early date western scribes had adopted the Byzantine practice of replacing eta and certain classical diphthongs with iota reflecting the contemporary pronunciation. Referring again to the Lord's Prayer in "the Schaffhausen Adomnán," we see at line 5, ΟΦΙΛΗΜΑΤΑ for ὀφειλήματα; line 7, ΠΙΡΑCΜΩΝ for πειρασμόν.[33] (Note as well the confusion of omega and omicron in the second word, a frequent occurrence in the orthography of western Greek.)

In the ninth century we find examples of complete biblical texts copied out in Greek. Much of this activity was under the purview of Irish scribes working on the Continent. Sedulius Scottus, active *c*. 860, produced an entire Greek psalter in Greek script interspersed with Latin *tituli*. We know it is his work because he appended the explicit: "CHΔΥΛΙΟC CΚΟΤΤΟC ΕΓΩ ΕΓΡΑΨΑ." "I Sedulius the Irishman wrote (this)."[34] Irish scholars of the same period were also responsible for a group of bilingual biblical books, in which the Greek text was written across the entire page (instead of in columns as it sometimes was) and given a complete interlinear running gloss. In other words, these manuscripts would have looked something like the copies of the Greek New Testament, still available in religious bookshops, which print the Greek text with a literal English crib between the lines. Three examples are known: the so-called "Basel Psalter," Basel, University Library A. vii. 3; the "St Gall Gospels," MS 48 in the Stiftsbibliothek of St Gall; and the "Codex Boernerianus," remains of St Paul's letters preserved in Dresden, Stadtbiblikothek (Municipal Library) Msc. A. 145 b.[35] The last-named manuscript, unfortunately, was heavily damaged in the last war, but the entire book is preserved in a photographic facsimile (Figure 5.4).[36]

I shall come back to this group of manuscripts when I discuss the question of reading and understanding. The extant interlinear bilinguals have been ascribed to Sedulius Scottus, though unconvincingly.[37] Whoever was responsible, these manuscripts are written in an Irish hand, and names of Irish scholars fill the margins.[38]

---

[33] See Herren 1988, esp. pp. 61–2; Kaczynski 1988a: 31–2.
[34] Paris, Bibliothèque de l'Arsenal, MS 8407, fol. 55. It is unfortunate that scholars continue to refer to this psalter as a bilingual book. The text of the Psalms is entirely in Greek, the only Latin being the Vulgate titles prefacing each psalm. I believe that the error goes back to Kenney 1966: 557: "All in Greek with Latin interlinear translation."
[35] Herren 1996; see also Kaczynski 1988a: 80–2, 85–6, who associates the interlinear bilinguals with the activity of Marcus and his nephew Moengal at St Gall.
[36] See Bischoff 1981: 45–7.
[37] For the controversy over the origin and provenance of these manuscripts, see Kaczynski 1988a: 85–6.
[38] For the identification of these marginal names, see Contreni 1982: 758–98.

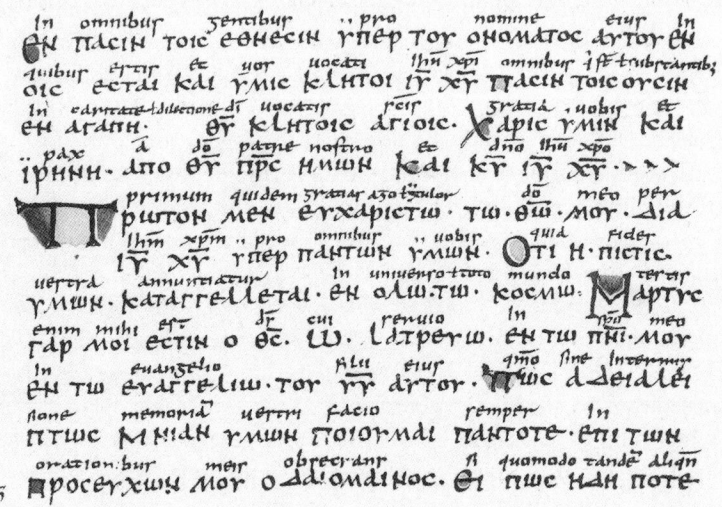

Figure 5.4: Dresden, Sächsiche Landesbibliothek, MS A 145b, f. 1r

Not all of the writing and glossing in Greek was the work of Irish scholars. Frankish scholars, especially ones associated with St Gall, also shared in this activity. Bernice Kaczynski's work (1988a) on the *graeca* of the St Gall manuscripts has turned up a number of examples of Greek texts written in a pure Carolingian hand lacking all trace of Irish influence. Texts include biblical books or portions thereof, prayers, doxologies, litanies, creeds, bilingual glossaries, and grammatical aids. The dates of these manuscripts range from the ninth to the eleventh centuries. Not all of the Greek texts are written in Greek letters; indeed, not a few have been transliterated into the Roman alphabet.

When we extend the notion of writing beyond alphabetical literacy to the ability to express one's thoughts in correct Greek, or something resembling it, the quantity of evidence shrinks exponentially. Until the late ninth century the Irish had a monopoly on this tiny enterprise. Beginning in the seventh century Irish scholars found pleasure in inserting bits of syntactically connected Greek into their verses. So we find in the seventh-century "Antiphonary of Bangor," which contains material dating to the late sixth and early seventh century, the alphabetical hymn that begins *Audite, pantes, ta erga*, "Hear, all ye, the deeds..." Of course, *audite* is Latin, but the writer has got his direct object, *ta erga*, right, and *pantes*, "all ye," will do nicely as a vocative. At a later stage, a few Irish poets were capable of more developed thoughts in Greek. Thus, in the "Rubisca," a satiric hisperic poem, we find two entire stanzas composed in macaronic Greek, written partially in Greek characters. I cite one of them:

YMNICTE ΠANTEC: TPINON, TON ETHNON
ΓEON THALACCON: MONON YPANON
<KTICTHN> TAΓMANON: KAI TON INΦEPON.
YMNICTE IONAC: IC TAC HONON.

All sing the one who is threefold,
Sole <Creator> of peoples, lands, seas, heavens,
(angelic) ranks, even those below,
Praise him unto ages of ages.[39]

This is pretty awful stuff, if one is a Hellenist! Yet it does attest to the author's desire to master Greek and prove his mastery by writing in that language. Nearly two centuries after the "Rubisca" was composed, another Irishman, John Scottus Ergiuena, also attempted to write poetry in Greek. Despite the fact that John was easily the greatest western Greek scholar between Boethius and Robert Grosseteste, his efforts in writing Greek poems fall well short of brilliance, as I learned when I re-edited them in 1993.[40] The impetus to write in Greek began to falter by the end of the ninth century. However, I should mention at least one non-Irishman who tried his hand at this craft, namely Hartmann of St Gall (*fl.* 883). Like Eriugena, Hartmann was not content to write just any kind of verse; no, it had to be of the classical quantitative type. Hartmann chose the elegiac distich:

KYRRIE pantocrator ysos sodisse te pantes
  Su basyleos ymon XPICTE eleyson ymas.[41]

This is doggerel, and does not scan according to quantitative rules, though it does more or less mimic the rhythm of the elegiac distich. Much more accomplished was the work of Liutprand of Cremona, who had the advantage of a sojourn in Constantinople. Liutprand did not attempt Greek poetry, but inserted Greek words, phrases, and grammatically correct sentences into his *Antapodosis*. Here is a short sample:[42]

Εξεπλισσαντο δε παντες περι του Ρομανου ταυτα ακουσαντες. *Unde factus est, ut tam pro ceteris quamque pro praeclaro praesenti hoc facinore* [!] *non multo post a*

---

[39] Herren 1987: 102–3.   [40] For the Greek poems, see Herren 1993a: 98–102.
[41] Cited from Kaczynski 1988a: 19.
[42] For more, see the text quoted in Berschin 1988a: 176–8.

Leone imperatore tanto donaretur honore. ὅπως παντα τα πλοια *suis essent in manibus eiusque iussionibus oboedirent.*[43]

Turning to the question of understanding, we need to look at scholars' ability to translate Greek and to compare Greek and Latin versions of the same work. This latter facility is particularly crucial for biblical exegesis. Much of our evidence for translation is to be found in glossed texts. However, evaluation of glossing can be tricky, for it is often impossible to tell whether a gloss or translation to a text was copied out – possibly from an ancient source – or was the work of the editor-scribe. This holds particularly true in the case of the fairly numerous parallel-column biblical texts. However, when we turn to the Irish interlinear biblical texts, the matter is different. While a parallel text can be copied without the scribe's understanding of his material, an interlinear version cannot be. The copyist must not only be concerned to write the proper Latin word overhead the proper Greek word, he must also allow for differences in grammatical structure. In other words, one cannot simply copy out a Greek text of a Gospel book and write the Vulgate translation between the lines. The scribe must be concerned with added and missing words in both versions, with matching word order, and with matching syntax insofar as this is possible between the two languages.[44] Here are examples of such practices from the St Gall Gospels, with the Vulgate text given for comparison:

	SG Greek	SG Latin	Vulg. +
Mt 2:1	ΤΟΥ ΔΕ ΙC ΓΕΝΝΗΘΕΝΤΟC	*autem Jesu nascente*	*Cum ergo natus esset Jesus*
Mt 2:21	ΛΕΓΟΜΕΝΗΝ	*dictam*	*quae uocatur*
Mt 3:3	ΥΠΟ ΗCΑΙΟΥ	*ab Esaia*	*per Esaiam*
Mt 3:13	ΒΑΠΤΙCΘΕΝΑΙ	*baptizari l.tur*	*baptizaretur*
Mt 4:1	ΠΕΙΡΑCΘΕΝΑΙ	*temptari*	*ut tentaretur*
Mt 5:4	ΠΕΝΟΥΝΤΕC	*lugentes*	*qui lugent*
Mt 5:17	ΜΗ ΝΟΜΙCΗΤΑΙ (= -ΤΕ)	*ne putetis*	*noli putare*
Mt 5:22	ΟΡΓΙΖΟΜΕΝΟC	*irascitur l.scens*	*irascitur*

Given the fact that there were no ancient models for interlinear translations of the Bible, we may assume that the ninth-century Irish examples that we possess were original productions, not copies. This hypothesis is

---

[43] "And all were astonished when they heard these things concerning Romanus. And not much later it came to pass that he (Romanus) was so greatly honoured by the Emperor Leo both for this remarkable deed [*facinus*!] as well as for others that all the ships were placed in his hands and obeyed his commands."

[44] Herren 1996: 311.

supported by the fact that scholars concerned with classifying Latin versions of the New Testament have been unable to classify the Latin interlinear translations. This is because they are truly *sui generis*. Although based on the Vulgate, they have been adjusted in many cases to meet the requirements of the Greek base texts.

A remarkable oddity, namely the interlinear glossing of a Latin text of the Psalms with Greek, occurs in Berlin, Phillipps 1674, where the scribe drew readings from his own copy of the Septuagint version of the Psalms and set them above the readings of Jerome's Gallican psalter:[45]

Fol. 208r,
to Ps. 26: ΚΑΙ ΝΥΝ ΙΔΟΥ ΥΨΩCΕΝ
 et nunc ecce exaltavit
 ΤΗΝΚΕΦΑΛΗΝ. ΜΟΥ
 caput meum

to Ps. 26: ΕΞΕΖΗΤΗCΑΤΟ ΠΡΟCΩΠΟΝ. ΜΟΥ
 exquisivit facies mea.

to Ps. 27: ΕΙCΑΚΟΥCΟΝ ΤΗC ΦΩΝΗC ΤΗC ΔΕΗCΕΩC
 exaudi vocem deprecationis
 ΜΟΥ
 meae.

to Ps. 28: ΚΑΙ ΕΝ ΤΩ.ΝΑΩ. ΑΥΤΟΥ.
 et in templo eius
 ΠΑCΤΙC ΛΕΓΕΙ ΔΟΞΑΝ
 omnis dicet gloriam.

to Ps. 28: K̄C̄ ΤΟΝΚΑΤΑΚΛΥCΜΩ̄ ΚΑΤΟΚΕΙ
 dominus diluvium inhabitat.

Of course, one must allow for the placement of the article without a space before the accompanying noun, a virtually universal practice of western scribes, and for not adjusting the Greek syntax to the Vulgate's Latin. However, Greek, after all, was the base text, so why would anyone wish to alter it to match a translation? The result is an impressive achievement.

Early medieval scribes not only copied and glossed Greek texts of the Scriptures, but also applied their knowledge of the Greek versions to their exegetical writings. Christian Stavelot made explicit reference to the Greek text of Luke when explicating a textual point in Matthew's Gospel.[46] Eriugena used a Greek text of John's Gospel for his commentary on that scriptural text.[47] This is not so surprising, as both of these Carolingian

[45] Kaczynski 1988b: 221. [46] Berschin 1988a: 131. [47] Bieler 1977.

scholars would have benefitted from the expanded distribution of Greek texts and the aids for learning Greek that became available in the later Carolingian period. More impressive in this regard is the achievement of the Venerable Bede, who, although working in England, did not enjoy the benefit of the education in Greek that was available in the south of his country in the earlier part of his lifetime. As Carlotta Dionisotti has shown, Bede was an autodidact, who learned what Greek he could acquire from a careful study of a bilingual, facing-page (Greek and Latin) text of the New Testament, in all probability the surviving codex Oxford Laud. Gr. 35, thought to have been written in Sardinia around 600.[48] In his *Retractatio in Actus Apostolorum* Bede alludes, in a number of passages, to the difference between the senses of the Greek and Latin texts. But even prior to this late work Bede sometimes took up the meaning of Greek words in his commentary.

After Boethius and before the thirteenth century only one scholar can be credited with making translations of entire Greek works (apart from biblical texts). I speak yet again of John Scottus Eriugena, the Irish scholar who spent most of mature life, as far as we know, in Francia; his years of activity overlap the reign of Charles the Bald. John made complete translations of Gregory of Nyssa's *De imagine*, Maximus the Confessor's *Ambigua* and the *Quaestiones ad Thalassium*, and the entire corpus of writing by Dionysius the Areopagite. Other translations, such as that of Epiphanius of Salamis's work *Ancoratus*, have also been attributed to him. The quality of John's translations and his overall ability as a Hellenist have been examined in recent years, especially by Edouard Jeauneau.[49] Flaws of various kinds have been noted.[50] Yet, whatever the final verdict on these translations, his work stands alone, surrounded by a vacuum of three to four hundred years in either direction.

An important general observation should be made at this stage. Works written in Greek that reached western scholars and libraries were limited to books of the Bible (primarily the Psalms and the books of the New Testament) and a few of the Church fathers. As far as the evidence goes, not a single classical literary text reached the west before the Renaissance. That is to say, no copies of Homer, Hesiod, the major Greek playwrights, or any of the lyric poets existed in western libraries. (Greek philosophical texts, especially those written by Aristotle, arrived in the twelfth century, but that is another story.) This serious deficiency notwithstanding, a western scholar, if he was interested, could find quotations of classical works in Greek. These were to be found chiefly in that great work of

[48] Dionisotti 1982b.   [49] Jeauneau 1979.   [50] See e.g. Pépin 1986.

Figure 5.5: Leiden B.P.L. 67, f. 32v

comparative grammar, Priscian's *Institutiones grammaticae*, which by the ninth century was already well represented in western libraries. Priscian liked to illustrate a grammatical point with an illustration from a Greek or a Latin poet.

Some years ago I examined a ninth-century copy of Priscian's *Institutiones grammaticae* written by the Irish scribe Dubthach (Leiden, Universiteitsbibliotheek, B.P.L. 67: Figure 5.5), which also contains a group of Eriugena's epigrams. However, as I worked my way through the manuscript of Priscian's work, I discovered short passages from Homer's *Odyssey* quoted by the grammarian that were recopied in the lower margin and provided with a Latin gloss. I suspected that both the recopied lines and the Latin gloss were from the hand known as I-1, that is, John Scottus's own hand. This suspicion was confirmed for me by Bernhard Bischoff.[51] The Homeric passages were in a highly corrupt state, thus not genuinely transmitted pericopes that might have been translated into Latin at an earlier point. The result was a fairly correct rendition of a badly mangled text. You can see the evidence below where I have given Homer's Greek text, Priscian's rendition of the same passage, and John's Latin gloss followed by an English translation.[52] Here is the text of *Odyssey* 1.163–5 as printed in modern editions:

εἰ κεῖνον γ' Ἰθάκηνδε ἰδοίατο νοστήσαντα
πάντες κ' ἀρησαίατ' ἐλαφρότεροι πόδας εἶναι
ἢ ἀφνειότεροι χρυσοῖό τε ἐσθῆτός τε.

Priscian's citation of the passage was omitted by Dubthach, but added (from another exemplar) by John at the bottom of the folio:

ΕΙΚΕΙΝΟΝ ΤΕ ΙΘΑΚΗΝ ΔΗΛΟΥΔΕ ΑΓΩΝΟΣ ΕΑΝΤΑ
ΕΑΝΤΟΣ ΚΑΡΗΣ ΔΙΑ ΤΗΛΑ ΦΡΟΝΩΤΕΡΟΙ ΥΓΘΛΗΙ (?)
ΕΙΝΑΙ ΑΦΝΕΙΟΤΕΡΟΙ ΧΡΥΣΟΙΤΕ ΣΘΕΤΟΥΤΕ

---

[51] I note that Paul Dutton had reached the same conclusion independently: see Dutton 1992: 15–45.
[52] Herren 1993b: 195–6 and plates.

John's interlinear translation runs as follows:

> *Illum que Ithaken* (gl. *insula*) *uero agone Eanta* (gl. *nomen herois*)
> *Eante Kares* (gl. *nomen proprium*) *per arma prudentior* ΥΓΘΛΗΙ (gl. *nomen proprium*)
> *Esse ditiore auro que pectore que*

And then he adds:

> *Talis sensus: Kares prudentior in armis Eante. Ditior et auro et pectore* ΥΓΘΛΗΙ. ("The sense of the passage: Kares is wiser in arms than Eas (Ajax). He is wealthier both in gold and in spirit than ΥΓΘΛΗΙ." [The last sentence alternatively:] "ΥΓΘΛΗΙ is wealthier in gold and spirit.")

The great mass of glosses on the text of Priscian's work has yet to be studied for what it may yield to students of early medieval humanism. I have examined a few copies of this work and can attest that medieval scholars had a special interest in glossing mythological names, even when written in Greek, as they often were in ninth-century Priscian codices. It is highly likely that the Priscian glosses to the *graeca* in Priscian's text go back to an archetypal set of glosses on Priscian that was excerpted and modified in different ways in a wide variety of codices. Dionisotti opined that the archetype is traceable to John Scottus's activity.[53]

I would like to look now at an earlier western figure that has received very little attention to date, but one that intrigues for his unusual knowledge of Greek and his imaginative manipulations of Greek mythology. I refer to the anonymous author of the *Cosmography of Aethicus Ister*, a forgery transmitted under the name of Jerome, written in the second quarter of the eighth century.[54] This work combines a description of the cosmos with a voyage around the described world, with special attention paid to the unexplored parts of the north. Jerome is presented as the editor and abbreviator of this *periplous*, allegedly written partly in Latin, partly in Greek, by a Scythian philosopher called Aethicus Ister. Our forger Pseudo-Jerome does all in his power to convince his readers that the barbarian Aethicus knew Greek by larding the work with numerous Greek words. Some of the neologisms are derived purely from Greek, others from Greek and Latin.[55] In addition to numerous words that had been granted citizenship in Latin (e.g. *aenigma, aether, physicus, anathema, neophytus, paradigma, paedagogus*), we find many other Greek words that occur in Latin

---

[53] Dionisotti 1988a: 50. See also Dutton and Luhtala 1994.
[54] See now Herren 2011: lv–lxxiii for date and provenance of this work.
[55] See Herren 2001: 184–200.

rarely, if ever: *acenaces* ("sword"), *aconiti* ("without a struggle"), *aspidiscus* ("surgical instrument"), *cataphractus* ("armoured"), *peripsima* ("scourings"), *asynchytus* ("unmixed bitumen"). Some of these words are attested in Graeco-Latin glossaries, but others are not. The author also invents a number of Graeco-Latin hybrids that remind us of similar inventions in the *Hisperica Famina*: *ideomochus*, *pachacomus*, *termofiles*, etc.[56] The text gives no concrete evidence that the author could speak Greek or even read it fluently, but a handful of words shows acquaintance with Byzantine lexica; *turma<r>chus* ("military commander") is an egregious example.[57] The copious employment of Greek lexica marks a point of continuity between the experiments of the Irish and Anglo-Saxons in the seventh and early eighth centuries and the activity of the Carolingians.

I shall conclude with this theme of important centres for the study of Greek. It should be clear from the foregoing that there was a *translatio studii* after the collapse of education in the Roman Empire. The recipients of this *translatio* were the monastic scholars of the British Isles, with Ireland leading the way, at least chronologically. It is difficult sometimes to pinpoint Irish centres of study; however, when it comes to Greek, the monks of Bangor can be identified as early pioneers, while the evidence from the Schaffhausen manuscript shows that Iona followed soon after. From the neighbouring island we now have good evidence of the study of Greek at Canterbury; more evidence may be forthcoming. However, Canterbury was not unique. In Jarrow, well to the north, the Venerable Bede pursued the study of Greek on his own using a bilingual version of the New Testament. Towards the middle of the eighth century the pseudonymous author of *The Cosmography of Aethicus Ister*, who I believe worked at a Continental centre with insular connections, revealed an extensive knowledge of Greek vocabulary.

With the onset of the Carolingian Renaissance, a fairly clear pattern emerges. We find one cluster of scholars pursuing Greek in northeastern France and Lotharingia. Particular places include Laon, Soissons, Rheims, and Auxerre – centres connected to John Scottus[58] – and Liège, where Sedulius worked. Corbie also comes into the picture vis-à-vis the study of Martianus Capella, a task that required Greek lexical and grammatical resources.[59] A second cluster can be located around Lake Constance in "the St Gall-Reichenau" area. St Gall, of course, was the more important of the two centres, as Kaczynski's work shows. In the last phase of the

---

[56] See the list in Herren 2001: 193.   [57] Herren 2001: 191–2.   [58] Jeauneau 1972.
[59] See generally the important collection edited by Teeuwen and O'Sullivan (2011).

Carolingian period Hellenic studies migrated southward to Auxerre, where Heiric and Remigius were active. A century later the map changed. Ottonian Germany became the focus of western interest in Greek, and Lombard Italy awoke from a long slumber. The old Carolingian foundations in Francia went into slow decline. However, it remains true that the ninth century was the *Blütezeit* of Greek studies in the west up to the time of Robert Grosseteste.[60]

---

[60] See Dionisotti 1988b.

CHAPTER 6

Out of the mouth of babes and Englishmen: the invention of the vernacular grammar in Anglo-Saxon England

Jay Fisher

The *Excerptiones de arte grammatica Anglice* of Aelfric has two features that make it unique for its time. Because it is a grammar of the Latin language written in a vernacular, its bilingual nature contrasts with the monolingual method of language education that had prevailed for centuries before Aelfric. He also innovates in another, less obvious manner, however, as he himself states. Aelfric has written a grammar of the Latin language explicitly aimed at children (p. 1 ii. 1–3). He therefore differs from previous grammarians not only in method but also in his explicitly intended addressees. Although at least some children must have learned Latin and used the grammars that were at hand, none of the previous grammars explicitly attempt to help children learn Latin through another language. In sum, the grammar is a, if not *the*, significant step towards the Latin textbooks that may now be found in classrooms all over the world, such as the *Cambridge Latin Course* (see Lister in this volume).

However different these two innovations may be, they share one common trait; they emerge from older texts and traditional ideas about language acquisition. Although Aelfric was the first to produce a Latin grammar in a vernacular language, there was already a tradition in place of translating Latin texts into Old English such as Alfred the Great's translation of the *De consolatione philosophiae* of Boethius. Glossaries of Latin words with vernacular equivalents are an even closer parallel. There also exist a number of learning texts in Latin or colloquies that serve the purpose of instructing children and that have some features of child-directed speech. Because there is also some overlap in the precedents of both the language and addressee of the grammar in colloquies that are glossed in the vernacular such as the *De raris fabulis* with its Welsh and Old English glosses, it is even possible that Aelfric's decision to write a Latin grammar in the vernacular and to address it to children are not independent of one another.

Out of the mouth of Englishmen: Aelfric and the vernacular Latin grammar

Although it may surprise some that a tenth-century grammar written on the fringes of the western world would be the first vernacular grammar of Latin, it was probably equally surprising to a medieval reader that a grammar of Latin would be written in any other language than Latin. After all, every grammar of the Latin language before Aelfric was written in Latin. Many of the authors of these grammars were native speakers of Latin who wrote when the Roman Empire still existed, such as Donatus the author of the *Ars grammatica major*, a text that was obscure enough to acquire a commentary by the time of the medieval period also written in Latin.[1] Many more grammars of Latin were written after the break-up of the empire by authors who were not native speakers of Latin. The grammatical tradition therefore belonged to those who could already read the language, while learners had recourse to *glossae*, a series of vocabulary lists in both languages, in lieu of a vernacular textbook.[2] These vocabulary lists could also be supplemented by vernacular interlinear glosses written in a second hand above the individual Latin words in manuscripts such as the Vespasian Psalter with its Old English interlineal glosses or the Old Irish "Wurzburg Glosses" of the Vulgate versions of the letters of Saint Paul. In addition, learners of Latin as a second language might have benefited from an emerging form of the Latin grammar that comprehensively illustrated paradigms of inflected words in a manner that earlier Late Antique grammars did not, such as the *Declinationes nominum*.[3]

If the grammar of Aelfric broke with tradition, it was also very much a product of this same, earlier grammatical tradition. The aforementioned *Declinationes nominum* is followed by a compendium of Old English and Latin glosses in an eleventh-century manuscript and may have inspired Aelfric's intuitive leap into a vernacular grammar.[4] The fact that Aelfric composed a glossary of his own and that it is attached to his grammar in some of the manuscripts may indicate a wish to soften the transition from the monolingual to the bilingual method. Although it is a reorganization of the descriptive facts found in earlier monolingual grammars, the grammar still treats the same facts as the earlier grammars, as Fabienne Toupin has observed.[5] Moreover, Aelfric's statement that his grammar is a translation

---

[1] Law 1997: 58.
[2] As Law (1997: 31) observes, Latin grammars, such as Tatwine's, also had interlinear glosses.
[3] Law 1997: 104.   [4] Law 1997: 105.   [5] Toupin 2010: 333–52.

of *Excerptiones de Prisciano*, an abridgement of the massive *Institutiones grammaticae* written by Priscian in the sixth century, implies that he saw his grammar as a continuation of the earlier tradition. The discovery of the eleventh-century manuscripts containing an abridgement of Priscian that served as the basis of Aelfric's grammar also suggests that Aelfric was imitating this abridgement, the *Excerptiones de Prisciano*, as much as innovating, if he did not abridge the grammar in Latin himself.[6] Aelfric goes so far, in fact, as to adapt the two appendices, and even keep the postscript of this abridgement. What is more, the monolingual method also must have been supplemented orally with a bilingual method to some extent, even if a negotiation between Latin and English had yet to surface in writing. As I have already suggested, the grammar of Aelfric did not appear *ex nihilo* and was as much a continuation of the medieval grammatical tradition as it was a break with it.

Although a Greek translation of the Latin grammar in the works of Dositheus could have had some influence on Aelfric's decision to write a grammar of Latin in the vernacular Old English, the evidence does not at present substantiate such a hypothesis. Vivien Law calls the transmission of Dositheus anomalous and suggests that it did not make many inroads outside of specific centers such as the St. Gall monastery.[7] Nor are there any manuscripts of Dosistheus listed in Michael Lapidge's exhaustive catalogue of insular manuscripts and reconstructions of Anglo-Saxon libraries, an absence that suggests that the grammar did not make it to England.[8] There is therefore no evidence that Aelfric had ever seen the anomalous Greek translation of the Latin grammar.

Even if Aelfric could have seen the grammar of Dositheus, there are crucial differences between the two texts that suggest that the Greek translation of the Latin grammar at St. Gall did not influence Aelfric. The manuscripts of Aelfric's grammar do not include the original Latin of his source as Dositheus does. There are also sociolinguistic differences between Greek and Old English that would have been a barrier to arriving at the idea of a vernacular grammar under the influence of Dositheus. Greek was as much of a sacred language as Latin, and therefore on more of an equal sociolinguistic footing with Latin, not to mention that Latin and Greek were equally foreign to speakers of Old English. What is more, the

---

[6] Although Law (1997: 203) does not believe that Aelfric compiled this amalgam of Latin texts, Porter (2002: 23–30) suggests that Aelfric did, in fact, put together the Latin text of the *Excerptiones de Prisciano*.
[7] Law 1997, p. 66 n 5. [8] Lapidge 2006: 133–342.

grammar in the corpus of Dositheus is not truly bilingual, but rather a translation from one language into the other, even though there are some bilingual paradigms. In contrast with the Greek text, Aelfric organically combines Latin and Old English into a single (and unprecedented) whole. For the same reasons other bilingual texts that include Greek and Latin, such as "St. Dunstan's Classbook" – a compendium of texts including parallel liturgical readings in Greek and Latin that made its way from Wales to England early enough to acquire an Old English homily – are not likely to have had any direct influence on Aelfric's decision to write a bilingual grammar.

Because no single impetus for writing a grammar of Latin in a vernacular can be identified, the grammar of Aelfric is more likely a product of the author's location, time, and experience. Aelfric wrote in a place where the vernacular was not descended from Latin, but rather a Germanic language, a fact that would have made it more difficult to maintain that Aelfric's Old English was somehow an imperfect form of Latin, as it was possible in areas where the romance dialects were spoken.[9] The vernacular in these areas was, in fact, a form of Latin that had changed over the centuries. Aelfric also lived at a time when the idea of the vernacular translation of Latin texts was familiar. Moreover, Aelfric himself translated Latin lives of saints, such as the Life of St. Edmund by Abbo of Fleury and other texts such as the *De consuetudine monachorum*, a text that was written by his teacher Aethelwold.

Although it is not impossible that a speaker of a romance language could have written the first vernacular grammar of Latin, there are factors that make it less likely than it would be for a speaker of a Germanic language such as Old English. The famous pronouncement at the Council of Tours urged that the Homilies be delivered or changed into (*transferre*) the *rusticam Romanam linguam* (*Monumenta Germaniae historica, Concilia* II, p. 288, canon 17) in order to be intelligible to the laity of the early ninth century, a phrase that betrays an assumption of a close relationship between the vernacular of Tours (i.e. *lingua Romana*) and Latin.[10] As Roger Wright has observed, the verb *transferre* in Carolingian Latin does not mean translate but rather "shift" or "change," a fact that suggests that Latin and the romance dialect of Tours were not yet perceived as different

---

[9] On beliefs concerning the relationship between Latin and the romance languages, see also Laird in this volume.

[10] Adams (2003b: 195) observes, "*Romanus* applied to language is already a synonym of *Latinus*" by the early empire.

languages.¹¹ The so-called *Reichenau Glossary*, from perhaps the late eighth century, simply gives Latin synonyms of words in the *Vulgate* influenced by the northern French dialect of Romance, a fact that suggests a speaker of Old French could puzzle out the Vulgate through similar forms in the northern French dialect of Romance.¹² In fact, the first example of the romance dialect that would become French only appears in the "Strasburg Oaths," oaths that were taken by the followers of Louis the Germanic and Charles the Bald and that were recorded in the ninth-century Latin text *De dissensionibus filiorum Ludovici Pii*.¹³ Even here the vernacular is again called the *romana lingua*, a name that again implies that the language of the oaths is somehow related to Latin.

Because Aelfric was a speaker of a Germanic language, he may have been more aware that there were significant differences between his vernacular and Latin, as other speakers of Germanic languages appear to have been. In contrast with the Reichenau Glossary, the Kassel Glossary, compiled only at a slightly later date at a monastery at Fulda in modern Germany, glosses Latin words with German rather than Vulgar Latin.¹⁴ Moreover, Einhard, the biographer of Charlemagne, assumes that his readers will be surprised that a barbarian, in other words a speaker of non-romance language, would have the temerity to compose a text in the *Romana locutione*:

En tibi librum praeclarissimi et maximi uiri memoriam continentem; in quo praeter illius facta non est quod admireris, nisi forte quod homo barbarus et in Romana locutione perparum exercitatus aliquid me decenter aut commode Latine scribere posse putauerim... (Einhard's Preface to the *Vita Karoli Magni*, 4)

Here is a book about the most famous and greatest of men, in which there isn't much of note other than his deeds, except perhaps that I, a barbarian not very practiced in Roman speech, would think myself able to write anything in an acceptable and pleasing Latin.

If the expression *Romanam linguam* in the acts of the Council of Tours is ambiguous, *Romana locutione* is unequivocally a reference to Latin.

Alcuin of York, another native speaker of a Germanic language, appears to have been a key figure in the changing perception of Latin as something distinct from Romance. Roger Wright not only suggests that the *De*

---

[11] Wright 1981: 356–8.
[12] Solodow 2010: 172–5 is a convenient and reliable introduction to the *Reichenau Glossary*. Studer and Walters (1962: 14–19) provide a more extensive list of "typical examples" from the *Glossary*.
[13] Solodow (2010: 175–6) provides a reliable introduction, text, and translation. I use his translation when quoting this text below.
[14] Solodow (2010: 268–76) is again a reliable introduction. Barber (1951: 4–6) provides a sampling of glosses of single words and phrases.

orthographia of Alcuin is a treatise on the proper pronunciation of Latin, but he also argues that Alcuin's encounter with the diversity of romance pronunciations of Latin texts led him to base his reforms "on the artificial one he had taught himself."[15] In other words, Alcuin had no preconceived idea of how to pronounce Latin based upon his native language of Old English. What is more, Joseph Errington goes as far as to imply that Alcuin of York was a major factor in the creation of the idea of Latin as a dead language, rather than a more correct form of the romance languages, because he was not a native speaker of a romance language.[16] If Errington's hypothesis is correct, it may be significant that Aelfric was also a speaker of Old English. The Anglo-Saxons not only "had to learn Latin as a foreign language" through grammars that were "unsuited ... to the task,"[17] they may have also been in a better position to evaluate the relationship between the living romance dialects and the dead Latin language, since Latin was, in fact, more of a foreign language to them.

The vernacular grammar was not inevitable outside of the geographical spread of the romance dialects, however, even though the perception of the romance languages as "incorrectly" spoken Latin would have impeded the development of a bilingual grammar. If the differences between the language of the Strasburg Oaths and classical Latin are not as drastic as those between Latin and Old English, there are still differences. It is likely that someone would eventually come to the conclusion that phrases such as *si cum om per dreit son fadra salvar dift*, "as one ought by right to succor his brother," were not Latin. Moreover, Latin was an object of intense interest in the British Isles that resulted in a number of monolingual grammars by Alcuin, Tatwine, and others. In light of this evidence, geography was only one factor that prompted Aelfric to write a Latin grammar in the vernacular.

Chronology was also likely a factor that helped produce the first bilingual Latin grammar. Although Alfred the Great died approximately fifty years before Aelfric was born, his educational reforms impacted how Aelfric interacted with Latin. As is well known, Alfred wished that all men who had the ability would be educated. In order to accomplish his ends he not only attempted to make English the language of primary education but also began a program of translation of Latin texts. Because Aelfric therefore had access to the vernacular translations of Latin texts that

---

[15] Wright 1981: 350–1.   [16] Errington 2008: 17–20.
[17] Gneuss 1990: 9, commenting on a similar observation made by Law (1983: 57–9). The article has been updated and represented in Law 1997: 91–123.

Alfred commissioned, he could compare the Old English translation with the Latin original. Moreover, these translations could then raise questions about the relationship of Old English to Latin for anyone who could read both languages, including Aelfric, who sometimes expressed discomfort with the act of translation of religious texts, as Melinda Menzer has observed.[18] Menzer has even raised the possibility that the grammar was intended as a guide for interpreting Old English texts, especially translations that are "potentially confusing and dangerous."[19] Whether or not Menzer is correct, the vernacular translation was a fact of life for Aelfric.[20]

The translation of Latin texts had reached a point where another previously unthinkable translation took place. At some point Aelfric translated part of Genesis from the Latin Vulgate. Although he expresses his misgivings about translating the Bible into the vernacular in his preface to the translation, he not only translated parts of Genesis and Numbers and all of Joshua, but someone else also translated the rest of Genesis and Numbers and the remaining books of the *Hexateuch* besides Joshua, into the vernacular. Because there are seven different (mostly fragmentary) manuscripts of this translation,[21] it seems that Aelfric's England was a place where any Latin text could be translated including the Bible and the vernacular grammar. Even if Aelfric did not translate Genesis, his ample experience as a translator would still have been yet another factor in his decision to write his grammar in the vernacular.

Whatever it might have been that led Aelfric to compose the first grammar of Latin in a vernacular, he is still very much steeped in the monolingual Latin tradition that preceded his grammar. Aelfric cannot, for example, match every synthetic Latin verb form with an English equivalent, a fact that forces him to resort to paraphrase rather than word-for-word translation. In other words, he must confront the difference between the multiplicity of tenses of Latin and the verbal system of Old English that consisted of only two synthetic tenses, the present and preterite. Whereas grammars such as the *Ars grammatica maior* of Donatus could simply cite a single form of each paradigm (*inperfecta, ut legebam, perfecta, ut legi, plusquamperfecta, ut legeram* (Keil *GL* iv, p. 384, l. 11)), Aelfric has

---

[18] Menzer 1999: 639. [19] Menzer 1999: 640.
[20] Although I am sure that the grammar did influence later interpretations of vernacular texts, I am not persuaded that Aelfric had this purpose in mind when he wrote his grammar. Nor is this a necessary precondition for Aelfric's use of grammar as a form of interpretation within his own vernacular works, as demonstrated in the excellent discussion of the use of grammar in the homilies in Menzer 1999: 637–52.
[21] Fox and Sharma 2012: 7.

to find an alternate way to express the meaning of the various synthetic forms of the Latin verb.

In order to supply Old English equivalents for the five tenses for Latin identified in his grammar, Aelfric employs adverbial expressions rather than repeating an Old English form that is most approximate to the Latin form, an indication that his purpose is to describe Latin usage in a vernacular:[22]

> PRAESENS TEMPUS ys andwerd tid: *sto* ic stande; PRAETERITUM TEMPUS ys forðgewiten tid: *steti* ic stod; FUTURUM TEMPUS ys towerd tid: *stabo* ic stande nu rihte oððe on sumne timan...
>
> PRAETERITUM INPERFECTUM... *stabam* ic stod. PRAETERITUM PERFECTUM... *steti* ic stod fullice... PLUSQUAM PERFECTUM... *steteram* ic stod gefyrn. (pp. 123–4 ll. 14–17, ll. 1, 3–9)

Praesens tempus is the present time; *sto* I stand; the preterite tense is the past time; *steti* I stood; Future tense is the approaching/future time; *stabo* I stand right now or at some time... The imperfect preterite... *stabam* I stood... the perfect preterite... *steti* I stood perfectly... the pluperfect... *steteram* I stood once.

Sto and *stabam* are translated *ic stande* and *ic stod*, while *stabo* is rendered *ic stande nu rihte oððe on sumne timan*, "I stand right now or at some time." The pluperfect *steteram* yields *ic stod gefyrn*, "I formerly stood" or "I stood long ago," and the perfect *steti*, *ic stode fullice*, "I stood completely." Vivien Law points out that expressions such as *ic stode gefyrn* cannot be found outside of the grammar, and suggests that Aelfric is not trying to recreate the Latin system in English but is only communicating the sense of the different forms.[23] Nor does Aelfric's grammatical terminology appear to be anything more than an attempt to explain the Latin terminology, as Edna Williams suggests.[24]

In spite of this tendency to translate idiomatic Latin by means of unidiomatic Old English, however, Aelfric will sometimes select a more idiomatic translation, even when a grammatically acceptable and literal translation was available. He begins his discussion of the passive voice, for example, by translating the Latin form *legor* into *ic eom geræd on sumum gewrite sum ðing to donne*, "I am read in some (cases) am written to do something" (p. 182 ll. 4–5). Although he begins with the literal *ic eom*

---

[22] All quotations of the grammar are from Zupitza 1880, still the standard text of the grammar as far as I am aware. Although there may be cases where Aelfric influenced English usage, such as the regular use of the accusative with the preposition *þurh*, as noted by Sisam (1953: 183–5), I cannot accept Sisam's thesis (*ibid.*, p. 301) that the grammar is an introduction to both languages, a position that is "not orthodox" in any case, as noted by Menzer (1999, p. 646 n. 6).
[23] Law 1997: 212–13.   [24] Williams 1958: 457.

geræd, he then expands into an alternate interpretation rather than a simple translation, perhaps because it is impossible literally to read a person. Because there is little semantic difference between "it is read by me" and "I read," Aelfric could have chosen to translate literally. He also translates *legitur a me* as *ic ræde*, "I read" (p. 127 ii. 1–2), even though he himself uses the verb *rædan* in the passive construction *ic eom geræd*. It seems likely that "I am read" by itself did not seem to be idiomatic Old English, even less so than *ic stod gefyrn*, "I formerly stood" or *ic stode fullice*, "I stood completely."

In addition to employing an Old English phrase in lieu of a single Latin word, Aelfric sometimes changes passive forms in Latin into active forms in Old English. He not only translates *legitur a me* as *ic ræde*, "I read" but also *amatur a me*, "he is loved by me," as *ic lufige*, "I love" (p. 127 ll. 1–2). Because Aelfric actually translates *amatur* as *he ys gelufed*, "he is loved," it cannot be suggested that a literal translation of *amatur*, "she is loved" is not idiomatic on the basis of grammatical structure. Nor does Aelfric seem to have any trouble expressing an agent for a passive form of the verb *lufian*, since he also translates *amor a te* as *ic eam gelufod fram ðe* (both mean "I am loved by you") (p. 120 l. 16). Instead of a syntactic constraint in Old English, it is likely that a passive construction for *rædan* and *lufian* simply sounded wrong to Aelfric in some contexts.

Such choices shed light on another of Aelfric's translations of a Latin passive construction in Old English. In one passage *doceo* corresponds to Old English *ic tæce*, (p. 120 l. 5), but *doceor* is translated as *ic eom gelæred* "I am instructed," (p. 158 l. 12). Although the Latin verb *docere* remains the same, the grammarian has changed his lexical selection. He employs the verb *tæcan* to translate *doceo*, but its synonym *læran* to translate the same Latin verb in the passive construction. Nothing prevents Aelfric from simply using *læran* in both the active and the passive, however, even though *tæcan* cannot be used idiomatically in Old English because it takes a dative object (such verbs are not normally found in the passive in Old English). Aelfric's choice therefore appears to have been motivated yet again by the semantics as well as the syntax of Old English.

Out of the mouth of babes: child-directed speech in the *Excerptiones de Arte Grammatica Anglice*

In addition to being a translator, Aelfric was also an educator who had to wrestle with the conflicting needs of the scholar and the student, an opposition that he expresses in terms of age. In his preface, Aelfric tells us that he has translated the excerptions for "you tender boys," *uobis puerulis tenellis*:

Ego Aelfricus, ut minus sapiens, has excerptiones de Prisciano minore uel maiore uobis puerulis tenellis ad uestram linguam transferre studui (p. 1 ll. 1–3)

I Aelfric, with no claims to great wisdom, was eager to translate the *Excerptiones de Prisciano* (*minore uel maiore*) for you tender boys into your tongue.

In doing so, Aelfric maps out and circumscribes a space for his grammar that does not replace the monolingual grammar, but rather trains the child unschooled in Latin grammar. Moreover he excludes "old men" from his intended audience:

... *sed ego deputo hanc lectionem inscientibus puerulis, non senibus aptandam fore* (p. 1 ll. 11–12)

... but I consider this tract to be appropriate for unknowing children not old men.

Aelfric's choice of addressees, and whom he includes and excludes from his addressees, is as unexpected as his use of the vernacular.

Aelfric not only states his intention to write a grammar for children, but he also follows through with that intention in at least one way. His grammar exhibits a number of features that conform with "child-directed speech," a simplified form of language used by adults when they speak to children.[25] Three features of child-directed speech that can be observed in the grammar are particularly helpful for understanding important aspects of Aelfric's work. Some claim that syntactic transformations are avoided in English "motherese," a characteristic of child-directed speech that may explain why Aelfric presents the Latin passive voice as he does. In at least one instance Aelfric explains the absence of a given form because it is a homonym of a common noun, perhaps under the impression that children avoid homonymy, a phenomenon that has been identified as a trait of the language of children.[26] Because the child's interests are the dominant subject matter of child-directed speech, Aelfric's choice of verbs in his illustration of the forms of the Latin verb, such as "I learn," and "I read," activities that children in a monastery presumably engaged in and perhaps sometimes enjoyed, may be another indication that he is employing child-directed speech. Finally, Aelfric's omission of a rather extensive discussion of pronunciation in his source may be a recognition that child-directed speech features a simplified pronunciation that would not be compatible with

[25] Field 2004: 54–5.   [26] Ingram 1975: 289–92.

the adult pronunciation of Latin, let alone an extended theoretical discussion of such issues.[27]

Before exploring the implications of the influence of child-directed speech on the treatment of the passive in Aelfric, there are some complications that need to be addressed. Although children who speak English apparently shun the passive voice,[28] this lack of passive constructions is not confined to child-directed speech in English, since the passive voice is used infrequently in Germanic languages such as English and its ancestor Old English.[29] Because there is agreement that children master the passive fairly late, however, any use of an active Old English form for a Latin passive form in the grammar may indicate that Aelfric noticed the same phenomenon and was shaping his grammar to accommodate the speech of children.

Aelfric does, in fact, occasionally substitute an active for a passive form, even though he does not normally avoid using a passive construction when translating a Latin passive. Aelfric translates the phrase *amatur a me*, "he is loved by me," for example, with *ic lufige*, "I love" (p. 127 ll. 1–2). Because the passive was a perfectly idiomatic form of the Old English verb *lufian*, Aelfric translates the passive construction in Latin with an active one without any apparent motivation. In addition to the translation of the Latin passive construction *legitur a me* with an active form of *rædan*, a verb that can be used idiomatically in the passive (p. 127 ll. 1–2), the expansion of *legor* into *ic eom geræd on sumum gewrite sum ðing to donne*, "I am read in some (cases) am written to do something," (p. 182 ll. 4–5) may also be a case of adding extra information to clarify a form that was thought to be unfamiliar to children. The use of *Ic eom gelæred* to translate *doceor* (p. 158 l. 12) may also have sounded more natural to children in a monastery because it also can mean "I am clerical." Because *amare*, *docere*, and *legere* are presented as the paradigmatic examples of three of the four Latin conjugations in the grammar and illustrated with full Latin paradigms for all forms of the verb, three of the four paradigmatic verbs are therefore handled in a manner that suggests that Aelfric was adjusting his language for his juvenile audience. When Aelfric's explicit statement that his grammar is intended for children is taken into account, it seems likely that these adjustments are accommodations to the language of children as Aelfric perceived it.

When Aelfric explains that the verb *urgeo* lacks a fourth principal part because the hypothetical form would be homonymous with *ursus*, "bear,"

---

[27] Field 2004: 54. [28] Peccei 2006: 27. [29] Frary 1966: 7–8.

he is also avoiding homonymy, another postulated characteristic of the speech of children:

Urgeo ic ðrafige, *ursi* (*ursum* is bera: *hic ursus* Þes bera, *hunc ursum*) (p. 155 ll. 12–13)

Urgeo, "I push," *ursi* (*ursum* is "bear"; *hic ursus*, "this/the bear," *hunc ursum*).

Although the *Excerptiones de Prisciano* also notes that *ursum* means something else, the language of Aelfric's source text is ambiguous: *Nam "ursum" aliud significat* (IV.88.III), "for '*ursum*' [bear] means something else."[30] For someone who did not know that *ursus* meant "bear," the explanation in the *Excerptiones* is almost meaningless, something that Aelfric is careful to avoid by pointing out that *ursum* would be the accusative of *ursus*, even though Old English *bera* makes the homonymy and its consequences clear for the speaker of Old English. Because Aelfric uses the synonyms *tæcan* and *læran* to translate the forms *doceo* and *doceor*, he avoids generating a weak homonymy by using the same root in Old English for two activities that a child may not see as two forms of the same activity even though they are expressed with the same Latin root.

Although the view that the avoidance of homonyms is characteristic of the language of children has been challenged,[31] the existence of such a thesis is evidence that at least some adults have perceived a lack of homonyms in the speech of children. If modern linguists have perceived such an absence, then it is not unreasonable to suggest that Aelfric also conceived of the speech of children as lacking in homonyms. Not only is it possible that he believed that children avoided homonyms, but Aelfric's explanation that there can be no fourth principal part for *urgeo* on the basis of homonymy with the noun *ursus* is also indicative of such a perception.

In addition to these two traces, there are two absences that suggest that child-directed speech has influenced the composition of Aelfric's grammar. As Porter has observed, "the higher theoretical studies of syntax have largely gone by the way" in the *Excerptiones de Prisciano*, possibly a recognition that the language of children and child-directed speech both employ simplified sentence structures.[32] Nor is pronunciation addressed in the *Excerptiones*, another aspect of language that adults alter significantly in child-directed speech by simplifying it. It is possible that Aelfric recognized that a discussion of pronunciation was out of place in a context where it may be altered for pedagogical purposes. If Aelfric compiled the

---

[30] The text and all citations of the *Excerptiones de Prisciano* are from Porter 2002.
[31] Backscheider and Gelman 1995: 107–27.   [32] Porter 2002: 13.

Excerptiones as Porter suggests,³³ then he actively removed material on syntax from his source material for the Latin *Excerptiones* that would interfere with the use of child-directed speech. Even if he is not the author of his Latin source text, he excludes the discussion of pronunciation in the *Excerptiones de Prisciano* in his grammar.

Because the topics of conversations with children also tend to center around their activities, Aelfric may have, in fact, deliberately chosen paradigmatic verbs that are germane to the interests of children, if, again, he compiled the Latin *Excerptiones*. The paradigmatic verbs *docere* and *legere* express the activities of the classroom and *amare* is an expression of affection, two spheres of activity that are likely to be familiar to children. Even if Aelfric is not responsible for the *Excerptiones*, there are differences between the two texts that emphasize the paradigmatic verbs in Aelfric. When Aelfric introduces the verb, the first examples encountered are *amo*, *doceo*, *lego*, and *audio* (p. 120 ll. 4–6), whereas the first examples in the *Excerptiones* are *metuo* and *timeo* because they are exceptions to the rule that active verbs are always transitive (IV. 5). The author of the Latin *Excerptiones* then goes on to reduce a variety of different verbs that illustrate the passive and active, including *benedico* and *oro* to a much smaller number that includes *amare*, *docere*, *legere*, and *audire*. Although the emphasis on the paradigmatic verbs has pedagogical advantages for teachers of students of any age, the fact remains that these verbs express activities performed by children. The demonstrable use of "strong local colouring of the vocabulary and examples" may also be an attempt to make the grammar more interesting to children, who would already be familiar with names such as *Eadgardus* (p. 8 l. 10) and titles such as *rex* and *episcopus* (p. 8 l. 11) rather than the traditional examples of nouns such as *Roma* or a community the size of an *urbs*.³⁴

Although the use of child-directed speech in a vernacular grammar of Latin is a partial break with tradition, it is very unlikely that Aelfric's assumptions about the language of children emerged *ex nihilo* any more than his decision to use the vernacular as the medium of his grammar. An anonymous note in a manuscript of Aristotle's *Categories* from St. Gall explicitly states that children learn meanings of a word before they learn the inflection of the same word.³⁵ This statement is essentially the

---

³³ Porter 2002: 24.   ³⁴ Law 1997: 208.
³⁵ Law (1997: 159) quotes the passage:
   Hunc ordinem in pueris natura ostendit, qui prius intellegunt ea uox que est homo unde praedicaetur quam in ipsa uoce fieri discant hanc flexionem (*Distributio* p. LXXXVI).

unspoken assumption that leads adults to emphasize the meaning of individual words over all other aspects of grammar. Because Aelfric is acting on an assumption that appears to motivate one aspect of child-directed speech that was remarked upon by at least one other medieval writer, his other implicit ideas about the language of children may not be idiosyncratic for his time. Moreover, if the Latin grammars themselves do not explicitly identify the intended age of their audience, a number of commentators on the *Ars minor* of Donatus claim that it is especially suited for children, including Pompeius (Keil *GL* v p. 98 ll. 6–8), Anonymus ad Cuimnanam (Keil *GL* v p. 326 ll. 12–15), and the *Cunabula grammaticae artis Donati* (Keil *GL* v p. 325 ll. 8–11). If nothing else, there are enough indications in the grammar to include it as yet more evidence that the Anglo-Saxons definitively had a concept of childhood as Sally Crawford has argued.[36]

Immediately following the statement that his grammar is intended for boys and not old men, Aelfric states that he has favored a "simple interpretation," perhaps an indication that his attitude towards the language of children was learned from his teacher and that his choice of addressee was traditional as far as he was concerned.

Scio multimodis uerba posse interpretari sed ego simplicem interpretationem sequor... si alicui tamen displicuerit, nostram interpretationem dicat, quomodo uult: nos contenti sumus, sicut didicimus in scola Adelwoldi, uenerabilis praesulis... (p. 1 ll. 13–17)

I know it is possible to understand words in many different ways but I will take the simple understanding... but if this displeases anyone let him say what he will of my interpretation, I am content, just as I was in Aethelwold's school, my venerable teacher...

Although Aelfric does not elaborate on what he means by a simple interpretation, he seems to associate the practice of *simplex interpretatio* with his instruction at the school of Aethelwold, presumably as a boy. If Aelfric has faithfully imitated the use of the *simplex interpretatio* from his teacher, then his method of instruction is grounded in the traditional means of teaching the Latin language, as he understood it. To judge from the grammar, this means of instruction included some accommodation to the speech of children or more accurately, the inclusion of characteristics of child-directed speech.

---

[36] Crawford 1999.

Out of the mouth of babes and Englishmen: tradition and originality in Aelfric

The use of the language of the classroom in the grammar not only conforms with the principle that adults will choose a topic of interest to children when addressing them, but it also recalls the colloquy that is attributed to Aelfric in some manuscripts,[37] a text that not only depicts a schoolroom scene but may also have formed a "grammatical triad" with his grammar and glossary, as Joyce Hill suggests.[38] Even if this triad emerged over time rather than from a predetermined plan, as Hill also suggests,[39] the progression from grammar to glossary to classroom scene in the colloquy works in reverse in comparison with the intuitive order for teaching a foreign language. Children must first have a teacher and a context where they can learn the language. In the classroom the first move is usually to teach individual words in the second language that have the same meaning as words in the first language. As the anonymous note from the *Categories* of Aristotle mentioned above implies, grammatical concepts would have been introduced after the meanings of words were learned. If the movement from grammar to colloquy is the reverse of what Aelfric experienced, then the use of the colloquy as a teaching tool may have influenced how he composed the grammar, since the grammar was the final step in a process that usually began with a colloquy.

Whether or not the colloquy, glossary, and grammar of Aelfric formed a coherent triad of educational texts, there is one aspect of at least one earlier colloquy, the *De raris fabulis*, which may have influenced his decision to compose a vernacular grammar and to address it to children. Because there are Welsh and Cornish glosses in the text of *De raris fabulis*, there may be a connection between these vernacular glosses and Aelfric's decision to translate a Latin grammar. If the practice of glossing, in effect translating, Latin colloquies was considered an effective way to teach Latin, then Aelfric may have taken the natural step of translating an entire grammar. The question and response format of the *Ars minor* of Donatus, a grammar that was seen as suitable for children as I have already observed, may have also helped bridge the distance between Latin grammar and a running gloss of a Latin colloquy. Given that one means of teaching them was a

---

[37] According to Stevenson (1929: 75) there are no titles in any of the manuscripts. One manuscript (Oxford, St. John's College, MS. 154) has the notice that Aelfric is the author of the text that Aelfric Bata has there expanded. Gwara (1996, p. 2 n. 5) adds that another version of the colloquy has the inscription *Æluricus Bate* in another manuscript (London, BL, MS. Cotton Tiberius A.iii).
[38] Hill 2007: 285–307.   [39] Hill 2007: 287–8.

Latin colloquy, the choice of addressees in Aelfric's grammar may have been influenced by the use of these texts as teaching tools. In sum, the two unique features of Aelfric's grammar are not only as traditional as they are innovative, they may also have been associated with one another in the context of learning Latin before Aelfric.

It should be evident that the *Excerptiones de arte grammatica Anglice* is the result of a series of individual interventions in a set of historical circumstances. Neither of the two significant changes in the grammar that I have discussed represents a complete break with the previous grammatical tradition, since Aelfric had access to texts that had been translated from Latin into Old English and to glossaries that served a similar if not an identical purpose as his grammar. Not only is it very likely that Latin grammars had been used to teach children how to read Latin, but also the tradition of Latin instruction before Aelfric almost certainly included some use of the vernacular. In other words we may ask if we should infer not only "the influence of the colloquies" on the glossary that accompanied the grammar but also upon the grammar itself, to answer David Porter's question, even if we cannot prove a relationship.[40] It is customary to quote the phrase "out of the mouth of babes and sucklings" when one is surprised by the precociousness of a child. It is not so surprising upon reflection, however, that the first vernacular grammar of Latin, in effect, came "out of the mouth of babes and Englishmen."

---

[40] Porter 2002: 33.

CHAPTER 7

First steps in Latin: the teaching of reading and writing in Renaissance Italy

Robert Black

The first stage of the Italian medieval, Renaissance and early modern school curriculum consisted of learning to read; this skill was always acquired through the medium of the Latin language. For pupils who continued to study Latin (grammar was a synonym for Latin), the next step was learning the parts of speech and memorizing the varying forms (morphology) of nouns, verbs, adjectives and participles (regarded, unlike today, as a separate element during antiquity, the Middle Ages and the Renaissance). Immediately after morphology, pupils were introduced to reading elementary Latin texts, and, at about the same time, they began learning how to write. The next stage for Latin pupils was syntax and learning how to write their own phrases, sentences and short compositions; this level was accompanied by reading more Latin texts. At the end of the Latin syllabus, pupils were composing their own letters and reading more advanced texts, including the classical authors. At this final stage, Latin stylistics, taught by reference to simplified rhetorical treatises, were introduced.[1] An alternative syllabus focused on elementary arithmetic, known as the *abaco*, involving not the instrument for calculation now known as the abacus (by the turn of the thirteenth century, *abacus* was a synonym for arithmetic[2]), but rather consisting of a course, beginning with elementary arithmetic and culminating in basic commercial knowledge (such as the monetary

---

This article reproduces pp. 37–9, 40–2, 44–5, and 57–9 of R. Black, *Humanism and Education in Medieval and Renaissance Italy: Tradition and Innovation in Latin Schools from the Twelfth to the Fifteenth Century*, Cambridge University Press, 2001; pp. 36, 43–4, 54–6, and 58–60 of R. Black, *Education and Society in Florentine Tuscany: Teachers, Pupils and Schools c. 1250–1500*, Brill, 2007; and pp. 107–9 of R. Black, "Italian education: languages, syllabuses, method," in L. Nauta (ed.), *Language and Cultural Change: Aspects of the Study and Use of Language in the Later Middle Ages and Renaissance*, Peeters, 2006. The editors are grateful to Peeters for granting non-exclusive rights to reproduce this material, and to Koninklijke Brill NV for the permission to republish the relevant pages.

[1] On the reading and grammar curriculum, see Black 2001; Rizzo 2002: 125–217; Grendler 1989: 107ff.; Gehl 1993.
[2] Ulivi 1994: 33.

system) and skills (occasionally, for example, double-entry book keeping); the abacus was taught entirely in the vernacular, and always followed elementary reading.[3] Often it was an alternative to the Latin curriculum: pupils, having learnt how to read through the medium of Latin, immediately progressed to the vernacular abacus syllabus; many children never learned Latin as such, simply acquiring the skills of reading on the basis of Latin texts and thereafter either leaving formal education or passing to a vernacular abacus school.[4] Sometimes, on the other hand, the abacus was learnt in addition to the more advanced Latin curriculum, either before[5] or after the study of grammar.[6] Pupils normally learned how to write after getting the knack of elementary reading, sometimes while studying the abacus syllabus but before more advanced work in grammar (Latin).[7]

The first textbooks were usually called *tabula* or *carta*, a sheet of parchment or paper which began with the alphabet and concluded with syllables to sound out; it was fixed on a wooden board and took its name either from the parchment or paper (*carta*) or from the board (*tabula*).[8] The introduction to reading by learning the alphabet and then syllables[9] was a technique going back to Greek and Roman antiquity;[10] the smallest Roman schoolboys were known as *abecedarii* ("alphabetizers") or *syllabarii* ("syllablizers").[11] In the earlier Middle Ages, too, children began with the alphabet and proceeded to syllables: as Remigius of Auxerre wrote in the ninth century, "the instruction of small children normally involves first the study of letters, then of syllables";[12] similar was Peter Damian's scheme articulated in the eleventh century: *In litterario quippe ludo, ubi pueri prima articulatae uocis elementa suscipiunt, alii quidem abecedarii, alii syllabarii,*

---

[3] The leading active scholar of abacus schools is Elisabetta Ulivi. See Ulivi 1993, 1994, 1996, 1998, 2000, 2001, 2002a, 2002b, 2003. See also the important contributions of Warren Van Egmond: Van Egmond 1976, 1977, 1978, 1980, 1986. Useful summaries are provided in Franci 1988, 1992, 1993, 1996, 1998. The foundations for study in this field were laid by Gino Arrighi: see Arrighi 2004 for a convenient anthology of his publications. The first important article in English was Goldthwaite 1972–3, which offered a major discovery, besides containing a still useful account of the topic in general. Grendler 1989: 306–19 provides an accessible introduction.

[4] E.g. the sons of Antonio Rustici (see Black 2007: 632–4) or Tribaldo de' Rossi (see below pp. 115–16 and Black 2007: 695–705).

[5] E.g. Niccolò Machiavelli: see Black 1996b.

[6] E.g. Donato Velluti's son (see Black 2007: 323) or Bartolomeo Valori (see Black 2007: 322–3).

[7] See Black 2007: 56–8.

[8] Lucchi 1978: 599; Grendler 1989: 142–6.

[9] In Recanati in 1404, beginning readers were called "abecedaristi" ("alphabetizers"): Boracini Verducci 1975: 129.

[10] Marrou 1964: 211–12, 364.   [11] Marrou 1964: 364.

[12] *Patrologia latina* (ed. Migne 1844–55), 131.845, cited by Riché 1979: 223.

quidam uero nominarii...appellantur.[13] ("In Latin schools, where boys take the first steps in reading the written word, some are called alphabetizers, others syllablizers, yet others nominizers.")

The next stage was reading words and phrases: in late Roman antiquity this was accomplished by reading and learning by heart the collection of aphorisms known as Cato's *Distichs*, a text going back to perhaps the third century CE.[14] In the early Middle Ages, however, a significant change of curriculum occurred: the *Disticha Catonis* were replaced as the first reading text by the Psalter.[15] This change of reading matter began first in monastic schools and soon spread to parish and ecclesiastical schools, as well as to lay education.[16] Throughout the Middle Ages, being *psalteratus* ("knowledgeable in the psalter") was synonymous with literacy.[17] In the early Middle Ages, novice monks had had to learn all 150 psalms, a process which could take up to three years for normal pupils, whereas the gifted might accomplish the task in as little as five months.[18] Even in the early Middle Ages it seems that this undertaking was considered too onerous for the whole of literate society;[19] by the later Middle Ages it is clear that the entire psalter was no longer serving as the introductory reading text.[20] This is not only suggested by the diminutive nomenclature in wide use (*salteruzzo, saltero piccolo, psalteriolus* ["little psalter"])[21] but also by the famous story recounted by Boccaccio, who was appalled on his visit to Montecassino to find the writing being erased from ancient codices in order to make psalters for boys.[22] It is obvious that several entire psalters could not be created out of the eight folios constituting a quaternion.

On the evidence of curriculum outlines, it is clear that in later medieval and early Renaissance Italy, the elementary pupil, having learned the alphabet from the *tavola* or *carta*, still went on to the *salterio*. By the later Middle Ages, it seems that prayers and devotional texts had definitively

---

[13] *Patrologia latina*, 145.698.   [14] Marrou 1964: 364.   [15] Riché 1953: 253–6; Riché 1976: 464.
[16] Riché 1953: 255–6; Riché 1979: 223.   [17] Riché 1979: 223.
[18] Riché 1976, p. 464 n. 117.   [19] Riché 1976: p. 464.
[20] The partial reading of the psalter by future clerks learning to read may have been occurring already in the early twelfth century: see Pasqui 1899: 525: *Presbiter Petrus de Monte Gerlone ... dixit: Citulus eram et iam legebam in psalterium* ("Priest Piero from Monte Gerlone ... said: I was a boy and already reading from the psalter"); p. 557: *Presbiter Pepo prepositus de Avegnone ... dixit: Puer eram et legebam in psalterio in plebe de Saturnino tempore Gualfredi episopi senensis* ("Priest Pepo prepositor of Avignon ... said: I was a boy and was reading from the psalter in the parish of Saturnia at the time of Gualfredo bishop of Siena").
[21] See the following note and Black 2001, p. 38 n. 34.
[22] Cited by Lucchi (1978: 601): *aliqui monachi uolentes lucrari duos uel quinque solidos, radebant unum quaternum et faciebant psalteriolos quos uendebant pueris.* ("Some monks wanting to make two or five soldi, rubbed out a quaternion and made little psalters which they sold to boys.")

replaced psalms in the *salterio*. In a letter about her daughter Tina to her husband Francesco Datini in 1393, Margherita Datini wrote: "La Tina àne letto il saltero; arebe di bisogno di qualche libricuolo che vi fosse suso i sette salmi e l'ufficio della Donna ch'avesse buona lettera."[23] In translation, this passage reads: "Tina has read the psalter; she needs a book containing the seven psalms and the office of our lady which is well-written [i.e. easily readable]."[24] The significant point about this passage is that it shows that, by the turn of the fifteenth century, the psalter no longer included the seven penitential psalms, but must already have contained various prayers and miscellaneous devotional texts.

In the Middle Ages, a pupil acquired the skills of basic reading by subjecting the psalter to a two-stage process. The first focused on a written text: the pupil had a psalm written on his waxed tablet and read it over and over again. The second involved memory: by reading the psalm from his tablet many times, the pupil eventually learned the text by heart and so was able to dispense with the written text. After appropriate examination by his teacher, he was then assigned another psalm, and the process was repeated. This procedure, involving first reading from a written text and secondly recitation from memory without the written text, is described in the sixth-century monastic *Regula magistri*.[25] The process changed little throughout the Middle Ages; indeed, boys might have been reading the psalter on the basis of a written text copied onto their waxed tablets in the fifteenth century, as is clear from a gloss, describing the use of the stylus ("graphium" or "pezelo") to read the psalter, in contrast to the quill pen

---

[23] Pampaloni 1981, p. 196 n. 2.
[24] The phrase "che vi fosse suso" is an archaic way of saying "nel quale ci sono" ("in which there are"). I should like to correct an error of interpretation in Black 1991b: 140–1. I suggested a regrouping of letters in this text, but after discussions with Silvia Rizzo, Teresa De Robertis and Alan Bullock, I realize that this was philologically impossible and that the original transcription must be correct.
[25] *La règle du maître*, ed. Vogüé 1964: 234–6: *alii legant, alii audiant, alii litteras discant et doceant, alii psalmos, quos habent superpositos, meditentur. Nam cum eos maturauerint et memoria perfecte tenuerint, adducti a prepositis suis ipsum psalmum aut canticum seu quamuis lectionem memoriter abbati restituant. Et cum perreddiderit, mox petat pro se debere orari. Et cum pro eo a circumadstantibus oratum fuerit, conplenti abbati genua osculetur qui reddidit. Cui mox aut ab ipso nouus [psalmus] aut a prepositis iubetur superponi, et postquam superpositum fuerit quoduis, antequam se meditet, item a circumadstantibus petat pro se orari et sic incoent meditare.* ("Let some read, others listen, other learn letters and teach, let others study psalms that they have written for them. For, when they have got to know them well and have memorized them perfectly, let them be taken by their prefects to the abbot to recite the psalm or canticle or any reading text from memory. And when he has done this thoroughly, then let him ask for prayers on his behalf. And when those nearby have prayed for him, let him kiss the knees of the officiating abbot. Then once a new psalm has been ordered to be written on the tablet by the abbot or by the prefects, and after it is written on the tablet, before he studies it, let him seek to have prayers said on his behalf by those nearby and then let him begin to study it.") French translation in Riché 1979: 349–50.

with which books were copied.[26] Indeed, the procedure of learning the psalter verse by verse and reciting it back piecemeal to the teacher was still used in Bolognese schools in the mid-Trecento, as is clear from a text by Giovanni Conversini da Ravenna.[27] The main technical development in the course of the thirteenth, fourteenth and fifteenth centuries was the substitution of ready-made psalters, such as those described by Boccaccio,[28] for versions copied onto waxed tablets, but the basic approach of first reading from a written text followed by memorization without the text remained unchanged.[29]

A curious fact in the history of Italian pre-university education during the thirteenth, fourteenth and fifteenth centuries is that the vernacular was not used at what must seem – given widespread literacy in the vernacular – the most obvious point (at least to us) in the curriculum: the elementary stages of learning to read. It may have been educationally problematic, if not impossible, to teach basic reading technique in a language without fixed orthography, such as the Italian *volgare* (vernacular) before the sixteenth century. Indeed, in the Middle Ages and early Renaissance, Latin was regarded as an artificial, created, unchanging language, an *ars* (discipline) suitable for teaching, whereas the vulgar languages were considered

---

[26] Florence Biblioteca Riccardiana (henceforth BRF) 809, fol. 2r (gloss to *Graecismus*, xv¹): *Notandum quod stilus dictus a sto stas. Assumitur dupliciter, scilicet proprie et improp[r]ie. Prop[r]ie assumitur pro graphio, id est pezelo quo pueri utuntur in legendo donatum psalterium. Improp[r]ie dupliciter assumitur primo modo pro pena qua libri scribentur, secundo modo assumitur tripliciter a poietis.* ("It is to be noted that stylus comes from I stand, you stand. It has two meanings, namely literally and loosely. Literally it means a writing stick, that is a rod that boys use to read the psalter [and] Donatus. Loosely it is used first for a pen with which books are written, secondly by poets in three senses.")

[27] See Giovanni Conversini da Ravenna's account of a schoolmate's failure to learn the psalter in this way: *cum semel nescisset psalterii uersum reddere* . . . "when once he did not know how to recite a verse of the psalter" (Sabbadini 1924: 130; Garin 1958: 107). *Reddere* here means "recite from memory": see the subsequent passage (Sabbadini 1924: 130; Garin 1958: 107): *complecti mente ac reddere compellebat* ("he forced him to memorize and recite"), cited in Black 2001: p. 174 n.12.

[28] Italian pupils were already owning their own psalters in the thirteenth century: see document dating from 1268 to 1277 in Venice, where at least one psalter (and possibly two: see Black 2001, p. 40 n. 48) was purchased for the sons of Marco Zambon (Cecchetti 1886: 363; Ortalli 1997: 890). By the end of the fourteenth century teachers seem to have been distributing psalters among their pupils: see the inventory dated 4 February 1398 of the recently deceased *Magister Lodisius Caluus de Vicheria regens scolas grammaticales in hac ciuitate Ianuensi* ("Master Lodisio Calvi from *Vicheria* running a grammar school in this city of Genoa"), which includes *salteria parua pro pueris* ("small psalters for boys") (Gorrini 1932: 90, 93). His other books consisted largely of standard grammar school fare for the end of the Trecento: Vergil's *Georgics*, *trauetum* (= Nicholas Trevet's commentary on Boethius' *Consolation*), Boethius [*Consolation*], three copies of Lucan, *Priscianus unus maior* [= books 1 to 16 of *Institutiones grammaticae*], Ovid's *Heroides*, two copies of Geoffrey of Vinsauf's *Poetria noua*, Henry of Settimello's *Elegia*, Seneca's *Tragedies*, Ovid's *Metamorphoses*. He also had copies of Seneca's letters to Lucilius, which were not normally read at grammar school: see Black 2001: 212–13.

[29] See Black 2001: 58ff. and below for vocabulary "al testo" ("reading from a written text") and "al senno" ("memorization") at use during the fourteenth and fifteenth centuries.

changeable and unstable, regarded literally as forms of babble, learnt naturally but formally unteachable; only with the triumph of the humanist view of Latin as itself a natural, historically changing language in the sixteenth century did it become conceivable to teach fundamental language skills in the vernacular. It is important to remember the close association, even identification, of *ars* and teaching in the Middle Ages; Latin was teachable precisely because it was considered an artificial language, whereas teaching the vernacular was inconceivable because it was regarded as natural, not artificial, not an *ars*.[30]

The final stages of elementary education in medieval and Renaissance Europe were presided over by Donatus.[31] But it has long been recognized that in Italy during the high and late Middle Ages the principal textbook in elementary schools was not Aelius Donatus' *Ars minor*[32] but the manual spuriously attributed to Donatus which Remigio Sabbadini christened *Ianua* after the first word of its verse prologue and which, as a parsing grammar, dominated the Italian manuscript tradition and early printing.[33]

Early manuscripts of *Ianua*, with their extensive paradigms, examples, mnemonics, rules and excursuses, offered texts to form the basis of an active knowledge of Latin, but the condensed *Ianua* of the fourteenth and fifteenth centuries was used, not primarily as a manual for learning the rudiments of Latin grammar, but rather as a reading text: it is clear that the specialist teachers of *Ianua* were elementary reading masters such as ser Dore di ser Giovanni, who was elected *magister ad docendum pueros legere et scribere* ("master to teach boys to read and write") in San Gimignano in 1359 and whose duties included teaching *omnes et singulos pueros ab eo*

---

[30] See Black 2001, pp. 41–4, and p. 378 n. 35 for a more detailed discussion.

[31] The fundamental importance of Donatus, even in sixteenth-century Italy, is illustrated by a vernacular annotation, in the hand of a (non-Tuscan) Cinquecento schoolboy, on a copy of Terence (Florence Biblioteca Medicea Laurenziana [henceforth BML] Pluteo 38.33, fol. 98v): "Poiché non volete imprare donato e le regole se<n>sa le quali non i<m>pareresti mai cosa alchuna" ("Since you do not want to learn Donatus and grammar rules without which you would never learn anything"). The "regole" here referred to correspond to the grammar rules of teachers such as Francesco da Buti and Guarino Veronese: the term was generic for a secondary grammar manual in the fourteenth and fifteenth centuries.

[32] In Carolingian Italy, the genuine *Ars minor* of Donatus was still being used as the basic text of elementary education, as suggested by the *Ars Donati* by Paul the Deacon, which was a reproduction of Donatus' text, with the interpolation of largely additional declensions and conjugations as normal in medieval versions of the *Ars minor* (for this practice, see Black 2001: 45). On Paul's *Ars Donati*, ed. Amelli (1899) from the unique version in the Vatican Library (Biblioteca Apostolica Vaticana Palatinus Latinus 1746), see also Lentini 1975: 121–2, 198–9, who points out that this work was an elementary treatise for beginners.

[33] Sabbadini 1896: 35, 42–4; Schmitt 1969: 45, 73–4; Garin 1958: 98; Grendler 1989: 174–82; Black 1991a: 101–15; Black 1991b: 141–5; Gehl 1993: 82–106; Black 1996c: 5–22; Pinborg 1982: 65–7; Rizzo 1986: 395; Law 1986: 138–41.

*audire et discere uolentes uz. tabulam, psalterium, donatum*³⁴ ("each and every boy wanting to attend his lessons and learn, namely the table, the psalter, Donatus"); indeed, in 1399 the Lucchese grammar teacher was forbidden to instruct anyone who had not already mastered Donatus,³⁵ while in 1469 the commune of Pistoia laid down an explicit division of labour: in his school the grammarian could not teach Donatus, which was to be the exclusive preserve of "uno o dua maestri che debano insegnare a fanciulli"³⁶ ("one or two masters who must teach children"). *Ianua* was not part of the grammar syllabus: in fourteenth-century Colle Valdelsa a distinction was drawn between schooling *in grammaticalibus* ("in grammar") on the one hand and *lettera seu doctrina donati, libricioli, carte* ("reading and learning Donatus, little books, alphabet sheets") on the other,³⁷ while fifteenth-century Bucine differentiated "gramaticha" ("grammar") from "el saltero o donadello"³⁸ ("the psalter and Donatus"), as did Bassano as early as 1259;³⁹ indeed, in Piedmont Donatus was distinguished even from *primum latinum*⁴⁰ ("first Latin"), while in Trecento Arezzo it was declared that elementary reading, including Donatus, was taught before the pupil was introduced to grammar.⁴¹ Donatus was *read*, Latin was *done*: *facientes latinum* ("doing Latin"), *legentes Donatum* ("reading Donatus") (Colle Valdelsa,⁴² San Gimignano⁴³); *lactinare* ("to write in Latin"), *legere Donatum* ("to read Donatus") (Pistoia,⁴⁴ San Gimignano⁴⁵); *legentes Donatellum* ("reading Donatus"), *lactinantes in latino* ("writing in Latin in Latin") (Volterra).⁴⁶ This vocabulary is making a point: *Ianua* was being used not so much as a manual to learn Latin but as a reading text. How *Ianua*

---

³⁴ San Gimignano Archivio comunale (henceforth ACSG), 123, fol. lxxviiii verso–lxxx recto (18 June 1359).
³⁵ Barsanti 1905: 120.   ³⁶ Zanelli 1900: 138–9.
³⁷ Siena Archivio di stato Comune di Colle Valdelsa (henceforth ASS Colle) 110, fol. 2v (March 1368): *tam in gramaticalibus quam in lettura seu doctrina donati, libbricioli, carte et aliis pertinentibus ad dictum ministerium seu artem* ("both in grammar and in reading or learning Donatus, the little book, the alphabet sheet and other things pertaining to his job and trade").
³⁸ Mazzi 1896: 186.   ³⁹ See Black 2001, p. 36 n. 14.   ⁴⁰ Gabotto 1895: 335–6.
⁴¹ See below p. 108 and n. 62.
⁴² ASS Colle 94, fol. lviiii recto (5 August 1352), lxvi recto (23 August 1352), ci verso (6 November 1357); 107, fol. lxxxxiii recto (31 March 1367).
⁴³ ACSG 131, fol. cxiii verso (5 April 1372).
⁴⁴ Pistoia Archivio di stato Provvisioni (henceforth ASPistoia Provv.) 22, fol. 55v–56r (4 June 1389).
⁴⁵ ACSG 160, fol. 45r (23 February 1407), fol. 150v–151v (31 October 1407: see Pecori [1853], p. 618); 162, fol. 27v–28v (8 March 1409); 164, fol. 161r–162r (1 December 1412); 168, fol. 14r–15r (14 October 1417).
⁴⁶ Battistini 1919: 34–5. In view of the evidence linking *Ianua* with the beginning reading texts (*tavola/carta, salterio*) and separating it from the grammar syllabus, Gehl's statement (1993: 84) seems puzzling: "In the trecento the Donatus was used almost exclusively as a propaedeutic to further Latin study. It was not given to students for whom the further Latin course was not planned."

was actually taught to boys who did not yet know Latin is suggested by the distinction frequently made between two stages of reading this text: "Donato per lo testo et per lo senno."⁴⁷ "Per lo testo" was sometimes rendered as "a veduta" ("by sight"),⁴⁸ *testualiter* ("textually"),⁴⁹ *cum textu* ("with the text"),⁵⁰ whereas "per lo senno" was often translated *cum sensu*⁵¹ or *sensualiter* ("with meaning").⁵² "Per lo testo" means reading with the aid of a written text, whereas *cum sensu*, *sensualiter*, "per lo senno" or "per l'insenno"⁵³ signifies using one's wits and not the written text, in other words, by memory. At first these *maestri di fanciulli* had their pupils simply sound out and read the words of *Ianua* directly from a written text, either copied onto a waxed tablet⁵⁴ or, beginning in the thirteenth century, from a copy of the text owned by the pupil;⁵⁵ the emphasis at this stage was on phonetic reading: hence, the rendering sometimes of "per lo testo" as

---

⁴⁷ Zanelli 1900: 139.   ⁴⁸ Klapisch-Zuber 1984: 767.
⁴⁹ ASS Colle 121, fol. lxiiii recto (29 January 1381).
⁵⁰ Lucchi 1978: 601; Borracini Verducci 1975: 129, 158.
⁵¹ Lucchi 1978: 601; Colini-Baldeschi 1900: 23; Borracini Verducci 1975: 129, 158.
⁵² ASS Colle 121, fol. lxiiii recto (29 January 1381).   ⁵³ Black 1996b: 392–3.
⁵⁴ Cf. BRF 809, fol. 2r: *graphio id est pezelo quo pueri utuntur in legendo donatum* (see above n. 26 for English translation).
⁵⁵ As early as the mid-thirteenth century, schoolboys were owning their own copies of *Ianua*: see the document published by Cecchetti 1886: 332 (see Ortalli 1997: 890) where *donatus* was purchased for sons of Marco Zambon c. 1270. There is substantial documentary evidence of *donadelli* purchased for schoolboys in Florence in the second half of the fourteenth century: Florence Archivio di stato (henceforth ASF) Carte Del Bene 32, fol. 7r: "Amerigho di Borghognione [Del Bene] dì xiiii de febraio '367 per uno donadello per se – L. 1 S. 15" ("Amerigo di Borgonione Del Bene on 14 February 1367 for a Donatus for himself – 1 lira 15 soldi"). Carte Strozziane iii.277, fol. 91v: "deono dare dì iii di gennaio 1379 ... sono per uno donadello et Catto che si comperò per Checcho" ("they have to pay on 3 January 1379 ... it is for a Donatus and Cato that was bought for Checco"); fol. 167v: "messer Pazino di messer Franciescho delgli Strozzi de' avere a dì 14 di gennaio 1379 ... sono per uno donadello che ssi conperò a Checcho di messer Palla – L. 1 S.ii D.V. De' avere dì xviii di gennaio 1379 ... per conperare uno donadello per Nani di misser Palla... – L.i S.iiii D.vii"; fol. 114r: "E deono dare detto dì [4 December 1381] L.2 S.quindici ... sono per uno donadello che ssi conperò per Simone... – L.1 S.ii d.ii"; fol. 181v: "e de' avere detto dì [4 December 1381] L. 2 S. quindici ... sono per uno donadello per Simone di misser Palla... – L.1 S.ii D.ii"; fol. 122v [7 February 1382 ab inc.]: "E deono dare dì vii di febraio ... L. due S. quindici ... demmo per conperare uno donadello – L.1 S.i d. vi"; fol. 189r: "E de' avere dì vii di febraio [1382] ... L. due e S. quindici ... sono per conperare uno donadello per Simone ... L.I. S.I. D.vi." ("messer Pazino di messer Francesco Strozzi has to receive on 14 January 1379 ... it is for a Donatus that was bought for Checco di messer Palla [Strozzi] – 1 lira 2 soldi 5 pence. He has to receive on 18 January 1379 ... to buy a Donatus for Nanni di messer Palla... – 1 lira 4 soldi 7 pence." "They have to pay on the said day [4 December 1381] 2 lire 15 soldi ... it is for a Donatus that was bought for Simone... – 1 lira 11 soldi 11 pence"; "and he has to receive on the said day [4 December 1381] 2 lire 15 soldi ... it is for a Donatus for Simone di messer Palla... – 1 lira 11 soldi 11 pence"; [7 February 1383] "They have to pay on 7 February ... 2 lire 15 soldi... We paid to buy a Donatus – 1 lira 1 soldo 6 pence." "And he has to receive on 7 February [1382] ... 2 lire and 15 soldi ... it is to buy a Donatus for Simone ... 1 lira 1 soldo 6 pence.").

donatum legens syllabicandum and *donatum legens syllabicando*[56] ("reading Donatus syllable by syllable"). At this textual stage, pupils were hardly yet learning Latin; here the emphasis was on phonetic technique, on *sillabicare* ("syllable by syllable") and *compitare* ("sounding out"),[57] on reading skills, rather than on the Latin language itself.[58]

Nevertheless, *Ianua* could also serve the small numbers of Italian boys who went beyond elementary reading and writing to the actual learning of Latin. If pupils went on to the next level, "al senno" or "per lo senno," the emphasis was on memory. There was a phrase "per lo senno a mente" signifying a knowledge so thorough as to know something by memory,[59] and so "Donato al senno" meant learning *Ianua* so well as to know the text by memory and without the written text. It is clear that *Ianua* must have been memorized at this stage by boys about to learn Latin, because there was no other manual in the grammar curriculum which included full declensions of nouns and pronouns and complete conjugations of regular and irregular verbs.[60] Guarino's *Regulae* and its medieval forerunners

---

[56] Massa 1906: 321.
[57] For *sillabicare* in Bonaventura's scheme of learning to read, see Manacorda (1914), II: 172; see also Lucchi 1978: 601. For *compito* and *compitare* (meaning "sounding out"), see Lucchi 1978: 600; Klapisch-Zuber 1984: 767. The first seven years of the education of the Pavian clerk Opicino de Canistris from 1304 to 1311 were divided into two stages: first three years for *legere vel sillabicare* ("reading and learning syllables"), the next four *in studio grammatice* [i.e. Latin] (Sasse Tateo 1992: 30–1).
[58] This type of phonetic reading without meaning often remained with Italians in later life: hence Peter Damian's accusation of those who babble syllable by syllable without understanding (*syllabatim . . . balbutiant* ["by syllables . . . babbling"]), cited by Reynolds 1996: 10.
[59] Tommaseo and Bellini 1861–79, vol. 4 pt. 1, p. 794, s.v. senno: "† **Saper per lo senno a mente**, *Aver piena e indubitata contezza, Saper benissimo, minutamente, Avere esattamente a memoria. Varch. Stor. 12. 419. (C)* In Firenze vivono ancora, se non più, diecimila persone, le quali le sanno . . . per lo senno a mente. *Galil. Sist.* 27. Ci sono molti, che sanno per lo senno a mente tutta la Poetica, e sono poi infelici nel compor quattro versi solamente." ("To know thoroughly by heart, to have full and undoubted security, to know extremely well, minutely, to have exactly by memory. Varchi, *Storie fiorentine.* 12.419. (C) In Florence there lived yet 10,000 persons, if not more, who knew them . . . thoroughly by heart. Galileo, *Sistema*, 27. There are many, who know thoroughly by heart the entire *Poetics* and who are ill at ease in composing only four verses.") This is the phrase used by Bernardo Machiavelli in his *Libro di ricordi*, fol. 14r: "R° q° dì detto di sopra chome insino a dì 5 del presente cominciò Nicholò mio andare a imparare da Ser Baptista di Filippo da Poppi. Insegnagli il donadello per lo insenno a mente." ("I record this day as above how on the fifth of the present month my Niccolò began to go to learn from ser Battista di Filippo da Poppi. He teaches him Donatus by heart.") See Black 1996b: 392. Also significant is the phrase "Donato a seno et a mente" ("Donatus by memory"), transcribed by Grendler (1989, p. 196 n. 117) from the Venetian Professioni di fede of 1587.
[60] Gehl's statement ("Full mastery of grammatical terms and paradigms could not have been learned from the *Ianua* alone. For that the student needed to work carefully through some of the Latin reading texts" [1993: 86]) needs amendment. Full mastery of the paradigms is what *Ianua* did offer; before the appearance of Perotti's *Rudimenta*, there was no other manual offering all the paradigms. As for grammatical terminology, there was much of this in *Ianua*, but it had to be complemented by

such as Goro d'Arezzo's *Regule parve* or Francesco da Buti's *Regule* included only partial paradigms and assumed a knowledge of declensions and conjugations.[61]

The elementary curriculum was often extended to include the *Disticha Catonis*. This syllabus – beginning with *tabula/carta*, progressing to *salterium* and culminating in *Donatus* and *Cato* – was considered distinct from Latin (in contemporary parlance, *grammatica*). Its purpose was generic reading skill, whereas the grammar syllabus was intended to teach Latin composition and introduce pupils to Latin literature. The division between elementary and grammar education was made clear by an Aretine document of 1396:

cum uideatur et sit utile ac necessarium habere in ciuitate Aretii unum magistrum qui instruat pueros in primis litteris ac etiam doceat Donatum et Catonem et alios libros antequam inttroducantur ad gramaticam.[62]

Since it seems and is useful and necessary to have in the city of Arezzo a teacher to instruct boys in their first letters and also to teach Donatus and Cato and other books before they are introduced to Latin.

This elementary curriculum remained untouched by humanist educators. Even a renowned humanist pedagogue such as Guarino Veronese relied heavily on *Ianua* in his school,[63] and curriculum outlines throughout Italy confirm that the traditional syllabus of *tabula/carta*, *salterium* and *Ianua* remained omnipresent in Italy throughout the fifteenth century.[64] The only significant change here had been the shortening of *Ianua*'s text in the course of the later thirteenth and fourteenth centuries in order to accelerate the initial reading process, but this was a development antedating the arrival of humanist pedagogues in the fifteenth century.[65]

The use of Latin *salteri* ("psalters") for imparting basic reading skills remained standard practice in Italy until the later eighteenth century, when educators began to demand that pupils learn to read in Italian. Thus the *Compendio del metodo delle scuole normali per uso delle scuole della Lombardia*, published in 1792 by the educational reformer Francesco Soave, insisted that "le prime cose, che hannosi a far leggere da' fanciulli ... esser debbono

---

secondary study of a text such as Francesco da Buti's or Guarino's *Regule*. Literary texts from the minor or major authors (see Black 2001, ch. 4) obviously contained no theoretical grammatical terminology.

[61] See Black 2001: 98ff.
[62] Arezzo Archivio di stato Deliberazioni del Consiglio Generale 3, fol. 105r. See Black 2007: 738 for the entire text and the context.
[63] Sabbadini 1896: 45ff.
[64] For Italy, see Black 2001, p. 36 n. 14; for Tuscany, see Black 2007: 77–118 *passim*.
[65] Black 2001: 55ff.

Italiane."[66] The call for such reform became particularly importunate in the case of lower-class children, who had hitherto been taught to read, like the upper classes, using traditional Latin *salteri* ("psalters"). Now, however, the Lombard reformer Pier Domenico Soresi, in *Dell'educazione del minuto popolo* (1775), called for "fanciulli plebei" to be excluded "dalle scuole e dagli studi di Latinità,"[67] since their humble station did not allow them to "passare molti anni negli'intralciati studi del latino":[68] "quanto più ignota è la lingua, tanto più lentamente progredirà chi vuol imparare leggere e scrivere," skills acquired "con maggior facilità ... instando sul solo italiano."[69] Similarly in Parma, the *Costituzione per i nuovi regi studi* of 1768 envisaged teaching only Italian in the lowest school classes (reserved for pupils who would not go on to further study): one would begin "fin dalle basse scuole ad insegnare la buona e corretta lingua Italiana, di cui quotidiano e necessario è l'uso."[70] Such new methods seem to have been inspired by Enlightened contempt for useless Latinity and the corresponding wish to substitute a more practical form of elementary education. As Ludovico Antonio Muratori wrote in *Della perfeta poesia*, "il lodevolissimo sì, ma troppo zelo d'instruire i giovani nel Linguaggio Latino, giunge a segno di non permetter loro l'esercizio dell'Italiano, e di lasciarsi uscir dalle pubbliche Scuole ignorantissimi della lor favella natìa ... Proprio de gli anni teneri è un sì fatto studio; e perciò dovrebbe con quel della Lingua Latina congiungersi l'altro dell'italiano ... affinché i giovani per divenir dotti in una Lingua straniera, e morta, non sieno sempre barbari, e stranieri nella propria, e viva loro favella."[71] Such ideas were incorporated into reform proposals for Lombardy submitted to Emperor Joseph II by the scientist Paolo Frisi, who argued that "non si perdesse tanto tempo nella lingua latina e in tante inutili questioni."[72]

[66] Cited in Matarrese 1993: 32 ("the first things that must be read by children ought to be Italian").
[67] Cited in Matarrese 1993, p. 29 n. 7: "lower-class children to be excluded from schools of and from the study of Latin."
[68] Cited in Matarrese 1993, p. 29 n. 7: "pass many years in the intricate study of Latin."
[69] Cited in Matarrese 1993, p. 29 n. 7 ("the less familiar the language, the more slowly will someone make progress in reading and writing, skills acquired with greater ease using Italian only").
[70] Cited in Matarrese 1993: 29 ("beginning in the most elementary schools to teach good and correct Italian, which is needed every day").
[71] Cited in Matarrese 1993: 26–7 ("the highly praiseworthy but excessive zeal to instruct young people in the Latin language has as a result their inadequate familiarity with Italian, allowing them to leave state schools ignorant of their native tongue. Study of language is needed in the early years, and therefore the study of Latin must be joined to that of Italian, lest young people, through becoming learned in a foreign and dead language, always remain barbarians and foreigners in their own, living tongue").
[72] Cited in Matarrese 1993: 30 ("one should not waste so much time on the Latin language and in such useless pursuits").

The monolingual approach for teaching elementary reading in medieval, Renaissance and early modern Italy has not always been understood. Especially misleading has been the view put forward by Paul Grendler that there were two streams of education in Italy from the fourteenth to the sixteenth century: vernacular and Latin.[73] But the only schools that taught overwhelmingly in the vernacular were abacus schools; when abacus teachers did occasionally teach beginners' reading (as in, for example, Colle Valdelsa, Arezzo or Pistoia), they did so on the basis of Latin, not vernacular texts, as is clear from appointment documents naming Latin (*salterium* and *donatum*), not vernacular, texts to be used. Elementary reading in Italy, as has already been seen, was always taught on the basis of Latin, not the vernacular, up to the end of the eighteenth century. The only evidence cited by Grendler substantiating the teaching of vernacular literature by abacus teachers before the sixteenth century comes from a "fifteenth-century contract [that] obliged an abbaco teacher in Volterra ... 'to teach reading to those who do not wish to study Latin but wish to learn to read vernacular books and written letters.'"[74] The source for this document is Battistini 1919: 29 and 45. However, a personal search for this document in the Volterra communal archives before 1500 has proved vain. In fact, the document post-dates 1530, when the new Florentine duchy issued a new gold coin: the *scudo*, mentioned in the document mistakenly attributed by Battistini to the fifteenth century and repeated by Grendler: "Il salario è di scudi ottantaquattro di moneta l'anno netti."[75] ("The salary is eight hundred and four scudi in money a year net.") In fifteenth-century Italy, abacus teachers did not yet teach vernacular literature, as they would eventually do in the sixteenth century, and, during the Renaissance period, there were never any elementary Italian schools teaching solely in the vernacular: it was never possible to choose a wholly vernacular education, in contrast to the entirely Latin curriculum offered in Italy's grammar schools.

Reading, grammar and abacus are well documented phases of education in Italy from the thirteenth to the fifteenth centuries, but little has been known hitherto about learning to write. In 1982, Piero Lucchi published a text from a Genoese notarial cartulary with the date March 1311, in which an apparent pupil wrote the following sentence four times: "Pero Pumoso de Zoane a fatto cosse inver lo maistro de le quae elo se pentirà." ("Pier Pumoso of Genoa has done things towards his teacher of which he will repent.") Lucchi regarded this as a writing exercise in the vernacular,

---

[73] Grendler 1995.   [74] Grendler 1995: 166.   [75] Batttistini 1919: 45.

handed out as a less violent punishment than the usual corporal variety,[76] but this interpretation is uncertain, especially in view of the grammatical construction in the sentence: if the sentence were translated into Latin, it would involve use of the impersonal verb *p[a]enitet*. The sentence looks more like deriving from an exercise in the translation of an active verb in the vernacular into an impersonal construction in Latin: a favoured topic in translation exercises intended to provide practice in Latin syntax (*themata*).[77] The fact that the sentence was repeated only four times suggests *probationes pennae* rather than punishment or indeed a writing exercise. The document can perhaps be interpreted more suggestively as associated with the teaching of Latin composition rather than of writing.[78]

There is no doubt, however, that the vernacular exercises published by Paolo Cherubini in 1996[79] were connected with learning to write. These consist of five fragments, including alphabets, simple Latin prayers and standard phrases ("de' dare," "de' avere") ("to pay," "to receive") from account books; the date 1481 and the locality Foligno are mentioned. Numerous repetitions of the same sentences, phrases and characters indicate that the principal concern was the teaching of writing: one of the alphabet exercises is repeated 13 times, another 17 times, a third 18 times, a fourth 7 times; the two prayers are repeated 16 times each; two of the accounting formulas are repeated 6 times, while the third is repeated 9 times. Because of the inclusion of accounting extracts, Cherubini suggests that the exercises came from an abacus school. This interpretation is supported by figures he summarizes[80] on the basis of the educational extracts published by Armando Verde from the Florentine 1480 Catasto.[81] These indicate that the age of learning to read preceded that of learning the abacus and writing; the latter two skills appear to have been learned at approximately the same age.[82] This interpretation is confirmed by a similar table based on Florentine pupils in pre-university education, as revealed by the Florentine Catasto of 1427.[83] Again, learning to read is

---

[76] Lucchi 1982: 106–7.   [77] See e.g. Black 1996a: 730, 732, 734–6, 739.
[78] Similarly, the other sentence written by "Pero" (cited by Lucchi 1982, p. 107 n. 17) also has the appearance of a syntactical exercise in translation, in view of its reference to a [school] "compagno" ("fellow pupil"), its artificial sense and its contorted construction. The "sgrammatico" *latinum* ("ungrammatical Latin"), referring to beatings by the teacher (*verbera magistri*), is obviously a translation exercise; without the text, it is hard to judge the fictitious letter, but epistolography with the translation of an entire letter from the vernacular into Latin was the ultimate goal of secondary Latin syntactical study. On this evidence and its meaning, see also Blasi 1993: 385.
[79] Cherubini 1996.   [80] Cherubini 1996: 237.   [81] Verde 1973–2010, vol. 2, pp. 1003–202.
[82] For the table (slightly modified), see Black 2007: 462–3.
[83] Based on Black 2007, Appendix 1. See Black 2007: 447 for the table.

concentrated before the abacus, which seems to have been roughly concurrent with learning to write. All this evidence suggests that, for pupils embarking into the educational stream where reading was followed by abacus, the teaching of writing took place after elementary reading and at the same time as the abacus.

A similar but considerably earlier document has recently been discovered and published by Irene Ceccherini.[84] This consists of a single folio, written on both sides and preserved within an account book of the Florentine merchant company owned by Francesco and Iacopo Del Bene, itself dated from 1361 to 1366. The sheet was not originally part of the book, since their sizes and watermarks differ, but the two documents are roughly contemporaneous, the folio's watermark approximating Briquet 3287 (a deer), found in Florence between 1359 and 1365. The writing exercises are, like those discovered by Cherubini, in the vernacular. A generic phrase typical of an account book ("Bartolo di Niccholò (et) suoi compagni deono dare contanti l(ire) m(ille)") ("Bartolo di Niccolò and his fellow pupils must pay in cash 1000 lire") is copied by the pupil 24 times, while a liturgical invocation, also in the vernacular ("Al nome sia di (Christo) benedetto (et) della madre vergine Maria") ("In the name both of the blessed Christ and of the Virgin Mary"), is repeated 22 times. The pedagogic technique employed is the same as that found in Cherubini's exercise sheets: at the top of the page an experienced hand writes the phrase, which the learner then copies, filling the side of paper. Again, as in the later example, it is arguable that the exercises came from an abacus school, given that the phrases are formulae typical of account books (which often opened with a religious invocation). What is particularly interesting about these examples is that none is written in typically mercantile script – *scrittura mercantesca*. Instead, Ceccherini's example is copied in a formal notarial script (known as *cancelleresca*) typical of the later thirteenth and fourteenth centuries, whereas Cherubini's is written in an ordinary semi-cursive script, used by both merchants and notaries. Writing in Italy was apparently taught in schools on the basis of a generic script (for example *cancelleresca* before the fifteenth century and ordinary semi-cursive thenceforth); specialization – into book hand (*littera textualis* [gothic] or humanist minuscule or italic), notarial cursive or *mercantesca* – took place subsequently, when the pupil would enter a profession or a trade. No writing exercises in Latin dating before 1500 have yet emerged, but it is likely that a similar pedagogic system teaching writing on the basis

---

[84] Ceccherini 2010.

Teaching reading and writing in Renaissance Italy 113

of a generic, non-specialized semi-cursive script was prevalent in Italy from the thirteenth to the mid-fifteenth century: Latin vocabulary and translation exercises written by schoolboys throughout this period are normally written in ordinary semi-cursive script.[85]

For pupils progressing to grammar (Latin) education, curriculum outlines confirm that writing was learnt after elementary reading (*tabula/carta, salterium*),[86] often simultaneously with *Ianua* or sometimes immediately thereafter; it was always taught before Latin composition (*lactinare*). Writing was taught by specialist elementary teachers (often called *doctores puerorum* ["teachers of boys"]),[87] abacus teachers[88] or grammar teachers;[89] on one occasion the writing teacher also taught

---

[85] See the texts in Belloni and Pozza 1987, Black 1996a and Black 2001: 109, 114–15, 331–6.

[86] De Blasi 1993: 93: "la scrittura ... era insegnata dopo la lettura" ("writing ... was taught after reading"). De Blasi (p. 386) gives a perceptive and suggestive analysis of how the phonetic technique of learning to read had an impact on the orthography of unskilled writers, citing the case of one Ghezzo Senese in 1314, whose spelling actually appears to have derived from his crude attempts to sound out (*compitare*) words.

[87] Fucecchio 1319 19 April, 1326 30 June, 1481 (Fucecchio Archivio comunale [henceforth ACF] 25 NN [= not numbered], 30 NN, 48 fol. 181v); Florence 1427 (ASF Catasto 17, fol. 341r [see Black 2007, Appendix 1]), 1456 (ASF Arte della lana 201, fol. 237r); Colle Valdelsa 1359–60 (ASS Colle 101, fol. xli verso); S. Croce sull'Arno 1390 (S. Croce sull'Arno Archivio comunale [henceforth ACSC] 2, 141r); Volterra 1370 (Volterra Archivio comunale [henceforth ACV] A nera 21 IV, fol. 5r); Prato 1358 (Prato Archivio di stato Comune Diurni [henceforth ASPrato CD] 64 parte 8, fol. 32r; 883 parte 7, fol. 3r), 1362 (ASPrato CD 65 parte 4, fol. 3v), 1366 (ASPrato CD 66 parte 1, fol. 32v), 1409–11 (ASPrato CD 82, fol. 27r, 41v; 83 fol. 38v–39r), 1413 (ASPrato CD 84, fol. 52v–53r); S. Miniato 1371 (S. Miniato Archivio storico Comunità di San Miniato Deliberazioni dei priori e del consiglio [henceforth ACSM Delib.] 2293 fol. 81r), 1378 (ACSM Delib. 2298, fol. 16r), 1379 (ACSM Delib. 2300, fol. 46r); Pistoia 1474 (ASPistoia Provv. 43, fol. 174r–v), 1476 (ASPistoia Provv. 43, fol. 439r–440r; 44, fol. 23r), 1483 (ASPistoia Provv. 47, fol. 30r); S. Gimignano 1359–61 (ACSG 123, fol. lxxvi recto, lxxviiii verso–lxxx recto).

[88] Volterra 1331 (ACV A nera 11, fol. 15v); Colle 1370–1 (ASS Colle 110 fol. 82v), 1373 (ASS Colle 116, fol. 6v); Prato 1362–3 (ASPrato CD 65 parte 4, fol. 3v), 1365 (ASPrato CD 65 parte 10, fol. 4v), 1366–8 (ASPrato CD 66 parte 2, fol. 4 parte 3v; parte 6 fol. 19v; parte 7, fol. 42v; parte 8, fol. 39r), 1373–5 (ASPrato CD 67 parte 11, fol. 7; parte 9, fol. 12r), 1377–8 (ASPrato CD 67 parte 5, fol. 14v), 1481 (ASPrato CD 102, fol. 382v); Pistoia 1461 (ASPistoia Provv. 41, fol. 239r–v).

[89] Fucecchio 1318 31 October (ACF 25 NN), 1484 (ACF 197, fol. 290v), 1491 (ASF Comune di Fucecchio Reformationes a. 1488–96 [not yet catalogued], fol. 96v); Buggiano 1385–8 (Buggiano Archivio comunale [henceforth ACB] 9, fol. 205r, 236r, 274v–275r, 331r); Pistoia 1353 (ASPistoia Provv. 11, fol. 17r), 1472 (ASPistoia Provv. 43, fol. 211r–v), 1487 (ASPistoia Provv. 48, fol. 139v), 1488 (ASPistoia Provv. 48, fol. 172v), 1493 (ASPistoia Provv. 50, fol. 30v); Pescia 1388 (Pescia Archivio di stato Deliberazioni [henceforth ASPescia Delib.] 10, fol. 163r), 1391 (ASPescia Delib. 11, fol. 171v), 1484 (ASPescia Delib. 38, fol. 39r); Bibbiena 1423 (ASF Statuti di comuni soggetti [henceforth SCS] 80, fol. 26v); Ripomarance 1476 (ASF SCS 718, fol. 38r); Volterra 1391 (ACV A nera 24, fol. 271v), 1398 (ACV A nera 24, fol. 428v); Poggibonsi 1373 (ASS Comune di Poggibonsi [henceforth Poggibonsi] 81, fol. 50v); Prato 1372–3 (ASPrato CD 67 parte 13, fol. 26r), 1374–5 (ASPrato CD 67 parte 9, fol. 12r), 1380 (ASPrato CD 78, fol. 118r), 1383 (ASPrato CD 79, fol. 322v); Sansepolcro 1394 (Sansepolcro Archivio comunale [henceforth ACSS] ser. 11, 1, fol. 79v); Colle Valdelsa 1352 (ASS Colle 94, fol. li recto); S. Gimignano 1372 (ACSG 131, fol. cxi verso – cxiiii verso, xcv recto–verso), 1379 (ACSG 136, fol. 34v–36r).

grammar and abacus.⁹⁰ There are rare instances of specialist writing teachers: Joachim Riß aus Rothenburg, later a famous illuminator,⁹¹ was appointed by the Ufficiali dello Studio to teach writing in Florence for the academic year 1444–5⁹²; he was reappointed, probably for the same purpose, in 1451.⁹³ A specialist writing teacher was also mentioned in Pescia in 1497.⁹⁴ Whoever the teacher in charge, however, the preceding evidence suggests that reading and writing were not taught simultaneously, and that writing followed elementary reading, was roughly concurrent with the abacus⁹⁵ and/or *donatus* and preceded Latin composition.

---

⁹⁰ Fucecchio 1327 26 July (ACF 50 NN: *Coram uobis . . . pro parte magistri Iohannis artis gramatice et abbaci . . . ciuitatis Pistorii . . . pro parte ser Iohannis notarii et magistri artismetice siue albaci . . . ciuitatis Pistorii et parte Guelfe, exponitur quod ipse paratus est manere Fucecchii tamquam terr(igin)a guelfa et docere pueros et quoscumque uolentes predictam scientiam adiscere et doctrinam scribendi et legendi, tamquam fidelis et devotus uester tam ratione sanguinitatis quam amore partis prefate que Domini uigeat in onore Dei, suplicat uobis humiliter ac etiam reuerenter quatenus uobis placeat et uelitis tenere consilium et in eo facere solempniter reformari quod camerarius comunis de pecunia et auere comunis possit et debeat dare et soluere pro pensione domus quam habitauerit illam pecunie quantitatem que ipso conpsilio uidebitur et placuerit, pro docendo et instruendo pueros et alios quoscumque de scientia prelibata et releuare ipsum ab honeribus.* "In your presence . . . on the part of Giovanni teacher of the art of grammar and abacus . . . from the city of Pistoia. . . on the part of ser Giovanni notary and teacher of arithmetic or abacus . . . of the city of Pistoia and of the Guelf Party, it is related that he himself is prepared to stay in Fucecchio as a Guelf native resident and teach boys and whoever wants to learn the above-mentioned skill and subject of writing and reading, as your faithful and devoted servant both by reason of blood and for the love of the aforesaid Party (which should thrive for the honour of the Lord God); he begs you humbly and also reverently that it should be pleasing to you and you should want to deliberate and solemnly to cause to be legislated that the treasurer of the commune from the money and property of the commune can and must give and pay for the rent of the house which he inhabits that quantity of money which seems appropriate and is pleasing, for teaching and instructing boys and any others in the aforementioned skill and to exempt him from taxes."

⁹¹ See now Böninger 2006: 286–91.   ⁹² Park 1980: 302.

⁹³ Gherardi 1881: 460, 462. He is referred to as *magister scolarum* ("school teacher") in an archival document from autumn 1452: Böninger 2006: 287.

⁹⁴ ASPescia Delib. 39, fol. 264r: *Item ut supra, obtinuerunt quod ser Antonius Michaelis Cialdini notarius de Piscia capiat mansionem et stantiam in palatio d. Priorum quam uolet pro retinendis pueris, et similiter magister . . . qui docet pueros ad scribendum capiet mansionem et locum in dicto palatio quem uolet*. ("Further as above, it is provided that ser Antonio di Michele Cialdini notary from Pescia assume the duty and residence in the palace of the said Priors which he desires for accommodating boys and similarly the teacher . . . who teaches boys to write should assume the duty and place in the said palace that he desires.)

⁹⁵ Pupils could learn to write remarkably late. For example, Matteo di Matteo Strozzi had evidently already learnt to read and been through abacus school, when, at the age of fifteen in 1447, he was learning to write, as recorded by Alessandra Macinghi Strozzi (Strozzi 1987: 63): "non può esser preso per le gravezze insino a sedici anni ed egli ebbe undici di marzo. Hollo levato dall'abbaco, e appara a scrivere; e porrolo al banco, che vi starà questo verno." ("He is not subject to taxes before the age of sixteen and he was sixteen on 11 March. I have taken him away from abacus school, and he is learning to write; and I shall put in a shop to work, which will take place this winter.") Matteo was still not an experienced and fluent writer at the age of sixteen, more than a year later, as Alessandra

Teaching reading and writing in Renaissance Italy 115

The vocabulary for learning to write was idiosyncratic. The key word was "littere" – "lictere" – "lettere". This is made clear by the diary of the Florentine Tribaldo de' Rossi, describing the beginnings of his son Guarieri's writing instruction in the spring and summer of 1493. Guarieri had already learned to read *Ianua* (*donadello*) phonetically "a veduta", "al testo":

A dì 17 d'aprile 1493 fe' lasciare el donadelo a Ghuarieri. Aveva lo imparato a veduta.

On 17 April 1493 I had Guarieri stop reading Donatus. He had learned to read it phonetically.

Now his father wanted him to learn to write, and so he had his son put aside the *donadello* and begin to learn writing: here, peculiarly, the phrase he used as a synonym for "[g]li inparasi le lettere e schrivere" was "leggere le lettere":

Vo' li inparasi le lettere e schrivere; però lo fe' abandonare el donadelo e detto [dì] chominciò legier le lettere, nel nome di dio.

I want him to learn to write; so I had him stop reading Donatus and begin to write, in the name of God.

The educational activity now was centred on writing, since Tribaldo now bought his son his first pen and inkpot in order to learn how to write soon after the lessons began:

Choperai penaiuolo e'l chalamaio a Ghuarieri, el primo per chominciare a 'nparare a scrivere; chostò S. 4. D. 4.[96]

I bought a pen and an inkpot for Guarieri, the first in order for him to begin to learn to write; it cost 4 soldi 4 pence.

It seems that the phrase "leggere e scrivere" could actually mean just writing. Tribaldo de' Rossi entitled one paragraph of his *ricordanza* "A scrivere di nuovo mando Guerieri" ("I send Guarieri again to learn to write"), but the ensuing text referred to "imparare a leggere e scrivere" ("to learn to read and write"), and, since Guarieri had already learned to read the *tavola*, *salterio*

---

wrote to her son Filippo in 1448: "fo iscriverti a Matteo; e si perchè s'avvezzi a dettare un poco le lettere; ché quando iscrive adagio, e che ponga il capo a quello ha fare, iscrive bene: e così dice Antonio Strozzi, e Marco (che ho mostro loro de' fogli ch' egli scrive), che ha buona forma di lettera: quando iscrive ratto, diresti che non fussi di suo' mano; e tal differenza è da l'una a l'altra, quanto il bianco dal nero: e no gli posso tanto dire, che voglia iscrivere adagio." Strozzi 1987: 66. ("I am having Matteo write to you, so that he will get used a bit to writing; because when he writes slowly and puts his mind to what he has to do, he writes well; and Antonio Strozzi says so, and Marco [and I have shown them some sheets that he has written], that he has good handwriting, when he writes quickly, you would say it is not his hand; and there is as much difference between the one and the other as between white and black; and I cannot tell you how much he should want to write slowly.")

[96] Florence Biblioteca Nazionale Centrale (henceforth BNCF) II.ii.357, fol. 99r. See Black 2007, Appendix 5, for the full text and context.

and *donadello al testo*, the activity that this phrase described was not learning to read but learning to write:

A scrivere di nuovo mando Ghuerieri:

... lo rimando anchora a la schuola a 'nparare a legiere e scrivere.[97]

I send Guarieri again to learn to write ... I am sending him again to school to learn to write.

Reading was taught first by sounding out letters and then syllables (*tabula/carta*), and then whole words, and apparently the same technique was used to teach writing. This "building-block" approach is described by Alberti in *De pictura*:

Voglio che i giovani, quali ora nuovi si danno a dipingere, così facciano quanto veggo di chi impara a scrivere. Questi in prima separato insegnano tutte le forme delle lettere, quali gli antiqui chiamano elementi; poi insegnano le silabe; poi apresso insegnano comporre tutte le dizione.[98]

I want the young, when they first begin to paint, to do what I see when they learn to write. At first they separately learn to form letters, which the ancients called elements; then they learn syllables; then learn to compose entire words.

Latinity had a special status for Italians during the Middle Ages, Renaissance and early modern period: unlike other cultures considered in this volume, in Italy the skills of reading and, to a large extent, writing were taught through the medium of a language that was not the culture's mother tongue. In the Greek-speaking ancient world,[99] in Anglo-Saxon England,[100]

---

[97] BNCF II.ii.357, fol. 99r. See Black 2007, Appendix 5, for the full text and context.
[98] Alberti 1960–73, II: p. 94, cited by Avesani (2001: 4). [99] See Dickey in this volume.
[100] This is suggested by Fisher in this volume, where it is pointed out that Aelfric's grammar was aimed explicitly at children. See also Asser's life of King Alfred (ed. Stevenson 1959), which describes the first steps in his passage from illiteracy to literacy in terms of learning to read a book of English poetry: (22) *indigna suorum parentum et nutritorum incuria usque ad duodecimum aetatis annum, aut eo amplius, illiteratus permansit.* (23) *Cum ergo quodam die mater sua sibi et fratribus suis quendam Saxonicum poematicae artis librum, quem in manu habebat, ostenderet, ait: "Quisquis uestrum discere citius istum codicem possit, dabo illi illum." Qua uoce, immo diuina inspiratione, instinctus Aelfredus, et pulchritudine principalis litterae illius libri illectus, ita matri respondens ... inquit "uerene dabis istum librum uni ex nobis, scilicet illi, qui citissime intelligere et recitare eum ante te possit?"... Tunc ille statim tollens librum de manu sua, magistrum adiit et legit. Quo lecto, matri retulit et recitauit:* "but alas, by the shameful negligence of his parents and tutors he remained ignorant of letters until his twelfth year, or even longer. One day, therefore, when his mother was showing him and his brothers a book of English poetry which she held in her hand, she said: 'I shall give this book to whichever one of you can learn it the fastest.' Spurred on by these words, or rather by divine inspiration, and attracted by the beauty of the initial letter in the book, Alfred spoke as follows in reply to his mother ... 'Will you really give this book to the one of us who can understand it the soonest and recite it to you?'... He immediately took the book from her hand, went to his teacher and learnt it. When it was learnt, he took it back to his mother and recited it" (tr. Keynes and Lapidge [1983]).

in nineteenth- and twentieth-century France,[101] in twentieth- and twenty-first-century Britain,[102] in the United States,[103] literacy was acquired through the medium of the native language; Latin was the second, not the first literate language. Not so for Italians up to the end of the eighteenth century: the close proximity of Italian to Latin meant that literacy in Latin was a transferable skill; phonetic reading, learned through the Latin language, could be immediately applied to the vernacular. For pre-modern Italians, basic literacy in Latin opened the door to vernacular reading on a utilitarian level as well as to Italian literature.

---

[101] See Waquet in this volume.   [102] See Lister in this volume.   [103] See Kitchell in this volume.

CHAPTER 8

The teaching of Latin to the native nobility in Mexico in the mid-1500s: contexts, methods, and results

Andrew Laird

Superbum ac pene improbum cuique uidebitur, Felicissime Rex, nos omnium infimos ad te inter homines supremum regem litteras destinare, ad quem non sat firmo animo scribere solent qui uel regia dignitate uel eruditione uaria sunt insigniti. At cum nos mancipia et quidem humillima simus, et litteras siue diuinas siue humanas necdum a limine salutauerimus, annon temerarium omnino fuerit nos scribere non ad principem quemquam sed ad te talem ac tantum Regem? Vt etiam si tuos seruos ultro nos offeramus uix digni iudicemur? Qui enim aut quales sumus? Nempe pauperes, miseri, barbari, tales denique quorum praedecessores suae tempore gentilitatis fuere admodum rustici, abiecti, nudi et corporis et animae dotibus, inter quas primas habent uirtutes ac litterae, quas profecto ne per somnium quidem nouere.

Most fortunate King, it will strike anyone as proud if not ill-judged, that we, the most lowly of all, are sending a letter to you, the supreme ruler among men, to whom even those distinguished with royal rank or a range of learning do not write with too firm a resolve. But as we are vassals and indeed of the lowliest sort, and as we have not hailed the realm of letters, whether divine or human, even from the threshold, is it not wholly presumptuous for us to write to any prince, let alone to a king such as yourself, who is so great, that even if we offer ourselves as your willing slaves we may scarcely be judged worthy? Who, then, or what are we? Nothing but paupers, wretches, barbarians, such as whose predecessors were altogether rustics, abject, bare of endowments for body and soul, amongst which the virtues and letters hold first place: things they did not even know in their dreams.[1]

This is the opening of a letter addressed to Philip II of Spain in 1561 by the rulers of Azcapotzalco, a pre-Hispanic principality to the west of the Valley of Mexico. This text alone shows how, within just a few decades after the Spanish conquest of Mexico in 1521, some members of the Nahuatl-speaking native nobility had not only learned Latin, but could compose

---

[1] The original manuscript of the letter is in the Archive of the Indies in Seville: AGI Legajo, Mexico 1842. Laird 2011 presents the text with an English translation.

in it with considerable accomplishment. In the passage excerpted above the writers indicate their esteem for literacy and literature in their evocation of the Spanish humanist Antonio de Nebrija's avowal that letters are necessary "to adorn human life."[2] Later parts of the elegant composition, which runs to more than 2,000 words, contain quotations from Virgil, Horace, and Silius Italicus, and allusions to Cassius Dio and Homer.

The achievements of indigenous Latinists in sixteenth-century New Spain (as colonial Mexico was known) have been extolled rather than explained by those scholars who have drawn attention to them.[3] This discussion aims (1) to give an account of the circumstances in the 1500s which prompted missionaries, particularly the Franciscans, to teach Latin to a select number of youths from the native nobility; (2) to make some conjectures about the methods and texts that were used; and (3) to consider the historical significance of this education as well as its consequences for humanism and cultural production in the colony.

Contexts

We have received great help and much light in the implanting of the faith in these parts, from those whom we have taught the Latin language. This people did not have letters nor any characters, nor knew reading nor writing; they communicated with one another by means of images and paintings.[4]

The Franciscan ethnographer Fray Bernardino de Sahagún thus explained in the 1570s that "implanting of the faith" was the reason for providing the native Mexicans with instruction in Latin. As early as 1535, the Dominican Fray Julián Garcés, the first bishop to be consecrated in Mexico, had already praised the Mexicans' readiness to learn Latin, also explaining "they used to paint instead of write, that is, they employed pictures instead of letters" (*pingebant enim, non scribebant, id est, non litteris sed imaginibus utebantur*).[5] In 1536, the Imperial College of Santa Cruz was established in Tlatelolco, to the north of Mexico City, in order to provide "Indians" with

---

[2] Nebrija 1492, book 1, chapter 2, "On the first invention of letters": "Among all the things that men discovered through experience or divine revelation to refine and *adorn human life* [*adornar la uida umana*] ... none was so necessary as the invention of letters."
[3] Kobayashi 1974, Gil 1990, Osorio Romero 1990, Aguilar Moreno 2002, George 2009, Laird 2010.
[4] Sahagún 1982: 82.
[5] Garcés 1537, fol. 9 adduces the account of Egyptian hieroglyphs in Lucan, *De bello civili* 3.220–4. The passage, transcribed from a later sixteenth-century copy of the original text in the John Carter Brown Library cited here, is in Acuña 1995: 12.

an advanced education in Latin and the liberal arts. The foundation of the college was enthusiastically supported by the Franciscan bishop of Mexico, Fray Juan de Zumárraga, but it appears to have been first prompted by Sebastián Ramírez Fuenleal, president of the Second Audience in 1531–5 (effectively the governor of New Spain).[6]

Missionaries attached great importance to Latin in the process of evangelization because it was the language of scripture, liturgy, and the church – like the city of Rome itself, it had a spiritual significance that transcended temporal history. But Latin was also the language of the *literati*, and it remained the medium of knowledge and education in Europe, in humanist circles as well as in the seminaries and universities. Erasmus' advocation of a refined and purified *lingua*, for the propagation of the Gospel and for the unification of mankind, was as influential in Iberia as it was in northern Europe in the early 1500s.[7] From a practical point of view, Latin served the friars with a means of communicating amongst themselves: the names of many prominent educators in the early colony, such as Arnaud de Bassac, Jean Faucheur, Maturino Gilberti, Peter of Ghent, and Johann Dekkers show that by no means all of them spoke Spanish as a first language.[8] That may have lent further weight to the emphasis Franciscans in the colony placed on Christianizing rather than Castilianizing the inhabitants, in spite of the Crown's insistence from 1550 that they should do the latter – the friars objected to the conquistadors' persistent referral to Spaniards as "Christians."[9] Finally, Latin was important in another way, which was both symbolic and practical. Since Late Antiquity, Latin had been conceived scientifically, not as the source of the "natural" and therefore corruptible romance languages, but as an artificial medium, which had been refined *from* them.[10] It thus possessed a special status and was commonly referred to in Spanish and Italian as *grammatica*, "grammar." In the New World Latin continued to provide the basis for organizing and comprehending other languages, including those that were not European, in what was called the process of *reducción*.[11]

---

[6] For sources, see n. 18 below.   [7] Erasmus 1975 [1533]; Bataillon 1998 [1937]; Egido 1998.
[8] Letters from Fray Cristóbal Cabrera to Zumárraga (1540) and to a "Fray Juan" [de Lagunas?] in the Vatican library and edited in Campos 1965 show Latin was used in communications between Spanish-speaking Franciscans in the colony.
[9] Baudot 1977, cited in Duverger 1987: 178–9. Heath 1972: 12, 15–17.
[10] The idea of Latin as ancestor of romance languages still had little currency in the 1500s. The idea of Latin [*gram[m]atica*] as an artificial medium refined from romance languages presented in Dante, *De uulgari eloquentia*, remained influential: Caruso and Laird 2009: 14–15. On beliefs concerning the relationship between Latin and the romance languages, see also Fisher in this volume.
[11] Mignolo 1992, 1995; Errington 2008; Hanks 2010.

It was for these reasons that knowledge of Latin was regarded as essential for the indigenous preachers, catechists, and interpreters who were being trained to assist in the conversion and ministry of peoples in New Spain and beyond.[12] Their training was in turn deemed necessary because, prior to the conquest, the population of the entire Mexican isthmus may have been as large as twenty-seven million, among which more than a hundred different languages were spoken.[13] Even though the missionaries made impressive progress with the most commonly used Mesoamerican languages, Nahuatl and P'urhépecha (or "Tarascan"), known as *lenguas generales*, they still faced an overwhelming challenge. Some might have envisaged the formation of an indigenous clergy, although the ideological ramifications of this would have been highly controversial:

> If the conquistador was capable of accepting the existence of an indigenous clergy, if, in other words, he was capable of recognizing the Indian's prerogatives in the sphere of religion, then he had to accept him on an equal footing in civil life. If, on the other hand, the conquistador opposed this possibility, then the Indian would be relegated, as in fact he was, to the level of subordination, and consequently, servitude. The polemic about the teaching of Latin to the Indians, and especially about their access to the priesthood, was the reflection, on the superstructural level, of another more grievous reality, the reality of the conquest.[14]

In practice Indians, *mestizos* and blacks had been prohibited from entering the priesthood since the beginning of New Spain's history – and the prohibition was formalized by the First Mexican Council of 1555.[15] Moreover in Europe, the 1545 session of the Council of Trent, the institutional embodiment of the Counter-Reformation, enjoined preaching in vernaculars (*vulgares linguae*) in order to combat Protestant influence in Europe, a move which also had the unintended effect of increasing Spain's power in its colonies in relation to that of the Catholic church, and diminishing further the need for providing native catechists with more advanced instruction in Latin.[16]

These considerations have led historians to consider the Imperial College of Santa Cruz de Tlatelolco as a failure in terms of its supposed purpose: the common view is that this was to train indigenous students for the priesthood.[17] A great deal of emphasis has been placed on this relatively unlikely objective, perhaps because the college was a Franciscan institution modelled on the European seminaries in which the friars themselves had

---

[12] Laird 2010; Gray and Fiering 2000. [13] Prem 1997: 124–5 reviews recent estimates.
[14] Osorio Romero 1990: v. [15] Poole 1981. [16] Laird 2010: 174–6; Ricard 1966: 235.
[17] Steck 1944; Ricard 1966: 217–24.

been educated. Yet the idea, expressed by the institution's founder, Sebastián Ramírez Fuenleal, was only for an unspecified "great fruit" to be born from training Indian students in "good Latinity and oratory" as well as in theology (*doctrina*).[18] Bishop Zumárraga's similar proposal was made in similarly general terms.

Something that occurred towards the end of Ramírez Fuenleal's presidency suggests that there was a political dimension to this educational initiative. In 1535, five years after the last *cazonci* or king of the P'urhépecha in the western Mexican region of Michoacán had been summarily executed by the rogue conquistador Nuño de Guzmán, the *cazonci's* two young sons were taken to Mexico City as hostages by their uncle, to guarantee the loyalty of the P'urhépecha nobility. Both boys became pages to the first viceroy Antonio de Mendoza who succeeded the auditor Ramírez Fuenleal, and they received an intensive tuition in Spanish and Latin at the viceregal court.[19] On their return to Michoacán in 1538, the elder son, Francisco Tariácuri become governor of the region, to be replaced on his death by his brother Antonio de Huitziméngari – who was renowned for his ability in Greek and Hebrew as well as Latin.[20] This indicates that the motive for providing the youths of the indigenous nobility with a more advanced education was not simply religious: it must have been to create a gubernatorial class imbued with Christian humanist principles. It is significant that both the auditor Ramírez Fuenleal and the viceroy Mendoza were present, along with Bishop Zumárraga, at the inauguration of the College of Santa Cruz de Tlatelolco on the feast of Epiphany 1536.[21] Fray Bernardino de Sahagún acknowledged in the 1570s that the college had only continued to exist because of the income bequeathed from the late viceroy Mendoza's estate.[22]

Sahagún gives a full account of his experience of working in the college, with which he was closely involved for more than forty years from the time of its foundation. He recalls its origins:

After we came to this land to implant the Faith we assembled the boys in our houses as is said. And we began to teach them to read, write, and sing. And as they did well in this, we then endeavoured to put them to the study of grammar

---

[18] Fuenleal, "Carta a la emperatriz, del obispo de Santo Domingo..." (Mexico, 8 August 1533), in Paso y Troncoso 1939, vol. 3, p. 118, translated in Laird 2010: 177–8, cf. Kobayashi 1974: 292. A royal *cédula* of 1536 credited Zumárraga with the idea: Ricard 1966: 221.
[19] Franco Mendoza 2000; see further n. 20 below.
[20] Miranda Godínez 1972: 150 assembles sources for Huitziméngari's accomplishments, see further Corona Núñez 1982 and Jiménez 2002; on his ownership of Perotti's *Cornucopia*, a Latin lexicon and concordance of Martial, see Laird 2012a.
[21] Mendieta 1993 [1870]: 414–15; Torquemada 1975–83 [1615], vol. 5 (1977), p. 175 (book 25, chapter 43).
[22] Sahagún 1982: 84–5; Torquemada 1977–83 [1615], vol. 5 (1977), p. 175.

[Latin]. For this training, a college was formed in the city of Mexico, in the Santiago de Tlatilulco [*sic*] section, in which [college] were selected from all the neighbouring villages and from all the provinces the most capable boys, best able to read and write.[23]

According to Sahagún, the Spaniards and members of other religious orders found the idea very amusing, because they assumed Latin could not be taught to a people apparently so incapable: other Franciscan chroniclers relay an anecdote about a priest who was himself shown up after attempting to make fun of an Indian for his knowledge of grammar.[24] After two or three years the students came to understand every area of grammar (*todas las materias del arte de la gramática*) and knew how "to speak Latin, and understand it, and to write Latin, and even to compose hexametric verses."[25] Sahagún makes no mention of any expectation that the college might have produced a native clergy: in fact he recalls that the principal objection to the provision of this Latin education to the Indians was that it might lead them into heresy, since it was taken for granted that they were not to become priests:

To these objections it was responded that, admitting they were not to be priests, we wished to know how far their capabilities might be expanded. Knowing this from experience we could bear witness what was in them, and in accordance with their capabilities, there would be done with them what would seem to be just as nearly as possible.[26]

Sahagún is now widely regarded as an anthropologist *avant la lettre*, although his detailed researches into Aztec thoughts and beliefs were conducted in order to extirpate them. But in commenting on his work as a *lector* and teacher he owns up to a remarkable curiosity about his students' capacities: the remarks quoted above suggest that the teaching of Latin grammar to the Indians may also have been a benign kind of pedagogical or ethnological experiment.

Methods

Rote-learning of the *Pater noster, Credo, Ave Maria,* and obligatory liturgical formulae would have been inflicted on all the natives converted and

---

[23] Sahagún 1982: 82.
[24] Torquemada 1975–83 [1615], vol. 5 (1977), p. 177. Compare Motolinía 2001 [1541]: 243; Mendieta 1993 [1596], book 4, chapter 15.
[25] Sahagún 1982: 82. Alonso de Zorita remarked later in the 1500s that one fomer student Pablo Nazareo was a good Latinist, rhetorician, logician, and philosopher "and not a bad poet in every genre of [Latin] verses": Zorita 1999: 103–4.
[26] Sahagún 1982: 83.

catechized by the religious orders. The Franciscan chronicler Fray Juan de Torquemada describes two techniques that were used to induce memorization of the right words in Latin, without providing any idea of what those words meant:

> Some proceeded by counting the words of the prayer [*Oración*] they were learning with pebbles or grains of maize, putting down a stone or grain, one after the other, for each word or each group of words they were pronouncing, so for the expression or word *Pater noster* (as we say it) there was a stone, for *qui es in coelis*, another, for *santifiquetur*, another; and, afterwards, signalling with the finger they began, by means of the first stone to say *Pater noster* and then *qui es in coelis* on the prompting of the second, and they went through all of them until the end; and they used to go through this several times until the whole prayer stayed in their memory...
>
> Another way (in my view very difficult, though remarkable) was to apply the words which in their language conformed and approximated to some extent with the pronunciation of the Latin words. They put them, in order, on a sheet of paper, not as written words formed in letters, but what those words conveyed; because they did not have letters of their own but paintings, and these were interpreted as characters. This will be more easily understood by an example. The word they have that comes closest to the pronunciation of *Pater* is *pantli*, which signifies a kind of little flag and that prompts them to say *Pater*. For the second word *Noster* the term they have closest to it in pronunciation is *nuchtli*, that is the name for what our people call *tuna* [prickly pear] or "fig of the Indies" in Spain. In order to align it with the word *Noster* they paint it next in sequence to the little flag, a *tuna*, which they call *nuchtli*; and in that fashion they go on until the end of their prayer; and by a similar means they find other corresponding characters that could be understood, to memorize what they had to recite in chorus.[27]

The methods missionaries used to convey the actual *meaning* of Latin prayers were also inspired by the common use of pictograms in Mesoamerican societies. According to the Spanish Jesuit historian José de Acosta, indigenous painters were encouraged to represent the content of the Latin prayer of confession *Ego peccator confiteor Deo*; and Fray Diego Valadés, a Franciscan missionary, described in the 1570s how the natives had made confession: "Using a picture they show ways they offended God and they place stones on a symbol denoting vices or virtues to signify repetition of the same sin" (*adhibita pictura demonstrant, in quibus Deum offenderint, & calculos ad significandum eiusdem peccati iterationem, ad signum quo uitia uel uirtutes denotantur reponunt*).[28] Stratagems of this kind may have met

---

[27] Torquemada 1975–83 [1615], vol. 5 (1977): 157–9 (book 15, chapter 36).
[28] Acosta 1880, vol. 2, p. 405, cited in Gray and Fiering 2000: 5; Valadés 1579, fol. 95.

the urgent needs of evangelists but they are a far cry from what would normally be regarded as linguistic instruction.

There are, however, numerous sources attesting to the readiness and ability of young Mexicans who were properly taught Latin. In a letter to Pope Paul III, later published in Rome in 1537, Fray Julián Garcés reported that the children not only wrote in Latin as well as Spanish, but also affirmed that "they know and speak Latin more elegantly than our own, and no less than our own people who have devoted themselves to the study of this subject" (*nostris pueris elegantius Latine sciant atque loquantur: non minus quam nostri qui se eius rei studio dedidere*).[29] Yet at first sight it seems odd that not one of the chroniclers who so effusively praised the progress of the indigenous students, ever gives any intimation at all of how it was they were taught – whilst the exotic practices of communicating prayers and catechisms to the illiterate by means of mnemonic devices and pictograms were explained in great detail. That could be because the latter practices were considered more remarkable and a novelty worth reporting to those who had not witnessed it.

It can be inferred from the lack of information the friars supplied about their teaching methods – whether for inculcating rudiments of grammar or the principles of rhetoric needed for composing speeches and letters – that those methods were the same as those used for youths and children in Europe: there was no need to describe systems of imparting Latin grammar to readers who were themselves well acquainted with them. Many of the Mexican pupils already knew Castilian, as members of the indigenous nobility had had sustained contact with the Spaniards and multilingualism had been a feature of Amerindian societies in Mexico prior to the conquest.[30] At the same time, many missionaries learned Nahuatl: Peter of Ghent for example acquired a command of the Mexican *lingua franca* some time before he began teaching Latin to native children in Texcoco in the early 1520s – he later founded the College of San Jose de los Naturales in Mexico City 1527. But once communication was established, Latin was largely taught in Latin. Erasmus' elementary textbooks such as the *Colloquia familiaria* which were used all over Europe involved what teachers of English as a foreign language today call the "direct method."

---

[29] Garcés 1537, fol. 9.
[30] Gibson 1964, Lockhart 1992. However Nahuatl glosses on a handwritten copy of a 1516 edition of Nebrija's Spanish-Latin dictionary, *Vocabulario de romance en latín* (Newberry Library, Chicago: Ayer MS. 1478) appear to be by a native scribe better versed in Latin than Castilian: Clayton 1989, 2003.

The direct method was made more effective still by a strategy of linguistic immersion: Sahagún makes clear that the students in Santa Cruz de Tlatelolco "slept and ate in the college itself, not going out except on a few occasions."³¹ Fray Juan de Torquemada who was guardian of the College emphasizes that "the collegial children were raised and instructed with great care" and offers a fuller picture of the environment and education they experienced: the youths would share meals with the friars in the refectory, but they slept in different quarters on platforms of timber, each with a blanket and mat, and a lockable trunk for books and clothing. There was a light in the dormitory all night, and wardens were on duty to ensure peace and quiet as well as propriety. In the morning the students sang matins, and heard mass before attending their lessons. They were taught by the most "renowned and weighty *maestros* of Latinity, after Fray Arnaud de Bassac": Fray Bernadino de Sahagún and Fray Andrés de Olmos, who wrote the earliest surviving grammar of Nahuatl. Lectures on rhetoric, logic, and philosophy were given by Fray Juan de Gaona, Fray Francisco de Bustamente, and Fray Jean Faucheur.³² Although Torquemada does not outline the syllabuses followed, it is clear that the medieval *trivium* of grammar, rhetoric, and logic or dialectic prevalent in European schools and universities provided their framework. No mention is made of the *quadrivium* (arithmetic, geometry, astronomy, music) but there was probably instruction in these fields as well as scripture, religion, medicine, art, and music.³³

The teaching of Latin was informed by the Renaissance humanists' view of grammar, not the more philosophical "speculative" linguistics of medieval scholasticism: Erasmus' pragmatic principles of pedagogy are evident in the writings of all the early Franciscan educators (including even Sahagún), just as his practical *philosophia Christi* inspired Zumárraga's Christian activism. Erasmus' proposals for school education in the *De ratione studii* of 1512, recalled in another seminal and encyclopaedic educational treatise, *De tradendis disciplinis* (1531) by the Spaniard Juan Luis Vives, were being implemented all over Europe in order to ensure pupils had spoken and written fluency in Latin.³⁴ In 1512, Erasmus had been invited by John Colet to devise a programme for St Paul's School in London; and his disciple Vives later developed similar pedagodical prescriptions while

---

[31] Sahagún 1982: 82.
[32] Details of these figures and of their works are in Ricard 1966 and García Icazblaceta 1954 respectively.
[33] Steck 1944: 25.
[34] Baldwin 1944: 75–93 discusses the *De ratione studii* and the curriculum at St Paul's.

based in Oxford in the 1520s. In Louvain, Vives wrote the *Exercitationes linguae latinae* – a fresh edition of that work, supplemented with additional dialogues by Francisco Cervantes de Salazar, was the first Latin textbook to be printed in Mexico City in 1554.[35] Thus, the intensive kind of learning that would have been imposed in a monastic educational institution like the Imperial College of Santa Cruz de Tlatelolco is likely to have been in line with this characterization of the routine in a sixteenth-century English grammar school:

> Grammar was studied first... Gradually pupils ascended to the writing of themes on a set subject and impromptu disputations in Latin, while working through Latin literature in stages of increasing linguistic difficulty... The curriculum was not large, but the teaching was incredibly thorough... after the master's explanation the pupil would repeat it, memorize it, be asked to recite it; be tested again, repeat it, and be made to use it over and over again until there was no chance of forgetting it... School hours were from 6 a.m. till 9, then breakfast; 9.15 till 11, then lunch; 1 till 5, then supper; 6 till 7, for pure repetition, for thirty-six weeks a year for six years. First thing in the morning pupils were tested on the facts they had been given to learn the previous day.[36]

It is thus striking but not surprising that the students of the College of Santa Cruz de Tlatelolco appear to have read the same classical Latin texts as those which Erasmus had prescribed for St Paul's: at elementary level Cato's *Distichs*, Aesop's *Fables*, and Ovid's *Tristia* as a model for verse composition; with Cicero, Sallust, Horace, and Virgil for the upper school.[37]

Many more Latin works could be consulted in the college library at Santa Cruz: Zumárraga had decided to donate his own books to the college in 1537 and by 1572 there were sixty-one volumes which increased to seventy-three in 1574 – a single volume might contain a number of complete or anthologized texts.[38] The material available included devotional, patristic, and Renaissance humanist and scientific works, as well as

---

[35] García Icazbalceta 1954: 157–8.
[36] Vickers 1989: 257, epitomizing parts of Baldwin 1944 (n. 34 above).
[37] According to Torquemada 1977 [1615], vol. 5, pp. 176–7 (book 15, chapter 43), Antonio Valeriano, a former collegian, translated Cato into Nahuatl. Valeriano alluded to *Tristia* 3.1.15 in his letter to Fray Juan Bautista (n. 50 below). This and other exile poems by Ovid were in *Tam de Tristibus quam de Ponticis*, Mexico City 1577, the first anthology of classical verse published in New Spain: Osorio Romero 1984: 192–200. A Nahuatl version of Aesop was produced in the 1500s: Kutscher, Brotherston, and Vollmer 1998. A 1578 Gryphius text of Sallust, *Coniuratio Catalinae et Bellum Jugurthinum*, was in the college library; Cicero, Horace, and Virgil are widely echoed e.g. in the Azcapotzalco letter and in the native Pablo Nazareo's Latin letter to Philip II (which also quotes Ovid's *Ars amatoria*: Laird 2010, p. 186 n. 42).
[38] Mathes 1982: 25.

editions of classical authors (Caesar, Livy, Seneca) which offered models for imitation as well as edifying content. There was also a 1527 Savetier text of Quintilian, Francisco de Vergara's 1537 grammar of Greek, Nicholas Cleynaert's *Institutiones in Graecam linguam*, and even Cleynaert's *Tabula* for Hebrew. The library also possessed standard works of Latin lexicography: Johannes Balbus's *Catholicon*, Ambrogio Calepino's *Dictionarium*, Nebrija's *Vocabularium*. A vocabulary of Nahuatl, on the model of Nebrija, Fray Alonso de Molina's *Diccionario en Castellano y Mexicano* was compiled in the college itself, but only one Latin grammar is recorded – a Granada 1540 edition of Nebrija's *Introductiones latinae*. The apparent absence of curricular staples such as Horace, Ovid, or Terence is even more surprising for an institution primarily devoted to the teaching of Latin, and could reflect the influence of the northern European current of "Christian humanism."[39] It can be assumed though that the range of books that could be obtained in practice, through lending, copying or private ownership, was far greater than the inventories of 1572–4 suggest.[40]

While friars with the linguistic gifts of Sahagún or Olmos would not have needed to use grammar books for their Latin teaching, there was a strong demand for grammars in New Spain by the mid-1500s. The Latin language was being studied all over the colony – in seminaries; in various colleges founded for Indians and *mestizos* as well as those for Spanish students; and by individuals pursuing private study. In the Royal University of Mexico, which opened its doors in 1553 (to Spanish students only), Latin was the language of instruction. Yet restrictions on the import of books prior to 1540 and the prohibitive cost of this must have meant that the few printed grammars to have reached the colony were circulating between different institutions in order to be copied by hand.[41] In 1559 however, a new grammar of Latin, the *Grammatica Maturini*, was published in Mexico City by Fray Maturino Gilberti, who had published an *arte* and a vocabulary of the P'urhépecha language the previous year. A Franciscan historian Agustín de Vetancurt maintained in the late 1600s that the *Grammatica Maturini* was specifically

---

[39] George 2009: 280.
[40] This is indicated by the vast range of classical, medieval and humanist sources cited in Torquemada 1975–83 [1615] which was completed in Tlatelolco in the 1590s. The sources are indexed in volume 7 of the UNAM edition.
[41] García Icazbalceta 1954 and Griffin 1991: 105–33 treat printing in the early colony; Osorio Romero 1980: 24–54 discusses grammars and rhetorical manuals imported from Europe. The Nahuatl glosses to Nebrija's *Vocabulario de romance en latín* considered above (n. 30) were added to a manuscript copy.

designed for the indigenous students at the College of Santa Cruz de Tlatelolco.[42] There is no evidence for this (Gilberti was based in Tzintzuntzan and had probably not visited Mexico City) and any notion that such a work could be projected exclusively for the teaching of Indians – whether P'uhrépechas in Michoacán or Nahuas in central Mexico – or of Spaniards is anyway misconceived: a Latin grammar in Latin would be equally useful to both Spanish and Mexican students learning the language.

The *Grammatica Maturini* shows more concretely than any other source how Latin was presented and taught in sixteenth-century New Spain. It drew from earlier Renaissance grammars, especially those of Niccolò Perotti and Antonio de Nebrija: Gilberti's colleague Fray Francisco Beteta praises him for "plucking his flowers from all sides, like bees" (*flores undique seligens apes ceu*).[43] Like its humanist antecedents, the *Grammatica Maturini* was designed to be practical. But it is a trimmer, clearer work, with no digressions, annotations or tedious enumerations of usage in ancient sources. Theory is eschewed altogether: not even *grammatica* is defined – its constituent *partes* are simply listed with illustrations in the opening sentence of the work.[44] Definitions of the parts of speech (ultimately derived from the ancient grammarians Donatus or Priscian) are given very briefly; terms like "declension" and "conjugation" are not defined at all.

Maturino Gilberti's aim, expressed in his dedication, was "to open up a route by which students might ascend almost to the summit of Grammar without squandering too much time" (*aperire uiam, qua citra tanti temporis iacturam Grammatices pene fastigium tenerent*). The contents, ascending in degrees of difficulty, are arranged to be of use to readers at different stages in their study of Latin. The work is in seven parts, the first five roughly corresponding to the five books of Nebrija's *Introductiones Latinae*: the eight parts of speech; agreement; gender, declension and conjugation; construction and "government" (*regimen*) of the verb and the eight parts of speech; accent and quantity. Elegant as well as correct language would have been a prerequisite for that ascent to the *Grammatices fastigium*, and matters of style are treated in the final two parts of the work. The sixth section is on "adornment" (*De ornatu linguae latinae*) and the seventh part

---

[42] Vetancurt 1697.   [43] Laird 2012a; Beteta in Gilberti 2003 [1559], fol. iv.
[44] "There are four parts of grammar, namely the letter, such as *a, b, c*; the syllable, such as *ba, be*; the word, such as *Pater*; and speech [*oratio*] such as *Pater noster qui es in caelis*." The Italian humanist grammarian Perotti had begun his *Rudimenta grammatices* with the *Pater Noster*: Laird 2012a.

is entitled "Some Exercises and Formulae for Greeting, Taking Leave, and Making Enquiries, for Pupils of the Latin language drawn from Erasmus of Rotterdam and other learned authors" (*Quaedam pro pueris linguae Latiné salutandi, ualedicendi, percontandi exercitamenta ac formulae ex Erasmo Roterodamo aliisue doctissimis*).

Gilberti had also incorporated excerpts from Erasmus' works into earlier parts of the grammar: the fourth section on construction amounts to a transcription of the Dutch humanist's guide to Latin syntax, *Libellus de octo orationis partium constructione* first published in 1513, although Nebrija's rules and terminology are retained in a couple of places.[45] Gilberti often uses his examples of recommended Latin usage to praise Erasmus himself:

For expressing praise, the verbs *praesto, floreo, polleo, exupero, antecello* are elegant, as in: *Pollet Erasmus latinitate* ("Erasmus excels in his Latinity") or *latinitatis gloria* ("in renown for his Latinity").[46]

The Erasmian material in the seventh part of the *Grammatica Maturini* is from *Colloquia familiaria* (1518), *De conscribendis epistolis* (the celebrated treatise on composing letters); the *Duplici copia uerborum ac rerum commentari*, "Notes on the double resource of words and themes" (1512); and also *Epitome in Elegantias Laurentii Vallae*, in which Erasmus reworked Valla's foundational study on Latin expression. Many of the oratorical and epistolary formulae transmitted by Gilberti in this final part of his grammar coincide with those employed in the Azcapotzalco letter and in texts by other native authors.[47] The *Grammatica Maturini* was not alone responsible for the diffusion of Erasmus' prescriptions on Latinity in New Spain: Erasmian linguistic pedagogy had such a pervasive influence in the early colony that it even informed missionaries' attempts to refine their command of indigenous languages to establish an *eloquium commune* for propagation of the gospel.[48]

---

[45] The instances noted by Lucas González in Gilberti 2003 [1559]: 62–3 are at 72v and 82v. At 72v Nebrija is invoked by name to authorize the use of the genitive after the impersonal verbs *interest* and *refert*, Gilberti retains Nebrija's terms *gerundum subtantiuum* and *gerundum adjectiuum*, resisting Despauterius' distinction between gerund and gerundive preferred by Erasmus.

[46] Gilberti 2003 [1559], fol. 123v.

[47] Compare e.g. Antonio Cortés Totoquihuaztli's letter of 1 December 1552 to Emperor Charles v in the Archive of the Indies: AGI Patr. 184,45.

[48] These opinions are clearly expressed in *Fray Maturino Gylberti al yllustrissimo y reverendissimo señor don Vasco de Quiroga: Dedicatoria* in Gilberti 2004 [1558], 58; see further Laird 2012a. Compare the Prologue of Molina 1944 [1571]; in the early 1600s Molina was praised in the *Séptima relación*, 219v–220r of the native chronicler Chimalpahin Quauhtlehuanitzin for finding Spanish correspondences to Nahuatl "with accuracy, with rectitude, with order [*neltilichtica, tlamellauhca, tlatecpanalixtica*]."

Results

It might be imagined that the Franciscan chroniclers were disingenuously exaggerating their pupils' accomplishments simply because their order stood to lose much ground if the venture of educating youths of the native nobility had not proved successful, given the controversies and expenditure it involved. However, the writings in Latin by Mexicans in mid-1500s provide direct and conclusive evidence that the friars did succeed, and some of that output was known outside Franciscan circles in the early colony: in 1554 the lay Spanish humanist Francisco Cervantes de Salazar, professor of rhetoric at the Royal University of Mexico, described the "Indian" Antonio Valeriano as being "in no way inferior to our own Latin grammarians ... and very devoted to cultivating eloquence" (*nostris grammaticis nequaquam inferiorem ... et ad eloquentiam auidissimum*). Some years later Cervantes also attested to the P'urhépecha Huitziméngari's ability to write elegantly in Latin as well as in Spanish.[49]

Most of the known Latin documents penned by members of the indigenous nobility, including Pedro de Montezuma, Antonio Cortés Totoquihuaztli, and Pablo Nazareo, were petitions to the crown for titles, pensions, restitution of lost land, or requests made in the interests of the wider communities they led. A more personal letter from Antonio Valeriano to Fray Juan Bautista accompanied a now lost translation made by the Azcapotzalcan scholar – probably from Latin to Nahuatl.[50] A translation that *is* extant was made in 1552 by Juan Badiano, a collegian from Tlatelolco: the *Libellus de medicinalibus indorum herbis* was a rendering of a Nahuatl herbal originally authored by another Mexican, Martín de la Cruz. Taken together, the texts by native Mexican Latinists produced between 1540 and 1580 share characteristics which distinguish them from the Latin compositions by Europeans in New Spain during the same period: the petitionary letters contain a good deal of genealogical and chronological information about pre-Hispanic Mexico; they include Nahuatl words and names, sometimes explaining their meanings or etymologies; and they can display structures and idioms that are more characteristic of Nahuatl courtly speech than of humanist epistolary

---

[49] Cervantes de Salazar 1554, fol. 267 r. and 1971, p. 282 col. 1 (book 6, chapter 28). See nn. 19 and 20 above.
[50] The letter was quoted in Fray Juan Bautista's Prologue to his *Sermonario en lengua mexicana* published in Mexico City by Diego López Davalos in 1606 and transcribed in García Icazbalceta 1954: 474–8.

Latin.⁵¹ It is also notable that pagan authors of classical antiquity were quoted or echoed more frequently in these letters than they were in the vernacular writings of the Franciscans.

The native Latinists had an early and enduring influence on the particular character of Latin humanism produced by Spaniards and *criollos* ("creoles," American-born Spaniards) in New Spain. Cervantes de Salazar's accommodation of Nahuatl vocabulary in a dialogue printed in 1554 is worth quoting for its striking resemblance to the hybrid Latin of *Libellus* produced by the native Badiano only two years earlier:

Semina item, uari[a]e uirtutis exposita sunt, qualia sunt chia, guahtli, herbarumq[ue] & radicum prostra[n]t mille genera, nam iztacpatli a phlegmate purgat: tlalcacaguatl, & izticpatli a febri liberant. culuzizicaztli, capitis grauedine[m] leuat, ololiuhqui, ulcera & latentia uulnera.

Seeds of various virtues are on display, such as *chía*, *guahtli* and a thousand kinds of herbs and roots are laid out; thus *iztacpatli* purges phlegm; *tlalcacaguatl* and *izticpatli* relieve fever; *culuzizicaztli* eases head catarrh; *olilouhqui* heals ulcers and internal injuries.

Whilst Nahuatl words for specifically Mexican commodities naturally passed into Spanish, it is remarkable that they could intrude into a Latin set text authored by a devotee of Vives for use in a university to which only Spaniards were admitted. More remarkable still is the fact that this could occur at a time when European humanists were striving to avoid contamination of their Latin diction with vocabulary from any vernacular language. Seventeenth- and eighteenth-century creole humanists in New Spain took evident delight in employing Nahuatl names and terms in Latin literary discourse, even fitting them into poetic hexameters. The accomplishments of the native Latinists also acquired symbolic importance for creole patriots in the 1700s who sought to affirm the richness of Mexico's cultural and classical heritage in the face of disparaging polemics from European intellectuals.⁵² And the classical learning of the collegians may well have inspired the comparisons between pre-Hispanic Mexico and ancient Rome made by native

---

[51] Compare the final lines quoted from the 1561 Azcapotzalco letter (p. 118 above) to the words in a contemporaneous Nahuatl text which Sahagún (1986 [1564]: 148) attributed to a prestigious group of Aztec priests: "Are we perchance something? Since we are only the poor class of the people, we are full of earth, of mud, we are ragged ones, we are wretches, we are infirm ones, we are afflicted ones..." For a similar effect in Badiano's Latin translation of Cruz's preface to the 1552 *Libellus*, see Laird 2010: 191–4.
[52] Laird 2012b.

chroniclers of the following generation including Fernando Alvarado Tezózomoc and Fernando de Alva Ixtlilxóchitl.[53]

Yet none of the Latin writings by indigenous scholars were printed in New Spain during the 1500s and they remained unpublished until the twentieth century. Even the Cruz-Badiano *Libellus* – though it was finely illustrated, dedicated to Francisco Mendoza (son of the viceroy), and passed from the Royal Library of Spain to the Vatican – only became widely known after English and Spanish translations appeared in the 1940s.[54] While more recent accounts of classical humanism in New Spain have continued to lay emphasis on these outputs in Latin and while the genealogies and other information they contain are of interest to specialists in pre-Hispanic Nahua society, the texts in themselves are of limited significance for colonial history. The publication of numerous Christian *Doctrinas* and *Sermonarios* in Nahuatl and other Amerindian languages following the establishment of a press in Mexico City in 1539 show that translation *from* Latin was by far the most conspicuous and highly valued outcome of the natives' acquisition of the language. The missionaries could not have produced these texts (or assessed them for their accuracy) without the help of Mexican collaborators. Pablo Nazareo, the native rector of the College of Santa Cruz de Tlatelolco, explained in his 1556 letter to Philip II that he "toiled to the utmost night and day, to translate into my mother tongue the Gospels and Epistles which are read in church over the course of the entire year." (*Sic noctes diesque summopere laboraui ut, que per anni totius discursum in Ecclesia leguntur, Euangelia et epistolas in linguam maternam traducerem.*)[55]

It should therefore be emphasized that the most important consequence of the indigenous scholars' training in Latin was not their contribution to colonial Latin literature, but the preservation and creation of literature in Nahuatl. Letters of the alphabet, literacy, and literature, secular and sacred, had been introduced almost all at once to the Franciscans' native pupils. From the perspective of those pupils, letters were inextricably bound up with Latin, or *grammatica*, a term which was known to be a cognate of the Greek words *gramma*, "letter" and *graphein*, "to write" or "to draw."[56]

---

[53] Alvarado Tezózomoc 1998 [1598]: 12–13; Alva Ixtlilxóchitl 1997 [1600–8]: 269–71 makes chronological comparisons between events in late antique Rome, Spain, and the Toltec capital of Tula.
[54] Clayton, Guerrini, and de Ávila 2009 treat the early European reception of the *Libellus*.
[55] Nazareo, letter of 11 February 1556 to Philip II in Osorio Romero 1990: 3.
[56] Irvine 2006; see also n. 10 above. The Greek etymology of *grammatica* may also explain the associative connection between Latin and native pictograms in Sahagún, Garcés, and other sources: nn. 4 and 5 above.

A fascination with the idea of *litterae* is evident from the Azcapotzalco letter quoted at the opening to this chapter: its authors were clearly struck by the unity underlying the term's different meanings. As Sahagún implied, it was really through learning of Latin that some members of the indigenous elite acquired the ability to record (or create) Nahuatl texts by means of the Roman alphabet, and thus to preserve (or at least interpret) their autochthonous traditions and forms of knowledge.[57] Moreover, Sahagún regularly signalled his debt to native Latinists for their assistance with the various redactions of his *Historia general* and with his *Coloquios*, even though both works were actually produced in Nahuatl and Spanish.[58] Other early colonial texts in Nahuatl, including the corpus of poems known as the *Cantares mexicanos*, the *Kalendario Mexicano, Latino y Castellano* and, not least, the *Çaçanillatolli ynquitlali ce tlamatini ytoca Esopo*, "The fable discourses composed by the wise man named Aesop," show, to varying degrees, evidence of their authors' capacities in Latin.[59]

Fray Juan de Torquemada summarized the beneficial outcomes of the education provided at Santa Cruz de Tlatelolco in his response to the argument that the Indians' knowledge of Latin "would be of no actual use to the republic." First, the friars acquired perfect knowledge of the Mexican language from the Latinists whom they had taught, and were thus able to translate works on doctrine and other religious treatises into Nahuatl, and to ensure they were printed correctly. Secondly, the Indians' knowledge of Latin enabled them to help the missionaries, in scrutinizing the legitimacy of marriages and in the administration of the sacraments. Thirdly, the Indians were appointed as judges and governors: "They did this better than others, as they were men who read, know and understand." Torquemada then elaborates on this point citing the example of Antonio Valeriano. His training in Latin, logic, and philosophy enabled him to be governor of the Indians of Mexico City for more than thirty-five years, securing the "the acclaim of the viceroys and the edification of the Spaniards." Again, there is no mention of any expectation that the students might have entered the priesthood, adding weight to the suggestion made

---

[57] Sahagún 1982: 82.
[58] Sahagún 1982, 55: "In all of [the siftings of my book] my collaborators were collegians expert in grammar [*gramatica*]. The principal and most learned of them was Antonio Valeriano, of Atzcapotzalco, and Alonso Vegerano of Cuauhtitlan; another was Martín Jacobita. I should add Pedro de San Buenaventura. All three were expert in three languages: Latin, Spanish, and Indian." Compare Sahagún 1986: 75.
[59] These texts were all copied in a single manuscript in the National Library of Mexico (BNM Ms. 1628) dating from the sixteenth or seventeenth century. Bierhorst 1985, Iguíniz 1918, and Kutscher, Brotherston, and Vollmer 1998 are editions of the individual works.

earlier in this chapter that the collegians' advanced education was really intended from the outset to prepare them for a career in public service, not the church. That would account for the greater emphasis on grammar, rhetoric, and philosophy than on theology in the curriculum, and it might also explain the propensity of Mexican Latinists to cite both classical and Christian sources in their writings.

CHAPTER 9

Ut consecutivum *under the Czars and under the Bolsheviks*

Victor Bers

In Chekhov's *Three Sisters*, Kulygin, a schoolteacher in the provincial town that his wife and her sisters long to escape, reflects with pleasure on the destiny that put him in the classroom:

> Fate is different for different people... In the excise office here there is a clerk called Kozirev. He was a fellow student of mine, and he was expelled from the fifth form because he could not understand the "ut consecutivum" in Latin. Now he's dreadfully poor, he's ill, and whenever I meet him I say to him "Good morning, ut consecutivum." "Yes," he says, "that's just it, consecutivum," and then he coughs... But for me, I've had good fortune all my life, I'm happy, I even have the Stanislav medal of the second class, and I teach others this very same thing, the "ut consecutivum." Of course I'm clever, cleverer than so many others... (trans. G.R. Ledger)[1]

This is one, fictional – and dismal – face of classical pedagogy. In the real Russian world, classical education of the young sometimes crossed paths with distinguished scholarship, though not often in the same era. Mikhail Ivanovich Rostovtsev (sometimes spelled *Rostovtzeff*), a numinous presence at Yale, where he taught from 1925 until 1944, had like many other important European scholars up to our own day worked as a high school teacher. Long before emigrating, Rostovtsev taught Latin in Russia's most famous school, the Imperial Lyceum, founded in 1810 by Alexander I at Tsarskoe Selo, just outside St. Petersburg.[2] Its most famous graduate was Pushkin, for whom the town is now named; Rostovtsev also taught at the Bestuzhevski Kursi, an institution for women, who were not yet admitted

---

The reader is notified that my interest in the topic is far more personal than professional (see n. 3), and that I have leaned heavily on colleagues in assembling this essay. My greatest debts are to Vasily Rudich and Alexander Gavrilov, both for substance and for translation from Russian. Two articles by Gavrilov deserve special mention: Gavrilov 1995 and 2002–8. Quoted translations are in each case attributed to their source.

[1] www.oxquarry.co.uk/Act4.htm (accessed 27 June 2013).
[2] The Lyceum was moved to St. Petersburg in 1843, where it survived until 1918.

to St. Petersburg University. Among his early students was Krupskaya, Lenin's wife;[3] at the university, Rostovtsev taught Alexander Kerensky, prime minister after the February Revolution. Kerensky writes that Rostovtzeff, "still very young at the time . . . thrilled us with his accounts of the Greek towns that flourished on the Black Sea before the birth of Rus (Ancient Russia) . . . His lectures on this pre-Russian world . . . clearly demonstrated that the roots of democracy in Ancient Rus went back much farther than had been thought, and that there was some connection between early Russian statecraft and the ancient Greek republics."[4] That sort of talk could have been seen by political authorities of the time as more than a stirring cliché.

To some degree, the Russian experience of classical pedagogy, admirable *and* repellent, resembles its counterpart in western Europe. In the thirty-first chapter of Samuel Butler's *Way of All Flesh*, the schoolboy, often punished by being made to copy out lines of Virgil, tells himself, "Latin and Greek is great humbug; the more people know of it the more odious they generally are; the nice people whom you delight in either never knew any at all or forgot what they had learned as soon as they could; they never turned to the classics after they were no longer forced to read them; then they are nonsense, all very well in their own time and country, but out of place here."[5] Vladimir Nabokov's father, a great liberal politician, thought of his gymnasium Latin teacher as "a half-witted despot [who] drummed in along with his wretched Latin a deep hatred and disgust of the subject, drying up our minds, killing [in his students] any interest in classical antiquity." Accordingly, he sent Vladimir and his other son to a school without Greek and Latin.[6] The elder Nabokov's hatred of his Latin teacher was not just a matter of an individual's bad luck, since the dominance of Latin in the curriculum and the emphasis on grammar were a pan-Russian phenomenon, owing to the extreme centralization of the system. As Minister of Education, one man, Count Dmitri Tolstoy (very distantly related to the novelist), imposed a curriculum quite deliberately meant to

---

[3] Another Rostovstev student at the Bestuzhevski Kursi was my paternal grandmother, one of the Jewish women whose presence in this city outside the Pale of Settlement was facilitated either by bribing the police or registering as a prostitute. My grandmother chose the first method as more expensive, but distinctly more dignified. Satina 1966: 101–9 gives a brief description of the academic and political atmosphere of this institution. In his brief overview of the limited educational opportunities offered women and girls under Dmitri Tolstoy (see pp. 141–3 below), Hans 1964: 127–31 remarks that "the first College for women in England – Girton College at Cambridge" was founded in the same year as the "first Russian Higher Courses for Women," and that no other European country could claim similar institutions.

[4] Quoted at Wes 1992: 20.   [5] Butler 1992: 118.   [6] Boyd 1993: 26, 87.

sustain imperial rule.⁷ Alexander Gavrilov gives an example of the sort of thing that "had to be memorized by every person aspiring to enter university: the genitive plural of χρήστης has a paroxytone accent to distinguish it from the genitive plural of χρηστός."⁸ Adherence to his ministry's commands was enforced by inspectors throughout the empire. Some schools run by churches or restricted to the nobility were exempt from this control, but in the main there was a uniformity in classroom practice far beyond the homogenizing effects achieved by standard university entrance exams in western Europe, where those were imposed. In Russia, as often happens elsewhere, language teaching can carry heavy ideological baggage.⁹ In this case, the baggage includes the very late acknowledgment and cultivation of the mother tongue. French was the *lingua franca* of the upper class, so one can really say that a Russian might regard learning Russian as "learning *their* language," that is, the language of the lower orders.¹⁰ Pushkin himself learned Russian mostly from household servants and his maternal grandmother. And of course that was in the Orthodox East, not the Catholic West, with its direct descent from Rome and its language. Going back even further than Peter the Great, who is often credited with "initiatives" that began classical philology in Russia, there was what we might call, in Plato's phrase, an "ancient quarrel" between Russia *per se* and the Ukraine, in particular the city of Novgorod, which is sometimes regarded as a medieval hotspot of democracy and rationalism. From the Slavophile point of view dominant in Moscow, Latin in its broadest cultural sense, *Latinstvo*, was associated with the dangers posed to Russia by Jesuits, Poles, and Lithuanians. In the mid-seventeenth century, the teaching of Latin was seen as a presage of the arrival of the Antichrist. By a sort of extended metonymy, syphilis was called "the Latin disease."¹¹

But in time, and for a variety of reasons, Russia had within its borders a number of influential humanists, persons with a grounding in the classical past, some of whom managed to exploit classical texts in the adulation of the Czar and the justification of his rule (a good example is Simeon Polotsky, a Ukrainian who enjoyed the patronage of Czar Aleksei, Peter's

---

[7] For Tolstoy's attempts to support the autocracy through his educational policies, cf. Alston 1969: 77–104 and Sinel 1973, *passim*.
[8] Gavrilov 1995: 63.
[9] Cf. in this volume Kitchell's discussion of the debate over what sort of education suited emancipated slaves and their progeny.
[10] Cf. Black in this volume, pp. 103–4: "A curious fact in the history of Italian..."
[11] Wes 1992: 21.

father).¹² The Czars themselves drew closer to Athens and Rome. Peter the Great did this – and of course much else – in an especially spectacular style. Among the many consequences of Peter's obsession with Holland, where he traveled incognito, was an influx of books printed there for the Russian market. These included a Latin grammar, in Latin, with an accompanying Russian translation, editions of Aesop's *Fables* in Latin and Russian, and the *Batrachomyomachia*. Peter's successor Catherine the Great is reported to have read Tacitus, and a celebration in her honor drew on Trajan's column and its iconography; also, on Virgil, *Eclogue* 4.6 *iam redit et Virgo, redeunt Saturnia regna*, though virgo she certainly was not. Her desire to expel the Turk from Constantinople was grounded, at least in propaganda, on her desire to redress the Turkish destruction of classical Greece.¹³

Through the eighteenth century, elementary education of aristocratic children was to a large degree administered at home by French tutors, among them Jesuit priests. The hero's tutor in Pushkin's *Eugene Onegin*, M. L'Abbé, may have been typical in diluting his pedagogy. The poem says, he "taught him all things in play, bothered him not with stern moralization." One consequence was Onegin's superficial knowledge of Latin. "In French impeccably he could express himself and write," but "Latin has gone at present out of fashion; still, to tell you the truth, he had enough Latin to make out epigraphs, expatiate on Juvenal, put at the bottom of a letter *vale*, and he remembered, though not without fault, two lines from the *Aeneid*." "Theocritus and Homer he disparaged, but read, in compensation, Adam Smith, and was a deep economist... His father could not understand him, and mortgaged his lands" (1.3, 6, 7 trans. V. Nabokov¹⁴). Pushkin's school was the Lyceum, or "lycée," an institution not just in its name molded far more along French than German lines. This was a school meant to train successive generations of the uppermost crust. Remarkably, the school operated without corporal punishment. Pushkin himself learned small Latin – and no Greek whatsoever. Nevertheless, he read classical texts voraciously, but in French translations. His feeling for Greek and Latin literature was profound, as can be seen in his *Monumentum*, a remarkable poem that takes off – and soars far away from – Horace 3.30. American classicists might call Pushkin the Poster Boy

---

¹² Wes 1992: 18–19, 25–7.
¹³ On Peter's and Catherine's classical enthusiasms, cf. Wes 1992: 8–67. For a discussion of how Petrov's first translation of the *Aeneid* into Russian exhibits marks of Catherine's "cultural politics," see Torlone 2011, esp. pp. 4f.
¹⁴ Pushkin 1964: 96, 98.

for the "Classical Civilization" major, where the study of Greek and Latin is given less, sometimes far less, emphasis than in traditional programs.[15]

Less glamorous than the Lyceum, yet of far wider importance, was Alexander I's evolving educational program for the entire country. A basic theme was an emphasis on the training and refinement of the students' intellects, rather than on the indiscriminate consumption of information. Classics, with Greek and Latin accorded equal roles, was seen as one of the few subjects that contributed to that aim by balancing logic and memorization. The other component was mathematics.[16] Here one sees the powerful influence of the German, more particularly Prussian, models advocated by Wilhelm Humboldt and others, but with a significant difference summarized by Brower: "Had the Russian schools performed as smoothly, they could easily have enjoyed the same rights as in Germany. But in Russia, educational spontaneity came to be associated in the minds of the political leaders with revolt."[17] When Alexander's death in 1825 precipitated the Decembrist Revolt against his successor, Czar Nicholas I regarded the home-schooling of the aristocracy and the relaxed tenor of boarding schools as working a subversive influence.[18] The Charter of 1828 made formal education a prerequisite for entering the civil service; Latin and mathematics dominated, but Greek fell to the side. The Czar allowed this policy, against the advice of many. The Minister of Education who worked to undo this error, Sergei Uvarov, makes an unappetizing ally for Hellenism: he was a reactionary ideologue, determined to make the schools buttress "the three pillars of the Russian state... orthodoxy, autocracy, and nationality."[19] Third, parity between the languages was never achieved, in part because there were too few qualified teachers of Greek, in part because a shift in 1849 maintained a requirement in Latin, even for those who planned to enter the university for training in practical subjects, leaving Greek as a mandatory subject only for those aiming for the philosophical division. Even worse, the revolutions of 1848 across

---

[15] For Pushkin's classical education and later relationship with the classics, cf. Wes 1992: 146–72.
[16] Cf. Waquet in this volume on the intellectual and moral advantages of a Latin education, namely a better knowledge of French, a better understanding of foreign languages, the development of logic and reasoning. And: "Around this time, the head mistress of the high school of Nevers voiced the same opinion: 'our students are intuitive, clever and spontaneous but, unlike boys, without coherence, thought and method. Latin can help girls acquire these qualities, by forcing them to slowly decipher other people's thoughts down to the most minute details'" (Maisani 1925: 424/ p. 152 below).
[17] Brower 1970: 129.
[18] Cf. Alston 1969: 31 on mistrust of aristocratic education at this time (citing the views of Pushkin).
[19] Sinel 1973: 15. On the policies of Uvarov, see in general Alston 1969: 33–41, Sinel 1973: 15–23, Wes 1992: 112–27.

Europe seemed to the Czar an indication that study of the ancient Greeks and Romans encouraged free thinking and republicanism.[20] In 1864 the gymnasia were divided into the classical sort and the "real-gymnasia"; the curriculum of the latter was composed of practical subjects, French, and German, but this arrangement did not bring harmony to the reign of Alexander II, Czar from 1855 to 1881. (Alexander II is best known to Americans for emancipating the serfs and selling Alaska to the United States.) A notable aspect of his reign was a passionate debate on educational reform – passionate because it reached deeply into the argument over the nature of Russia itself. Ideologies of earlier days became confused, as Slavophiles and westerners, "idealists" and "utilitarians," scientists and humanists took up surprising positions on the meaning and value of classical education.[21] I have mentioned the view of classics as potentially subversive, but it was a conservative, Mikhail Katkov, who insisted that classical education was a vehicle Russia could ride to a new status as a truly European country.[22] Konstantin Ushinksky (1824–70), Russia's most famous writer on pedagogy and a champion of the Russian language, saw classics differently, as incompatible with the Russian national character: "The study of the classical languages is to us a specialty necessary only for some kinds of learned occupations."[23] The revolutionary Dmitri Pisarev, a man famous for his disdain for Pushkin, rejected classical education as a waste of time: "To learn two languages in order to be able to read in the original two poems and four historical works, of which excellent translations exist – that, whatever you may say, is a heroic act of self-denial, which may be undertaken by free decision, but why make it compulsory for innocent pupils?"[24] In 1866, participation by students of the non-classical gymnasia in the attempt to assassinate Alexander II was seen by the authorities as showing that the time had come to elevate classical education to a dominance even beyond what it had under Uvarov.[25]

Onto the stage comes Dmitri Tolstoy, the new Minister of Education. He does not stride, but sidle in, knowing there would be fierce opposition to his program. Under the Charter of 1871, the *realgymnasium* was demoted

---

[20] Sinel 1973: 20–3.   [21] On the educational debate under Alexander II, cf. Sinel 1973: 130–70.
[22] For Katkov, cf. Alston 1969: 78–91.
[23] Hans 1963: 75. For Ushinsky's views on classical education, see also Alston 1969: 88–92.
[24] Quoted in Hans 1963: 123. For more general treatments of Pisarev, see Lampert 1965 and Pozefsky 2003.
[25] For the assassination attempt as a catalyst for the promotion of classical learning in the gymnasia, cf. Morrison 1969, Alston 1969: 78–91, Sinel 1973: 35ff.

to the level of a lower school, and the word *gymnasium* was now reserved to institutions preparing students for university with instruction in the two classical languages and mathematics (basically the curriculum of the state-funded high school described in this article's last paragraph).

Tolstoy was strategically deft, yet he reveals an interesting bias in stating the basis of his policy: "The choice between a classical course and other academic programs as the basis for all higher education is not only a choice between serious and superficial teaching, but also a choice between moral and materialistic instruction, and thus concerns all society. In fact, study ... can either act upon all aspects of the human spirit, enriching and ennobling it (as does the study of the classical languages and their literature) or it can educate students one-sidedly and influence neither their moral nor their aesthetic development, but turn their attention prematurely and exclusively to political and social questions ... the nature of the classical languages and also of much of mathematics is such that teachers can continually verify the students' knowledge of these subjects, ... while they find it almost impossible to check their pupils' understanding of all other disciplines, and particularly of the natural sciences; and this explains both the growth of egotism and the formation of the most erroneous concepts."[26]

This narrow-minded and arrogant manifesto was not mere bluster. Students certainly learned *something* from the grammatical exercises and composition, some of it done *ex tempore* from Russian into Greek and Latin, or Greek into Latin, or *vice versa*, but the portion of their time devoted to these exercises was bound to create the antipathy that made Nabokov's father find something better for his sons. And besides the arid, grotesquely narrow curriculum, Tolstoy's program sought to enforce its moral desiderata by creating the position of "class manager" or "mentor," whose responsibility was to supervise the students' public, and sometimes private, behavior. The notions of proper behavior, which included a stern prohibition on walking in public with one's hands in one's pockets, were enforced, with increasing frequency, by corporal punishment.[27] This practice brings to mind the legendary prominence of τύπτω in teaching Greek, or the sadistic practices of teachers in *kheders*, the traditional Jewish elementary schools. A majority of these martinet "class managers" were instructors of Greek and Latin. With friends like that, who needs enemies?

---

[26] Sinel 1973: 145.
[27] On Tolstoy's educational policies, see in general Sinel 1973, esp. pp. 130–213 on the importance of classical languages in Tolstoy's blueprint for gymnasia.

Very few descendants of serfs, very few girls, very few Jews, could aspire to gymnasium education, such as it was.[28] And in the provinces, the picture was bleaker for everyone. It was bad enough that Kulygin, proud master of *ut consecutivum*, was cuckolded; one must also doubt that he had any knowledge of ὥστε *consecutivum*. Despite this miserable backdrop of compulsion and rigidity, many of the Russians who could go to gymnasia, especially in St. Petersburg and Moscow, came away with great intellectual, and sometimes emotional, strengths.[29] One sees that in extraordinary scholars educated before the 1917 Revolution like Rostovtsev (1870–1952), Vyacheslav Ivanov (1866–1949), and Tadeusz Zielinski (1859–1944); Mikhail Bakhtin (1895–1975), one of the few classicists well known in the wider world of literary scholars, was Zielinski's student; two of the greatest Russian poets, Osip Mandelstam (1891–1938) and Anna Akhmatova (1889–1966), were both strongly influenced by Innokenti Annensky (1855–1909), Greek teacher at the Lyceum and himself a poet (his *oeuvre* takes death as its exclusive theme).

The second part of the story my title promises can be much shorter. As Alexander Gavrilov puts it in an essay published by the American Philological Association, "A system that had its deficiencies, but served as a basis of solid culture, was partially dismantled ... by the beginning of the [twentieth] century, and remained in a primarily defensive posture... The old gymnasium, though not entirely inaccessible to the lower classes, certainly favored the upper ones. It was only logical ... that the Bolsheviks destroyed the system with the thoroughness of which only they were capable. The execution was theirs, the project was not."[30]

Though the Bolsheviks eliminated Greek and Latin from the secondary schools, at the university and institute level some aspects of classical antiquity were still pursued, and indeed with great expertise, particularly in the archaeology of the Black Sea colonies; but the field as a whole suffered immeasurably from crude ideological control, and I think it must be said that in the post-Soviet period literary studies and social history still get less attention than strict philology, history of science, and the like. But expertise in classical languages did not utterly disappear in Soviet times, and this happy fact can be seen in the high philological standard of Russian scholars trained in that era and now training younger people

---

[28] Cf. Waquet in this volume on the education of girls in France: "Charles Rollin, rector of the University of Paris ... whether they should be taught Latin" (pp. 145–6 below).
[29] Soon after the start of the twentieth century Greek was taught only in a single gymnasium in each of the cities of St. Petersburg, Moscow, Warsaw, Kiev, Odessa, and Riga: Alston 1969: 166.
[30] Gavrilov 1995: 63–4.

who, in turn, train secondary school children. The portion of the story I know best from autopsy is a public institution in St. Petersburg, the Gymnasium Classicum Petropolitanum (*alias* "School Number 610"), founded in 1989 during the last days of *perestroika*. The Gymnasium teaches classics, including substantial Greek and Latin, and mathematics. Here I saw thirteen-year-old children get a precise first lesson in the optative, and then heard them in the cafeteria happily chattering about this interesting feature of the language as they ate their lunches. τοιαῦτα γένοιτο καὶ ἡμῖν.

CHAPTER 10

Latin for girls: the French debate

Françoise Waquet

It was only in 1925 that high school girls in France finally gained access to the same Latin classes as boys. Public high schools (*collèges* and *lycées*) for girls had already been established in 1880, but they offered only a modern curriculum, without Latin. At the end of their studies, girls obtained a diploma of limited value and prestige, which did not grant them access to higher education. To attend university, one needed a baccalaureate (*baccalauréat*), a diploma obtained at the end of the male high school curriculum, and this required Latin.

In this article, I want to address the circumstances and the reasons behind the late introduction of Latin in French public education for girls. I will first trace the long road leading from 1880 to 1924–5, from the creation of public high schools for girls to the unification of boys' and girls' curriculums. In the process, I will examine the arguments put forward by those who wished to legitimize girls' access to Latin, and by those who opposed it.

What happened during those years – between 1880 and 1925 – cannot be understood without first reviewing the arguments traditionally put forward against Latin education for girls. To this end, I must go back to the Ancien Régime, that is, before the Revolution. Education for girls was then extremely limited and consisted only of three elements: religion and morals; reading, writing, and counting; and needlework. Girls who had access to a more complete education were few, and they received it through homeschooling. As for those who learned Latin, they were extremely rare: only a handful are known, starting with the future Madame Dacier (1647–1720).

This limited education for girls (and then only girls of a certain social status) reflected the proper place of women in Ancien Régime society, and the role they were expected to play in it. This is made plain by Charles Rollin, rector of the University of Paris from 1694, whose pedagogical writings we could call rather modern. In a *Supplément* appended to his famous *Traité de la manière d'enseigner et d'étudier les belles-lettres* (1734), he pondered the education of women and whether they should be taught Latin. He established that this issue was not an intellectual problem. Women were able to pursue advanced studies, and this meant studying Latin; he put forward the example of Madame Dacier to show that "sex, in itself, makes no difference between minds." The issue was a social one. Rollin mentioned that "the world is not governed by chance... There is a Providence that determines each and every one's condition and duties." If men were destined for careers for which Latin was a prerequisite, this was not the case for women, who had other vocations. "They are not destined," wrote Rollin, "to educate nations, to govern states, to wage war, to render justice, to plead cases nor to practice medicine. Their lot is confined to the house..." This rule was, remarked Rollin, the same in all countries and through all the ages. Therefore, in the name of a division of labor fixed by Providence and certified by universal practice, Latin was useless to women. Useless and dangerous. Indeed, Latin and knowledge derived from Latin fostered dangerous ambitions in women, and distracted them from their duties; this would have doomed their families and, eventually, all of society. Therefore, in the name of a providential and conservative view of society, Latin instruction, the purview of men, was off limits to women, who were confined to the domestic space and the vernacular.[1]

This view of society did not end with the Ancien Régime. It was still current during the Revolution, a time of great social change. We can read in a report on public education submitted to the *Assemblée nationale* in 1791 that: "Men are destined to live on the world's stage. Public education is for them... The father's house is more suitable for the education of women..., who are destined for domestic duties."[2] This is a classic statement of the division of society between a public male sphere and a private female sphere, the domain of those destined to become wives and mothers. Consequently, men should receive an education outside of the home – and a few years later, 1802, *lycées* for boys were established. Women, for their part, would only receive some basic training, but no real education. This view of the respective roles of men and women endured throughout the nineteenth century and justified the imbalance between male and female educational levels. Girls' schooling remained basic and, for the most part, prepared them for their future domestic duties.

This started to change in the second half of the nineteenth century however, when people began to feel the need to give a more complete

---

[1] See Waquet 1998: 264–6.   [2] Baczko 1982: 170.

education to girls – or at least girls of the bourgeoisie. We note, however, that in 1850 a third of French girls had no access to any kind of education, and years later, under the Third Republic, workmen and farmers almost never sent their daughters to high schools. As for Latin, it was gradually and parsimoniously introduced into public female education, and not without debate and a few false starts. Opponents rarely doubted girls' capacity to learn the language; they mainly argued along the same lines as Rollin or the report of 1791. Advocates of Latin proceeded from a similar logic: they invoked the traditional role of women to legitimize the study of Latin, even contending that Latin instruction helped foster some feminine qualities for the common good of the whole society.

Before proceeding any further, let me trace the evolution of secondary education in France between the Camille Sée law of 1880 and the Bérard decree of 1924, that is, between the creation of a public secondary education system for girls and its assimilation to that of boys.[3] For a long time, there had been no secondary education for girls organized by the state. Nevertheless, young girls of the bourgeoisie received some instruction in private institutions, Catholic for the most part. The goal of this mode of education was mostly to turn a young woman into a proper lady of the house. The level of this private instruction improved constantly, although it did not normally lead to a degree. Some girls succeeded in obtaining the *brevet supérieur* of the male curriculum – even if they did not plan any professional career. Fewer attempted the much more difficult *baccalauréat*. This evolution revealed a need for a secondary system for girls organized by the state instead of leaving it to the private sector, mainly the church. I remind the reader that the Third Republic was characterized by a confrontation between church and state: education was a major issue in this confrontation, and the Republicans' goal was to get girls out of the church's hands.

The Republicans who came to power in 1870 set themselves to work. In 1880, the Camille Sée law instituted a public female secondary education system. However, the way in which the curriculum was organized in 1882 made female instruction inferior to that of the male curriculum. It did not lead to a *baccalauréat* but to a school diploma. Latin and Greek were excluded; the curriculum was based on French literature and science, one foreign language, and a little history and geography. It was in fact an improved elementary education, the product of conflicted thinking. On the one hand, the government wanted to give girls a different education

---

[3] My presentation of these developments is based on Mayeur 1977.

that respected their womanliness; on the other hand, it also wanted to bridge the intellectual chasm between both sexes, or, as it was proclaimed, to avoid an "intellectual divorce" that might separate an educated man and his uneducated wife, and which would be disastrous for the couple and then for all of society. A number of factors raised and transformed the level of public female instruction: success, intense competition from the private sector, and a social demand bolstered by economic hardships and World War I. In 1924, after intense debates, the minister Léon Bérard "assimilated" female and male secondary education; courses and schedules were harmonized the next year. Although girls could still pursue a high school diploma (*diplôme*), the more prestigious route was the *baccalauréat*. Young women studying for the *baccalauréat* followed the same curriculum as boys, for the same number of years and with the same schedule.

Latin was one of the stakes in this "assimilation" or "identification," to employ the vocabulary of the times. We will get some sense of its importance by looking at the years following the Camille Sée law of 1880. There were no mandatory Latin classes, but some optional Latin was introduced in 1882. These classes were limited in scope: up to one hour per week in the last two years of high school. Their goal was not to further girls' intellectual development but to prepare them for their role as mothers. As it was said, "future mothers would be happier overseeing the first studies of their sons."[4] This was not a new argument. It had been put forward some forty years before (in 1838) by a Latin teacher called Maritan, who had developed a Latin course. He had shown the usefulness and necessity of a well-rounded education for women, and he insisted that knowing Latin would be profitable to them, to their children, and to society as a whole. In the present situation, a young boy who needed help with his Latin studies could only get it from strangers, with all the dangers that this could bring. And Maritan, after evoking a grim scenario, concluded: "Nowadays, knowing Latin cannot be a luxury for women, nor a vanity; it is on the contrary an essential complement to motherhood."[5]

In 1897, the optional Latin classes introduced in 1882, which amounted to little and had been more or less successful, were cancelled altogether. Nevertheless, girls still aspired to the *baccalauréat*, both for its prestige and for economic reasons. For this, they needed a specific training and therefore Latin. Private schools met the challenge, organizing preparatory courses with Latin for the *baccalauréat*. This was limited to Paris and affected only a very small number of students. Still, this private initiative

[4] Marion 1900: 477.   [5] Maritan 1838: 2–3.

forced public institutions to react. Already in 1908, preparatory courses to the *baccalauréat* were set up in high schools for girls, although many directors of *lycées* were originally opposed to this idea. These preparatory courses included Latin classes to be paid for by the students themselves, but they nevertheless met with success. At Lille, in 1908, twenty-two girls were taking Latin classes; there were forty-seven in 1911. On the eve of World War I, there were preparatory programs for the *baccalauréat* in all Parisian high schools and many provincial institutions as well, Lyon being a notable exception.

The socio-economic impact of World War I brought even more girls to attempt the *baccalauréat*, and the preparation for it became the major goal of secondary female education. Yet schools were faced with a shortage of money and teachers. Latin classes for girls consisted of "short Latin" (*latin court*), so-called because it was offered for three years only and less intensively than in the male curriculum; also, students had to pay for this instruction. This remained the case until 1924–5, when the Bérard reform harmonized male and female secondary education.

This reform reorganized female secondary education into two sections: the *baccalauréat* section, where girls received the same education as boys – Latin included – and the *diplôme* section, without Latin, but featuring instead courses exclusively for girls such as home economics, women's handiwork, and music. At this point I must recall two principles that inspired the Bérard reform. First, the *baccalauréat* was reserved for a minority of students; the majority of girls were to enroll in the diploma section. Here are the words of Minister Bérard himself: "My ambition has been to make classical culture accessible to elite children, and to offer the improved education promised by the government of 1880 to the vast majority of the girls in our high schools, who are destined for a life at home." Second, the minister made it clear that girls who enrolled in the *baccalauréat* section would still receive "their part of feminine culture"; in fact, schools' programs show that girls had to take drawing, sewing, and music lessons.[6] Thus, while giving girls or rather a minority of them the possibility of receiving the same instruction as boys, their "feminine specificity" was very much put to the fore.

Feminine specificity and assimilation were the two terms in a long-standing debate. In 1903 a wish was expressed at the *Conseil supérieur de*

---

[6] In his *Rapport au Président de la République française précédant la proposition de décret soumise par le ministre de l'Instruction publique et des Beaux-Arts*, 25 March 1924, and *Arrêté* [same day] *fixant la répartition hebdomadaire des matières*. It is clear that the reform is elitist, and concerns a minority of students (on elitism in Latin education, see Kitchell in this volume).

l'Instruction publique that the optional Latin classes abolished in 1897 be restored, so that girls might have access to careers requiring a knowledge of Latin. This wish was rejected since it would have led to the assimilation of female secondary education to the male one, and would violate the very spirit of secondary education for girls. It was then recalled that the government in 1880 intended "this education to prepare girls to fulfill with dignity their roles as women, wives, and mothers, both in society and at home; it was not to lead them to this or that profession." There was no desire to deviate from this principle. The *Conseil* nevertheless proposed optional Latin classes, which were not intended as a preparation for the *baccalauréat* or for a future career, but as a "complement to education."[7] This underlined the cultural and disinterested character of female secondary education.

It was with these perspectives that the debate concerning girls' access to Latin took place. Of course, advocates of Latin used the traditional arguments invoked since the eighteenth century: that women should enjoy the intellectual and moral advantages of a Latin education, namely a better knowledge of French, a better understanding of foreign languages, the development of logic and reasoning, knowledge of a model civilization, acquisition of moral norms, etc.[8] These arguments were occasionally put forward by the students themselves. Girls from the *lycée* at Aurillac interviewed by their Latin teacher in 1911 declared that "what little Latin they knew was already helping them understand seventeenth-century French better, and Spanish as well." Their comrades at Lille echoed these remarks, and one of them wrote: "Latin develops judgment and reasoning better than mathematics."[9]

These traditional arguments played only a secondary role in the debate over girls' access to Latin education. They were superseded by a social demonstration of the usefulness of Latin instruction. Opponents argued from the point of view of the traditional role of women in society to refuse Latin instruction to girls. Advocates of Latin, for their part, showed that Latin was particularly suited to girls, and that its acquisition could not only develop feminine qualities but also correct some feminine shortcomings, and above all reinforce women's social role as wives and mothers.

It is this debate that I will now explain, taking as a focal point the *Revue universitaire*, a journal founded in 1892 to promote reform in secondary

---

[7] Mayeur 1977: 394–5.
[8] On these arguments, see Waquet 1998, chapter 7; for an example of the mental discipline provided by the study of Latin, see Kitchell in this volume, p. 173.
[9] Cayrou 1911, p. 4, n. 2.

education; it contains both an official point of view and contributions from teachers of various backgrounds. In 1909, a section entitled *Bulletin d'enseignement secondaire des jeunes filles* was established, echoing a rising interest in women's issues. This *Bulletin* was a journal within the journal, and contained information concerning female education as well as reviews of studies or articles on this topic. People writing in the *Bulletin* were not amateurs or self-made pedagogues but professional teachers, both men and women, and headteachers of high schools for girls. The *Bulletin* on the whole favored the assimilation of girls' and boys' curriculums, defended it, and tracked its progress.[10] Arguments remained the same between 1909 and 1925, only to be supplemented by fresh evidence. I will give some representative examples of such arguments.

Part of what the advocates of assimilation and Latin did was to respond to attacks launched against Latin education for girls, which was until 1925 the "short Latin" taught in three years. Some said that this mode of education favored mindless memorization, would lower the standard of male Latin instruction, and brought anarchy to the girls' education. Here is how M. Druesnes, a teacher in the *collège* for girls at Lille, responded to these accusations in 1911. The first risk – mindless memorization – did not exist when education was conducted well. It was also out of the question to use the girls' curriculum as a pretext to reduce boys' Latin instruction to three years. The pool of students was different: it was much more selective in female institutions, and three years sufficed to prepare girls for the *baccalauréat*. Finally, there was no reason to fear anarchy resulting from the girls being pulled in three directions – the *diplôme*, the *brevet*, and the *baccalauréat* – if girls were to be led down only one of these paths, while preparation for the *baccalauréat* remained "exceptional, reserved for an elite."[11] Advocates of Latin education brushed aside the charge that Latin instruction and preparation for the *baccalauréat* caused overwork. Although boys were also at risk, girls were thought to be particularly vulnerable.[12] First of all, they were believed to be more fragile than boys and were prone to study harder than them. Second, some feared that intellectual effort would make women even weaker than they were by nature, and cause a decline in fertility.[13] Teachers of Latin answered these allegations in a series of articles in which they debated the proper teaching

---

[10] On the *Bulletin*, see Mayeur 1977: 385.
[11] Druesnes' article, originally published in the *Bulletin de l'Académie de Lille*, was summarized in the *Bulletin de l'enseignement secondaire des jeunes filles* of the *Revue universitaire*, xx.2 (1911), 53–4.
[12] Héry 2003: 85–6.   [13] Maisani 1925: 422–6.

method to adopt in order to prevent overwork among female students. These teachers focused on the essentials and did not try to make girls erudite, as they did for boys, who were submitted to a more rigorous curriculum. It was important to avoid unnecessary exercises and simplify the teaching of grammar. In this way, Latin did not cause overwork among girls but, on the contrary, improved the feminine mind.[14]

This was an important aspect of the cause for female Latin instruction. Studying Latin rectified intellectual deficiencies inherent in young women. This is what a teacher from Paris, M. Thévenin, declared in 1911, based on his experience: after two or three years of Latin, he had seen "futile and loose minds become more balanced and tame..., the creation of a thinking mind, and a self-disciplined consciousness."[15] The headmistress of the *Université catholique* de Neuilly, a private institution which had offered Latin instruction to girls from early on, observed in 1925 that "ancient languages are even more useful to girls than to boys: they rectify typically feminine deficiencies such as a lack of general ideas and objectivity; properly taught, they provide an uprightness and solidity of spirit akin to wisdom."[16] Around this time, the headmistress of the *collège* at Nevers voiced the same opinion: "our students are intuitive, clever and spontaneous but, unlike boys, without coherence, thought and method. Latin can help girls acquire these qualities, by forcing them to slowly decipher other people's thoughts down to the most minute details."[17]

Young girls also brought to the study of Latin some welcome dispositions made manifest in their study of living languages. English and German had been introduced in the early years of female secondary education and they had been made compulsory with the promulgation of the Camille Sée law. Girls, many noticed, learned languages more easily than boys. This was due to a better organization of language instruction in high schools for girls. Some, for example the headmistress of the *lycée* Fénelon in Paris, added that feminine character traits were also at work. Here is what she said in 1924: "Girls are chatty, and this failing allows them to learn foreign languages quicker. They also play music more than boys and their memory of sounds is more developed than their brothers'. They are also better at mimicking; they are more given to playing riddles and

---

[14] For an example, see Cayrou 1911.
[15] Thévenin's article originally published in the *Mercure de France* was summarized in the *Bulletin de l'enseignement secondaire des jeunes filles* of the *Revue universitaire*, XX.2 (1911), 52.
[16] Mrs Daniélou quoted in "Un bilan de l'enseignement secondaire féminin," in *Bulletin de l'enseignement secondaire des jeunes filles* of the *Revue universitaire*, XXXIV.1 (1925), 155.
[17] Maisani 1925: 424.

comedies, at least in high schools, and are better at it than boys."[18] These dispositions could be put to good use in learning Latin, a better cause. The *Bulletin* published in 1920 an apology for Latin by an English teacher, M. Duchemin, an article that was quite persuasive since it was not written by a professional Latinist. According to him, learning living languages had a practical goal and was the equivalent of "mastering a mechanism"; Latin offered more. This teacher contrasted the quick reading of stories, tales, and novels in classes of English and German to meditating upon ancient literature in Latin classes. "A child embarking on Latin studies is plunged into the study of great literary works, greatly profitable on account of its slow pace." Because of their strong language skills, girls were particularly qualified for studying Latin; this study was also morally profitable and did not put the feminine mind at risk the same way modern romantic literature did.[19]

If Latin studies were intellectually and morally profitable to girls, they were even more advisable from the point of view of disinterested learning – one of the goals of female education – and from the point of view of a feminine specificity that had to be preserved and cultivated in the name of a traditional view of society. Advocates of Latin and assimilation routinely used this argument, for example M. Thévenin, whose views on the beneficial character of Latin studies I have already mentioned. He also insisted on disinterested studies as suitable preparation for the future woman's social role. "This Latin education brings no material benefits; who can deny that this aristocratic culture, pursued by itself and for itself, is in our democracy more suited to a young woman than to a young man?" Such an education makes women learned and "re-establishes harmony between the genders," but it also preserves the different social roles imparted to men and women: "It is necessary," said Thévenin, "for men to be directed toward bold enterprises, innovation and possible futures, while women steeped in tradition should represent conservatism and virtues assembled around the cult of Vesta."[20]

The most sustained argument was presented by a zealous advocate of Latin, M. Druesnes, a teacher at the *lycée* at Lille whom we have already seen responding to opponents of Latin. In 1913, in a public presentation entitled "The young woman Latinist at home," he made a powerful plea in

---

[18] Caron 1924: 325.
[19] Duchemin's article, originally published in the *Revue de l'enseignement des langues vivantes*, was summarized in the *Bulletin de l'enseignement secondaire des jeunes filles* of the *Revue universitaire*, XXIX.1 (1920), 52–3.
[20] Article quoted in n. 15, pp. 52–3.

favor of Latin education for girls. Citing Fénelon – the *lycée* at Lille was named after this French writer of the seventeenth century – he gave Fénelon's views on women's role in society: "a house to manage, a husband to please and children to raise." This definition was still valid (we only have to think about the underlying principles of the Sée law and the Bérard decree) and justified Latin education for young women. Druesnes showed that "Latin literature prepares a woman for the important and charming duties of family life." He dismissed the objection that Latin made girls pedantic. This was not the case. On the contrary, Latin studies reinforced a woman's modesty. Here is his reasoning: "Do we *know* Latin? No, we study it, we taste it ... Latin is the thing in this world that we *know* the least. A Latin student can glimpse the splendor of antiquity through the difficulty of a language that doesn't always give away its secrets, but she also learns that she doesn't know as much as she could: Latin breeds modesty... A Latin student feels her perpetual and painful inadequacy." Druesnes then rejected a second objection to Latin education for girls, namely that teaching high culture to young women guaranteed "many misunderstandings among future couples, or wives who would despise their family and even their husband if he is less educated." For Druesnes, this was very unlikely. If it ever happened, a cultivated woman would then discern the qualities of a hard-working and industrious husband, even if he had not reached the baccalaureate and learned Latin. Druesnes was more concerned with a third objection: Latin is useless. He did not answer by invoking the traditional arguments on the intellectual and moral usefulness of Latin, nor did he justify Latin instruction by pointing out that it led to liberal careers. He rather showed – and this is an important part of his presentation – that Latin is especially useful to young women because it prepares them for their roles as wives, mothers, and ladies of the house. "Is it not true that reason, good sense, wisdom, method, an ordered spirit and discipline are necessary qualities for the management of a household? Well then! All of these qualities are also qualities of the Latin spirit and of the Latin language ... Latin is wise, methodical and disciplined, it is a living example of reason and good sense." Druesnes then conjured up episodes of Latin literature featuring feminine models, such as Cornelia or Arria, as well as texts blaming feminine failings such as a romantic character, vanity or idle chatter. He capped his advocacy of domestic Latin by evoking the moving scene of a "mother making her son recite his Latin lessons."[21]

[21] Public presentation summarized in the *Bulletin de l'enseignement secondaire des jeunes filles* of the *Revue universitaire*, XXII.2 (1913), 250–2.

Whether it was due to these arguments, economic necessity or simply ambition, more and more girls opted for the *baccalauréat* section and Latin education. But as soon as they obtained the right to study Latin, they encountered another classical obstacle: Greek. Prior to the Bérard decree, it had been proposed that girls should have access to both Greek and Latin, but parents' associations were opposed. Even more than Latin, Greek was thought to make people pedantic, and some feared that if Greek became mandatory for the *baccalauréat*, many families would pull their daughters from the curriculum. Latin was the "reasonable limit." Feminine specificity and the social role of women were once again invoked, but this time to deny them access to Greek. Adding Greek to the curriculum would have overburdened the girls and led them to overwork. Either this, or it would have been necessary to reduce the number of hours assigned to sewing and home economics, and so deprive young women of studies "better fitted to their own calling." At the time of the "assimilation," Greek was made optional for girls and taught one hour less than in high schools for boys. It was therefore more difficult for girls to be admitted to the Latin and Greek section of the *baccalauréat*, and this section became the elite section.[22]

Latin and Greek remained predominantly male school subjects; this situation endured up until 1968 – an important date in French history and for Latin as well since it was then abolished in grade 6. However, the picture was quite different at university: the feminization of classical studies was noticeable already in the 1950s, when there were two or three women for each man enrolled in Latin studies at the Sorbonne. The rise of women in classics at university was perceived as signaling the decline of the discipline, or alternatively, as a symbol of women's advancement.[23] After the Bérard reform, advocates of Latin for girls thought that it was now "their duty to guard the torch of the humanities that men, too concerned by material life and too prone to imitate America, had let escape from their hands."[24] The great number of women in the auditoriums of the Sorbonne is proof that women rose to the challenge. I will not, however, comment on the use of America as a negative example!

---

[22] On the debate about Greek for girls in the years before the "assimilation," see "Autour de la réforme: questions posées," in *Bulletin de l'enseignement secondaire des jeunes filles* of the *Revue universitaire*, XXXII.2 (1923), 345–7. On the Latin and Greek section, see Héry 2003: 83.
[23] Cf. the opposite points of view of Flacelière (1957: 134) and Boyancé (1953: 129).
[24] "Les humanités pour les jeunes filles", in *Bulletin de l'enseignement secondaire des jeunes filles* of the *Revue universitaire*, XXXVII.1 (1928), 445–6.

CHAPTER 11

Women's education and the classics
Fiona Cox

Maggie found the Latin Grammar quite soothing after her mathematical mortification; for she delighted in new words, and quickly found that there was an English Key at the end, which would make her very wise about Latin, at slight expense. She presently made up her mind to skip the rules in the Syntax – the examples became so absorbing. The mysterious sentences snatched from an unknown context – like strange horns of beasts and leaves of unknown plants, brought from some far-off region – gave boundless scope to her imagination, and were all the more fascinating because they were in a peculiar tongue of their own, which she could learn to interpret.[1]

George Eliot's Maggie Tulliver has achieved iconic status as the nineteenth-century girl, denied access to the classical education bestowed upon her brother, Tom, even though he is far less able and interested than she is. Maggie's approach to the learning of classical languages is characterised both by a keen sense of injustice at her exclusion from a full education, and a sense of wonder at these worlds of learning in which women were forbidden to be explorers. One hundred and fifty years later, at a time when the teaching of Latin and Greek risks virtual eradication from mainstream education, the classical world is increasingly dependent upon reception studies, and is being revitalised through new interpretations in film, television, translations, fiction and poetry. For the first time in the history of western culture it is women writers who are shaping the contemporary response to the classical world. There is an abundance of such writers in the United Kingdom alone, such as Josephine Balmer, A. S. Byatt, Margaret Drabble, Carol Ann Duffy, Helen Dunmore, Jeanette Winterson, Ali Smith, Jenny Joseph, Alice Oswald, Michèle Roberts, Ruth Fainlight, Jo Shapcott and the late U. A. Fanthorpe. The list is not exhaustive. It is the purpose of this chapter to examine

---

[1] Eliot 1980: 129. For a discussion of the role of Eliot in shaping Victorian women's imagination, see Hurst 2006.

the responses by women writers to the classical education they received in the course of the twentieth century, to the reactions provoked by their increased access to Latin and Greek, and to the burgeoning of female responses to the classics from the 1980s onwards, when the teaching of Latin and ancient Greek really began to wane in schools. The spirit of Maggie Tulliver – resentful and fired by wonder – haunts the responses of her twentieth-century descendants.

A. S. Byatt's novel *The Children's Book* (2009) offers a vivid and detailed account of life in the middle-class household of a children's author at the turn of the nineteenth and twentieth centuries. In 1896 the girls of the house are still confined to an education devoted to accomplishments rather than learning, in contrast to their brothers who receive tutoring in history, literature and Latin in preparation for the entrance exams of Eton and Marlowe: "Basil and Katharina felt that what young women needed was accomplishments – music, manners, painting and drawing. They offered to invite Dorothy to share Griselda's art lessons. Griselda had been reading *The Mill on the Floss* and had persuaded Dorothy to read it too. They sat in Griselda's bedroom, indignant Maggie Tullivers, for whom maths and Latin and literature were not considered."[2] These girls are fictional contemporaries of Virginia Woolf, who was also educated at home, and for whom the learning of ancient Greek symbolised her exclusion from a male world of knowledge and privilege. Her essay "On Not Knowing Greek" (1925) begins:

For it is vain and foolish to talk of knowing Greek, since in our ignorance we should be at the bottom of a class of schoolboys, since we do not know how the words sounded, or where precisely we ought to laugh, or how the actors acted... All the more strange, then, is it that we should wish to know Greek, try to know Greek, feel for ever drawn back to Greek, and be for ever making up some notion of the meaning of Greek...[3]

Hurst points out that the knowledge for which Woolf yearns – hearing the intonations and accents of ancient Greek – is unattainable, whether by schoolboy, academic or self-educated females.[4] Nevertheless, the passage both highlights Woolf's sense of inadequacy as she compares her abilities to those of schoolboys, while also conveying a passionate interest in the subject from which she is excluded. Even as Woolf was writing, however, classical languages were beginning to become available to girls in school.

---

[2] Byatt 2009: 167. For a discussion of this passage and its relation to women's education and the classics, see Cox 2011: 2–3.
[3] Woolf 1992: 93.   [4] Hurst 2006: 220.

Betty Radice, who was to become one of the most distinguished figures in British literary circles both as a commentator on Pliny, as well as editor of Penguin Classics from 1964 until her death in 1985, was one of the first girls able to learn both Latin and Greek at her high school in the 1920s. Margaret Wynn recalls that:

> Betty and her sister Nancy went to Newland High School in Hull. She broke with school tradition in specializing in Latin and insisting on reading Greek in the sixth form in order to apply to Oxford, again a break with traditions. She spoke of coming home to tea "with my new worlds of Greece and Rome in my satchel." She was made a scholar at St Hilda's, the only classicist of her year.[5]

Radice, too, conveys her passion for the subject by evoking the sheer excitement of being able to explore these "new worlds." It is striking just how often women writers who have benefited from a classical education recall, when looking back to their schooldays, the thrill of learning, and in particular of learning subjects that had been denied to their female ancestors for so long. A. S. Byatt (born 1936) describes the way in which she felt the language of *Aeneid* VI "singing in her blood"[6] as she studied for her Latin A-Level,[7] and thrilled to the feeling of power which the description of the Sibyl gave her,[8] and yet her awareness of the challenges facing intellectual women in the twentieth century is evident in her short story "The Djinn in the Nightingale's Eye," where the narratologist Gillian Perholt is suddenly afflicted by a sense of powerlessness during her delivery of a paper which reflects on the representation of women's lives in fiction and observes that they are "the stories of stopped energies – the stories of Fanny Price, Lucy Snowe, even Gwendolen Harleth ... all come to that moment of strangling, willed oblivion."[9] That this is directly connected to her status as a woman is indicated by the appearance of a ghostly sibyl who does not represent power on this occasion, but rather the void of empty lives and unfulfilled dreams:

> And Gillian Perholt stared out of glassy eyes and heard her voice fail. She was far away and long ago – she was a pillar of salt, her voice echoed inside a glass box, a sad piping like a lost grasshopper in winter. She could move neither fingers nor

---

[5] Wynn 1987: 32.   [6] Byatt 2000: 132.
[7] A-Levels are advanced examinations usually taken at the age of eighteen.
[8] "When I read *Aeneid VI*, where the golden bough shines on the shores of the underworld, and the Sibyl writhes in her cave, I felt a shiver down my spine which was recognition of power" (Byatt 2000: 137).
[9] Byatt 1995: 121.

lips, and in the body of the hall, behind the grey-scarved women, she saw a cavernous form, a huge, female form, with a veiled head bowed above emptiness and long slack-sinewed arms, hanging loosely around emptiness, and a draped, cowled garment ruffling over the windy vacuum of nothing, a thing banal in its conventional awfulness, and for that very reason appalling because it was there, to be seen, her eyes could distinguish each fold, could measure the red rims of those swollen eyes, could see the cracks in the stretched lips of that toothless, mirthless mouth, could see that it was many colours and all of them grey, grey. The creature was flat-breasted and its withered skin was exposed above the emptiness, the windy hole that was its belly and womb.[10]

The Welsh poet Deryn Rees-Jones recalls the thrill of scandal permeating the rows of schoolgirls, in a poem called "Loving the Greeks" that explicitly connects gender with the classical material that was on offer and how it was taught:

> Being girls, we thought it best to love the Greeks. . .
>   We were always
> fast to learn, scorning the rhetoric of Cicero
> for the travels of Herodotus; and being *outré*
> Ovid's Book of Love, which was, by then,
> allowed us, was considered "out" in favour
> of the Sapphic fragments. . .[11]

The impact of being able to study Latin in school is evidenced not only by the abundance of these schoolgirl memories in autobiographical accounts but also by a dramatically increased range of references to Latin texts in the burgeoning field of schoolgirl fiction.[12] In 1940 Elinor M. Brent-Dyer included an untranslated citation from Virgil in *The Chalet School in Exile*, which indicates that by that time her schoolgirl readers could be expected to understand the Latin for themselves. Similarly Antonia Forest frequently refers to the Virgil that her schoolgirl characters are following in their lessons. Her characters are able to perceive parallels between the lines of ancient text and situations that they are experiencing in their everyday lives. In *The Cricket Term* the young Ginty Marlow is gratified when her prowess at swimming is acknowledged through reference to the *Aeneid*:

"Megan, no matter whether it is the postman or a herd of giraffes in the drive, your attention should be *here*. We shall be hearing your version of lines 583–587 and today, I hope, you won't take us too far from the original." Lower V.A.

---

[10] Byatt 1995: 117–18.   [11] Rees-Jones 1994: 15.
[12] For a discussion of this see Cox 2011: 4–5.

grinned; Megan Reeves looked pained. "And Virginia can take us as far as line 595. I imagine neither she nor Monica will find difficulty in translating,

> *delphinum similes qui per maria umida nando/Carpathium Libycumque secant luduntque per undas –"*

Like dolphins who, swimming through the drenching seas sail past Carpathia and Libya, playing in the waves...[13]

In an earlier book *Peter's Room* (1961), when Ginty and her sisters fabricate a make-believe world along the lines of the Brontës' Angria, Ginty tries to think herself into the skin of her chosen hero by remembering her Latin lessons:

He had taken his commission because – because his family always would *do*, but there ought to be something else as well... Because of Rupert, perhaps? Because Rupert was his friend as David was Jonathan's or – she remembered last term's Virgil lessons – Nisus was Euryalus'? Both were splendidly tragic stories in the end – and, for some moments, combing her hair more and more slowly in the intensity of her thought, she tried to decide whether it would be more fun if only one of them died and was mourned by the other (David and Jonathan) or they died together killed by the enemy (Nisus and Euryalus).[14]

What is of significance here is that Ginty is subconsciously performing one of the functions of a traditional classical education, which is to emulate the heroic behaviour promoted in the epics. While it was becoming unremarkable in the 1960s for girls to assume masculine modes of behaviour, Dorothy L. Sayers probed the same phenomenon in her detective story *Gaudy Night* (1935) set in a women's college in Oxford. The college is being plagued by a series of vindictive acts and murderous threats, which have been accompanied by a quotation from the *Aeneid*:

Harriet watched her go, and then took out a piece of paper from a drawer. The message upon it was pasted up in the usual way, and ran

tristius haud illis monstrum nec saevior ulla pestis et ira deum Stygiis sese extulit undis. Virginei volucrum vultus foedissima ventris proluvies uncaeque manus et pallida semper ora fame.

"Harpies," said Harriet aloud. "Harpies. That seems to suggest a train of thought. But I'm afraid we can't suspect Emily or any of the scouts of expressing their feelings in Virgilian hexameters."

She frowned. Matters were looking rather bad for the Senior Common Room.[15]

---

[13] Forest 1979: 124. [14] Forest 2004: 140–1. [15] Sayers 2003: 180.

It is notable from this extract that the dons assume that Latin belongs to a highly select and elite category of women. The presence of the note appears to exonerate the serving staff, and points the finger of suspicion back to the academic community. Harriet Vane, Sayer's female sleuth, correctly identifies the quotation as the passage from Book 3 of the *Aeneid* (214–18) describing the Harpies: "The fury of the gods has raised no horror,/No plague more cruel out of the streams of Styx./They have girls' faces, but their stomachs drip/Revolting filth, their hands have claws, their faces/Are always pale with hunger."[16] In the context of an all-women's Oxford College the quotation evokes the stereotype of the unattractively ambitious female undergraduate or don, who foregoes food and sleep in order to pursue her learning.[17] However, Lord Peter Wimsey modifies the view that it could only be a learned woman who had left the note by pointing out that any schoolchild would have had ready access to the passage:

> There was one consideration which inclined Miss Vane to exonerate all the scouts, and that was, that no woman in that position would be likely to express her resentment in the Latin quotation from the *Aeneid* found attached to the dummy.
>
> This objection had some weight with me, but not a great deal. It was the only message that was not in English, and it was one to which any school child might easily have access. On the other hand, the fact that it was unique among the other scripts made me sure that it had some particular significance. I mean, it wasn't that X's feelings habitually expressed themselves in Latin hexameters. There must be something special about that passage besides its general applicability to unnatural females who snatch the meat from men's mouths. (pp. 528–9)[18]

It is notable that all of the female dons slip unthinkingly into elitism when they assume that the perpetrator has to belong to the college, a clear indication of the divisions that education created between the classes. Eventually it transpires that the culprit is the widow of a man who committed suicide after his dishonest research practices had been exposed by a female don. When confronted with irrefutable evidence, the perpetrator rounds on the entire female community:

---

[16] Virgil 2008: 54.
[17] For a parody of this see Rosamond Lehmann's (1936: 113) description of a female undergraduate's first night at Cambridge, meeting her fellow students: "Earnestly her eyes beamed and glinted behind their glasses. Presumably she was kind and well-meaning, but her skin was greasy and pink was not her colour; and her lank hair smelt; and when she talked she spat. The colourless face had nothing of youth in it. Perhaps this was what really clever girls looked like."
[18] For a discussion of Virgilian reception in *Gaudy Night*, see Hurst 2006: 207–11.

I say you murdered him. What had he done to you? What harm had he done to anybody? He only wanted to live and be happy. You took the bread out of his mouth and flung his children and me out to starve. What did it matter to you? You had no children. You hadn't a man to care about... What business had you with a job like that? A woman's job is to look after a husband and children. I wish I had killed you. I wish I could kill you all. I wish I could burn down this place and all the places like it – where you teach women to take men's jobs and rob them first and kill them afterwards. (p. 539)

In *Gaudy Night* Latin quotation is used as an emblem of the hard-hearted bluestocking whose educational ambitions lead her to warp and deform her womanly nature. Privileged, clever girls may have been able to begin to enjoy the educational opportunities that their brothers took for granted, but there was still a price to be paid. That mindsets are more stubbornly resistant than educational policies is indicated by the fact that A. S. Byatt vividly recounts her headmistress's admonishments to girls who favoured Latin and Racine over needlework, and in her fictionalised account of this episode she goes on to describe negotiating similar difficulties on behalf of her daughter in the 1970s.[19]

The educational systems in place, once girls were able to enjoy educational opportunities on an equal footing with boys, meant that the learning of classics was only available for a relatively short period to a privileged few. Antonia Forest's fictional characters may have been able to take it for granted, but Forest's books were banned for a period from a number of public libraries on the grounds that their protagonists were too privileged and elitist. Classics was associated in the public mind with the grammar schools which educated the most academically able for the top universities, while secondary modern schools trained the others for employment.[20] It was in 1960 that Oxford and Cambridge abolished their requirement for O-Level Latin,[21] a move that stripped Latin of its central status in a

---

[19] Byatt 1988: 31: "You may very well – with the best of intentions, naturally – be confusing Sarah's best interests with your own unfulfilled ambitions. Sarah may not be an academic child. Emily dared not ask him, as she should have done, as furious Sarah, frustrated and rebellious, was expecting her to do, if he *knew* Sarah, on what he was founding this judgement. Sarah's French, she said, is very good indeed; it is my subject, I know. She has a natural gift. He smiled his thin disbelief, his professional dismissal, and said that was her view, but not necessarily the school's. We are here to educate the whole human being, he told Emily, to educate her for life, for forming personal relations, running a home, finding her place in society, understanding her responsibilities. We are very much aware of Sarah's needs and problems – one of which, if I may speak frankly, is your expectations. Perhaps you should try to trust us? In any case, it is absolutely impossible to arrange the timetable so that Sarah may do both maths and French."
[20] See Bulwer 2006: 126. [21] O-Levels were examinations taken at the age of sixteen.

grammar school curriculum almost overnight.[22] In a recent novel *The Seven Sisters* Margaret Drabble evokes a classics lesson for girls held around this time, making it clear that the teaching of Latin was already a fragile and doomed enterprise:

> At school, Julia, Janet and I all studied Latin up to A and then S level standard,[23] only the three of us in the class. We had an excellent teacher. Maybe all Classics teachers are excellent. They sing in the dark and shore up the ruins. They play with tragic brilliance the endgame.[24]

Drabble's novel serves as a kind of parable for the relationship between women and the classics in the contemporary world. Its protagonist, Candida Wilton, decides to take an evening class on Virgil's *Aeneid* when she arrives in London, newly divorced and in late middle age. The evening class does not last long, as the building in which it is held is renovated as a sleek new gym, but Candida manages to keep in touch with some of the class's few pupils as well as with their teacher, the sibylline Mrs Jerrold. Each of the ladies feels exiled from the Latin they studied at school, or else they didn't study it at all, yet each of them feels a longing for the very world from which they have become disconnected. When they travel to Carthage and Naples in the footsteps of Aeneas, the journey they take is metaphorical as well as physical. There is a sense in which we have come full circle – the yearning that fired Maggie Tulliver is palpable in the twenty-first century, despite the increased equality in the education of both sexes. The diminished opportunities to study the classics at school have led to a feeling of rootlessness, of being divorced from our origins. That this is not a phenomenon that is exclusive to the United Kingdom is indicated by Ursula Le Guin's fear, expressed in the afterword of her book, *Lavinia*:[25]

> From the Middle Ages on, the so-called dead language Latin was, through its literature, intensely alive, active and influential. That's no longer true. During the last century, the teaching and learning of Latin began to wither away into a scholarly specialty. So, with the true death of his language, Vergil's voice will be silenced at last.

Paradoxically, however, as the teaching of classical languages waned the interest in classical civilisation flourished. Bulwer points out that the

---

[22] See Lister in this volume on the abolition of this requirement as a catalyst for reform of the Latin curriculum.
[23] A- and S-Levels are advanced examinations usually taken at the age of eighteen.
[24] Drabble 2003: 83. For a discussion of this book see Cox 2011: 115–35.
[25] Le Guin 2008: 273.

training of our classics teachers, who had to study history, art and architecture, religion and philosophy and literature as well as the classical languages as part of their degree, puts them in an excellent position to deliver a broad curriculum. He also highlights the success of the Open University in wooing interested members of the public to courses which cover both Latin and Greek language, as well as classical reception.[26] Le Guin's enterprise forms part of the same phenomenon. She is not simply rescuing Virgil's most overlooked female character from oblivion by giving her her own story, but she is also reminding the contemporary world of just how strongly our existence continues to be shaped by antiquity. At the same time she is injecting new life into this ancient epic by representing it from a female perspective. Her book represents an attempt to ward off a new Dark Age in which nobody will understand Latin and its importance to today's world, and one of its desired effects is, of course, to encourage her readers to learn Latin in institutions such as the Open University.

It is, above all and for the first time, women writers who are leading the resurgence of the classical world in contemporary literature, and inevitably their readership is predominantly female. Often their attempts are governed by a need to rework the Western canon so that a woman's voice and perspective can be accommodated. Carol Ann Duffy's *The World's Wife* (1999) offers the female perspective on the lives of Tiresias, Orpheus, Pygmalion and Penelope, among others. Writers such as Ali Smith remould the myths so that they encompass the experiences of lesbians also. Her contribution to the Canongate "Myths" series, *Girl Meets Boy* (2007) joyfully reworks the myth of Iphis from Ovid's *Metamorphoses*, so that the ancient tale is played out by two lesbians on the twenty-first-century streets of Scotland. In this book Smith probes contemporary anxieties about our treatment of the earth and its natural resources, a concern that also expresses itself in the mythical reworkings of Duffy in her poem "Atlas" (2010)[27] and Jeanette Winterson's own contribution to the Canongate series, *Weight: the Myth of Atlas and Heracles* (2006).[28] More recently Jo Shapcott has evoked her experience of breast cancer and her medical treatment in a book of poetry entitled *Of Mutability* (2010). The ghost of Ovid's *Metamorphoses* haunts the collection, as Shapcott depicts not just metamorphosis, the changing form of her body, but the

---

[26] Bulwer 2006: 129–30.
[27] The poem was commissioned for National Poetry Day and appeared in *The Daily Telegraph* on 3 October 2009. See www.telegraph.co.uk/culture/books/bookreviews/6250955/Carol-Ann-Duffy-Interview.html, accessed 9 April 2013.
[28] See Cox and Theodorakopoulos 2013.

uncontrolled and exuberant mutability of cancerous cells. Ovid is invoked to chart the transformation of the body after the attack of both illness and chemotherapy. The volume won the Costa Book of the Year award, after the judges decided that "the book was so accessible, and the subject matter so relevant, that if any poetry book could capture the spirit of life in 2011, this would be it."[29] At the beginning of the twenty-first century the future of the classical world and its capacity to rekindle interest in the learning of its languages depends upon the capacity of ancient literature to adapt itself to new environments and new tongues, to learn to speak in new tongues. The daughters of Maggie Tulliver have moved from the sidelines from which they resentfully watched others discovering the languages of antiquity to the centre of a new stage on which the future of Latin and Greek depends.

---

[29] Higgins, Charlotte, "Jo Shapcott takes Costa book of the year award for Of Mutability," *Guardian* 25 January 2011. See www.guardian.co.uk/books/2011/jan/25/costa-book-award-jo-shapcott-INTCMP=SRCH, accessed 9 April 2013.

CHAPTER 12

"Solitary perfection?" The past, present, and future of elitism in Latin education

Kenneth J. Kitchell, Jr.

The name of the conference, from which this article arises, comes from Shakespeare's *Tempest*. Caliban rants at Prospero for his servitude, attacking his master with the very tool that the master has taught his slave – language.

> You taught me language; and my profit on't
> Is, I know how to curse. The red plague rid you
> For learning me your language!
> (1.ii.364–6)[1]

Caliban clearly bears quite a grudge against Prospero and the source for this bad blood lies in what at first would seem to be an act of kindness. When Prospero first came to the island, exiled by his brother Antonio, Caliban showed him how to get food and water. In return, Prospero taught Caliban his language, thus raising him up from the animal state in which he resided despite having a human shape. This, one would think, was a blessing for Caliban, but his essentially low nature won out and he next tries to pass beyond the limits set for him by his master. He longs for equality with Prospero and desires to possess the special magical powers that give his master power over him. He strives even further – too far, in fact – in his quest for equality, when he tries to rape Prospero's daughter, Miranda. For this his master has turned against him and now binds him with his magic, forcing him do all the manual labor for Prospero, whose magical knowledge renders him immune from work. And where is the knowledge of this magic located? It clearly lies in Prospero's books, which, he says, are "dukedom large enough" (1.ii.110) for him, and which he has brought to his island. The power that binds Caliban lies in these books, especially those on magic, which, given the time period in question, were almost certainly written in

---

[1] Quotations from *The Tempest* are taken from Shakespeare 2005.

Latin.[2] Caliban can come as far as English, but Latin, as a symbol of formal education and power, is forbidden to him.

When Caliban later plots with Stephano to topple Prospero from power, he lays out his plan:

> Why, as I told thee, 'tis a custom with him,
> I' th' afternoon to sleep: there thou mayst brain him,
> Having first seized his books.
> (III.ii.87–9)

Prospero's books have to be seized first or the coup will not work. The real knowledge, and thus the real power, resides in those books of Prospero and the ability to understand them. And the key to all this lies in knowing Latin. Thus, while Prospero "learned" Caliban English, one can be fairly sure that he is not about to "learn" Caliban any Latin, for to do so would be to empower him.

It is interesting to compare Caliban and Pedro Gonzales, born in the Canary Islands in the late sixteenth century and given to King Henri II to rear. Gonzales possessed excessive body hair and thus "looked more like a beast than a man."[3] Gonzales was educated at court, progressing to the point where he eventually wrote his autobiography in Latin, as if to announce that he now had left savagery behind and was a full member of the "human," classically educated elite. This is but an exaggerated instance of the taint of elitism that has dogged the study of the classics for generations.

American elitism – overview

What better paradigm than Caliban for the topic of elitism and American Latin studies? For too many centuries and in too many countries, those with the insider's knowledge of Latin have always managed to make the acquisition of the language something to be kept for the few and not to be shared with the many, and the pattern was followed with vigor in America. The full history of Latin pedagogy in America has yet to be written, and it will be a large task. In this article I hope merely to offer a series of snapshot looks at a few important junctures in time where this division of power, firmly rooted in the acquisition of learning Latin, has been in play during America's history. I will conclude with some projections for our future,

---

[2] But see the discussion by post-colonial scholars cited by Emily Greenwood below.
[3] Waquet 2001: 230. Cf. Sherrow 2006: 212. Compare the study of Atherton (1998) who links the acquisition of grammar with the elevation of elite children from the status of the beast.

because elitism in Latin pedagogy is still quite prevalent in American education and, I submit, threatens its continued existence in the curriculum.

The phenomenon of using Latin as a way to keep "undesirables" out of higher education (and thus higher society) is quite old. From the infancy of European universities, Latin was the language both of admission and of instruction. The lower classes need not apply. Françoise Waquet has chronicled admirably much of the history of Latin "as the expression of a power exerting dominance over others" in her excellent *Latin: Or the Empire of a Sign*,[4] and elsewhere in this volume she demonstrates the way Latin was used to exclude females in France from higher education. Walter Ong went so far as to equate the learning of Latin in the Renaissance with a rite of initiation such as those practiced by tribal societies.[5] Recently, in a study of classics at Oxford, Isobel Hurst has shown the same misogynistic bias against women learning the classics in England and Edmund Richardson has used Hardy's *Jude the Obscure* to paint a poignant picture of the fate of what he calls the English "classical outcasts."[6]

Similar dichotomies between the educated "haves" and the classically deprived "have-nots" crossed the Atlantic with our first European settlers and have existed in America since its founding. Many scholars have pointed out that this inherited elitism drew heated attacks from the very beginning of our Republic. Some colonists, believing firmly in their new country as a land of equal opportunity, raised heavy opposition to a classics-based education, deeming it antithetical to "useful education."[7] A handful of examples will have to suffice.

Meyer Reinhold first shed light on the move to oust Latin and Greek from American curricula in favor of useful knowledge from the early 1700s on. Benjamin Rush (1745–1813) is often cited as the most outspoken leader in the attacks on the classics-based curriculum. Consider this:

Under the circumstances to spend four or five years in learning two dead languages, is to turn our backs upon a gold mine, in order to amuse ourselves in catching butterflies... The next ray of truth that irradiates human reason upon

---

[4] Waquet 2001: 243 and see, in general, chapter 9, "The power to say and to conceal," (pp. 230–56).
[5] Ong 1959.
[6] Hurst 2007, Richardson 2007. On women in the sixteenth and seventeenth centuries, see Stevenson 1998.
[7] Reinhold 1984. Chapter 2, "The quest for useful knowledge in eighteenth-century America," is an excellent treatment of this movement and chapter 4, "Opponents of classical learning," describes well the opposition. The debate began long before colonial America: see Kitchell 1998.

this subject, I hope will teach us to reject the Latin and Greek languages altogether, as branches of liberal education.[8]

and

Were every Greek and Latin book (the New Testament excepted) consumed in a bonfire, the world would be the wiser and better for it.[9]

and

Many sprightly young boys of excellent capacities for useful knowledge have been so disgusted with the dead languages as to retreat from the drudgery of schools to low company, whereby they have become bad members of society and entailed misery upon all who have been connected with them.[10]

And listen to the pragmatic, ever so American words of one William Livingston in 1768:

We want hands, my lord, more than heads. The most intimate acquaintance with the classics, will not remove our oaks; nor a taste for the *Georgics* cultivate our lands. Many of our young people are knocking their heads against the *Iliad*, who should employ their hands in clearing our swamps and draining our marshes.[11]

Benjamin Franklin himself, in his proposal for a Philadelphia academy, argued against making Latin and Greek mandatory for all students. And in so doing he quoted the educator George Turnbull, who said that "Few think their Children qualified for a Trade till they have been whipt at a Latin School for five or six years, to learn a little of that which they are oblig'd to forget."[12] In an interesting parallel to the stories of Caliban and Gonzales, Franklin also relates the story of some Iriquois leaders who rejected the white man's offer of a traditional classical education as being utterly useless. They had previously seen Iroquois youths go off for such an education only to come back totally unprepared for any useful occupation. Instead, the Iroquois offered to train some English boys in their ways so that the boys would at least have some useful skills when done.[13]

Some saw the elitism inherent in the study of Latin as directly opposed to the basic American ideal of equal opportunity. Lee Pearcy uses the bestowal of an honorary degree upon Andrew Jackson by Harvard as an example of what he calls "the dialectic opposition of classical studies and

---

[8] Reinhold 1984: 130. Early American vagaries of punctuation and spelling are preserved as they are in Reinhold's original.
[9] Reinhold: 1984: 136.   [10] Richard 1994: 199.   [11] Reinhold 1984: 36.
[12] Richard 1994:197. Note that Richard is arguing that the effectiveness of the anti-classics backlash during this period is overstated. See his chapter 7, "The myth of classical decline," pp. 196–231.
[13] Richard 1994: 197–8.

democracy," a condition in which opposition to classical learning ran parallel to a growing faith in the democratic "American Dream." During the ceremony, held in 1833, Emerson held forth at length in Latin, while the populist Jackson, according to widely held lore, uttered all the Latin he knew: "Ex post facto; e pluribus unum; sic semper tyrannis; quid pro quo."[14] The story may be apocryphal, but it well represents the sentiment behind the attacks on Latin and Greek. If a rough-hewn, backwoods person such as Andy Jackson could become president, what actual advantage lay in a classical education?

As such attacks continued, defenders of the classical tradition countered either by staunchly defending tradition (thus preserving their elitist position) or by declaring that Latin and Greek were indeed utilitarian, preparing young men for an active and successful life in their culture. A trustee of Franklin's school, one Richard Peters, declared that the study of Latin and Greek offered "Instruction of Youth in Piety, Virtue, and Useful Knowledge," and that there was "an Abundance of Useful Knowledge which can be acquired in no other Language."[15] Indeed, as I have shown elsewhere, there has been, from Roman times on, a constant cycle of attacks on the non-utilitarian nature of Latin followed by responses which defend Latin as utterly utilitarian.[16]

The debate continued, of course, but the elite are always slow to relinquish their power to a newer elite, and Latin remained supreme in the curriculum. If a person wanted to enter a serious profession, Latin was a prerequisite and Greek was almost as important. If nothing else, both remained important in college admissions. When, for example, Northwestern University was founded in 1855, Latin and Greek were required for admission to the classical curriculum; the science curriculum required Latin alone.[17] One can see the tension building in the influential report of the "Committee of Ten," under the leadership of Charles Eliot (1834–1926), the famed educator and president of Harvard. In 1892, the National Education Association formed the committee to study the chaotic state of contemporary high school curricula and charged the committee with creating recommendations designed to standardize America's high school curricula. In order to fulfill their task, the committee needed to study college entry requirements as well, since then, as now, college admissions requirements exerted great influence on what was studied in high school. The report of the subcommittee on Latin is very telling for two reasons.[18] First, the subcommittee toyed with the idea

[14] Pearcy 2005: 60–1. [15] Richard 1994: 222. [16] Kitchell 1998: 8–9
[17] Winterer 2002: 101. [18] National Education Association 1894: 60–74.

that perhaps the number of pre-collegiate courses in Latin ought to be increased, the better to prepare students for entry exams. Yet they concluded that there simply was no more room in the curriculum and that for this reason Latin had to be taught better, and earlier.[19] This shows first that college admissions still rested heavily upon the possession of Latin, but it also hints that the high school curriculum was filling up with more, ostensibly "relevant" courses. Their second conclusion was that Latin was being taught very poorly across the nation. The language was hard and the students seemed to make slow progress. The first part of this problem lay in the teachers themselves:

> It is a common practice to put the teaching of beginners into the hands of the youngest and most poorly paid teachers, that is to say, of those who have the slenderest equipment of knowledge and experience...
>
> If, then, the results of the study of Latin often seem absurdly meagre in proportion to the time spent upon the subject, we must look for the cause very largely in the fact that, at the most critical point in his study, the student is given over to an instructor of the least experience and knowledge.[20]

Moreover, the committee believed that the colleges and universities established entrance requirements that demanded familiarity with authors and works which were overly difficult and profoundly uninteresting. They longed for change, but, they lamented, "Thus far, the colleges have in general left the schools very little liberty of choice." One author mandated for study was Caesar who, they say, is "altogether too difficult for beginners." Vergil's *Bucolics* they call "the least original, and, to the school-boy, least interesting, and most difficult, part of the poet's works."[21]

The committee called for the substitution of Nepos for Caesar and, prior to reading Nepos, they felt the students should ease into complex prose with works such as Eutropius or selections from two transitional readers of the day such as the fairly recent *Gradatim* and the decidedly more venerable *Viri Romae*.[22] We will return to these sensible suggestions below, when we discuss the future, but for now it is well to review the lay of the Latin landscape in 1894 America. First, Latin was being taught by inept teachers. Second, the authors read after the first year of study were

---

[19] National Education Association 1894: 60–1.
[20] National Education Association 1894: 64–5.
[21] National Education Association 1894: 64.
[22] National Education Association 1894: 74. For *Gradatim*, cf. Heatley 1889. *Viri Romae* (Lhomond 1779) was revised by Andrews (1842) to accompany his Latin textbook and was the version the Committee would have known.

too difficult for the average student. Third, there was no room in the high school curriculum for more study of Latin due to the filling of the curriculum with more modern courses.

In their report on Greek, the subcommittee was equally plain:

> However unfortunate it may be thought, the fact remains that few schools will do more for their pupils in preparation for college than the college requirements for admission demand, so that the college determines in large measure the amount of work done in the school, as well as controls to some extent by the rigor or laxity of its entrance examinations the quality of the preparatory instruction.[23]

The members of the subcommittee clearly saw the hard reality of the driving force college admissions exerted on secondary school curricula, and once colleges and universities abandoned Latin and/or Greek as a criterion for admission, the decline of these languages was assured. Indeed, there was already some reason for unease.[24] In 1824, "Hobart College was established as the first college in the United States (or England for that matter) with no instruction in Greek or Latin." In 1827, reports issued at Amherst College proposed a parallel, non-classical track, and similar contemporary reforms were discussed at both Harvard and the University of Virginia.[25]

As LaFleur reports, "Harvard abandoned its Greek admissions in 1886, and by the end of the century most colleges had followed suit; Yale dropped the Latin requirement in 1931 ... and most other American colleges did likewise during the 1930s and 1940s."[26]

Yale's eventual capitulation was hard fought, however, for it was at Yale University, the site of the conference that led to this volume, that a major battle in the war against classics was fought in 1828, five years before Jackson's speech at Harvard.

The Yale Report

In 1827 Judge Noyes Darling, a former Yale tutor and at the time a state senator, rose at Yale's commencement and delivered a speech which must have been rather shocking to many in the audience. Darling openly called for the removal of Latin and Greek from the Yale curriculum. The university immediately did what universities have always done, and formed a committee to study the problem. In 1828 the committee issued the

---

[23] National Education Association 1894: 76.
[24] What follows is based on Urofsky 1965: 54–8.   [25] Kliebard 1992: 7; cf. Urofsky 1965: 54–8.
[26] LaFleur 1991: 124. Cf. Urofsky 1965: 53–7, Kennedy 1984: 341–2.

renowned "Yale Report," which solidly defended the classical curriculum and its central role in education.[27]

The authors of the report were well aware of the current thinking, the crux of which was that American education was following moss-covered European models not at all suited to the realities of nineteenth-century America. The report sums up the argument perfectly: "The same systems, however, with slight alterations, have been brought down to the present day, and now reign in our public seminaries,— while the general circumstances of the country have become totally changed."[28]

The authors of the report strenuously defend Yale, claiming that it *had* changed over the years. But at no point do they even hint that the teaching of Latin should be part of that change.

> The committee, however, do not rest their opposition to the proposed plan solely on the considerations already suggested. The thorough study of the ancient languages, particularly the Latin and Greek, not only before but subsequently to an admission into college, they are fully satisfied, is, in many respects decidedly and positively useful to the pupil.[29]

One way to view the report is to celebrate it as "the definitive expression of the philosophy of liberal arts education as seen by nineteenth-century American scholars."[30] By continuing to require classical languages for college admission, Yale helped ensure that other colleges would keep them and this, in turn, as the Committee of Ten had foreseen, ensured that high schools throughout the country kept them in their curricula, at least for a while.

That, of course, is the good news. But the bad news resides in the fact that it is equally possible to view the report as a reaffirmation and reinforcement of a tradition of educational exclusion and elitism. The report repeatedly makes a plea to the utility of Latin and Greek, but it does so by stressing over and over how the mental discipline and overall knowledge obtained through their study will help current students with their future careers in theology, law, medicine, and the like – undeniably the professions of the few.[31] As it had been in the Middle Ages, Latin continued to be the secret handshake that allowed one into the halls of the privileged. It would take the Civil War to push this sort of thinking to a *reductio ad absurdum*.

---

[27] Yale University 1828: 36–7. [28] Yale University 1828: 43. [29] Yale University 1828: 52.
[30] Herbst 2004: 213. [31] Urofsky 1965, Herbst 2004, Pearcy 2005: 60–72.

Reconstruction

Let us turn now to another fascinating episode in this battle between utility and elitism, one that is especially relevant in these heady days after the nation has elected its first African-American president. I am referring to the period of Reconstruction when North and South alike struggled with the question of how best to deal with the millions of slaves now declared free by the recently assassinated Abraham Lincoln. The classics had long been used as a source for arguments both for and against slavery[32] and, now that it had been abolished, they found themselves once more at the heart of the debate.

Chief among the problems was the matter of education. The issue of the educational philosophies dealing with this recently freed population is extraordinarily complex, but can probably be viewed for the present purposes in rather broad ways.[33] Only the diehard racists believed that not educating the recently freed slaves was an option. It is a simple matter to keep slaves, Caliban for example, ignorant, and, when slavery is legal, one may do so with impunity. In fact, during slavery, most southern states had prohibited teaching slaves to read and write, often by actual legislation.[34] But free people, even those consigned by Jim Crow laws to live a repressed and segregated life, could no longer be denied education without eventual civil unrest, either from the oppressed minority or from their privileged northern supporters. Some course of action was called for. But which course to follow?

The debate over how to implement the education of freedmen seems to have brought out the best and the worst in the debaters, often uncovering deeply ingrained prejudices. None other than Matthew Arnold, upon visiting Oberlin College, was invited to the classroom in which Mary Church Terrell (1863–1954), later the renowned author of *A Colored Woman in a White World*, was studying Greek. She relates in her book that he listened as the talented young woman recited and translated a passage. He was astonished at what he had seen, because, he said, "he thought the tongue of the African was so thick he could not be taught to pronounce the Greek correctly."[35] Well prior to this time, in 1833, John

---

[32] Richard 2009: 182–203.
[33] For a brief history of the exclusion of Blacks from classical learning, see Malamud 2011a: 281–3.
[34] Nieman (1994: vii) states that Tennessee was an exception. But Ashmore (1954: 6–7) and Bond (1970: 21) claim the ban was universal and had been in place for three decades, adding that even free persons of color could not be educated in Mississippi.
[35] Quoted by Cook and Tatum (2010: 98). My thanks to Joy Connoly of New York University and Helen Morales of University of California, Santa Barbara for pointing this book out to me.

C. Calhoun had claimed that only if and when a black man learned ancient Greek, an event he thought impossible, would he believe that the black man was the intellectual equal of the white man.[36]

The role that the classics played in Reconstruction has begun to be studied in depth by classicists in recent years, and there is much more to be done.[37] For now, let me only sketch the outlines of the arguments. At opposite ends of the debate stood those who promulgated either industrial or classical education. Industrial education was a practical education, one that would obtain jobs and social stability for the African-American community. S. C. Armstrong, a northern officer who fought at Gettysburg in 1863 and later in the same year gained command of the "8th US Colored Troops," became interested in the welfare of African Americans after the war. He championed the cause of an industrial education when he founded the Hampton Normal and Agricultural Institute, now known as Hampton University. Armstrong's student, one Booker Taliaferro Washington, carried the message to his own institution – the Tuskegee Institute, where he prepared recently freed slaves to learn a trade that would ensure them work following graduation.

Other people, even some of good intent, used racism to justify reserving a classical curriculum to whites. Atticus G. Haygood, born the same year as Armstrong, and later the president of Emory College, served as "chief agent" of the John Fox Slater fund, begun in 1882 for the industrial education of the recently freed African Americans along industrial lines. He truly believed that this sort of education was the salvation of the former slaves' race and labored hard to make this happen. He may have been a bit naive when he said, "Alas, that there ever was any hinderance to their education! God be thanked! There is now, January, 1881, next to no opposition to their instruction. Where one benighted neighborhood can be found where their education is opposed, twenty may be found where it is encouraged."[38]

W. E. B. DuBois himself called Haygood "the fairest minded of White Southerners,"[39] but beneath his apparent benevolence lurked some odd beliefs. Consider this explanation of why the freedmen could not suddenly be given a liberal arts education.

If some power could feed and clothe and shelter them by the distribution of all things needful for their bodies, could dismiss them from their toils and send the

---

[36] Cook and Tatum 2010: 95.
[37] The work of Ronnick (2005; cf. bibliography there) is especially notable in this regard as is the recent work of Cook and Tatum (2010), Hall *et al.* (2011), Orrells *et al.* (2011).
[38] Haygood 1881: 15.   [39] DuBois 1903: 67.

whole race to school for a term of years, the problem of the Negro's right education would not be solved, although every one mastered a liberal course of studies. Such schooling would create new and harder problems; under such conditions their moral and social education could not keep pace with their mental development, and thus a new and deadly virus would be introduced into their very blood. One obvious result would be, such education would multiply vagabonds and sharpers by the million. For true education means far more than "book learning"; there must be education of the instincts, the feelings, the habits, the will, the conscience.[40]

Clearly, in the minds of some, the goal of an industrial education was, at least in part, to tame savagery and create decent citizens. Its job was, as Gustavus Glenn, the Commissioner of Education in Georgia, put it, to "educate the beast out of the Negro."[41] The wrong kind of education, Haygood argued, would destroy black docility and set loose what he saw as the inherent savagery of an inferior race upon the South, claiming that "education in the liberal arts would merely breed discontent among members of the race and ill prepare them for their role." That role, of course, was to take menial jobs and remain subservient to whites – that is to say, to have the role of Caliban, a savage refused the higher knowledge of a classical education.[42] There was also an undercurrent of belief that a study of ancient rhetoric overly empowered Blacks, giving them tools to fight slavery and abolition, which could prove troublesome.[43] No less a figure than Basil Lanneau Gildersleeve said after the end of the Civil War: "We of the South have little left except our systems of higher education," and his overt sympathy with slavery and antipathy toward Reconstruction make it clear that to lose the classical curriculum to freedmen would be the ultimate indignity.[44] Michelle Ronnick has recently traced the vitriol heaped upon those intrepid educators who dared to teach such subjects to newly freed slaves.[45]

Others, black and white alike, felt that industrial education was settling for too little. Merely to teach the freedman useful skills was to consign him or her (and the entire race) perpetually to the lower rungs of society. Some black leaders saw it as a way to continue a form of slavery in which the African American was to be relegated to roles that would mean he or she worked for whites, continuing to further Caucasian well-being just as they had when they were enslaved. W. E. B. DuBois called this a "proposal to educate black boys and girls simply as servants and underlings, or simply

---

[40] Haygood 1881: 136–7.   [41] Quoted by Finkenbine 1994: 76.
[42] Finkenbine 1994: 76–81.   [43] Lupher and Vandiver 2011: 99–101, Malamud 2011a.
[44] Lupher and Vandiver 2011: 332–3.   [45] Ronnick 2011.

for the use of other people."⁴⁶ What was needed, he and others before him claimed, was what had been, up to that point, the almost exclusive bailiwick of the white man – a classically based education. Many black educational leaders saw the classical curriculum as a way to claim the white man's education and to prove that blacks were able to rise to its challenges. Coupled with this was the beginning of an argument that would eventually culminate in Martin Bernal's 1987 *Black Athena*. Recent work by Margaret Malamud and an article by Kenneth Goings and Eugene O'Connor have studied the movement within black educational circles to use classical texts to trace the beginnings of African-American culture to classical times. The latter pair claim that because such educators were convinced "that the Classics were their inheritance and their right," the classical curriculum remained strong in the curricula of traditionally black colleges and universities.⁴⁷

Everyone seems to have had an opinion about this educational divide. Dubois is commonly proclaimed the champion of the classically based education and to a large extent he was. But a new book by Alridge re-evaluates DuBois' position and offers great insight into the double-edged sword that is elitism.⁴⁸ DuBois, he claims, held a mixed view concerning education for the freedmen and understood full well that there was a place for industrial education. People, after all, have to make a living. But, DuBois stressed, this was not the path to advancement of the race. For the advancement of his race, DuBois looked to what he called the Talented Tenth, the most intellectually gifted 10 percent of the race, male and female alike, who would become the leaders, scientists, physicians and lawyers who would lead the way.⁴⁹ Dubois had no problem with openly calling this Tenth, who would receive the classically based, liberal education, an "aristocracy."⁵⁰ The white elitists would now have the competition of a black elite. Different ends, but the same means – the study of Latin and Greek.

There is so much to pursue here that I am tempted to go further, but space restrictions force us to come to the present, for charges of elitism continued to follow the classics in later years.

Decline of Latin and movement away from elitism

Most classicists in the field are aware that Latin studies fell off sharply in the 1970s. But it is clear that the decline in Latin studies began, not in the

---

⁴⁶ Alridge 2008: 63. The quote is taken from a speech of 1905.
⁴⁷ Malamud 2011b; Goings and O'Connor 2011: 102–3.   ⁴⁸ Alridge 2008.
⁴⁹ DuBois 1903. Cf. Cook and Tatum 2010: "The making of the talented tenth" (chapter 3), 93–124.
⁵⁰ Alridge 2008: 63.

70s as so often thought, but, as Carl Richard traces, much earlier. In 1886 Harvard eliminated Greek as an entry requirement and by 1912 two-thirds of colleges and universities required neither Latin nor Greek.[51] The effect quickly trickled down to the high school level. In 1910 an all-time high of 83.3% of high school students studied languages and Latin was the king – 49% of students studied Latin while all other modern languages combined accounted for only 34.3% of the 915,061 high school students of the time.[52] Spanish, today's most popular language, comprised but 0.7% of students. But things were to change quickly.

By 1922 Latin (27.5%) was in a dead heat with modern foreign languages (27.4%) and by 1928 Latin lagged behind them (22% to 25.2%) and has never overturned this trend. Increasingly, "relevance" seems to have taken precedence over tradition. For a while German rose to the fore, Russian was deemed crucial during the Cold War, and now it is Spanish. Soon it may be Arabic, Chinese, or even Korean. The specifics change according to the politics and demographics of a given era, but the trend is clear. For over thirty years Latin has been studied by 2% of the school population or less.

My own career can serve as an illustration. I entered high school in 1961, when Latin was studied by 7.5% of all high school students, a raw number of 680,234. In 1962, my second year of Latin in high school, the raw number was 702,135, but this amounted to only 7.1% of students. I graduated college as a classics major in 1969, completely unaware that this year marked the seventh straight year of Latin enrollment decline. By 1970, when I was in graduate school, they numbered 265,293 (2%).

In 1974 I entered the world of teaching high school Latin. By 1976, the year I left high school teaching to begin my college teaching career, Latin enrollments had fallen to 150,470 (1.1%), the lowest point they have hit to date. I had entered the field when Latin studies were at their modern peak but now, as I began my college teaching career, they were at their lowest point ever, having sustained an overall fall of about 78.5%.

Why did this happen? Of course, there are many reasons. The United States were in turmoil. The sixties and seventies brought massive social disruption, with the Vietnamese War, assassinations of political and social leaders, and the Civil Rights movement. The voice of youth became louder and more demanding as the voice of the establishment, of received wisdom, of the elite, grew faint and mistrusted. "Out with requirements!" the young demanded, and this included foreign language requirements

---

[51] Richard 2009: 207.
[52] Data for this and for what follows were taken from Draper and Hicks 2002: 5, Table 1.

and, most especially, difficult, non-utilitarian, dead languages. Education for its own sake was equally suspect. It was time for relevant, practical curricula and for electives rather than requirements. It was time, in short, to toss out Latin on its elitist ear.

Amid this turmoil Latin and her advocates did not "go gentle into that good night." We fought back against the revolution in what I have called elsewhere the "Great Counter-offensive." If you have ever heard of the Committee for the Promotion of Latin, have used one of the new Latin textbooks, or have read an article about Latin pedagogy, you have benefited from the Great Counter-offensive.

Thanks to this movement, born, it is admitted, out of dire necessity, the decline in enrollment has been checked and the teaching of Latin has changed dramatically. A trinity of new textbooks (*Cambridge Latin Course*, *Oxford Latin Course*, and *Ecce Romani*) arose in the late sixties and early seventies in an effort to modernize our approach for the high school level and earlier.[53] (Elsewhere in this volume Bob Lister clearly outlines the causes that led to the *Cambridge Latin Course*.) My own *Disce!* is now attempting to do the same for college students.[54] The common theme of all these books is that Latin can and should appeal to the masses on its own merits. It is interesting *per se* and can be taught in an interesting manner.

The precipitous decline in Latin enrollments finally forced our discipline to begin to understand that Latin and Greek could no longer bring in the crowds as they had – by dictating the rules from an elite position in the curriculum. Gone was the power of college entrance requirements. Gone, in far too many places, was a meaningful language requirement. Be it at the collegiate or the pre-collegiate level, Latin now had to attract students on its own merits. As a result, we began to advertise our courses, to try to make them interesting and attractive and to fight for every credit hour we could get. We fought back with groups such as the Committee for Latin and Greek, National Latin Recruitment Week, and the Committee for the Promotion of Latin.

To some extent, this counter-offensive or counter-revolution has worked. The decline in enrollments has ceased and we are seeing modest gains. But a serious threat to our profession has arisen of late and, I submit, it is, as it so often has been, rooted in an inherently accepted elitism. This problem concerns the current state of upper division Latin, and it is to be found equally in high schools and colleges.

---

[53] Cambridge School Classics Project 2007, Balme and Morwood 1996, Lawall 2009.
[54] Kitchell and Sienkewicz 2011.

The new elitism – the AP exam and college curricula

We are all well aware that while a program may be thriving at the Latin 1 and 2 levels (usually the first and second years of study), there is a terrible drop-off in enrollment at the Latin 3 and 4 level. This phenomenon plagues all Latin programs, be they at the high school or college level and, I think, the causes are more alike than they are different.

At the high school level the culprit is the Advanced Placement (AP) exams[55] and the fundamental elitism upon which they are built. Parents demand AP so that their above average children can get into above average schools. The students demand AP courses to add luster to their transcripts. School districts want them so that they look "good" to legislatures and voters. Many colleges have been forced to grant college-level credit for high school work because if they do not, the brightest students will go elsewhere. Finally, teachers want AP courses because after two years of teaching "made up" Latin, they long to teach "real Latin."

But to whom can they teach this "real Latin?" Only to the best and brightest, those able to do AP work – classics' "Talented Tenth." Far too high a percentage of high school Latin 3 and 4 classes are AP only. Amid all our hard work we have constructed a system that entices students of all abilities and backgrounds into the language at its beginning levels. The "trinity readers" were designed to do just this. But in far too many schools those who are able to go on are only those of the highest ability, because the students must jump from the comfortable world of a text such as *Ecce Romani* directly into the maelstrom of Caesar or Vergil. It is like asking a third year English as a Second Language [ESL] student to jump from a primer into Dickens or Milton. Darwinism rules the day and only the elite survive. Without intending to do so, we have said, "This far shall you come, and no further." Unless you are our "Classical Talented Tenth," you cannot continue to study Latin.

At the collegiate level, much the same is true, but for different reasons. Most colleges can only offer one or two upper division Latin courses a

---

[55] The Advanced Placement program in the United States and Canada is run under the auspices of the College Entrance Examination Board. High school students take approved AP courses, which are supposed to be of college-level difficulty. Participating colleges and universities offer college credit for students who score well on the AP exams offered by the organization at the end of these courses. There formerly were two Latin AP courses, Latin Literature and Vergil. In 2012 these were reduced to a single course, which focuses on Vergil's *Aeneid* and Caesar's *Gallic Wars*. Many high schools that are able to offer only one advanced Latin course for third- and fourth-year students structure this course to conform to the AP curriculum.

semester. These typically are courses in authors that will help a student attend graduate school and perpetuate the existence of college-level classics departments. I certainly admit that we must provide for the future instructors of classics at the college level. And I admit that these are fine authors – Cicero, Tacitus, Livy, Horace, Vergil, Ovid. But, as the Committee of Ten pointed out long ago, they are also difficult. Do Spanish 3 students leap into Cervantes? Do ESL students in their third semester read Faulkner? No, they read material appropriate for their current level of language acquisition – short stories, novels, and plays written in ability-appropriate language – things that can be read, not things that have to be deciphered. Is there no room in our world for the student of average ability who simply likes Latin and wishes to continue in it? Is advanced literature study the only goal of our language classes? Are we not clever enough at long last to listen to the Committee of Ten and find ways to be able to accommodate both the elite student and the one who likes Latin and wishes to continue in it? What has happened is ironic. The loosening of the iron grip of college admissions policies, coupled with social unrest, led to the inclusion of students of divergent ability levels into our classrooms. Yet the constraints of the AP now too often dictate what our Latin 3 and 4 students should read and AP constraints have merely replaced those formerly imposed by college admissions rules. On our college and university campuses overly traditional curricula for classics majors do much the same. In short, we have once more reverted to reserving the fruits of learning Latin for the elite and have seen to it that the drudgery of grammar and inflection are all that is held out to the average students. It need not be so.

As the Committee of Ten recommended, there are other texts that the average student can read in a Latin 3 class. Dorothy Sayers, the creator of the noble detective Lord Peter Wimsey, advocated, for example, for the inclusion of Medieval Latin texts in such courses.

Those whose pedantic preference for a living language persuades them to deprive their pupils of all these advantages might substitute Russian, whose grammar is still more primitive. Russian is, of course, helpful with the other Slav dialects. There is something also to be said for Classical Greek. But my own choice is Latin. Having thus pleased the Classicists among you, I will proceed to horrify them by adding that I do not think it either wise or necessary to cramp the ordinary pupil upon the Procrustean bed of the Augustan Age, with its highly elaborate and artificial verse forms and oratory. Post-classical and mediaeval Latin, which was a living language down to the end of the Renaissance, is easier and in some ways livelier; and a study of it helps to dispel the widespread notion that learning and literature came to a full-stop when Christ was born and only woke up again at the Dissolution of the Monasteries.[56]

And classical texts do exist which are fairly straightforward and more easily read than others. Regular-level Latin 3 students could benefit (and feel more confident) from graded readers such as *Fabulae Graecae* (based on the older *Fabulae Faciles*)[57] or even from the older *Viri Romae*. The *Legamus* series of transitional texts, published by Bolchazy-Carducci, could be utilized in a survey course for those just emerging from learning the basics. This entirely parallels what is done in modern languages and is pedagogically sound. But, one may object, "these are not original authors." That is undeniable. But they are ability-appropriate for many students who would otherwise be driven away in fear and trembling at Sayer's "Procrustean bed of the Augustan Age." If authentic ancient authors are required, some candidates might be Nepos, Phaedrus, and the shorter poems of Catullus. Nepos, we recall, was recommended by the Committee of Ten as far back as 1894.[58]

So, without thinking very much about it, we have allowed another sort of elitism to get into our system – this time the elitism of what is considered to be appropriate for our students to read. Yet we have been warned. First it was the Committee of Ten and then, in 1924, The American Classical League Investigation, the largest and most comprehensive study of the state of Latin teaching in America ever undertaken, came to the same conclusions. They, too, felt that the curriculum needed adjustment and suggested, for the entire second year of study (i.e. after all basic grammar had been presented) that the readings be taken from a very interesting list of transitional readers then in print. Even in the third semester, they recommended adapted readings from standard authors and reserved unchanged readings for the fourth semester.[59] In short, they chose to treat Latin like a language and not like a code or a grammar book. They advised that we move the students along at a proper pace and that we value the solid acquisition of the language more highly than a forced march through a set number of pages of incomprehensible prose or poetry from certain highly valued authors. They felt we should make reading and

---

[56] Sayers 1979: 94.
[57] The first manifestation of this book was Ritchie 1884. Much as Andrews (*Viri Romae*, 1842) revised the older book of Lhomond (1779), Lawall (1991) has produced the excellent *Fabulae Graecae*.
[58] National Education Association 1894: 63–4. The committee recommended this because "Caesar is altogether too difficult for beginners."
[59] American Classical League 1924: 144–51.

comprehension skills more important than translation skills. Since that time this advice has been repeated, and ignored, frequently.[60]

This brings me at last to the title of my paper. In my view Latin is definitely standing at a crossroads. We will choose our future or our lack of it depending on which path we follow. We can continue the current, inherently elitist mainstream view that only the best authors should be studied and only by the best students. We can do this. It is our choice. But if we choose this path then we stand in danger of existing in "solitary perfection" – quite good at what we do but few in number and rather alone. The term "solitary perfection" comes from a chance encounter while browsing the internet, where a web page devoted to the natural world of Robertson, NSW, Australia, shows a picture of a beautiful flower, a clematis, and states that it is "a fairly weak plant, which struggles to produce, every year, a few flowers. But what stunning flowers!"[61] Will that be us?

I might also have used the words "splendid isolation." The term was most famously used at the end of the nineteenth century by Viscount George Goschen to refer to the Britain which, splendid as it was, preferred to remain aloof from most European politics. We can be splendid. We can, in elitist isolation, offer advanced Latin only to the Talented Tenth and the future classics professors who will replace us. In short, we can see to it that the best is read only by the elite. But if we do this we must also be prepared to watch our empire shrink and dwindle as we are drawn inevitably into the next, diminished, phase of our pedagogical history.

It is time for the profession as a whole to study the problem of upper division Latin studies. Are we here only for the few? Is our task to continue the exclusion of all but the best from the study of the hardest and best, or shall we once and for all ensure the future of our profession by thinking, and acting upon, a simple thought – Latin can and should be enjoyed by everyone.

---

[60] Cf. the thorough study of the report's goals and influence by Wraga (2009).
[61] http://peonyden.blogspot.com/2007/11/whte-clematis-solitary-perfection.html (accessed 28 March 2013).

CHAPTER 13

Exclusively for everyone – to what extent has the Cambridge Latin Course *widened access to Latin?*

Bob Lister

Historical context

Fifty years ago, Latin was a subject for the elite, available only to the few as a passport to the most prestigious universities in Britain and thence to positions of power in the law, the civil service and government. Together with Greek it was the cornerstone of the academic curriculum and its continued pre-eminence was in part due to a myth, that "of the effortless superiority of the classically educated man, able, by virtue of his training, to master any problem in any sphere of life so long as it was amenable to intellectual analysis (and what problem – so went the myth – was not?)."[1] In this paper I will first examine the educational changes in the 1960s that marked the end of the domination of the traditional curriculum by the classical languages and then consider the role of the *Cambridge Latin Course* from the 1970s to the present in making Latin accessible to a wider range of students. I will begin, however, with some contextual information about the education system in England.

The 1944 Education Act established three types of state-maintained secondary school in England and Wales, and divided children by academic achievement at the age of eleven: grammar schools for the academically gifted; secondary modern and technical schools for the less able students. An examination (known as the 11-Plus), taken in the last year of primary education, determined which type of secondary school students attended, with 25 percent going on to grammar schools. This examination also determined whether or not a student would have the opportunity to study Latin and Greek since the classical languages were offered only in grammar schools. Thus three-quarters of the population never had the opportunity to study Latin or Greek, merely because they had failed an examination at the age of ten. The only way that children not deemed able enough to go

---

[1] Sharwood Smith 1977: 1.

to grammar school could study Latin (and perhaps Greek) was by attending an independent school (attended by 5 percent of students in the early 1960s). But in this paper I am going to focus on Latin in state-funded schools because this is where there have been most changes in Latin provision in the last forty years.

Latin, then, was an exclusive subject, doubly so, in fact, because, even in the exclusive world of the grammar schools, the weaker and less well motivated students were either not offered Latin at all, gave it up of their own accord as soon as they were given the chance to do so, or were ruthlessly weeded out. In 1958, for instance, less than one third of students in grammar schools nationally took Latin O-Level.[2]

In the grammar schools Latin was typically a diet of Kennedy's *Revised Latin Primer*, Caesar's *Gallic Wars* and prose composition. Promoted for the mental discipline and academic rigour it instilled, Latin was taught exclusively as a linguistic subject, with little or no consideration given to the cultural and historical context in which the language flourished. It is not surprising, therefore, that many students struggled with the subject; and many only continued their study to O-Level because it was a compulsory requirement for entry to Oxford and Cambridge for all subjects. Yet there was little attempt to change the Latin curriculum in spite of the subject's unpopularity. Most classics teachers, it seems, were unmoved by the fact that their students were bored or bemused by Latin. An article in an educational publication in 1958 encapsulated the prevailing justification for Latin in the curriculum:

> Latin's claim to a place in the school curriculum must rest on the mental discipline it offers to the pupils in grappling with an inflected tongue. In short it is not SENECA but the subjunctive that makes Latin the subject for the school. The pity is that so few teachers realize this. Even if they do realize it, they too often look on the linguistics as a necessary evil... Latin will not survive like that. It needs teachers who believe in the ablative absolute. It needs men and women who have convictions about the gerund.[3]

As the leader writer acknowledges, however, not all teachers shared these views about the aims and priorities of Latin teaching. Opponents of the traditional approach had a number of concerns about traditional Latin. In particular they complained that there was an over-emphasis on teaching

---

[2] O-Levels were national examinations taken only by academically gifted students at the end of the year in which they were sixteen. They were replaced in 1988 by the General Certificate of Secondary Education (GCSE).
[3] A leading article in *The Times Educational Supplement*, 24 October 1958, cited in Forrest 1996: 11–12.

grammar at the expense of developing reading skills; that too many tasks depended merely on memorization; that teaching methods were at best inefficient and at worst totally ineffective; and that most of the students who started Latin never got as far as reading any Latin literature – which many considered the strongest argument for studying Latin in the first place. In fact these, and similar, concerns had been expressed at regular intervals for almost one hundred years to no avail. But when, in 1960, Oxford and Cambridge separately reached the same decision, to remove Latin as a compulsory matriculation requirement, suddenly the growing pressure for change turned into a wave of reform.

A clear change of mood was already evident at the annual general meeting of the Classical Association in April 1960 when the association passed a resolution calling for a general reconsideration of the aims and syllabus of the O-Level examination. There were two notable aspects to this resolution: first, the margin by which it was passed (200 for and 1 against), indicating a remarkable degree of unanimity on what had previously been a contentious and divisive issue; and second, the fact that the resolution had been proposed not, as might have been expected, by a school teacher but by a university professor, Charles Brink, the Kennedy Professor of Latin at Cambridge. This resolution heralded the beginning of a period of very close co-operation between school and university, particularly over what Brink himself called "small" Latin, i.e. Latin as experienced not by future classics scholars but by students for whom O-Level Latin was the summit of their classical education. He was alarmed by the high drop-out rate of pupils from Latin courses before reaching O-Level and concerned that small Latin was nothing more than "the preliminary to a classical education which never follows."[4] In short, he was arguing that Latin courses must offer some surrender value: each year of a course must be able to stand as a discrete unit with its own achievable learning goals.

However, of greater significance to the future of Latin in schools than the removal of Latin as a matriculation requirement at Oxford and Cambridge was the Labour Government's move in 1965 to implement its election promise to restructure the whole of secondary education, abolishing grammar schools and introducing a single, comprehensive, system of secondary education. Since Latin was so closely associated with grammar schools – in the words of Chris Stray, "Latin was the symbolic exemplar of the academic world of the grammar school,"[5] – many classicists saw this as the death knell for Latin. Discussion no longer centred on ways of

---

[4] Brink 1962; quotation from p. 8.   [5] Stray 2003: 3.

improving lower school Latin courses and methods but on how to prevent the subject's total extinction.

The *Cambridge Latin Course* and the story-based approach

But while pessimists saw the proposed reorganization of secondary schools as a potential disaster, optimists saw it, on the contrary, as an opportunity for expansion: as long as classics was offered in some form in the new comprehensive school curriculum, then many more students than previously would have the chance to learn Latin. What was needed for the new type of school was a new type of Latin course in keeping with the spirit of the age. In early 1966 a new organization, the Cambridge School Classics Project (CSCP), was set up, with a grant of £50,000 from The Schools Council, a government organization, and matching funding from the Nuffield Trust, an educational charity that championed inductive learning and the child-centred classroom. David Morton, the first Director of CSCP, saw it as a principal aim of the new organization to "investigate ways of improving the teaching of Latin at the early stage, i.e. up to O-Level, with special reference to the task of improving reading fluency."[6]

The challenge was to create a Latin course, which was sufficiently accessible, at least in the early stages, to engage and motivate less able students while at the same time challenging and rewarding enough to stretch and inspire the next generation of classics scholars. This was linked with a fundamental shift in priorities: the new course would present language not as an end in itself, but as a means of gaining access to the literature and the culture from which it sprang. To deliver the new priorities the dominant grammar-based approach to Latin was replaced by a story-based approach, which had the students reading connected, meaningful Latin from the very beginning of the course. Out went disconnected sentences about Roman leaders and the wars they fought; in came stories built round a "typical" Roman family living in Pompeii in the second half of the first century CE. Out went detailed explanations of grammar, followed by exercises of Latin into English and English into Latin sentences to practise the new grammar (and prepare the way for prose composition); in came stories embedding the new grammar – with students given the opportunity to acquire the new grammar for themselves – with subsequent explanation of the grammar, and technical terminology, kept to a minimum.

[6] CSCP/Advisory Panel Minutes, 4 December 1965, cited in Forrest 1996: 50.

In fact these changes were not quite as radical as many believed at the time. Many of the principles enshrined in the *Cambridge Latin Course* (CLC), as the course was called, were already to be found in *Latin for Today*, published in the late 1920s. It too was built round stories about a Roman family and it too emphasized the importance of studying the language in its cultural context. *Latin for Today* was an American textbook written by a high school teacher, Mason DeWitt Gray, and its design had been informed by the findings of a major research project into Latin teaching undertaken in 1921 by the American Classical League (ACL).[7] Interestingly, one of the main concerns raised in the ACL report was that raised nearly forty years later by Professor Brink, the high drop-out rate from Latin courses. The ACL report noted that 69% of all the pupils who began Latin in the secondary schools studied Latin for one or two years only and recommended "better adaptation of the content of the course to the ability and interests of the pupils."[8]

One feature of the CLC, however, which did mark it out as a radical departure from traditional courses was the model sentences that opened each new stage, presenting the new linguistic feature in what might be called a cartoon strip. In Figure 13.1 we see the introduction of the perfect passive participle. (This is the second in a series of six pictures with accompanying text.)

The recommended approach would be to tackle the model sentences as a whole class activity and

1. read through the sentences in Latin (in this example taking particular care to bring out the phrasing in the third sentence);
2. ask questions, in English, to establish key elements of the picture to aid subsequent translation of the sentences (here, for example, bringing out the evident approval of the architect – whose status is indicated by the toga – will help elicit the meaning of the verb, *laudō*, for those students who have forgotten it);
3. seek volunteers to translate the first two sentences (taking particular care to ensure that all the students know how to translate "*architectus fabrum laudāvit*" correctly);
4. read the last sentence again in Latin, drawing attention to the new language feature through stress and intonation;
5. after establishing that the craftsman was very happy, ask students to suggest meanings for the phrase "*ab architectō laudātus.*"

---

[7] American Classical League 1924.   [8] American Classical League 1924: 31.

Exclusively for everyone

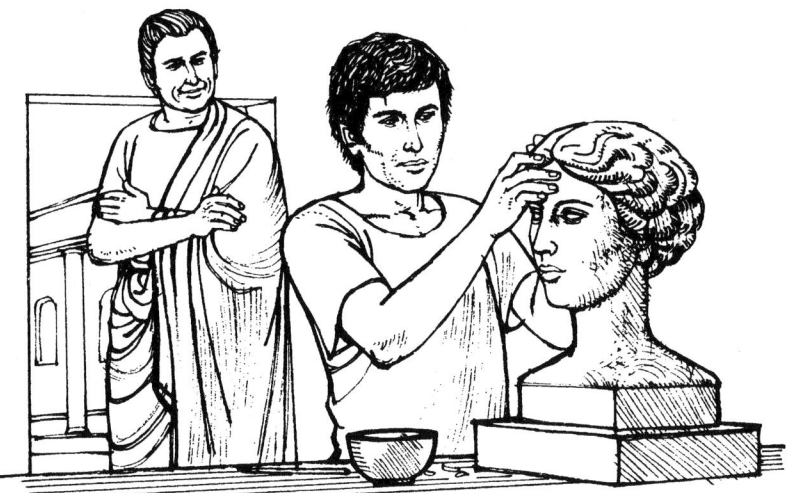

faber prīmus statuam deae Sūlis faciēbat.
architectus fabrum laudāvit, quod perītus erat et dīligenter labōrābat.
faber, ab architectō laudātus, laetissimus erat.

Figure 13.1: *Cambridge Latin Course* Stage 21 model sentence

With a little prompting, students will come up with a range of translations for the last sentence, such as:

> The craftsman, (having been) praised by the architect, was very happy.
> The craftsman was very happy when/because/after the architect praised him.
> The craftsman was very happy when/because/after he had been praised by the architect.

Once the examples have been pooled, many teachers will at this point highlight the new form of the verb and provide a literal translation ("having been...") before moving on to the next set of sentences to reinforce the new feature. But the key point about this approach is that concrete examples precede abstract explanation, giving the students themselves the chance to assimilate and, as it were, discover the new point of grammar. In the model sentences introducing the perfect passive participle, exactly the same pattern is used with three successive pictures, with a statement in one sentence immediately re-expressed as a participial phrase in the next. In the example above we have *architectus fabrum laudāvit* re-expressed as *faber, ab architectō laudātus*; then, with the next picture, *architectus fabrum incitāvit* followed by *faber, ab architectō incitātus*; and finally *architectus fabrum vituperāvit* followed by *faber, ab architectō vituperātus*. Able students are very quick to see patterns and by the third example will be able to identify the perfect passive participle immediately and confidently translate the participial phrase.

Opponents of the CLC argue that such an approach encourages guesswork and leaves students without the security of a grammatical explanation far too long after they have first encountered them in the model sentences. The Chief Examiner for O-Level Latin, Colin Dexter, was a leading critic of the CLC when it was first published and in a detailed critique argued that:

> its greatest weakness is that it does not give the learner very much in the way of grammatical and syntactical knowledge so necessary, as I see it, for the understanding of languages so highly inflected and so complex as Latin and Greek. I am suggesting, in short, that the languages are difficult and that they demand, on the technical level, a pretty rigorous discipline.[9]

But from the outset there were many supporters of the new course. In their eyes any deficiencies in the rigorous discipline offered by the CLC were more than outweighed by its benefits. For example Jill Simpson, an experienced Latin teacher, wrote in 1973:

> That the pupils themselves respond to the *Cambridge Latin Course* is evident. Many more want to stay the course, even though they find the language difficult, and reach a higher level of achievement than they otherwise might. Interest flows into free time and holidays when the Romans are zealously pursued by the most un-classical people! Even some of the less able want to continue Latin in the sixth form.[10]

A great strength of the CLC was its ability to reach out to students who would have struggled from an early stage with a grammar-based course. This made it a viable course to use in the newly created comprehensive schools where children were taught in mixed ability classrooms. Book One in particular, set in Pompeii and coming to a climax with the eruption of Vesuvius, was accessible to a much wider range of students than had ever been contemplated by the authors of traditional Latin courses. This was achieved not only through the design of the textbook but also through the supplementary resources that accompanied it. These included audio tapes

---

[9] Dexter 1973: 9.   [10] Simpson 1973: 5.

of key stories and slide sets (later replaced by film strips) to illustrate the cultural background.

Even Colin Dexter admitted that students were engaged by the stories in the CLC, and John Sharwood Smith, the leading classics reformer of the 1960s, explained, in a response to Dexter, *why*, in his view, students were so engaged. It was because, he said:

> the language material is embedded in what one might, by stretching the term a little, call an historical novel; and not a bad historical novel at that. The characters are, considering the limitations imposed, well-drawn and their doings interestingly conceived and related with skill.[11]

The CLC goes digital

Forty years on the CLC has changed little in terms of structure, emphasis, and narrative, and the storyline remains a key selling point. In presentation, however, the CLC has undergone a major makeover. In the light of a teacher survey in the late 1970s there was a substantial revision of the text in the early 1980s, resulting in the removal of some of the Course's more radical ideas (for example, in the first edition the traditional names of the cases had been replaced by Form A, B, C etc.); some pruning of longer stories in recognition of the limited time available in schools to cover the course; and the introduction of some improvements such as the use of macra. Then, in 1998, the CLC was published in colour for the first time in the United Kingdom: as well as sharpening the layout and freshening the general appearance of the course, this opened up new opportunities for the use of photographs and photo-essays to illustrate the cultural background.

But in terms of widening access to Latin, the most radical change to the CLC has come since 2000, with the creation of DVDs of digital resources for the first two books and a web site providing electronic support for all five books. These resources cover both linguistic and cultural aspects of the CLC. There is, for instance, an electronic dictionary, which not only provides the definition but also the correct pronunciation of every word in the course and every form of the word encountered. Furthermore all stories are available in interactive format, so that students can look up any word in any story with the click of a mouse. The resources also include many hours of video clips, with dramatizations of key stories in Latin and a

[11] Sharwood Smith 1975: 50–1.

wide range of 3–5 minute mini-documentaries on Roman life presented by leading academics.

But in many ways the most important aspect of the digitization of the CLC lies not so much in the enriched learning it has given existing students but the opportunities it has provided for new learners who have no access to a specialist teacher to take up Latin. The E-Learning Resources DVDs come with a built-in course for home-schooled and post-school learners (referred to as "independent" learners by CSCP) as well as students in schools with no specialist teacher. In addition the CSCP web site provides detailed advice and guidance both for schools wishing to start up Latin and for independent learners. Drawing on lessons learnt from a pilot project with two schools and a small group of independent learners in 2000–1, CSCP gained a very clear understanding of the infrastructure required to provide effective support for school students and independent learners. At a school level, for instance, even if students are learning Latin outside the school curriculum with an online tutor, there still needs to be a named member of the teaching staff who can liaise with the online tutor and help monitor students' progress.[12] Ten years on from the initial pilot, there are now more than 250 schools in England with no classics specialist offering a beginners' course in Latin using the DVDs, and more than 400 independent learners on the CSCP's e-tutoring programme, including 76 students taking the GCSE Latin course, and 44 the A-Level course.[13]

To what extent has the CLC extended access to Latin?

But in spite of the success of the CLC in traditional and, more recently, digital format, Latin in comprehensive schools has struggled to survive the unremitting pace of educational change of the last twenty years. The introduction in 1988 of a national curriculum for England and Wales was particularly damaging. This set out the school curriculum from 5 to 16 in highly prescriptive fashion, identifying a long list of compulsory subjects and leaving virtually no space for optional subjects such as the classical languages. As a result, in many state schools Latin was either forced off the curriculum or left with a minimal lesson allocation, making

---

[12] For a detailed discussion of teaching Latin *via* the internet, see Lister and Seranis 2005.
[13] Figures provided by CSCP, February 2009. GCSEs are the national examinations which replaced O-Levels and are generally taken by students at the end of year in which they are sixteen. A-Levels are advanced-level national examinations generally taken by pupils at the age of eighteen.

Table 13.1: *Latin GCSE entries by school type, 1988–2008*

	Comprehensive	Grammar	Independent
1988	4778	3715	7460
1989	4568	2807	8323
1990	3991	2627	7774
1991	3440	2292	8019
1992	3140	2008	8127
1993	2842	1964	7552
1994	2759	2031	7973
1995	2621	1905	8332
1996	2749	1985	7845
1997	2317	2083	7409
1998	2133	1772	6966
1999	1905	1833	6669
2000	1973	1915	6642
2001	1998	1852	6500
2002	1830	1834	6431
2003	1933	1825	6227
2004	1749	1719	6360
2005	1802	1586	6340
2006	1807	1820	6551
2007	1548	1638	6757
2008	1614	1703	6541

it very difficult to complete the GCSE syllabus in the time available. The effect on numbers taking Latin to GCSE is all too evident from Table 13.1.

In 1988 state school students accounted for just over half of the GCSE entries. By 2008 the state school entry had shrunk to just over a third of entries, with comprehensive schools particularly hard hit. Entries in independent schools, on the other hand, held up, mainly because, as a result of their independent status, they were not required to adopt the national curriculum.

Recent changes in the GCSE examination itself seem likely to have a further detrimental effect on comprehensive school Latin. Until 2000 there were two separate Latin GCSE examinations: a traditional GCSE with the emphasis on language, and a specially tailored *Cambridge Latin Course* GCSE with the emphasis on literature and culture. Even when these two examinations were merged into a single examination in 2000, there were still sufficient options to accommodate both a traditional and a CLC pathway through the qualification. But in 2008 the options were reduced and the literature/culture route, always the most popular route, was no longer available. It remains to be seen what impact this will have on entries from comprehensive schools.

So, how successful has CSCP's attempt been, to open up Latin to a wider audience? The writers never claimed to be creating a course for the *whole* ability range, but they did hope to make Latin accessible to the average student in the average comprehensive, at least to GCSE, and, speaking as someone who has used the CLC with a wide range of students in three different comprehensive schools over a period of fifteen years, I would argue that they have achieved this goal. (But then, as a past Director of CSCP, I would say that, wouldn't I?) Certainly the digitization of the course has undoubtedly opened up access to the subject in a way unimaginable forty years ago.

But the hard fact remains that only 14.9 percent of schools in England (and a mere 3.1 percent in Wales) offer Latin.[14] There are also signs that CSCP is losing the battle to sell Latin as a literary and cultural as well as linguistic subject. In the eyes of critics the CLC, in making Latin accessible, has made it easy, and "easy" does not fit well with the revitalized traditional branding of Latin as, in the words of Boris Johnson, the Mayor of London, "the ultimate crunchy subject."[15] Such views are, perhaps, to be expected from the Mayor, who was, after all, educated at Eton and Oxford. It is more disappointing, however, to find a Cambridge professor, described in the publicity for her blog as "a wickedly subversive commentator," publicly questioning whether Latin should be offered to any but the most able students. Although she asserts the importance of studying Latin in order to access the literature, she argues that:

Latin is an extremely self-selecting subject, chosen by some of our very brightest kids... The question is should Latin be the subject of choice for the less bright too? People – we classicists included – sometimes get in a muddle here. There is no question at all that Latin and Greek should be available to the talented of whatever wealth and class... But is it actually a sensible educational goal to try spread Latin and Greek right across the ability range?[16]

---

[14] Figures are taken from *A Survey of Access to Latin in UK Secondary Schools*, published in 2008 by CSCP. Available as a download from www.cambridgescp.com/downloads/Access_to_Latin.pdf; accessed 25 July 2013.

[15] Boris Johnson, quoted in "Vivat Latin, vox pop for a new age," *The Telegraph*, 8 September 2007. Accessed on 21 March 2013 at www.telegraph.co.uk/education/3354575/Vivat-Latin-vox-pop-for-a-new-age.html.

[16] Mary Beard in "A Don's Life," 28 June 2006, TimesOnline; accessed on 18 March 2013 at http://timesonline.typepad.com/dons_life/2006/06/index.html.

Mary Beard believes the answer to the last question is "no." Why does she believe that? Because, in her words,

> The central point of learning Latin is to be able to read some of the extraordinary literature written a couple of millennia ago. It can be formidably hard... But it is what makes the whole enterprise intellectually worthwhile. Make the whole thing easier (up the multiple choice and down play the real literature) and you've removed the very point of learning the language in the first place.[17]

Reading formidably hard authors, then, is the central goal of studying Latin. It may be the "central" point of *university* courses (though how many undergraduates are likely to agree with that?), but within the constraints of the school curriculum, with state schools lucky to have 240 hours to take pupils from scratch to GCSE, getting the students to a point when they can reach any literature in the original is an achievement. Whatever happened to the concerns raised by Professor Brink about "small" Latin? Whatever happened to the concept of "surrender value" in course design? It is as if the debate of the 1960s – and the close partnership between schools and universities – never took place. There is another issue: whereas in the 1960s the debate about the place of classics in the curriculum and how the classical languages should be taught was conducted behind closed doors in academic meetings and in the pages of scholarly journals, through her blog Mary Beard's views reach a much wider audience, an audience unlikely to be aware of the subtle intricacies of the academic debate over the aims and principles of teaching Latin in schools. Beard's views therefore affect public understanding of what classics is in a much more direct way than was possible before the advent of the internet; and the message is clear, Latin is for the few not the many.

Conclusion

The title for this paper is taken from a very successful advertising campaign in 2001 for Marks and Spencer, which neatly captured the company's aspiration to provide luxury products at a price anyone could afford. It has been a similar challenge for the classics community, finding a way to extend access to Latin without diluting its unique selling points. With the publication of the CLC and the subsequent creation of DVDs and web site to support the course, CSCP has played a central role in meeting this challenge. The key to its success has been the creation of a story-based

---

[17] "A Don's Life," 28 June 2006, TimesOnline; accessed on 18 March 2013 at http://timesonline.typepad.com/dons_life/2006/06/index.html.

course that engages the learner in a way that no grammar-based course could ever expect (or would ever wish!) to do. No other Latin course has evoked such strong feelings. The writer and columnist, Natalie Haynes, for instance, opens a recent book with fond reminiscences of her schooldays:

> When I turned twelve, Roman Life became Latin, and the *Cambridge Latin Course* took over. These brightly coloured books introduced a new generation of classical scholars to Caecilius and his wife Metella, who lived in Pompeii and so had a death sentence hanging over them from Book One. "Caecillius est in horto," we would chant, before grimly observing that he wouldn't survive the impending eruption from the garden, no matter how nice his triclinium was.[18]

To get a real flavour of the way the CLC has entered the popular consciousness one only has to visit the Facebook web site and see how many groups have been formed to celebrate Caecilius – or in some cases condemn him. The names alone of the groups tell a story: on the positive side "Caecilius Rocks," "Caecilius est optimus," "Caecilius appreciation society," "Caecilius fan club"; on the negative side "CAECILIUS NOOOOOOOOO," "I hate Caecilius," "CAECILIUS IS DEAD SO GO GET A LIFE U STUPID LATIN teachers." Remarkably, while most groups have between 10 and 50 members, one group ("Caecilius est in horto") has 19,754 members. However, the greatest recognition for Caecilius, Metella and Quintus came with their appearance in an episode of the British science fiction television series, *Doctor Who*.[19]

While some classicists may see a guest appearance by Caecilius in an episode of *Dr Who* as incontrovertible evidence of the dumbing down of Latin, I welcome this acceptance of characters from the CLC into mainstream popular culture as clear proof that CSCP has achieved its aim of widening access to Latin, not Latin as narrowly defined by traditionalists, but Latin as a language and culture. Nevertheless in a climate when there has been a swing back to traditional values in education and traditional approaches to teaching and learning, I remain very uneasy about the future of Latin in secondary schools and worry that it will once more become the preserve only of the rich and the most able.

Postscript

Much has happened since the paper on which this chapter is based was delivered in 2009. On the positive side, WJEC (Welsh Joint Education

---

[18] Haynes 2010: 1.
[19] "The Fires of Pompeii," with Caecilius played by Peter Capaldi, was first broadcast on 12 April 2008.

Committee) has introduced new qualifications which provide many students with a much more realistic examination than the existing GCSE. On the negative side, there is a proposal (currently out to consultation) that English into Latin exercises be reintroduced as a compulsory element of the GCSE. This proposal reflects the wishes of Michael Gove, the Secretary of State for Education, who wants to see the return of the "rigorous" standards of the O-Level examinations of the 1960s. If this proposal is implemented, on the evidence of a survey undertaken by CSCP, it will have a highly deleterious effect on the number of students taking the subject.

CHAPTER 14

Epilogue

Emily Greenwood

A well-known apocryphal anecdote about Dionysios Solomos, the "national" poet of Greece, records that when the poet returned from a ten-year stay in Italy, where he had established himself as an Italian poet, and had determined to write poetry in his native language (demotic Greek), he would buy dialect words from children in the countryside of Zakynthos in order to enrich his Greek vocabulary.[1] Solomos' poetic economy illustrates the potential of language as inexhaustible cultural and social capital: a native speaker buying (or buying back) his own language. The case of Solomos, author of the poem "The Hymn to Liberty," which was adopted as the Greek national anthem, shows up the sliding scale of language use where fluency among native speakers is always relative. And yet, because the Greek language was his birthright, Solomos was able to profit on language in a way that Shakespeare's Caliban apparently cannot. Yet another anecdote has the diplomat Spyridon Trikoupis (later to become the first prime minister of Greece in 1833) exhorting Solomos to "write in the language that he had imbibed with his mother's breast milk." Conversely, Caliban, who should have had native rights to his island, is alienated and displaced by the colonial technologies of Prospero, which include the colonizer's language.

This volume began with Shakespeare's Caliban weighing up and rejecting the benefits of learning the colonizer's language, and yet – with the exception of Eleanor Dickey's chapter which examines Greek speakers in Rome's eastern empire labouring to learn Latin (the colonizer's language) in order to facilitate their participation in Rome's empire, and Andrew Laird's account of Jesuit instruction in Latin for the Mexican nobility with a view to more efficient colonial government – the language

---

[1] Solomos was born in 1798 on the island of Zakynthos, formerly under Venetian rule, but then under French rule, and grew up speaking Greek and Italian. He was sent to study in Italy in 1808, at the age of ten, and returned to Zakynthos at the age of twenty.

learning scenarios explored in this volume involve a different dynamic where the "foreign" language is not a hegemonic language. These scenarios include citizens of the Roman Empire learning Greek (Hanson), the patchy knowledge of Greek amongst Servius and other Roman scholars in the fifth century CE (Racine), pupils learning Greek in the "Latin West" in the early Middle Ages (Herren), Aelfric's grammar offering Latin instruction to pupils in the eleventh century (Fisher), pupils learning Latin in Renaissance Italy (Black), girls and women learning Greek and Latin in England and France (Cox and Waquet), the politics of classical paedagogy in Russia with the transition from the Czars to the Bolshevik Revolution (Bers), and the study of the classical languages in the contemporary British classroom (Lister). So how relevant is Caliban's predicament for the study of Greek and Latin as second languages?

One argument might be that, although they were not hegemonic in the conventional sense, these "second" languages were not wholly secondary. Although a Roman citizen learning Greek in Egypt in the second century CE, or a student learning Greek or Latin in medieval England was not learning the language of the colonizer, they were learning languages with vast cultural capital, knowledge of which represented considerable power and promised, even if it did not always deliver, social mobility. Under the Roman Empire, as one of the *linguae francae* of culture, the Greek language had been prised apart from Greek ethnic identity as demonstrated by the coexistence of admiration for the "ancient" Greeks and contempt for contemporary Greeks in Cicero's corpus.[2] Authors such as Lucretius, Cicero, and Seneca strove to own ancient Greek to a greater extent than most of their contemporaries, Greeks included. One may see partial analogies with the conscious linguistic exuberance of Indian, Nigerian, or Barbadian writers under the British Empire who proved by their flair that they could out-English the English. The crucial difference is that the cultural exclusivity of the larger hinterland of English culture was policed by a web of intricate exclusions, whereas educated Romans were generally not seeking inclusion in Greek culture; if they prized Greek language and learning, it was in pursuit of Roman goals.[3]

Even in spite of the seismic shifts that have taken place in the British educational system in the past century, including the abolition of Latin as an entrance requirement for the universities of Oxford and Cambridge in

---

[2] See Swain 2002: 136.
[3] See Swain on Cicero again: "He mastered Greek in order to conquer the cultural high ground with Latin by giving the Romans the best of Greek culture" (*ibid.*).

1960,[4] Latin and Greek still retain a high degree of prestige value and exclusivity in the contemporary classroom, as Bob Lister observes in this volume. The view from America is presented in Kenneth Kitchell's chapter, where he explores the residual prestige and indeed elitism of the classical languages through the prism of Advanced Placement Latin exams in American high schools.

Kitchell offers us another argument for the relevance of Caliban's outcry for the study of the teaching of Greek and Latin: namely the argument that the books that are the repository of Prospero's magical power would have been written in Latin, the language of science and sorcery alike in the Renaissance. Indeed Ernest Rénan chose to exploit this circumstantial detail in his sequel to the *Tempest*, *Caliban, suite de La tempête, drame philosphique* (1878), giving Caliban the following lines (I quote from an 1896 English translation):

"War to the books! They are our worst enemies, and those who possess them will have power over all their fellows. The man who knows Latin can control and command the people to his service. Down with Latin!"[5]

Whether or not Shakespearean audiences conceived of Prospero's books in the *Tempest* as Latin books is open to debate.[6] Post-colonial adaptations and studies of this play in the context of the British Empire have treated the books as though they were written in Shakespeare's English or the so-called Queen's English – the language of the colonizer.[7] In a recent study of the relevance of Caliban for post-colonial literatures in English, Bill Ashcroft has explored the significance of Caliban's outcry in terms of two divergent conceptions of language: on the one hand "language as a communicative tool," and on the other hand "language as a cultural symbol."[8] He argues that although post- and anti-colonial writers have rejected the language of Prospero for its cultural symbolism, they have embraced and owned it as a tool of communication, transforming what it symbolizes in the process. In practice this distinction between these two conceptions of language is messy, since languages are imbued with historical associations

---

[4] Tristram 2003: 7. On broader shifts in the teaching of classics in Britain in the twentieth century, see Morwood 2003, in which Tristram's chapter appears.
[5] Rénan 1896: 42.
[6] See Mowat 2001 for discussion of Renaissance conjuring books as a model for Prospero's authority in the play.
[7] The *Tempest* has also had a distinguished anti-colonial Francophone reception history, including Aimé Césaire's *Une Tempête* (1969). For the reception of *The Tempest* in general, see Hulme and Sherman 2000.
[8] Ashcroft 2009, quoting from p.2.

with the result that linguistic communication will usually convey a larger force field.⁹ Surveying the different instances of language learning explored in this volume, all involve language as a cultural symbol including those chapters that focus on the acquisition of Greek and/or Latin as a tool of communication.

To my mind what both scenes reveal – Solomos buying words of dialect and Caliban cursing Prospero – is the mythical state of linguistic insiderism concealed in the phrase "native speaker." Caliban learns English but still finds himself despised and dispossessed, and the young Solomos, who was later heralded as the poet of the Greek nation, finds his Greek not Greek enough – i.e. not local and vernacular enough – and sets about authenticating it with dialect words. One can learn a language proficiently and flawlessly, and yet still find oneself relegated to secondary status, because language belongs to a larger nexus of cultural identity; alternatively, one can be born into a language and still find oneself displaced from the larger cultural community to whom the hegemonic version of the language belongs. Or, since both formulations are phrased in negative terms, which see language users being rejected by linguistic communities, in positive terms a language user might possess a "second language" but find it uncongenial, cursing and rejecting the culture that it evokes. Similarly, in cases of bilingualism, a language user might privilege one language over another for reasons of affect or sentiment, regardless of their relative competence in that language.

The role of sentiment in language use is implied by the phrase "mother tongue," which hints at a scale of intimacy and familiarity according to which a bilingual or multilingual speaker might identify with one language over another based on criteria that have nothing to do with proficiency in the conventional sense. All of the terms used to describe bilingualism, multilingualism, or learning languages introduce metaphors that colour the terms of the debate. A *mother* language, a *native* language, a *first* or *second* language, a *vernacular* language, a *standard* language, a *foreign* language... These potent metaphors are reinforced in the case of classical Greek and Latin, where the languages in question are underwritten by powerful myths of cultural priority that trump the native language. We see this happen with the influence that ancient Greek exerted over Latin and, in turn, the influence that Latin exerted over many modern European languages. How many students have laboured over Latin and Greek grammars convinced that, not only will knowledge of Latin and

---

⁹ Ashcroft acknowledges this, remarking that language is a practice (2009: 14).

Greek make them better educated all round, but also that their command of their own language (English, French, Italian) will improve as a result of learning these languages? There is some truth in this, but expectations of social mobility as a result of learning the classical languages have often been cruelly disappointed. Here one can think of Thomas Hardy's character, Jude Fawley, whose knowledge of Latin is not sufficient to gain him entry to Oxford University faced with the barriers of class and wealth,[10] or the working-class Caribbean students who "ascended" to the lowly grades of the colonial civil service as a result of their knowledge of Latin – a condition satirized by authors such as V. S. Naipaul and Austin Clark.[11] In her 1892 manifesto arguing for the education of the black woman in America, Anna Julia Cooper, herself a Latin teacher at M Street High School in Washington, commented on the pressure on black Americans to gain a classical education in the decades after the Civil War: "'Scale the heights!' was the cry. 'Go to college, study Latin, preach, teach, orate, wear spectacles and a beaver!'", only to conclude "...we began at the wrong end. Wealth must pave the way for learning."[12]

Not only are students of the classical languages not, and can never be, native speakers, but they are also destined never to be fluent in these languages. In reply to the perfectly obvious and intelligent question often posed of classicists by non-classicists "Do you speak Greek?" or "Do you speak Latin?" the response is often a slightly patronizing explanation that, no, these languages are not spoken (although there are those who are committed to Latin as a spoken language). This insider's response conceals a fascinating history, aspects of which are explored in this volume, in which "dead" languages have been preserved and renewed under the auspices of "classics," an invented tradition that has successively adapted and assimilated the cultures and literatures of Greece and Rome making familiar what is, in essence, desperately foreign. For not only do "we" not speak Greek or Latin, but the very conception of "Greek" and "Latin" as single, stable languages is an artificial construct. Which dialect of ancient Greek, whose Latin, and who is to say with confidence how the literary

---

[10] See Richardson 2007 *passim* and 35: "...ignorance of Latin, in nineteenth-century Britain, did not bar a person from becoming a socially acceptable classical scholar, nor did knowledge of it automatically allow one to be recognised as such." Hardy's *Jude The Obscure* was serialized in 1895 and published in book form in 1896.

[11] See Greenwood 2010: 73–5 (on V. S. Naipaul's satire on Latin education in colonial Trinidad in chapter 4 of *Miguel Street* (1959)), and p. 76 (on Austin Clark's depiction of the horizon of social expectations for working class schoolboys in colonial Barbados).

[12] Cooper 1988: 260–1.

form of these languages corresponded to the dialects that people spoke on the streets?[13] For centuries now the model of fluency in Greek and Latin has been the ability to compose artful pieces in the manner of a Greek or Roman author (so-called prose or verse composition), or to use great linguistic ingenuity to make these languages express the ideas and subjects of other ages and cultures (rendering passages from a speech by Abraham Lincoln into Demosthenic Greek, or turning Harry Potter into Ciceronian Latin). Meanwhile the degree of competence that most students are expected to attain in reading Greek and Latin is suggested by the use of verbs such as "construe" rather than "read," as in "how do you construe this sentence?" The gulf between the approach to teaching and learning a dead language, as opposed to a living one, is evident in Lytton Strachey's satirical portrait of Thomas Arnold, headmaster of Rugby School (a British independent school), from 1828 to 1841:

"I assume it," he wrote, "as the foundation of all my view of the case, that boys at a public school never will learn to speak or pronounce French well, under any circumstance." It would be enough it they could "learn it grammatically as a dead language."[14]

The reason why Arnold's schoolboys would never learn to speak or pronounce well was the infrequency of their French lessons, because the curriculum was crowded out by classics. The paedagogical model espoused by Thomas Arnold is remarkable on (at least) two counts: first, the modest linguistic competence with which students emerged was out of all proportion to the labour that they had expended on Greek and Latin and, second, in spite of the joyless learning environment many of the students developed an interest and affinity for Greek and Roman authors. In her recent study of classical receptions in British poetry of the Great War, Elizabeth Vandiver observes, "Perhaps most interestingly (and this should not be a surprise), a great many old boys of public schools retained an imperfect understanding of the ancient languages but also retained a passionate love of their literatures, and returned to read ancient texts in later years, often with the help of a translation."[15]

That an interest in classics can survive such experiences is illustrated by the case of Robert Graves (1895–1985), the soldier, classical scholar, novelist, poet (and poet laureate). Graves's credentials as a classicist are

---

[13] Adams, Janse, and Swain 2002: 2.
[14] Strachey's biography of Thomas Arnold is contained in his *Eminent Victorians*, first published in 1918. I quote from Strachey 1986: 171.
[15] Vandiver 2010: 38.

undeniable. His translation of Suetonius' *The Twelve Caesars* – a biographical study of twelve Roman emperors first published in 1957 – is still in print, and was republished by Penguin Classics in a revised edition in 2007. His bestselling historical novels based on the Emperor Claudius, *I, Claudius* (1934) and *Claudius the God* (1935) are also still in print. Although many classicists are disdainful of his highly idiosyncratic study of Greek myth, *The Greek Myths* (1955), it remains widely read and is often the guide of choice for poets and novelists. From Graves's biography *Good-bye to All That* (1929), we learn that spontaneous Latin verse composition was a casual pastime for Graves.

Writing about the last church service he ever attended, Graves recalls how he whiled away the duration of the service by composing Latin epigrams. The context is the First World War and Graves's leave from the Front in April 1916. He describes the Good Friday service, which he attended out of a sense of filial duty, already disillusioned about the Church by the failure, in his opinion, of the Anglican chaplains attached to the British regiments to give any practical spiritual guidance and support to the troops.[16] In Graves's account the vicar conducting the three-hour-long service preaches a glibly patriotic sermon about divine sacrifice and the glory of death in war, leading Graves to wonder why the vicar has not enlisted himself:[17]

> I stayed and tried to compose Latin epigrams, which was, in those days, my way of killing time – on ceremonial parades, for instance, or in the dentist's chair, or at night in the trenches when things were quiet. I composed a maledictory epigram on the strapping young curate – besides myself, my father, the verger, and an old, old man with a palsied hand sitting just in front of me, the only male in the congregation, though there were sixty or seventy women present. I tried to remember whether the *i* of *clericus* was long or short, and couldn't; but it did not matter, because I could make alternative versions to suit either case:

O si bracchipotens qui fulminat ore clericus...

and:

O si bracchipotens clericus qui fulminat ore...

The first line of the epigram translates as "O cleric with arms so powerful who releases lightning bolts from his mouth." *Bracchipotens* ("powerful in his arms") is a coinage, punning on the Latin adjective *armipotens* ("powerful in weapons," "warlike"). The tone is mock-heroic, with the connotations of divine strength serving as an ironic contrast to the fact that

---

[16] Graves 1998: 189–90. [17] Graves 1998: 200–1.

the cleric has not enlisted and instead lisps feeble homilies about the glory of war from his pulpit.

Reading this passage the reader might suppose that Graves had a natural affinity for classics, or that this kind of Latin versifying was normal in the first decades of the twentieth century. But Graves records that his early introduction to Latin at the King's College School, Wimbledon (in London) at the age of seven years, was inauspicious. Like many schoolchildren, Graves was introduced to classics with no explanation of what he was studying, or why he was studying it:[18]

> My father took me away after a couple of terms because he heard me using naughty words, and because I did not understand the lessons. I had started Latin, but nobody explained what "Latin" meant; its declensions and conjugations were pure incantations to me.[19]

The idea of Latin for Latin's sake, or classics for classics' sake are all too familiar. Countless writers in several different cultures have testified to the absurdity of being made to learn Latin and ancient history by rote, stripped of any historical or cultural context. In such circumstances, the conjugation of Latin verbs and declension of Latin nouns become synonymous with tedium and punishment.

We tend to assume that this is a modern phenomenon, and that each successive generation slides further away from pristine knowledge of Latin and Greek. However, as several studies have shown, schoolchildren have always struggled with the study of Latin (let alone Greek) as a second language and arcane statutes decreeing that Latin must be spoken, or requirements that university entrants or members of certain professions must be conversant in Latin are no guarantee that they actually are. In her study of the teaching of Latin in Europe from the sixteenth to the twentieth centuries, Françoise Waquet cites intimidating examples of the fluency in Latin expected at all levels of the educational system, including instances where proficiency in Latin was a prerequisite to receiving further schooling and then deflates them with evidence of the poor linguistic competence of those who had gone through this very system.[20]

---

[18] Graves 1998: 17.
[19] Compare the sardonic observation of L. E. Jones on the way in which he was taught Latin at school. Arguing that cribs should have been allowed, he contends, "is it not more sensible to read Virgil knowing what he means than not knowing what he means?" Jones 1955: 214, quoted in Vandiver 2010: 56.
[20] Waquet 2001.

Dismal as this sounds, it was the joyless grind of grammar drills in Greek and Latin that threatened the very place of these ancient languages in the curriculum and subsequently led to a thorough reappraisal of how the languages should be taught in order to halt their disappearance from the classroom. The discipline today is still in the process of reappraisal, two results of which are the focus on the history of classical paedagogy and an increased awareness of the construction of the classical. This volume is very much a product of this shift away from classics as an inherited tradition towards an understanding of the different political, social, and cultural factors that have shaped the teaching and study of Greek and Latin. In particular, the topic of second language learning intersects with three areas of current interest in classical scholarship: the study of bilingualism in the ancient Mediterranean;[21] research into education in classical antiquity particularly in Hellenistic Egypt; and classical reception studies, specifically the ways in which subsequent readers and learners have related to Greek and Latin and the cultures of classical antiquity, whether in educational or artistic contexts. To take the latter, recent work in classical receptions has examined approaches and responses to Virgil in the curriculum of Renaissance England, and Victorian women's access to classics.[22] In addition to fictional characters such as Maggie Tulliver in Eliot's *Mill on the Floss* (discussed by Fiona Cox above), in the past two decades classical reception studies have explored the deeply ambivalent testimonies about learning classical languages at school on the part of writers such as Tony Harrison in England, Christopher Okigbo in Nigeria, and Derek Walcott in St Lucia, to cite just a few examples from the twentieth century.

The question of the cultural imperialism and power dynamics involved in learning Greek and Latin also intersects with translation studies, which exert a considerable influence on current classical scholarship, both in classical reception studies and beyond.[23] Translation studies can teach us a good deal about linguistic insiderism and perceived secondariness, not just in modernity, but also in antiquity itself. Classical antiquity, often treated in its entirety for the sake of convenience, is profoundly chronologically stratified. How did an educated Roman of the first century CE relate to and measure their language in relation to that of Livius Andronicus, Ennius, and Naevius? Is Virgil closer to the roots of Latin than, say,

---

[21] Adams *et al.* 2002, Adams 2003.
[22] On Virgil in the curriculum of Renaissance England, see A. Wallace 2011; on Victorian women learning classics, see Hurst 2006, especially ch. 2 on learning classical languages.
[23] See Hardwick 2000, and Lianeri and Zajko 2008.

Seneca, as implied by Seneca's 58th letter where he cites Virgil as a source for what the ancients used to say (*dicebant antiqui*)?[24] Meanwhile, Lucian gives us ample testimony of the posturing and manoeuvring that went on in the rhetorical schools in Rome's eastern empire in the second century CE, as people vied to prove their impeccable knowledge of Greek as it was spoken in the fifth century BCE.

The figure of Caliban brings social and political dimensions of second language learning to the foreground and puts this volume squarely within the domain of sociolinguistics. When we attempt to do a sociolinguistic history of both the perception and practice of second language learning in classical antiquity there are several glaring lacunae, over and above the very poor data for ancient literacy and the fact that subliterary written works have survived extremely haphazardly. One of these lacunae is the occlusion of women as language users in the written records that have been preserved from the cultures and societies of Greece and Rome. Two chapters in this volume (Cox and Waquet) focus on the experience of girls and women learning Greek and Latin in modern classrooms and of women authors wielding their knowledge of these languages, a focus that serves to highlight the almost total absence of such data from classical antiquity.[25] Outside of the fragmentary corpus of Sappho's poetry, the songs written for Alcman's female choirs, and isolated evidence for female literacy in ancient Greece, Rome, and to a greater extent in Hellenistic Egypt,[26] we know little about how women experienced linguistic education in the ancient world, but we do have tantalizing glimpses of what we are missing. For instance, drawing on socio- and ethno-linguistics, Laura McClure's research on women's speech and verbal genres in Athenian drama has shown that male playwrights attempted to represent patterns and genres of women's speech in their depiction of female characters.[27] Although such differentiation of speech along gendered lines may serve hegemonic ends, it is nonetheless a reflection of the gendering of speech and the difficulties which male authors faced in writing women. The eloquence of Roman female speech genres is given a backhanded compliment in the work of Quintilian when he cites the case of squabbling little women (*iurgantes*

---

[24] Seneca *Epistulae Morales* 58.4. Seneca thrice cites Virgil as a source for ancient Latin word usage in sections 1–4 of this letter.
[25] On modern women as students and scholars of Greek and Latin outside of the academy, in addition to Hurst 2006, cited in n. 22 above, see also Prins 2006, Winterer 2007, J. Wallace 2011, and Prins forthcoming.
[26] See, e.g., Cavallo 1995, Bagnall and Cribiore 2008, Glazebrook 2005, and Flemming 2007.
[27] McClure 1999.

mulierculae) as an example of the verbal coherence of impassioned, improvised speech.[28] This example raises the question of language use in the case of social groups for whom a language is not a *second* language, but who are regarded as secondary users of that language. Like Caliban, the lowly women whom Quintilian envisages here could presumably have taught his orator several choice expressions that would have enlarged his command of the Latin language.

---

[28] Quintilian *Institutio Oratoria* 10.7.13; the diminutive *muliercula* is derogatory and may imply "mere" women or women of the street; the compliment is further dimmed by the use of the concessive conjunction *etiam* (*iurgantibus etiam mulierculis*: "*even* squabbling women...").

Bibliography

Acosta, J. de. (1880) *Natural and Moral History of the Indies*, ed. and trans. **E. Grimston** (2 vols.). London.
Acuña, R. (1995) *Fray Julián Garcés. Su Alegato en Pro de los Naturales de Nueva España*. Mexico City.
Adams, J. N. (2003a) *Bilingualism and the Latin Language*. Cambridge.
  (2003b) "'*Romanitas*' and the Latin language," *CQ* 53.1: 184–205.
  (2007) *The Regional Diversification of Latin 200 BC – AD 600*. Cambridge.
Adams, J. N., **Janse, M.**, and **Swain, S.** (eds.) (2002) *Bilingualism in Ancient Society: Language Contact and the Written Text*. Oxford.
Aguilar Moreno, M. (2002) "The *Indio ladino* as a cultural mediator in the colonial society," *Estudios de Cultura Náhuatl* 33: 149–84.
Alberti, L. B. (1960–73) *Opere Volgari*, ed. **C. Grayson**. Bari.
Allen, W. S., and **Brink, C. O.** (1980) "The old order and the new: A case history," *Lingua* 50: 61–100.
Alridge, D. P. (2008) *The Educational Thought of W.E.B. DuBois: An Intellectual History*. New York.
Alston, P. L. (1969) *Education and the State in Tsarist Russia*. Stanford.
Alva Ixtlilxóchitl, F. de. (1997) *Obras Históricas*, ed. **E. O'Gorman** (2 vols.). Mexico City.
Alvarado Tezózomoc, F. (1998) *Crónica Mexicáyotl, Texto en Náhuatl y Español, Paleografía y Traducción*, ed. **A. León**. Mexico City.
Amelli, A. (ed.) (1899) *Ars Donati quam Paulus Diaconus Exposuit*. Montecassino.
American Classical League (1924) *The Classical Investigation*. Princeton.
Amsler, A. (1989) *Etymology and Grammatical Discourse in Late Antiquity and the Early Middle Ages*. Amsterdam.
Andrews, E. A. (1842) *Lhomond's Viri Romae: Adapted to Andrews and Stoddard's Latin Grammar*. Boston.
Arrighi, G. (2004) *La Matematica dell'Età di Mezzo. Scritti Scelti*, ed. **F. Barbieri**, **R. Franci** and **L. Toti Rigatelli**. Pisa.
Ashcroft, B. (2009) *Caliban's Voice: The Transformation of English in Post-Colonial Literatures*. New York.
Ashmore, H. S. (1954) *The Negro and the Schools*. Chapel Hill.

Atherton, C. (1998) "Children, animals, slaves, and grammar," in **Y. L. Too** and **N. Livingstone** (eds.), *Pedagogy and Power: Rhetorics of Classical Learning*. Cambridge: 214–44.
Avesani, R. (2001) "La storia della scuola. Aspetti, problemi e prospettive di ricerca," in *Scuola e Insegnamento. Atti del XXXV Convegno di Studi Maceratesi. Abbadia di Fiastrai (Tolentino) 13–14 Novembre, 1999*. Pollenza: 1–21.
Axer, J. (1983) "Reedition of the Viennese fragments of Cicero, *In Catilinam* I," in *Festschrift zum 100-jährigen Bestehen der Papyrussammlung der österreichischen Nationalbibliothek, Papyrus Erzherzog Rainer*. Vienna: 468–82.
Backscheider, A., and **Gelman, S.** (1995) "Children's understanding of homonyms," *Journal of Child Language* 22: 107–27.
Baczko, B. (ed.) (1982) *Une Education pour la Démocratie. Textes et Projets de l'Epoque Révolutionnaire*. Paris.
Baehrens, A. (ed.) (1874) *Panegyrici Latini*. Leipzig.
Bagnall, R. S. (2011) *Everyday Writing in the Graeco-Roman East*. Berkeley.
Bagnall, R. S., and **Frier, B. W.** (1994) *The Demography of Roman Egypt*. Cambridge.
Bagnall, R. S., and **Cribiore, R.** (2008) (ACLS E-book edition) *Women's Letters from Ancient Egypt 300 BC – AD 800*. Ann Arbor.
Baldwin, T. W. (1944) *William Shakespeare's Small Latine and Lesse Greeke* vol I. Urbana, IL.
Balme, M., and **Morwood, J.** (1996) *Oxford Latin Course*, 2nd edn. Oxford.
Barber, C. C. (1951) *An Old High German Reader: With Notes, List of Proper Names, and Vocabulary*. Oxford.
Barsanti, P. (1905) *Il Pubblico Insegnamento in Lucca*. Lucca.
Bataille, A. (1967) "Les glossaires gréco-latins sur papyrus," *Recherches de papyrologie* 4: 161–9.
Bataillon, M. (1998) *Érasme et l'Espagne: Recherches sur l'Histoire Spirituelle du XVIe Siècle*. Geneva. [orig. Paris 1937]
Battistini, M. (1919) *Il Pubblico Insegnamento in Volterra*. Volterra.
Baudot, G. (1977) *Utopie et Histoire au Mexique: Les Premiers Chroniqueurs de la Civilization Mexicaine 1520–1569*. Toulouse.
Becker, J. (1908) *Textgeschichte Liudprands von Cremona*. Munich.
Belloni, G., and **Pozza, M.** (1987) *Sei Testi Veneti Antichi*. Rome.
Berschin, W. (1980) *Griechisch-lateinisches Mittelalter. Von Hieronymus zu Nikolaus von Kues*. Bern and Munich.
  (1988a) *Greek Letters and the Latin Middle Ages*, trans. and rev. **J. C. Frakes**. Washington, D.C.
  (1988b) "Greek elements in medieval Latin manuscripts," in **M. Herren** (ed.) with **S. A. Brown**: 85–104.
Bieler, L. (1977) "Observations on Eriugena's 'Commentary on the Gospel of John': A second harvest," in **R. Roques** (ed.), *Jean Scot Érigène et l'Histoire de la Philosophie*. Paris: 235–41.
Bierhorst, J. (ed.) (1985) *Cantares Mexicanos: Songs of the Aztecs*. Stanford.

Bischoff, B. (1951) "Das griechische Element in der abendländischen Bildung des Mittelalters," *Byzantinische Zeitschrift* 44: 25–55
  (1967) "Das griechische Element in der abendländischen Bildung des Mittelalters," in *Mittelalterliche Studien: Ausgewählte Aufsätze zur Schriftkunde und Literaturgeschichte* vol. II. Stuttgart: 246–75.
  (1981) "Irische Schreiber in Karonlingerreich," in *Mittelalterliche Studien: Ausgewählte Aufsätze zur Schriftkunde und Literaturgeschichte* vol. III. Stuttgart: 39–54.
  (1984) "Vulgärgriechisches-lateinisches Glossar (Zehntes bis elftes Jahrhundert)," in *Anecdota Novissima: Texte des vierten bis sechzehnten Jahrhunderts.* Stuttgart: 248–9.
Bischoff, B., and **Lapidge, M.** (1994) *Biblical Studies from the Canterbury School of Theodore and Hadrian*, Cambridge Studies in Anglo-Saxon England 10. Cambridge.
Biville, F. (2009) "Le latin expliqué par le grec. Les Institutions de Priscien," in **B. Bortolussi** *et al.* (eds.), *Traduire, Transposer, Transmettre dans l'Antiquité Gréco-romaine.* Paris: 47–60.
Black, Robert (1991a) "An unknown thirteenth-century manuscript of *Ianua*," in **I. Wood** and **G. Loud** (eds.), *Church and Chronicle in the Middle Ages.* London: 101–15.
  (1991b) "The curriculum of Italian elementary and grammar schools, 1350–1500," in **D. Kelley** and **R. Popkin** (eds.), *The Shapes of Knowledge.* Dordrecht: 137–63.
  (1996a) "The vernacular and the teaching of Latin in thirteenth- and fourteenth-century Italy," *Studi medievali* 3.37: 703–51.
  (1996b) "New light on Machiavelli's education," in **J.-J. Marchand** (ed.), *Niccolò Machiavelli, Politico, Storico, Letterato.* Rome: 391–8.
  (1996c) "*Ianua* and elementary education in Italy and northern Europe in the later middle ages," in **M. Tavoni** (ed.), *Italia ed Europa nella Linguistica del Rinascimento.* Ferrara and Modena: 5–22.
  (2001) *Humanism and Education in Medieval and Renaissance Italy: Tradition and Innovation in Latin Schools from the Twelfth to the Fifteenth Century.* Cambridge.
  (2006) "Italian education: Language, syllabuses, method," in **L. Nauta** (ed.), *Language and Cultural Change: Aspects of the Study and Use of Language in the Later Middle Ages and Renaissance.* Leuven: 91–112.
  (2007) *Education and Society in Florentine Tuscany: Teachers, Pupils and Schools, c. 1250–1500* vol. I. Leiden.
Blanchard, M., and **A.** (1973) "La mosaïque d'Anacréon à Autun," *REL* 75: 268–79.
Blasi, N. de. (1993) "L'italiano nella scuola," in **L. Serianni** and **P. Trifone** (eds.) *Storia della Lingua Italiana,.* Turin: 387–423.
Boland, E. (1995) *Object Lessons – The Life of the Woman and the Poet in Our Time.* London.
Bond, H. M. (1970) *The Education of the Negro in the American Social Order.* New York.

Böninger, L. (2006) *Die deutsche Einwanderung nach Florenz im Spätmittelalter*. Leiden.
Bonnet, G. (2005) *Dosithée: Grammaire latine*. Paris.
Borracini Verducci, R. (1975) "La scuola pubblica a Recanati nel sec. xv," Università di Macerata. *Annali della facoltà di lettere e filosofia* 8: 121–62.
Boyancé, P. (1953) "Le latin, discipline de base," *Revue de la Franco-Ancienne* 105: 128–30.
Boyd, B. (1993) *Vladimir Nabokov: The Russian Years*. Princeton.
Brent-Dyer, E. M. (1979) *The Chalet School in Exile*. London.
Brink, C. O. (1962) "Small Latin and the classics," in T. W. Melluish (ed.), *Reappraisal: Some Thoughts on the Teaching of Classics*. Oxford: 6–9.
Brok, M. (1975) "Die Quellen von Ammians Exkurs über Persien," *Mnemosyne* 28: 47–56.
Brower, D. (1970) "Reformer and rebels: education in Tsarist Russia," *History of Education Quarterly* 10: 127–36.
Bulwer J. (2006) "United Kingdom," in J. Bulwer (ed.), *Classics Teaching in Europe*. London: 124–31.
Butler, S. (1992) *The Way of All Flesh*. London.
Byatt, A. S. (1988) "Racine and the tablecloth," in *Sugar and Other Stories*. London.
  (1995) "The Djinn in the nightingale's eye," in *The Djinn in the Nightingale's Eye: Five Fairy Stories*. New York: 93–277.
  (2000) "Arachne," in T. Philip (ed.), *Ovid Metamorphosed*. London: 131–57.
  (2009) *The Children's Book*. London.
Cambridge School Classics Project. (2007) *Cambridge Latin Course*. 4th edn. Cambridge.
Cameron, A. (1966) "The date and identity of Macrobius," *JRS* 56: 25–38.
  (2004) *Greek Mythography in the Roman World*. Oxford.
  (2011) *The Last Pagans of Rome*. Oxford.
Campos, L. (1965) "Métodos misionales y rasgos biográficos de don Vasco de Quiroga según Cristóbal Cabrera, Pbro.," in M. Ponce (ed.), *Don Vasco de Quiroga y Arzobispado de Morelia*. Mexico City: 107–55.
Cannon, C., Copeland, R., and Zeeman, N. (eds.) (2009) New Medieval Literatures 11: *Medieval Grammar and Literary Arts*. Oxford.
Caron, M. (1924) "Quelques remarques à propos de l'enseignement secondaire des jeunes filles," *Revue universitaire* 33.1: 322–6.
Caruso, C., and Laird, A. (2009) "The Italian classical tradition, language and literary history," in C. Caruso and A. Laird (eds.), *Italy and the Classical Tradition. Language, Thought and Poetry 1300–1600*. London: 1–25.
Cavallo, G. (1995) "Donne che leggono, donne che scrivono," in R. Raffaelli (ed.), *Vicende e Figure Femminili in Graecia e a Roma: Atti del Convegno di Pesaro 28–30 Aprile 1994*. Ancona: 517–26.
Cavenaile, R. (1958) *Corpus Papyrorum Latinarum*. Wiesbaden.
Cayrou, G. (1911) "L'enseignement du latin dans un collège de jeunes filles (difficultés et résultats)," *Revue universitaire* 20.2: 1–10.

Ceccherini, I. (2010) "Teaching, function and social diffusion of writing in thirteenth- and fourteenth-century Florence," in **P. R. Robinson** (ed.), *Teaching Writing, Learning to Write: Proceedings of the XVIth Colloquium of the Comité International de Paléographie Latine.* London: 177–92.
Cecchetti, B. (1886) "Libri, scuole, maestri, sussidii allo studio in Venezia," *Archivio Veneto* 32.1: 329–63.
Cervantes de Salazar, F. (1554) *Ad Ludovivi Vivis Valentini Exercitationem, Aliquot Dialogi.* Mexico City.
Cervantes de Salazar, F. (1971) in **M. Magallon** (ed.), *Crónica de la Nueva España* (2 vols.). Madrid.
Césaire, A. (1969) *Une Tempête: D'après "La tempête" de Shakespeare. Adaptation pour une Théâtre Nègre.* Paris.
Chavez, M. (2001) *Gender in the Language Classroom.* Boston.
Cherubini, P. (1996) "Frammenti di quaderni di scuola d'area umbra alla fine del secolo XV," *Quellen und Forschungen aus italienischen Archiven und Bibliotheken* 76: 219–52.
Chin, C. (2008) *Grammar and Christianity in the Late Roman World.* Philadelphia.
Clanchy, M. (1984) "Learning to read in the Middle Ages and the role of mothers," in **G. Brooks** and **A. K. Pugh** (eds.), *Studies in the History of Reading.* Reading: 33–9.
Clarke, M. (2010) "Semantics and vocabulary," in **E. J. Bakker** (ed.), *Blackwell Companion to the Greek Language.* Malden: 120–33.
Clarysse, W., and **Rochette, B.** (2005) "Un alphabet grec en charactères latins," *Archiv für Papyrusforschung* 51: 67–75.
Clayton, M. L. (1989) "A trilingual Spanish-Latin-Nahuatl dictionary sometimes attributed to Bernardino de Sahagún," *International Journal of American Linguistics* 55: 392–416.
  (2003) "Evidence for a native-speaking Nahuatl author in the Ayer *Vocabulario Trilingüe*," *International Journal of Lexicography* 16: 99–119.
Clayton, M., **Guerrini, L.**, and **de Ávila, A.** (2010) *Flora: The Aztec Herbal.* Turnhout.
Colini-Baldeschi, L. (1900) "L'insegnamento pubblico a Macerata," *Rivista delle biblioteche e degli archivi,* 11: 19–26.
Contreni, J. J. (1978) *The Cathedral School of Laon from 850 to 930: Its Manuscripts and Masters.* Munich.
  (1980) "Inharmonious harmony: Education in the Carolingian world," *Annals of Scholarship: Metastudies of the Humanities and Social Sciences,* 1: 81–96.
  (1982) "The Irish in the western Carolingian empire," in **H. Löwe** (ed.), *Die Iren und Europa im früheren Mittelalter.* Stuttgart: 758–98.
Cook, W. W., and **Tatum, J.** (2010) *African American Writers and Classical Tradition.* Chicago.
Cooper, A. J. (1988) *A Voice from the South.* Oxford. [orig. Xenia, Ohio 1892]
Corona Nuñez, J. (1982) "Antonio Uitziméngari, primer humanista Tarasco," in **Centro de Estudios sobre la Cultura Nicolaita** (ed.), *Humanistas Novohispanos de Michoacán.* Morelia: 49–61.

Corso, L. del, and **Pecere, O.** (eds.) (2010) *Libri di Scuola e Pratiche Didattiche dall'Antichità al Rinascimento*. Cassino.

Courcelle, P. (1943) *Les Lettres Grecques en Occident de Macrobe à Cassiodore*. Paris.

Cox, F. (2011) *Sibylline Sisters – Virgil's Presence in Contemporary Women's Fiction*. Oxford.

Cox, F., and **Theodorakopoulos, E.** (2013) "Female voices: The democratic turn in Ali Smith's classical reception," in **L. Hardwick** and **S. J. Harrison** (eds.), *Classics in the Modern World: A Democratic Turn?* Oxford: 287–98.

Crawford, S. (1999) *Childhood in Anglo-Saxon England*. Stroud.

Cribiore, R. (1996) *Writing, Teachers, and Students in Graeco-Roman Egypt*. Atlanta.

(2001) *Gymnastics of the Mind: Greek Education in Hellenistic and Roman Egypt*. Princeton.

(2009) "Education in the papyri," in **R. S. Bagnall** (ed.), *The Oxford Handbook of Papyrology*. New York/Oxford: 320–37.

Crouzet-Ben-Aben, J. P. (1928) "Les humanités pour les jeunes filles," *Bulletin de l'Enseignement Secondaire des Jeunes Filles* of the *Revue universitaire* 37.1: 445–6.

Cuvigny, H. (2003) *La Route de Myos Hormos: l'Armée Romaine dans le Désert Oriental d'Égypte*. Cairo.

Daly, L. W. (1967) *Contributions to a History of Alphabetization in Antiquity and the Middle Ages*. Brussels.

Daris, S. (1991) *Il Lessico Latino nel Greco d'Egitto*. Barcelona.

Debut, J. (1987) "Les *Hermeneumata Monacensia*," *LEC* 55: 180–93.

Desmond, M. (1994) *Reading Dido: Gender, Textuality, and the Medieval Aeneid*. Minneapolis.

Dexter, C. (1973) "The changing pattern of examinations," *Latin Teaching* 35.1: 8–16.

Dickey, E. (2010a) "The creation of Latin teaching materials in antiquity: A re-interpretation of P.Sorb. inv. 2069," *Zeitschrift für Papyrologie und Epigraphik* 175: 188–208.

(2010b) "Greek Dictionaries Ancient and Modern," in **C. Stray** (ed.), *Classical Dictionaries*. London: 5–24.

(2012) *The Colloquia of the Hermeneumata Pseudodositheana I: Colloquia Monacensia-Einsidlensia, Leidense-Stephani, and Stephani*. Cambridge.

(forthcoming), *The Colloquia of the Hermeneumata Pseudodositheana II: Colloquia Harleianum, Montepessulanum, and Celtis*. Cambridge.

Dickey, E., and **Ferri, R.** (2010) "A new edition of the Latin-Greek glossary on P.Sorb. inv. 2069 (verso)," *ZPE* 175: 177–87.

(2012) "A new edition of the *Colloquium Harleianum* fragment in P.Prag. 2.118," *ZPE* 180: 127–32.

Dickey, E., **Ferri, R.**, and **Scappaticcio, M. C.** (2013) "The origins of grammatical tables: A reconsideration of P.Louvre inv. E 7332," *ZPE* 187: 173–89.

Dionisotti, A. C. (1982a) "From Ausonius' schooldays? A schoolbook and its relatives," *Journal of Roman Studies* 72: 83–125.
  (1982b) "On Bede, grammars and Greek," *Revue Bénédictine* 92: 111–41.
  (1988a) "Greek grammars and dictionaries in Carolingian Europe," in **M. Herren** (ed.) with **S. A. Brown**: 1–56.
  (1988b) "On the Greek studies of Robert Grosseteste," in **A. C. Dionisotti**, **A. Grafton**, and **J. Kraye** (eds.), *The Uses of Greek and Latin: Historical Essays*. London: 19–39.
Drabble, M. (2003) *The Seven Sisters*. London.
Draper, J. B., and **Hicks, J. H.** (2002) *Foreign Language Enrollments in Public Secondary Schools, Fall 2000*. www.actfl.org/files/public/Enroll2000.pdf.
DuBois, W. E. B. (ed.) (1903) "The talented tenth," in *The Negro Problem: A Series of Articles by Representative American Negroes of Today*. New York: 31–76.
Duffy, C. A. (1999) *The World's Wife*. New York.
Dümmler, E. (ed.) (1881) *Poetae Latini Aevi Carolini* vol. 1. Berlin.
Dutton, P. E. (1992) "Evidence that Dubthach's Prisician codex once belonged to Eriugena," in **H. J. Westra** (ed.), *From Athens to Chartres: Neoplatonism and Medieval Thought: Studies in Honour of Edouard Jeauneau*. Leiden: 15–45.
Dutton, P. E., and **Luhtala, A.** (1994) "Eriugena in Priscianum," *Mediaeval Studies* 56: 153–63.
Duverger, C. (1987) *La Conversión de los Indios de la Nueva España*. Mexico City.
Egido, A. (1998) "Erasmo y la Torre de Babel. La búsqueda de la lengua perfecta," in *España y América en una Perspectiva Humanista*, ed. **J. Pérez**. Madrid: 11–34.
Eliot, G. (1980) *The Mill on the Floss*, ed. **G. S. Haight**. Oxford.
Erasmus, D. (1975) *La Lengua de Erasmo Nuevamente Romançada por Muy Elegante Estilo*, trans. **B. Pérez de Chinchon**, ed. **D. S. Severin**. Madrid.
Errington, J. (2008) *Linguistics in a Colonial World: A Story of Language, Meaning, and Power*. Malden, MA.
Farrell, J. (2001) *Latin Language and Latin Culture*. Cambridge.
  (2008) "Servius and the Homeric scholia," in **S. Casali** and **F. Stock** (eds.), *Servio. Stratificazioni Esegetiche e Modelli Culturali/Servius: Exegetical Stratifications and Cultural Models*. Brussels: 112–131.
Ferri, R. (2008) "Il latino dei *Colloquia scholica*," in **F. Bellandi** and **R. Ferri** (eds.), *Aspetti della Scuola nel Mondo Romano*. Amsterdam: 111–77.
Feissel, D. (2008) "Deux modèles de cursive latine dans l'ordre alphabétique grec," in **F. A. J. Hoogendijk** and **B. P. Muhs** (eds.), *Sixty-five Papyrological Texts Presented to Klaas A. Worp on the Occasion of his 65th Birthday*. Leiden: 53–64.
Field, J. (2004) *Psycholinguistics: The Key Concepts*. New York.
Finkenbine, R. E. (1994) "'Our little circle': Benevolent reformers, the Slater Fund, and the argument for black industrial education, 1882–1908," in **D. G. Nieman** (ed.), *African Americans and Education in the South 1865–1900*. New York: 70–86.

Fitzgerald, R. (trans.) (1981), *The Aeneid: Virgil*. New York.
Flacelière, R. (1957) "Enquête de l'Unesco [Rapport]," *Revue de la Franco-Ancienne* 122: 134–6.
Flamant, J. (1977) *Macrobe et le Néo-platonisme Latin, à la Fin du IVe Siècle*. Leiden.
Flemming, R. (2007) "Women, writing and medicine in the classical world," *CQ* 57: 257–79.
Forest, A. (1979) *The Cricket Term*. London.
  (2004) *Peter's Room*. Bath.
Forrest, M. (1996) *Modernising the Classics: A Study in Curriculum Development*. Exeter.
Fox, M., and **Sharma, M.** (2012) "Introduction," in **M. Fox** and **M. Sharma** (eds.), *Old English Literature and the Old Testament*. Toronto: 3–22.
Fraenkel, E. (1949) "Review of E. Rand et al., *Servianorum in Vergilii Carmina Commentariorum Editionis Harvardianae Volumen II*," *JRS* 39: 145–54.
Franci, R. (1988) "L'insegnamento della matematica in Italia nel Tre-Quattrocento," *Archimede* 40: 182–94.
  (1992) "Le matematiche dell'abaco nel Quattrocento," in *Contributi alla Storia delle Matematiche. Scritti in Onore di Gino Arrighi*. Modena: 53–74.
  (1993) "La matematica dell'abaco in Italia dal XIII al XVI secolo," in *Il Pensiero Matematico nella Ricerca Storica Italiana*. Ancona: 62–7.
  (1996) "L'insegnamento dell'aritmetica nel medioevo," in **R. Franci**, **P. Pagli** and **L. Toti Rigatelli** (eds.), *Itinera Mathematica. Studi in Onore di Gino Arrighi per il suo 90° Compleanno*. Siena: 1–22.
  (1998) "La trattatistica d'abaco nel Quattrocento," in *Luca Pacioli e la Matematica del Rinascimento. Atti del Convegno Internazionale di Studi, San Sepolcro, 13–16 Aprile 1994*. Città di Castello: 61–75.
Franco Mendoza, M. (ed.) (2000) *Relación de Michoacan*. Zamora.
Frary, L. G. (1966) *Studies in the Syntax of Old English with Special Reference to the Use of Wesan and Weorðan: University of Minnesota Dissertation*. New York.
Fressura, M. (2009) "Revisione di POxy VIII 1099 e POxy L 3553," *Studi di Egittologia e di Papirologia* 6: 43–71.
Funaioli, G. (1930) *Esegesi Virgiliana Antica. Prolegomeni alla Edizione del Commento di Giunio Filagrio e di Tito Gallo*. Milan.
Funari, R. (2008) "2 Sallustius 2 F: Catil. 10, 4–5; 11, 6–7," in [no ed.] *Corpus dei Papiri Storici Greci e Latini, Parte B.1.2: Caius Sallustius Crispus*. Pisa: 51–62.
Gabotto, F. (1895) *Lo Stato Sabaudo da Amedeo VIII ad Emanuele Filiberto vol. III: La Cultura e la Vita in Piemonte nel Rinascimento*, Turin.
Gaebel, R. E. (1970), "The Greek word-lists to Vergil and Cicero," *Bulletin of the John Rylands Library* 52: 284–325.
Garcés, J. (1537). *De Habilitate et Capacitate*. Rome.
García Icazbalceta, J. (1954) *Bibliografía Mexicana del Siglo XVI*. Mexico City.
Garin, E. (ed.) (1958) *Il Pensiero Pedagogico dello Umanesimo*. Florence.
Gavrilov, A.K. (1995) "Russian classical scholarship," in **V. Bers** and **G. Nagy** (eds.), *The Classics in East Europe: Essays on the Survival of a Humanistic Tradition*. Worcester, MA: 61–81.

(2002–8) "Russia," in **H. Cancik** and **H. Schneider** (eds.), *New Pauly: Encyclopaedia of the Ancient World: Antiquity* vol v. Leiden.
Gehl, P. (1993) *A Moral Art. Grammar, Society, and Culture in Trecento Florence.* Ithaca, NY.
(1994) "Preachers, teachers, and translators: The social meaning of language study in trecento Tuscany," *Viator* 25: 289–323.
George, E. V. (2009) "Humanist traces in early colonial Mexico: Texts from the Colegio de Santa Cruz de Tlatelolco," in **F. Grau Codina**, **J. M. Maestre Maestre**, and **J. Pérez Dura** (eds.), *Litterae Humaniores del Renacimiento a la Ilustración*. Valencia: 279–91.
Gherardi, A. (ed.) (1881) *Statuti della Università e Studio Fiorentino*. Florence.
Gibson, C. (1964) *The Aztecs Under Spanish Rule*. Stanford.
Gignac, F. T. (1976) *A Grammar of the Greek Papyri of the Roman and Byzantine Periods vol. 1, Phonology*. Milan.
Gil, J. (1990) "El latín en América: Lengua general y lengua de élite," in *Il Simposio de Filología Iberoamericana. (Sevilla, 26 al 30 de Marzo de 1990)*. Seville: 97–135.
Gilberti, M. (2003) *Grammatica Maturini* (2 vols.), ed. **R. Lucas González**. Zamora. [orig. 1559]
(2004) *Arte de la Lengua de Michuacan*, ed. **C. Monzón**. Zamora. [orig. 1558]
Glazebrook, A. (2005) "Reading women: Book rolls on Attic vases," *Mouseion* 5: 1–46.
Gneuss, H. (1990) "Language in Anglo-Saxon England," *Bulletin of the John Rylands University Library of Manchester* 72.1: 3–32.
Goetz, G. et al. (1888–1923), *Corpus Glossariorum Latinorum a Gustavo Loewe incohatum* (7 vols.). Leipzig.
Goings, K. W., and **O'Connor, E.** (2011) "Black Athena before Black Athena," in **D. Orrells**, **G. K. Bhambra**, and **T. Roynon** (eds.), *African Athena*. Oxford: 90–105.
Goldthwaite, R. A. (1972–3), "Schools and teachers of commercial arithmetic in Renaissance Florence," *Journal of European Economic History* 1: 418–33.
Goold, G.P. (1970) "Servius and the Helen Episode," *HSCP* 74: 101–68.
Görler, W. (1987) "*Obtrectatores*," in **M. Geymonat** and **F. della Corte** (eds.), *Enciclopedia Virgiliana* vol. III. Rome: 807–13.
Gorrini, G. (1931–2) "L'istruzione elementare in Genova durante il medio evo," *Giornale storico e letterario della Liguria* 7: 265–86; 8: 86–96.
Grafton, A., and **Jardine, L.** (1986) *From Humanism to the Humanities: Education and the Liberal Arts in Fifteenth- and Sixteenth-Century Europe*. London.
Graves, R. (1998) *Good-bye to All That: An Autobiography*. New York.
Gray, E. G., and **Fiering, N.** (eds.) (2000) *The Language Encounter in the Americas*. New York/Oxford.
Greenwood, E. (2010) *Afro-Greeks: Dialogues Between Anglophone Caribbean Literature and Classics in the Twentieth Century*. Oxford.
Grendler, P. F. (1989) *Schooling in Renaissance Italy: Literacy and Learning, 1300–1600*. Baltimore.

(1995) "What Piero learned in school: Fifteenth-century vernacular education," in **M. A. Lavin** (ed.), *Piero della Francesca and his Legacy*. Hanover and London: 161–74.

Griffin, C. (1991) *Los Cromberger. La Historia de una Imprenta del Siglo XVI en Sevilla y Méjico*. Madrid.

Grotans, A. (2006) *Reading in Medieval St Gall*. Cambridge.

Gwara, S. (1996) *Latin Colloquies from Pre-Conquest Britain Edited from Oxford, St John's College, MS. 154 and from Oxford, Bodleian Library, MS. Bodley 865*. Toronto.

Hagedorn, U., Hagedorn, D., Youtie, L. C. and **Youtie, H. C.** (eds.) (1968) *Das Archiv des Petaus* (= *P.Petaus*), Köln and Opladen.

Hall, E., et al. (eds.) (2011) *Ancient Slavery and Abolition*. Oxford.

Hanks, W. F. (2010) *Converting Words: Maya in the Age of the Cross*. Berkeley.

Hans, N. A. (1963) *The Russian Tradition in Education*. London.

(1964) *History of Russian Educational Policy (1701–1917)*. New York.

Hanson, A. E. (1984) "Caligulan month-names at Philadelphia and related matters," *Atti XVII Congress* 3: 1107–18.

(1986) "The keeping of records at Philadelphia in the Julio-Claudian period and the 'economic crisis under Nero,'" *Proceedings XVIII Congress* 2: 261–77.

(1991) "Ancient illiteracy," in **J. H. Humphrey** (ed.), *Literacy in the Roman World*. Ann Arbor, MI: 159–98.

(1992) "Egyptians, Greeks, Romans, Arabes and Ioudaioi in the first-century A.D. tax archive from Philadelphia: P.Mich.inv. 880 recto and P.Princ. 111 152, revised," in **J. Johnson** (ed.), *Life in a Multi-Cultural Society* (= *Studies in Ancient Oriental Civilization 51*). Chicago: 133–45.

(2001) "Sworn declaration to agents from the centurion Cattius Catullus: P.Col.inv. 90," in **R. S. Bagnall** and **T. Gagos** (eds.), *Essays & Texts in Honor of J. David Thomas*. Oakville, CT: 91–7.

(2010) "Doctors' literacy and papyri of medical content," in **H. F. J. Horstmanshoff** (ed.), *Hippocrates and Medical Education. Selected Papers Presented at the XII International Hippocrates-Colloquium, Universiteit Leiden, 24–26 August 2005*. Boston and Leiden: 187–204.

Hardwick, L. (2000) *Translating Words, Translating Cultures*. London.

Hardy, T. (1896) *Jude the Obscure*. London.

Harris, W. V. (1989) *Ancient Literacy*. Cambridge, MA/London.

Haygood, A. G. (1881) *Our Brother in Black: His Freedom and His Future*. New York.

Haynes, N. (2010) *The Ancient Guide to Modern Life*. London.

Heath, S. B. (1972) *Telling Tongues. Language Policy in Mexico: Colony to Nation*. New York.

Heatley, H. R. (1889) *Gradatim, an Easy Latin Translation Book for Beginners*. Boston.

Herbst, J. (2004) "The Yale Report of 1828," *IJCT* 11: 213–31.

Herren, M. W. (ed.) (1974) *Hisperica Famina I: The A-Text: A New Critical Edition with English Translation and Philological Commentary*. Toronto.

(ed. and trans.) (1987) *The Hisperica Famina II. Related Poems*. Toronto.

(1988) "Evidence for 'Vulgar Greek' from early medieval Latin texts and manuscripts," in **M. Herren** (ed.) with **S. A. Brown** *The Sacred Nectar of the Greeks: The Study of Greek in the West in the Early Middle Ages.* London: 57–77.
(1993a) *Iohannis Scotti Eriugenae Carmina.* Dublin.
(1993b) "The humanism of John Scottus', in **C. Leonardi** (ed.), *Gli Umanesimi Medievali: Atti del II Congreso dell'Internationales Mittellateinerkomitee.* Florence: 191–9.
(1996) "John Scottus and the Biblical manuscripts attributed to the circle of Sedulius," in **G. van Riel**, **C. Steel**, and **J. McEvoy** (eds.), *Iohannes Scottus Eriugena: The Bible and Hermeneutics: Proceedings of the Ninth International Colloquium of the Society for the Promotion of Eriugenian Studies Held at Leuven and Louvain-la-Neuve June 7–10, 1995.* Louvain: 303–17.
(1999) "Literary and glossarial evidence for the study of classical mythology in Ireland A.D. 600–800," in **H. Conrad-O'Briain**, **A. D'Arcy** and **J. Scattergood** (eds.), *Text and Gloss: Studies in Insular Latin and Literature Presented to Joseph Donovan Pheifer.* Dublin: 49–67.
(2001) "The Greek element in the *Cosmography of Aethicus Ister*," *The Journal of Medieval Latin* 11: 184–200.
(2010) "The study of Greek in Ireland in the early Middle Ages," in *L'Irlanda e gli Irlandesi nell'Alto Medioevo.* Spoleto: 511–28.
(2011) *The Cosmographia of Aethicus Ister: Edition, Translation, and Commentary.* Turnhout.
(2012) "The Graeca in the *tituli* of Lucretius: What they tell us about the archetype," *Wiener Studien* 125: 107–24.
Herren, M. (ed.) with **Brown, S. A.** (1988) *The Sacred Nectar of the Greeks: The Study of Greek in the West in the Early Middle Ages.* London.
Héry, E. (2003) "Quand le baccalauréat devint mixte," *Clio* 18: 77–90.
Hill, J. (2007) "Ælfric's grammatical triad," in **P. Lendinara**, **L. Lazzari** and **M. A. D'Aronco** (eds.), *Form and Content of Instruction in Anglo-Saxon England in the Light of Contemporary Manuscript Evidence.* Turnhout: 285–307.
Honey, M. T. (1939) "The classics in America," *G&R* 9: 36–42.
Horsley, G. H. R. (1989) *New Documents Illustrating Early Christianity 5: Linguistic Essays.* North Ryde, Australia.
Hulme, P., and **Sherman, W. H.** (eds.) (2000) *"The Tempest" and Its Travels.* Philadelphia.
Hunt, T. (1991) *Teaching and Learning Latin in Thirteenth-Century England.* 3 vols. Cambridge.
Hurst, I. (2006) *Victorian Women Writers and the Classics – The Feminine of Homer.* Oxford.
(2007) "'A fleet of ... inexperienced Argonauts': Oxford women and the classics, 1873–1920," in **C. Stray** (ed.), *Oxford Classics: Teaching and Learning 1800–2000.* London: 14–27.
Iguíniz, J. B. (1918) "Calendario atribuido a fray Bernardino de Sahagún," *Boletín de la Biblioteca Nacional* 12: 189–232.
Ingram, D. (1975) "Surface contrast in children's speech," *Journal of Child Language* 2: 289–92.

Irvine, M. (2006) *The Making of Textual Culture: "Grammatica" and Literary Theory 350-1100*. Cambridge.
Jeauneau, E. (1972) "Les écoles de Laon et d'Auxerre au ixe siècle," in *La Scuola nell'Occidente Latino dell'Alto Medioevo* vol. ii. Spoleto: 495–522; 555–60.
(1979) "Jean Scot Érigène et le grec," *Archivum Latinitatis Medii Aevi* 41: 5–50.
Jiménez, N. (2002) "'Príncipe' indígena y latino. Una compra de libros de Antonio Huitziméngari (1559)," *Relaciones* 23.91: 133–62.
Johanson, C. (1987) *Women's Struggle for Higher Education in Russia*. Kingston.
Johnson, R. K., and Swain, M. (eds.) (1997) *Immersion Education: International Perspectives*. Cambridge.
Kaczynski, B. (1988a) *Greek in the Carolingian Age*. Cambridge, MA.
(1988b) "Greek glosses on Jerome's *Ep. CVI ad Sunniam et Fretelam* in E. Berlin, Deutsche Staatsbibliothek. MS Phillipps 1674," in M. Herren (ed.) with S. A. Brown: 215–27.
Kalb, J. E. (2008) *Russia's Rome: Imperial Visions, Messianic Dreams, 1890–1940*. Madison.
Kaster, R.A. (1978) "Servius and *idonei auctores*," *AJP* 99: 181–209.
(1988) *Guardians of Language*. Berkeley.
(2011) "Honor culture, praise, and Servius' *Aeneid*," in W. Brockliss, P. Chaudhuri, A. Haimson-Lushkov and K. Wasdin (eds.), *Reception and the Classics: An Interdisciplinary Approach to the Classical Tradition*. Cambridge: 45–56.
Keil, H. (ed.) (1855–80) *Grammatici Latini*. 8 vols. Leipzig.
Kelly, L. G. (2002) *The Mirror of Grammar: Theology, Philosophy, and the Modiastae*. Amsterdam and Philadelphia.
Kennedy, G. (1984) "Afterword: An essay on classics in America since the Yale Report," in M. Reinhold (ed.): 325–51.
Kenney, J. F. (1966) *The Sources for the Early History of Ireland: Ecclesiastical*, rev. L. Bieler. New York.
Keynes, S., and Lapidge, M. (1983) *Alfred the Great: Asser's Life of King Alfred and Other Contemporary Sources*. London.
Kitchell, K. (1998) "The great Latin debate: The futility of utility?" in R. LaFleur (ed.), *Latin for the 21st Century: From Concept to Classroom*. Glenview, IL: 1–14.
Kitchell, K., and Sienkewicz, T. (2011) *Disce! An Introductory Latin Course*. Boston.
Klapisch-Zuber, C. (1984) "Le chiavi fiorentine di barbablù. L'apprendimento della lettura a Firenze nel xv secolo," *Quaderni storici* 57: 765–92.
Kliebard, H. M. (1992) *Forging the American Curriculum*. New York.
Knauer, G. (1964) *Die Aeneis und Homer. Studien zur poetischen Technik Vergils, mit Listen der Homerzitate in der Aeneis*. Götingen.
Kobayashi, J. M. (1974) *La Educación como Conquista. Empresa Franciscana en México*. Mexico City.
Korhonen, K. (1996) "On the composition of the *Hermeneumata* language manuals," *Arctos* 30: 101–19.

Kramer, J. (1983) *Glossaria Bilinguia in Papyris et Membranis Reperta.* Bonn.
  (1996) "I glossari tardo-antichi di tradizione papiracea," in **J. Hamesse** (ed.), *Les Manuscrits des Lexiques et Glossaires de l'Antiquité Tardive à la fin du Moyen Âge.* Louvain: 23–55.
  (1999) "Zwei lateinische Alphabete für Griechischsprachige: Neuausgabe von P. Ant. 1, fr. 1 Verso," *Archiv für Papyrusforschung* 45: 32–8.
  (2001) *Glossaria Bilinguia Altera (C.Gloss.Biling. II, APF Beiheft 8).* Leipzig.
  (2004) "Essai d'une typologie des glossaires gréco-latins conservés sur papyrus," *Archiv für Papyrusforschung* 50: 49–60.
  (2010) "Neuedition des lateinisch-griechisch-koptischen Gesprächsbuchs von Berlin (P. Berol. inv. 10582, LDAB 6075)," in **H. Knuf, C. Leitz**, and **D. von Recklinghausen** (eds.), *Honi Soit qui Mal y Pense. Studien zum pharaonischen, griechisch-römischen und spätantiken Ägypten zu Ehren von Heinz-Josef Thissen.* Louvain: 557–66.
Krashen, S. (1981) *Second Language Acquisition and Second Language Learning.* Oxford.
Kraus, T. J. (2000) "(Il)literacy in non-literary papyri from Graeco-Roman Egypt: Further aspects of the educational ideal in ancient literary sources and modern times," *Mnemosyne* 4th series, 53: 322–42 (reprinted (2007) in *Ad Fontes: Original Manuscripts and their Significance for Studying Early Christianity*, Boston, MA and Leiden: 107–24, with Addenda 125–9).
Kutscher, G., Brotherston, G., and **Vollmer, G.** (eds.) (1998) *Stimmen indianischer Völker III. Aesop in Mexico.* Berlin.
LaFleur, R. (1991) "The classical languages and college admissions," *CO* 68: 124–32.
  (ed.) (1998) *Latin for the 21st Century.* Georgia.
Laird, A. (2010) "Latin in Cuautémoc's shadow: Humanism and politics of language in Mexico after the conquest," in **Y. Haskell** and **J. Feros Ruys** (eds.), *Latinity and Alterity in the Early Modern World.* Tempe, Arizona: 169–99.
  (2011) "Aztec Latin in sixteenth-century Mexico: A letter from the rulers of Azcapotzalco to Philip II of Spain, February 1561," *Studi Umanistici Piceni* 31: 293–314.
  (2012a) "Niccolò Perotti nel Nuovo Mundo: I *Rudimenta grammatices* e le *Cornu copiae* nel Michoacán del XVI secolo," *Studi Umanistici Piceni* 32: 51–70.
  (2012b) "Patriotism and the rise of Latin in eighteenth-century New Spain: Disputes of the New World and the Jesuit construction of a Mexican legacy," *Renaessanceforum* 8. www.renaessanceforum.dk/rf_8_2011.htm.
Laistner, M. L. W. (1923) "Notes on Greek from the lectures of a ninth-century monastery teacher," *Bulletin of the John Rylands Library* 7: 421–56.
Lampert, E. (1965) *Sons against Fathers: Studies in Russian Radicalism and Revolution.* Oxford.
Lanham, C. D. (ed.) (2002) *Latin Grammar and Rhetoric: From Classical Theory to Medieval Practice.* London and New York.

Lapidge, M. (1986) "The school of Theodore and Hadrian," *Anglo-Saxon England* 15: 45–72.
  (1988) "The study of Greek at the school of Canterbury in the seventh century," in **M. Herren** (ed.) with **S. A. Brown**: 169–94.
  (ed.) (1995) *Archbishop Theodore*. Cambridge.
  (1996) *"The school of Theodore and Hadrian," Anglo-Latin Literature 600–899*. London/Rio Grande, OH: 141–68.
  (2006) *The Anglo-Saxon Library*. New York/Oxford.
Law, V. (1983) "The study of Latin grammar in eight-century South Umbria," *Anglo-Saxon England* 12: 43–71.
  (1984) "The first foreign-language grammars," *The Incorporated Linguist* 23: 211–16.
  (1986) "Panorama della grammatica normativa nel tredicescimo secolo," in **C. Leonardi** and **G. Orlandi** (eds.), *Aspetti della Letteratura Latina nel Secolo XIII*. Perugia and Florence: 125–45.
  (1997) *Grammar and Grammarians in the Early Middle Ages*. London.
  (2003) *The History of Linguistics in Europe: From Plato to 1600*. Cambridge.
Lawall, G., et al. (ed.) (1991) *Fabulae Graecae: A Revised Edition of Ritchie's Fabulae Faciles*. New York.
  (ed.) (2009) *Ecce Romani* 4th edn. Boston.
Le Guin, U. (2008) *Lavinia*. Orlando.
Lehmann, R. (1936) *Dusty Answer*. London.
Lendinara, P. (2011) "The *Scholica Graecarum* and Martianus Capella," in **M. Teeuwen** and **S. O'Sullivan** (eds.), *Carolingian Scholarship and Martianus Capella: Ninth-Century Commentary Traditions on "De nuptiis" in Context*. Turnhout: 301–61.
Lentini, A. (1975) *Ilderico e la sua "Ars grammatica."* Montecassino.
Lewis, N. (1983) *Life in Egypt under Roman Rule*. Oxford.
  (1997) *The Compulsory Public Services of Roman Egypt* 2nd edn. Florence.
Lhomond, C. F. (1779) *De Viris Illustribus Urbis Romae a Romulo ad Augustum*. Paris.
Lianeri, A., and **Zajko, V.** (eds.) (2008) *Translation and the Classic: Identity as Change in the History of Culture*. Oxford.
Lister, B. (ed.) (2008) *Meeting the Challenge: International Perspectives on the Teaching of Latin*. Cambridge.
Lister, B., and **Seranis, P.** (2005) "Access to specialist knowledge through information and communications technology," in *Teacher Development* 9.1: 97–114.
Lockhart, J. (1992) *The Nahuas after the Conquest: A Social and Cultural History of the Indians of Central Mexico, Sixteenth through Eighteenth Centuries*. Stanford.
Lucchi, P. (1978) "La santacroce, il salterio e il babuino. Libri per imparare a leggere nel primo secolo della stampa," *Quaderni storici*, 38: 593–630.
  (1982) "Leggere, scrivere e abbaco. L'istruzione elementare agli inizi dell'età moderna," in *Scienze, Credenze Occulte, Livelli di Cultura. Convegno Internazionale di Studi (Firenze 26–30 Giugno 1980)*. Florence: 102–19.

Lupher, D., and **Vandiver, E.** (2011) "Yankee she-men and octoroon *Electra*: Basil Lanneau Gildersleeve on slavery, race, and abolition," in **E. Hall** *et al.* (eds.): 320–51.
Maehler, H. (1979) "Zweisprächiger Aeneis-Codex," in **J. Bingen** and **G. Nachtergael** (eds.), *Actes du XVe Congrès International de Papyrologie*. Brussels: 18–41.
Maisani, H. (1925) "Des anciens aux nouveaux programmes féminins," *Revue universitaire* 34.1: 422–6.
Majer-Leonhard, E. (1913) *ΑΓΡΑΜΜΑΤΟΙ in Aegypto qui Litteras Scriverint qui Nesciverint ex Papyris Graecis Quantum Fieri Potest*. Frankfurt.
Malamud, M. (2011a) "The *auctoritas* of antiquity: Debating slavery through classical *exempla* in the antebellum USA," in **E. Hall** *et al.* (eds.): 279–317.
  (2011b) "Black Minerva: Antiquity in antebellum African American history," in **D. Orrells**, **G. K. Bhambra**, and **T. Roynon** (eds.), *African Athena*. Oxford: 70–89.
Manacorda, G. (1914) *Storia della Scuola in Italia. Il Medioevo*. Milan, Palermo and Naples.
Marion, H. (1900) Rapport in *Lycées et Collèges de Jeunes Filles. Documents, Rapports et Discours à la Chambre des Députés et au Sénat. Décrets, Arrêtés, Circulaires, etc.* Paris.
Maritan, C. (1838) *De l'Etude du Latin en Général et par les Femmes en Particulier. Diverses Méthodes d'Enseignement. Cours en Dix Mois. Résultats Définis et Garantis*. Paris.
Marrou, H. (1964) *A History of Education in Antiquity*, trans. **G. Lamb**. New York.
Marshall, P. K. (1997) *Servius and Commentary on Virgil*. Asheville.
Massa, A. (1906) "Documenti e notizie per la storia dell'istruzione in Genova," *Giornale storico e letterario della Liguria* 7: 169–205, 311–28.
Matarrese, T. (1993) *Il Settecento*. Bologna.
Mathes, M. (1982) *Santa Cruz de Tlatelolco. La Primera Bibliotheca Académica de las Américas*. Mexico City.
Mayeur, F. (1977) *L'Enseignement Secondaire des Jeunes Filles sous la IIIe République*. Paris.
Mazzi, C. (1896) "Cartiere, tipografie e maestri di grammatica in Valdelsa," *Miscellanea storica della Valdelsa* 4: 181–8.
McClure, L. (1999) *Spoken Like a Woman: Speech and Gender in Athenian Drama*. Princeton.
McKitterick, R. (1994) "Women and literacy in the early Middle Ages," in *Books, Scribes and Learning in the Frankish Kingdoms, 6th–9th Centuries*. Aldershot: 1–43.
McNamee, K. (2007) *Annotations in Greek and Latin Texts from Egypt*. New Haven, Conn.
Mendieta, G. de. (1993) *Historia Eclesiástica Indiana* 4th edn., ed. **J. García Icazbalceta**. Mexico City.
Menzer, M. (1999) "Ælfric's *Grammar*: Solving the problem of the English-language text," *Neophilologus* 83: 637–52.

Merrilees, B. (1987) "Teaching Latin in French: Adaptations of Donatus' *Ars minor*," *Fifteenth-Century Studies* 12: 87–98.
Meyer von Knonau, G. (ed.) (1877) St. Gallische Geschichtsquellen, III. *Ekkehart's (IV.) Casus S. Galli*. St. Gall.
Migne, J. P. (ed.) (1844–55) *Patrologia Latina*, 217 vols. Paris.
Mignolo, W. D. (1992) "On the colonization of Amerindian languages and memories: Renaissance theories of writing and the discontinuity of the classical tradition," *Comparative Studies in Society and History* 34.2: 301–30.
 (1995) *The Darker Side of the Renaissance*. Ann Arbor, MI.
Miller, E. (1860) "Glossaire grec-latin de la Bibliothèque de Laon," *Notices et extraits de la Bibliothèque nationale* 29.2: 1–230.
Miranda Godínez, F. (1972) *Don Vasco de Quiroga y su Colegio de San Nicolás*. Morelia.
Molina, A. de. (facsimile) *Vocabulario en Lengua Castellana y Mexicana. Obra Impresa en México por Antonio de Spinola en 1571*. Madrid.
Mommsen, T. (1909) "T. Livii ab urbe condita lib. III–VI quae supersunt in codice rescripto Veronensi," in *Gesammelte Schriften* vol. VII. Berlin: 96–148.
Montevecchi, O. (1988) *La Papirologia. Ristampa, Riveduta e Corretta con Addenda*. Milan.
Moran, P. (2012) "Greek in early medieval Ireland" in **A. Mullen** and **P. James** (eds.), *Multilingualism in the Graeco-Roman Worlds*. Cambridge.
Morgan, T. (1998) *Literate Education in the Hellenistic and Roman Worlds*. Cambridge.
Morrison, J. D. (1969) "Educational expansion and revolution in Russia, 1801–1917," *Paedagogica historica* 9.1–2: 400–24.
Morwood, J. H. W. (ed.) (2003) *The Teaching of Classics*. Oxford.
Moscadelli, S. (1991) "Maestri d'abaco a Siena tra medioevo e rinascimento," in *L'Università di Siena: 750 Anni di Storia*. Siena: 207–16.
Motolinía (=Fray Toribio de Benavente) (2001) *Historia de los Indios de la Nueva España*, (ed.) **E. O'Gorman**. Mexico City.
Mowat, B. A. (2001) "Prospero's book," *Shakespeare Quarterly* 52.1: 1–33.
Mustard, W. P. (1892) "The etymologies in the Servian commentary to Virgil," *Colorado College Studies* 3: 1–37.
Naipaul, V. S. (2000) *Miguel Street*. Portsmouth, NH. [orig. 1959]
National Education Association of the United States (1894) *Report of the Committee of Ten on Secondary School Studies with the Reports of the Conferences Arranged by Committee*. New York.
Nebrija, A. de. (1492) *Grammática de la Lengua Castellana*. Salamanca.
Nieman, D. G. (ed.) (1994) *African Americans and Education in the South, 1865–1900* (= African American Life in the Post-Emancipation South, 1861–1900 vol. X.) New York.
Oates, J. F., **Bagnall, R. S.**, **Clackson, S. J.**, **O'Brien, A. A.**, **Sosin, J. D.**, **Wilfong, T. G.**, and **Worp, K. A.**, *Checklist of Greek, Latin, Demotic and Coptic Papyri, Ostraca and Tablets*, http://scriptorium.lib.duke.edu/papyrus/texts/clist.html

O'Hara, J. J. (1996) *True Names: Virgil and the Alexandrian Tradition of Etymological Wordplay.* Ann Arbor, MI.
Ong, W. J. (1959) "Latin language study as a Renaissance puberty rite," *SPh* 66: 103–24.
Orme, N. (2006) *Medieval Schools: From Roman Britain to Renaissance England.* New Haven.
Orrells, D. et al. (eds.) (2011) *African Athena: New Agendas.* Oxford.
Ortalli, G. (1997) "L'istruzione," in G. Arnaldi, G. Cracco and A. Tenenti (eds.), *Storia di Venezia dalle Origini alla Caduta della Serenissima*, III. Rome: 889–910.
Osgood, J. (2011) *Claudius Caesar: Image and Power in the Early Roman Empire.* Cambridge.
Osorio Romero, I. (1980) *La Floresta de Gramática, Poética y Retórica en Nueva España (1521–1727).* Mexico City.
  (1984) "Tres joyas bibliográficas para la enseñanza de latín en el siglo xvi novohispano," *Nova Tellus* 2: 165–200.
  (1990) *La Enseñanza de Latín a los Indios.* Mexico City.
Pampaloni, G. (1981) "La vita cittadina," in *Storia di Prato*, II. Prato: 195–203.
Papaconstantinou, A. (ed.) (2010) *The Multilingual Experience in Egypt from the Ptolemies to the Abbasids*, Farnham-Burlington, VT.
Park, K. (1980) "The readers at the Florentine studio," *Rinascimento* 2.21: 249–310.
Parker, D. C. (1992) *Codex Bezae: An Early Christian Manuscript and its Text.* Cambridge.
Paso y Troncoso, F. (ed.) (1939) *Epistolario de Nueva España 1505–1818* 16 vols. Mexico City.
Pasqui, U. (1899) *Documenti per la Storia della Città di Arezzo nel Medio Evo* vol. 1. Florence.
Pearcy, L. T. (2005) *The Grammar of Our Civility. Classical Education in America.* Waco, TX.
Peccei, J. S. (2006) *Child Language: A Resource Book for Students.* New York.
Pecori, L. (1853) *Storia della Terra di San Gimignano.* Florence.
Pépin, J. (1986) "Jean Scot traducteur de Denys. L'Exemple de la lettre IX," in G.-H. Allard (ed.), *Jean Scot Écrivain: Actes du IVe Colloque International Montréal, 28 Août – 2 Septembre 1983.* Montreal and Paris: 129–41.
Petschenig, M. (1883) "Ein griechisch-lateinisches Glossar des achten Jahrhunderts," *Wiener Studien* 5: 159–63.
Pinborg, J. (1982) *Remigius, Schleswig 1486: A Latin Grammar in Facsimile Edition with a Postscript.* Copenhagen.
Poole, S. (1981) "Church law on the ordination of Indians and Castas in New Spain," *Hispanic American Historical Review* 61.4: 637–50.
Porter, D. (ed.) (2002) *Excerptiones de Prisciano: The Source for Ælfric's Latin-Old English Grammar.* Cambridge.
Pozefsky, P. C. (2003) *Nihilist Imagination: Dimitri Pisarev and the Cultural Origins of Russian Radicalism (1860–1868).* New York.
Preisendanz, K. (1933) *Papyrusfunde und Papyrusforschung.* Leipzig.

Prem, H. J. (1997) *The Ancient Americas: A Brief History and Guide to Research*, trans. **K. Kurbjuhn**. Salt Lake City.
Prins, Y. (2006) "'Lady's Greek' (with the accents): A metrical translation of Euripides by A. Mary F. Robinson," *Victorian Literature and Culture* 34: 591–618.
(forthcoming) *Ladies Greek: Translations of Tragedy*. Princeton.
Priscian. (1855–9) *Institutionum Grammaticarum Libri XVIII*, 2 vols., (ed.) **H. Keil**. Grammatici Latini vols. II, III. Leipzig.
Pushkin, A. (1964) *Eugene Onegin, Translated from the Russian with a Commentary by Vladimir Nabokov*, vol. 1. New York.
Quintilian (2002) *The Orator's Education, IV, Books 9–10*, trans. **D. Russell**. Cambridge, MA.
Radice, W., and **Reynolds, B.** (eds.) (1987) *The Translator's Art – Essays in Honour of Betty Radice*. London.
Rees-Jones, D. (1994) *The Memory Tray*. Bridgend.
Reichardt, A. (1909) *Der Codex Boernerianus. Der Briefe des Apostels Paulus*. Leipzig.
Reichmann, V. (1943) *Römische Literatur in griechischer Übersetzung*. Leipzig.
Reinhold, M. (ed.) (1984) *Classica Americana: The Greek and Roman Heritage in the United States*. Detroit.
Rénan, E. (1878) *Caliban, Suite de la Tempête, Drame Philosphique*. Phalsbourg.
(1896) *Caliban: A Philosophical Drama Continuing 'The Tempest' of William Shakespeare*, trans. **E. Grant Vickery**. New York.
Reynolds, S. (1996) *Medieval Reading: Grammar, Rhetoric and the Classical Text*. Cambridge.
Ricard, R. (1966) *The Spiritual Conquest of Mexico*. Berkeley and London.
Richard, C. J. (1994) *The Founders and the Classics: Greece, Rome, and the American Enlightenment*. Cambridge, MA.
(2009) *The Golden Age of the Classics in America: Greece, Rome, and the Antebellum United States*. Cambridge, MA.
Richardson, E. (2007) "Jude the Obscure: Oxford's classical outcasts," in **C. Stray** (ed.), *Oxford Classics: Teaching and Learning 1800–2000*. London: 28–45.
Riché, P. (1953) "Le Psautier, livre de lecture élémentaire d'après les vies des saints mérovingiens," in *Études Mérovingiennes*, Paris: 253–6.
(1976) *Education and Culture in the Barbarian West: From the Sixth through Eighth Centuries*, trans. **J. Contreni**. Columbia, SC.
(1979) *Écoles et Enseignement dans le Haut Moyen Âge de la Fin du Ve Siècle au Milieu du XIe Siècle*. Paris.
(1988) "Le grec dans les centres de culture d'occident," in M. Herren (ed.) with S. A. Brown: 143–68.
Ritchie, F. (1884) *Ritchie's* Fabulae Faciles*; a First Latin Reader*. London.
Rizakis, A. (2008) "Langue et culture ou les ambiguïtés identitaires des notables des cités grecques sous l'Empire de Rome," in **F. Biville, J.-C. Decourt**, and **G. Rougemont** (eds.), *Bilinguisme Gréco-latin et Épigraphie*. Lyon: 17–34.
Rizzo, S. (1986) "Il latino nell'umanesimo," in **A. Asor Rosa** (ed.), *Letteratura italiana* 5: 379–408.

(2002) *Ricerche sul Latino Umanistico* vol. 1. Rome.
Rochette, B. (1990) "Les traductions grecques de l'*Énéide* sur papyrus. Une contribution à l'étude du bilinguisme gréco-romain au Bas-Empire," *LEC* 58: 333–46.
(1996) "Papyrologica bilinguia Graeco-Latina," *Aegyptus* 76: 57–79.
(1997) *Le Latin dans le Monde Grec. Recherches sur la Diffusion de la Langue et des Lettres Latines dans les Provinces Hellénophones de l'Empire Romain.* Brussels.
Rollin, C. (1734) *Traité de la Manière d'Enseigner et d'Etudier les Belles-lettres, par Rapport à l'Esprit et au Cœur.* Paris.
Ronnick, M. V. (ed.) (2005) *The Autobiography of William Sanders Scarborough: An American Journey From Slavery To Scholarship.* Detroit.
(2011) "'Saintly souls': White teachers' instruction of Greek and Latin to African American freedmen," in **T. Ramsby** and **S. Bell** (eds.), *Free At Last! The Impact of Freed Slaves on the Roman Empire.* London: 177–95.
Rowlandson, J. (ed.) (1998) *Women and Society in Greek and Roman Egypt.* Cambridge.
Russell, P. (2000) "Graeco-Latin glossaries in early medieval Ireland," *Peritia* 14: 406–20.
Rutilius Namatianus. (2007) *Sur Son Retour*, (ed.) **E. Wolff**. Paris.
Sabbadini, R. (1896) *La Scuola e gli Studi di Guarino Guarini Veronese.* Catania.
(1924) *Giovanni da Ravenna, Insigne Figura d'Umanista (1343–1408).* Como.
Sahagún, B. de. (1982) *Florentine Codex: Introductions and Indices*, (eds.) **A. J. O. Anderson** and **C. E. Dibble**. Salt Lake City.
(1986) *Coloquios y Doctrina Cristiana*, (ed.) **M. León-Portilla**. Mexico City.
Sandy, G. N. (1997) *The Greek World of Apuleius.* Leiden.
Sasse Tateo, B. (1992) "Forme dell'organizzazione scolastica nell'Italia dei comuni," *Archivio storico italiano* 150: 19–56.
Satina, S. (1966) *Education of Women in Pre-Revolutionary Russia*, trans. **A. F. Poutschine**. New York.
Sayers, D. L. (1979) "The lost tools of learning," *National Review* January 11: 90–9. Reprint from 1947.
(2003) *Gaudy Night.* London.
Scappaticcio, M. C. (2009) "Appunti per una riedizione dei frammenti del Palinsesto Virgiliano dell'Ambrosiana," *Archiv für Papyrusforschung* 55: 96–120.
(2013) *Papyri Vergilianae. L'Apporto della Papirologia alla Storia della Tradizione Virgiliana (I–VI d.C).* Liège.
Schironi, F. (2009) *From Alexandria to Babylon: Near Eastern Languages and Hellenistic Erudition in the Oxyrhynchus Glossary (P.Oxy. XVII 1802 + LXXI 4812).* Berlin.
Schmitt, W. (1969) "Die Ianua (Donatus)," *Beiträge zur Inkunabelkunde* 3.4: 43–80.
Scot Eriugena, J. (1993) *Iohannis Scotti Eriugenae Carmina*, (ed.) **M. W. Herren**. Scriptores Latini Hiberniae 12. Dublin.

Seneca. (1965) *Epistulae Morales Ad Lucilium*, (ed.) **L. D. Reynolds**, 2 vols. Oxford.
Servius Honoratus, M. (1864) *Commentarius in Artem Donati*, (ed.) **H. Keil**. Grammatici Latini 4: 403–48. Leipzig.
Shakespeare, W. (2005) *The Tempest*, (eds.) **V. Mason Vaughan** and **A. T. Vaughan**. London.
Shapcott, J. (2010) *Of Mutability*. London.
Sharwood Smith, J. E. (1975) "Changing Patterns and Mr Dexter," *Latin Teaching* 35.2: 48–52.
  (1977) *On Teaching Classics*. London.
Sherrow, V. (2006) *Encyclopedia of Hair*. Westport, CT.
Simpson, J. (1973) "Teaching the Cambridge School Classics Project Latin course," *Dialogue* 13: 3–5.
Sinel, A. (1973) *The Classroom and the Chancellery: State Educational Reform in Russia under Count Dmitry Tolstoi*. Cambridge, MA.
Sisam, K. (1953) *Studies in Old English Literature*. Oxford.
Slade, C., and **Möllering, M.** (eds.) (2010) *From Migrant to Citizen: Testing Language, Testing Culture*. Basingstoke.
Smith, A. (2007) *Girl Meets Boy*. Edinburgh.
Solodow, J. (2010) *Latin Alive: The Survival of Latin in English and the Romance Languages*. New York/Cambridge.
Speyer, W. (ed.) (1963) *Epigrammata Bobiensia*. Leipzig.
Steck, Francisco de Borgia (1944) *El Primer Colegio de América*. Mexico City.
Stern, L. C. (1908–9) "Ueber die irische Handschrift in St. Paul," *Zeitschrift für celtische Philologie* 6: 546–55; 7: 290–1.
Stevenson, J. (1998) "Women and classical education in the early modern period," in **Y. L. Too** and **N. Livingstone** (eds.), *Pedagogy and Power: Rhetorics of Classical Learning*. Cambridge: 83–109.
Stevenson, W. H. (ed.) (1929) *Early Scholastic Colloquies*. Oxford.
  (1959) *Asser's Life of King Alfred*. Oxford.
Strachey, L. (1986) *Eminent Victorians*. New York.
Stray, C. (1998) *Classics Transformed: Schools, Universities, and Society in England, 1830–1960*. Oxford.
  (2003) "Classics in the curriculum up to the 1960s," in **J. Morwood** (ed.), *The Teaching of Classics*. Cambridge: 1–5.
  (ed.) (2007) *Oxford Classics: Teaching and Learning, 1800–2000*. London.
Strozzi, A. (1987) *Tempo di Affetti e di Mercanti. Lettere ai Figli Esuli*. Milan.
Studer, P., and **Walters, E. G. R.** (1962) *Historical French Reader: Medieval Period*. Oxford.
Sullivan, R. E. (ed.) (1995) *The Gentle Voices of Teachers*. Columbus.
Swain, S. (2002) "Bilingualism in Cicero? The evidence of code-switching," in Adams, Janse, and Swain (eds.): 128–67.
Teeuwen, S., and **O'Sullivan, S.** (eds.) (2011). *Carolingian Scholarship and Martianus Capella*. Turnhout.
Terry, P. (ed.) (2000) *Ovid Metamorphosed*. London.

Thomas, E. (1879) *Scholiastes de Virgile: Essai sur Servius et son Commentaire sur Virgile d'après les Manuscrits de Paris et les Publications les Plus Récentes.* Paris.
Thomas, J. D. (2007) "Latin texts and Roman citizens," in **A. K. Bowman** *et al.* (eds.), *Oxyrhynchus: A City and its Texts.* London: 231–43.
Thomas, R. (1992) *Literacy and Orality in Ancient Greece.* Cambridge.
Tollefson, J. W. (1995) *Power and Inequality in Language Education.* Cambridge.
Tommaseo, N., and **Bellini, B.** (1861–79) *Dizionario della Lingua Italiana.* Turin et alibi.
Too, Y. L., and **Livingstone, N.** (eds.) (1998) *Pedagogy and Power: Rhetorics of Classical Learning.* Cambridge.
Torlone, Z. (2011) "Vasilii Petrov and the first Russian translation of the *Aeneid*," *Classical Receptions Journal* 3.2: 227–47.
Torquemada, J. de. (1975–83) *Monarquía Indiana*, 7 vols. Mexico City.
Toupin, F. (2010) "Exploring continuities and discontinuities between Ælfric's *Grammar* and its antique sources," *Neophilologus* 94: 333–52.
Tristram, D. (2003) "Classics in the curriculum from the 1960s to the 1990s," in **J. Morwood** (ed.), *The Teaching of Classics.* Cambridge: 6–19.
Tristram, H. L. C. (1999) "Die irischen Gedichte im Reichenauer Schulheft," in **P. Anreiter** and **E. Jerem** (eds.), *Studia Celtica et Indogermanica: Festschrift für Wolfgang Meid zum 70. Geburtstag.* Budapest: 503–29.
Turner, E. G. (1968) *Greek Papyri, An Introduction.* Princeton. (Reprintings by OUP in 1980 and later added supplementary bibliography.)
Uhl, A. (1998) *Servius als Sprachlehrer. Zur Sprachrichtigkeit in der exegetischen Praxis des spätantiken Grammatikerunterrichts.* Göttingen.
Ulivi, E. (1993) *"I maestri Biagio di Giovanni e Luca di Matteo e la 'Bottega d'abaco del Lungarno,'" Rapporto Interno no. 11, Dipartimento di Matematica.* Florence: 1–17.
  (1994) "Luca Pacioli. Una biografia scientifica," in **E. Giusti** and **C. Maccagni** (ed.), *Luca Pacioli e la Matematica del Rinascimento.* Florence: 21–78.
  (1996) "Per una biografia di Antonio Mazzinghi, maestro d'abaco del xiv secolo," *Bollettino di storia delle scienze matematiche* 16: 101–50.
  (1998) "Le scuole d'abaco a Firenze (seconda metà del sec. xiii–prima metà del sec. xvi)," in **E. Giusti** (ed.), *Luca Pacioli e la Matematica del Rinascimento.* Città di Castello: 41–60.
  (2000) "Le scuole d'abaco e l'insegnamento della matematica a Firenze nei secoli xiii–xvi," in **F. Freguglia**, **L. Pellegrini** and **R. Paciocco** (eds.), *Scienze matematiche e insegnamento in epoca medioevale.* Naples: 85–110.
  (2001) "Mariano di Maestro Michele, un maestro d'abaco del xv secolo," *Nuncius. Annali di storia della scienza* 16: 301–45.
  (2002a) *Benedetto da Firenze (1429–1479), un Maestro d'Abaco del XV Secolo.* Florence.
  (2002b) "Scuole e maestri d'abaco in Italia tra medioevo e rinascimento," in *Un Ponte sul Mediterraneo. Leonardo Pisano, la Scienza Araba e la Rinascita della Matematica in Occidente.* Florence: 121–59.

(2003) "Maestri e scuole d'abaco a Firenze. La bottega di Santa Trinita," *Bollettino di storia delle scienze matematiche* 23: 9–57.
Urofsky, M. I. (1965) "Reforms and response: The Yale report of 1828," *History of Education Quarterly* 5: 53–67.
Valadés, D. (1579) *Rhetorica Christiana*. Perugia.
van den Berg, R. M. (2007) "What's in a divine name? Proclus on Plato's Cratylus," in **J. H. D. Scourfield** (ed.), *Texts and Culture in Late Antiquity: Inheritance, Authority, and Change*. Swansea: 261–78.
Vandiver, E. (2010) *Stand in the Trench, Achilles: Classical Receptions in British Poetry of the Great War*. Oxford.
Vandorpe, K. (2009) "Archives and dossiers," in **R. S. Bagnall** (ed.), *The Oxford Handbook of Papyrology*. Oxford: 216–55.
van Egmond, W. (1976) *The Commercial Revolution and the Beginnings of Western Mathematics in Renaissance Florence, 1300–1500*, Ph.D. Thesis. Bloomington, IN.
(1977) "New light on Paolo dell'abbaco," *Annali dell'Istituto e museo di storia della scienza di Firenze* 2.2: 1–21
(1978) "The earliest vernacular treatment of algebra: The *Libro di ragione* of Paolo Gerardi (1328)," *Physis* 20: 155–89.
(1980) *Practical Mathematics in the Italian Renaissance. A Catalog of Italian Abacus Manuscripts and Printed Books to 1600*. Florence (Supplemento agli annali dell'istituto e museo di storia della scienza di Firenze, 1).
(1986) "The contributions of the Italian Renaissance to European mathematics," *Symposia mathematica* 27: 51–67.
Verde, A. (1973–2010) *Lo Studio Fiorentino*, 6 vols. Florence and Pistoia.
Vergil. (2008) *The Aeneid*, trans. **S. Ruden**. New Haven and London.
Vetancurt, A. (1697) *Teatro Mexicano. Crónica de la Provincia del Santo Evangelio de México, Menologio Franciscano*, 5 parts. Mexico City.
Vickers, B. (1989) *In Defence of Rhetoric*. Oxford.
Vogüé, A. de. (ed.) (1964) *La Règle du Maître*. Paris.
Voigts, L. E. (1996) "What's the word? Bilingualism in late-medieval England," *Speculum* 71: 813–26.
Wallace, A. (2011) *Virgil's Schoolboys: The Poetics of Pedagogy in Renaissance England*. Oxford.
Wallace, J. (2011) "Classics as souvenir: L. E. L. and the annuals," *Classical Receptions Journal* 3.1: 109–28.
Waquet, F. (1998) *Le Latin ou l'Empire d'un Signe (XVIe–XXe siècle)*. Paris.
(2001) *Latin or the Empire of a Sign: From the Sixteenth to the Twentieth Centuries*, trans. **J. Howe**.
Washington, B. T. (1903) "Industrial education for the Negro," in *The Negro Problem: A Series of Articles by Representative American Negroes of Today*. New York: 7–30.
Werner, S. (2009) "Literacy studies in classics: The last twenty years," in **W. A. Johnson** and **H. N. Parker** (eds.), *Ancient Literacies. The Culture of Reading in Greece and Rome*. Oxford: 333–52.

Wes, M. (1992) *Classics in Russia 1700–1855: Between Two Bronze Horsemen.* Leiden, New York, Cologne.
Wessner, P. (1929) "Lucan, Statius und Juvenal bei den römischen Grammatiken," *PhW* 49: 296–303, 328–35.
Williams, E. (1958) "Aelfric's grammatical terminology," *Publications of the Modern Language Association of America* 73.5: 453–62.
Winterer, C. (2002) *The Culture of Classicism: Ancient Greece and Rome in American Intellectual Life, 1780–1910.* Baltimore, MD.
  (2007) *The Mirror of Antiquity: American Women and the Classical Tradition, 1750–1900.* Ithaca, NY.
Winterson, J. (2006) *Weight: The Myth of Atlas and Heracles.* Edinburgh.
Wolf, E. (ed.) (2007) *Rutilius Namatianus. Sur Son Retour.* Paris.
Woolf, V. (1992) *A Woman's Essays,* (ed.) **R. Bowlby**. London.
Wraga, W. (2009) "Latin literacy redux: The classical investigation in the United States, 1921–1924," *History of Education* 38: 79–98.
Wright, R. (1981) "Late Latin and early Romance: Alcuin's *De Orthographia* and the Council of Tours (AD 813)," in **F. Cairns** (ed.), *Papers of the Liverpool Latin Seminar: Third Volume.* Liverpool: 343–61.
Wynn, M. (1987) "Betty Radice: A memoir" in **W. Radice** and **B. Reynolds** (eds.), *The Translator's Art – Essays in Honour of Betty Radice.* London.
Yale University. (1828) *Reports on the Course of Instruction in Yale College; By a Committee of the Corporation, and the Academical Faculty.* New Haven.
Youtie, H. C. (1966) "Pétaus, fils de Pétaus, ou le scribe qui ne savait pas écrire," *Chronique d'Égypte* 41: 127–43 (reprinted 1973 in *Scriptiunculae* 2, Amsterdam: 677–95).
  (1971a) "ΑΓΡΑΜΜΑΤΟΣ: an aspect of Greek society in Egypt," *HSCP* 75: 161–76 (reprinted 1973 in *Scriptiunculae* 2, Amsterdam: 611–27).
  (1971b) "βραδέως γράφων: Between literacy and illiteracy," *GRBS* 12: 239–61 (reprinted 1973 in *Scriptiunculae* 2, Amsterdam: 629–51).
  (1976) "P.Cornell inv. I 11: Σουβρικός," *ZPE* 22: 53–6 (reprinted 1981 in *Scriptiunculae posteriores* 1, Bonn: 335–8).
Zanelli, A. (1900) *Del Pubblico Insegnamento in Pistoia dal XIV al XVI Secolo.* Rome.
Zetzel, J. (1981) *Latin Textual Criticism in Antiquity.* Salem.
Zorita, A. de. (1999) *Relación de la Nueva España.* Mexico City.
Zupitza, J. (ed.) (1880) *Aelfrics Grammatik und Glossar.* Berlin.

Index

abacus, 99, 110
Ælfric of Eynsham
   Excerptiones de arte grammatica Anglice, 83–98
Aeschylus, 56
Aesop
   Fables, 127, 139
Aethelwold, 96
Aethicus Ister
   Cosmography, 80–1
African Americans
   and the classics, 174–7
Alberti, Leon Battista
   De pictura, 116
Alcuin of York, 87
   De orthographia, 87
American Civil War, 173
Aristotle, 57
   Categories, 95
Arnold, Matthew, 174
Arsinoite nome, 5, 10, 15, 20, 26
Augustine
   Locutiones in Heptateuchum, 63–4

Bede, 78
   Retractatio in Actus Apostolorum, 78
Bérard, Léon, 148–9
Boccaccio, Giovanni, 101
Brent-Dyer, Elinor M.
   The Chalet School in Exile, 159
Butler, Samuel
   The Way of All Flesh, 137
Byatt, A. S., 158, 162
   "The Djinn in the Nightingale's Eye," 158
   The Children's Book, 157

Caesar, Gaius Julius, 171
   Gallic Wars, 185
Calhoun, John C., 174
Caliban, 166, 198–201, 207–8
Cambridge Latin Course, 184–97
Cambridge University, 186

Camille Sée law, 147
Canary Islands, 167
Catherine the Great, 139
Cervantes de Salazar, Francisco, 131
Chekhov, Anton, 136
Christian of Stavelot, 77
Cicero, 43, 57
conversion, 121
Cooper, Anna Julia, 202
Coptic, 33
Cornish, 97
curricula, 99, 127

Datini, Margherita, 102
De raris fabulis, 83, 97
discipline, 7
Disticha Catonis, 101, 108, 127
Donatus, Aelius, 54–5, 58–9, 104
   Ars maior, 84, 89
   Ars minor, 96–7
Dositheus, 41, 85
Drabble, Margaret
   The Seven Sisters, 163
DuBois, W. E. B., 175–6
Duffy, Carol Ann
   The World's Wife, 164

education
   in families, 13–15, 148, 154
   of adults, 14
   of children, 83, 92, 99–117
Education Act of 1944, 184
Einhard
   Vita Karoli Magni, 87
Ekkehart IV of St Gall, 66
Eliot, Charles, 170
Eliot, George, 156
Emerson, Ralph Waldo, 170
Epicurus, 72
Erasmus, Desiderius, 126, 130
   Colloquia familiaria, 130

De conscribendis epistolis, 130
De ratione studii, 126
Duplici copia verborum ac rerum commentari, 130
Epitome in Elegantias Laurentii Vallae, 130
Libellus de octo orationis partium constructione, 130
Eriugena, John Scottus, 69, 75, 77, 79–81
ethnology, 123
etymologies, 59–61
Eustathius, 56
Eutropius, 171
Eutyches, 67

fables, 49–50
Forest, Antonia, 159
  Peter's Room, 160
  The Cricket Term, 159
France, 145–56
  Aurillac, 150
  Lille, 150
Franklin, Benjamin, 169
French Revolution, 146

Garcés, Julián, 119
Gilberti, Maturino
  Grammatica Maturini, 128–9
Gildersleeve, Basil Lanneau, 176
Graves, Robert, 203, 205
Guarino Veronese, 107–8

Hartmann of St Gall, 75
Harvard University, 170, 172
Hermeneumata Pseudodositheana, ix, 14, 36, 68, 214
Herodotus, 58
Hisperica Famina, 67, 81
Homer, 56
  Odyssey, 79–80

Ianua, 104–8
idioms, 63
instructional materials, 5, 9, 13–14, 31
  alphabets, 35, 67, 70, 100
  colloquies, 14, 36–7, 83, 97. See also *De raris fabulis*, *Hermeneumata Pseudodositheana*
  composition exercises, 49–50
  glossaries, 14, 37–8, 44–8, 67–9, 83–4, 87
  glosses, 77–8, 80, 83–4
  grammatical texts, 33–5, 38–43, 67, 104, 128
  literature, 43–6, 48–9
  modern textbooks, 179, 185
  paradigms, 69, 84
  phrasebooks, 31–5, 68

pictograms, 124
tabula, 100
writing exercises, 13, 17, 35, 111–12
Iroquois, 169
Italy, 99–117
  Arezzo, 108
  Colle Valdelsa, 105
  Florence, 111, 114
  Lucca, 105
  Parma, 109
  Pistoia, 105

Jackson, Andrew, 169

Latin
  as *grammatica*, 6, 120
  Latin for Today, 188
Le Guin, Ursula
  Lavinia, 163
libraries, 127
literacy
  definitions of, 12, 19, 74, 101
  in antiquity, 13, 35
  in Greek, 63, 70
  in vernacular languages, 133
Liutprand of Cremona, 75
  Antapodosis, 71, 75

Macrobius, 53
Martianus Capella, 70, 81
Martin of Laon, 67, 69
memorization, 102, 106, 123, 127
methods of instruction, 123
Mexico, 118–35
multilingualism, 2
  and status, 2, 138, 199
  definitions of, 70, 201
  in antiquity, 30–1
  in medieval Europe, 65–82
  in the Roman Empire, 11, 52–3

Nabokov, Vladimir, 137
Nahuatl, 121, 132
National Education Association, 170
Nepos, Cornelius, 171, 182
Northwestern University, 170
numeracy, 99

Old English, 83–98
Open University, 164
Ovid
  Metamorphoses, 164
  Tristia, 127
Oxford, 161
Oxford University, 186

Paul the Deacon, 66
pedagogy
  bilingual, 2, 5, 83, 116
  child-directed speech, 92–7
  monolingual, 103, 110
  techniques, 14, 17, 50
Peter Damian, 100
Peter the Great, 139
Priscian, 63
  Excerptiones de Prisciano, 84
  Institutiones grammaticae, 79–80, 85
Psalter, 101–2, 108
Ptolemy, 57–8
Pushkin, Alexander
  Eugene Onegin, 139
  Monumentum, 139

quadrivium, 126
Quintilian, 128

Radice, Betty, 158
Ramírez Fuenleal, Sebastián, 122
Rees-Jones, Deryn, 159
Regula magistri, 102
Reinhold, Meyer, 168
Remigius of Auxerre, 68, 100
Rénan, Ernest
  Caliban, Suite de la tempête, 200
Rostovtsev, Mikhail Ivanovich, 136
Rush, Benjamin, 168
Russia, 136–45

Sahagún, Bernardino de, 119, 122–3
Sallust, 48–9, 57
Sayers, Dorothy L., 181
  Gaudy Night, 160, 162
scribes, 15, 18
  duties of, 18
second language acquisition, 2
Sedulius Scottus, 67, 73, 81
Servius, 52–64
Shakespeare, William
  The Tempest, 1, 166, 198–201, 207–8
Shapcott, Jo
  Of Mutability, 164
Smith, Ali

Girl Meets Boy, 164
Soave, Francesco, 108
Solomos, Dionysios, 198
Soresi, Pier Domenico, 109
St. Gall, 66, 85
Strachey, Lytton, 203

Terrell, Mary Church, 174
Theocritus, 57
Theodore, Archbishop of Canterbury, 66
Thesaurus linguae Graecae, 67
Thucydides, 57
Tolstoy, Dmitri, 141
translation, 76, 78, 83, 89, 111, 133
  of the Bible, 76, 89
trivium, 126
Turnbull, George, 169
universities, 31, 168
  admissions, 171
  Latin and Greek requirements, 178

Ushinksky, Konstantin, 141

Varro, 60
Virgil, 43–8
  Aeneid, 43, 56
  Eclogues, 57, 139, 171
Vives, Juan Luis
  De tradendis disciplinis, 126
  Exercitationes linguae latinae, 127

wax tablets, 102
Welsh, 83, 97
Winterson, Jeanette
  Weight: the Myth of Atlas and Heracles, 164
women
  and access to classics, 7, 155–6, 158
  education of, 3, 28, 102, 136, 145–65
  literacy of, 20–1, 23–9, 207
Woolf, Virginia
  "On Not Knowing Greek," 157

Xenophon, 57

Yale University, 172–4
"Yale Report," 172